Lovesick Ellie

3

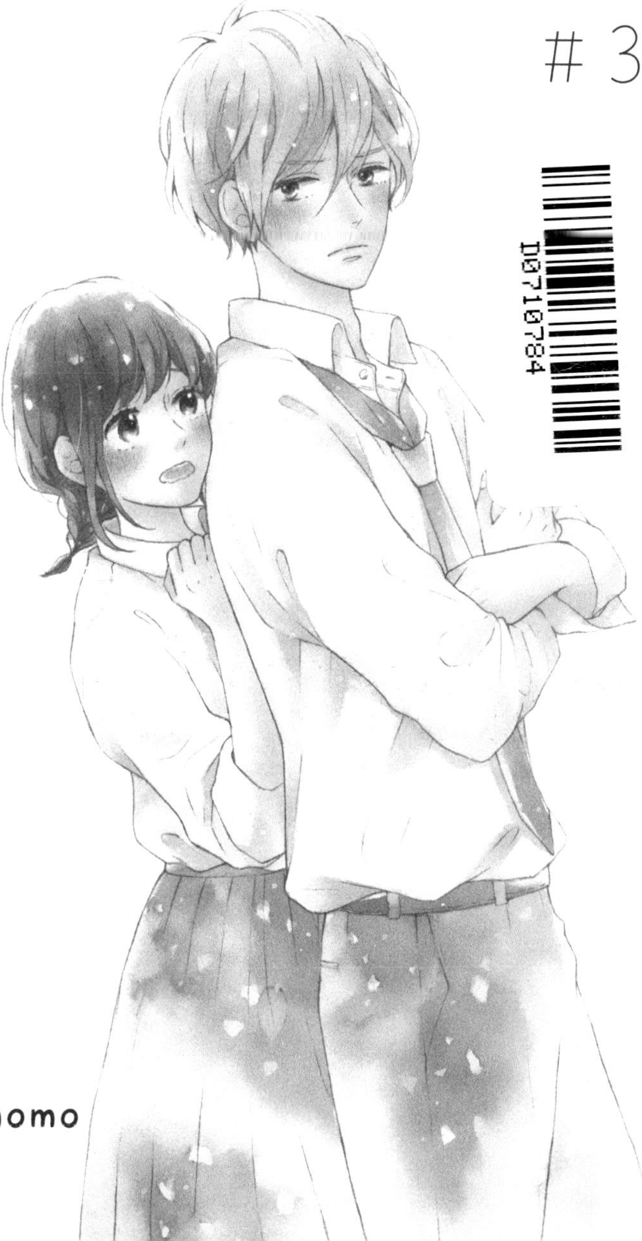

Fujimomo

Lovesick Ellie
contents

characters

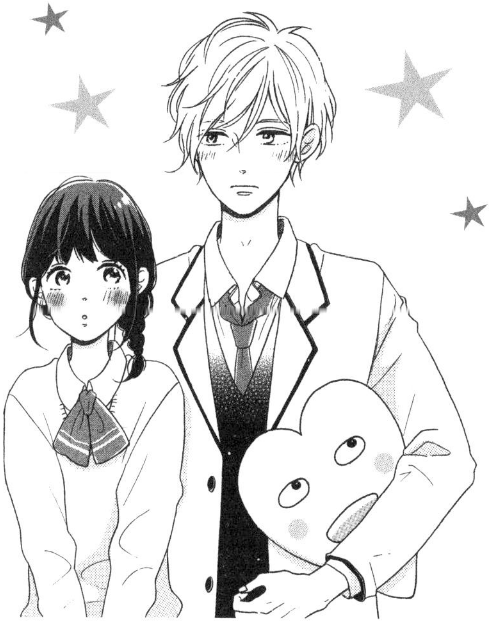

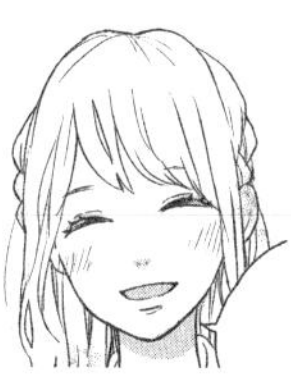

SARA-CHAN
Ellie's first friend.

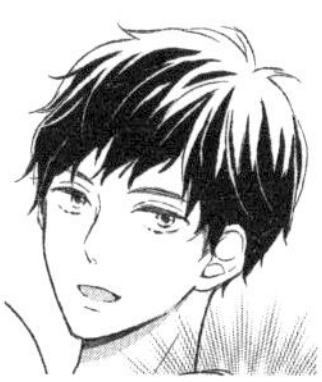

SHIOTA-SENSEI
Ellie's homeroom teacher and Omie-kun's uncle.

ERIKO ICHIMURA
Ellie
A plain high school girl. Spends her days tweeting Omie-kun-centric fantasies.

AKIRA OHMI
Omie-kun
Everyone's favorite popular boy on the outside. Irritable and childish on the inside.

story

Ellie spends her high school days in complete obscurity, but she has a hobby: tweeting fantasies about handsome, smooth-spoken Omie-kun. One fateful day, Omie-kun discovers her tweets, and Ellie finds herself in hot water! However, not only does Omie-kun find her interesting, they go to the festival and study together and get extremely close! Despite Ellie's perverted nature, Omie-kun can't help but find himself more and more pulled in by her charm. When their intimate moment is interrupted at the library, Omie-kun assures Ellie that they will "continue after passing her exam," and Ellie's fantasies explode!! What does he mean by "continue"...?!

9 #GimmeMyPrize

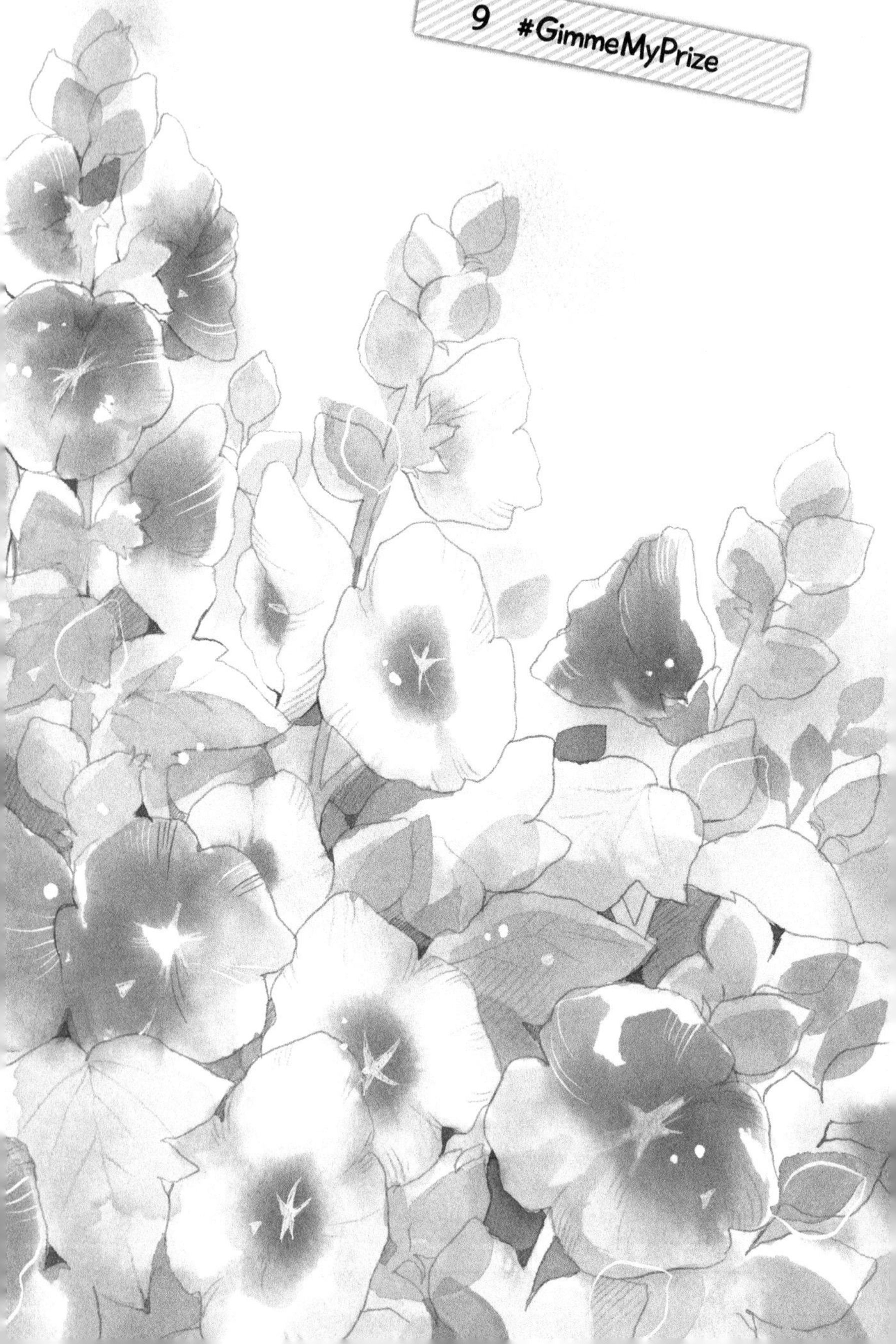

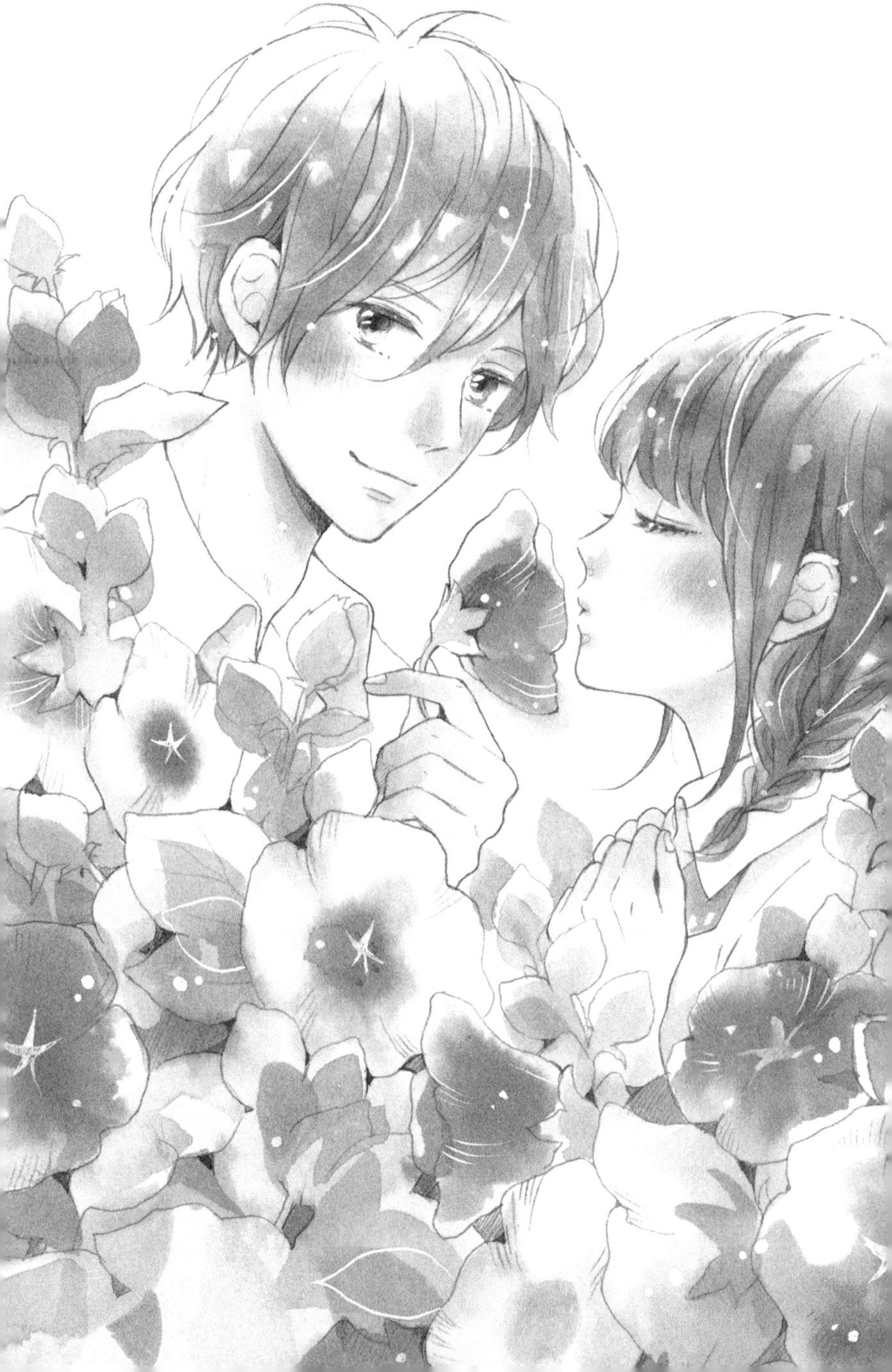

Lovesick
Ellie

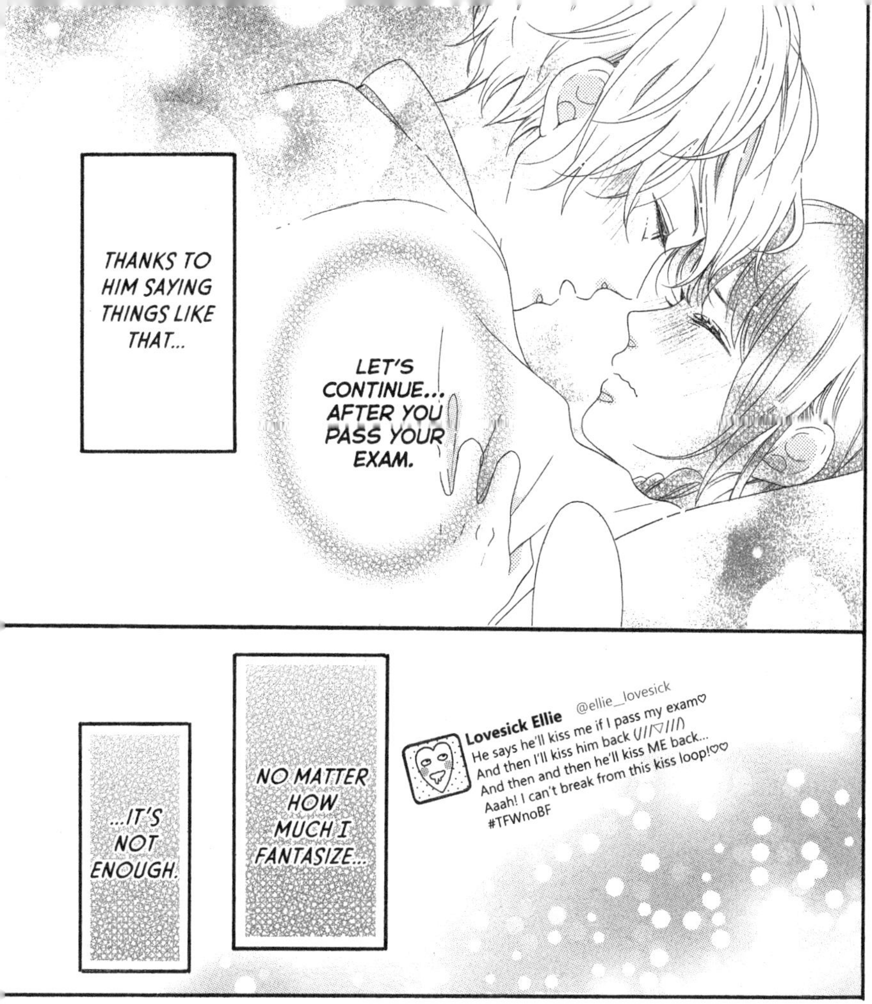
LET'S CONTINUE... AFTER YOU PASS YOUR EXAM.
THANKS TO HIM SAYING THINGS LIKE THAT...
Lovesick Ellie @ellie__lovesick
He says he'll kiss me if I pass my exam♡
And then I'll kiss him back (///▽///)
And then and then he'll kiss ME back...
Aaah! I can't break from this kiss loop!♡♡
#TFWnoBF
NO MATTER HOW MUCH I FANTASIZE...
...IT'S NOT ENOUGH.

Hello! Fujimomo here.
Thank you so much for reading the third volume!
Pervy Ellie and Bratty Omie: full speed ahead to lovey-dovey action (?)
I hope you enjoy Volume 3!!

Check out Ellie's twitter, too!

@ellie__lovesick
(that's two underscores)

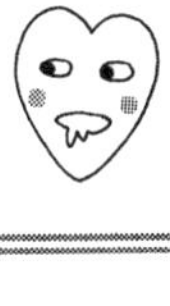

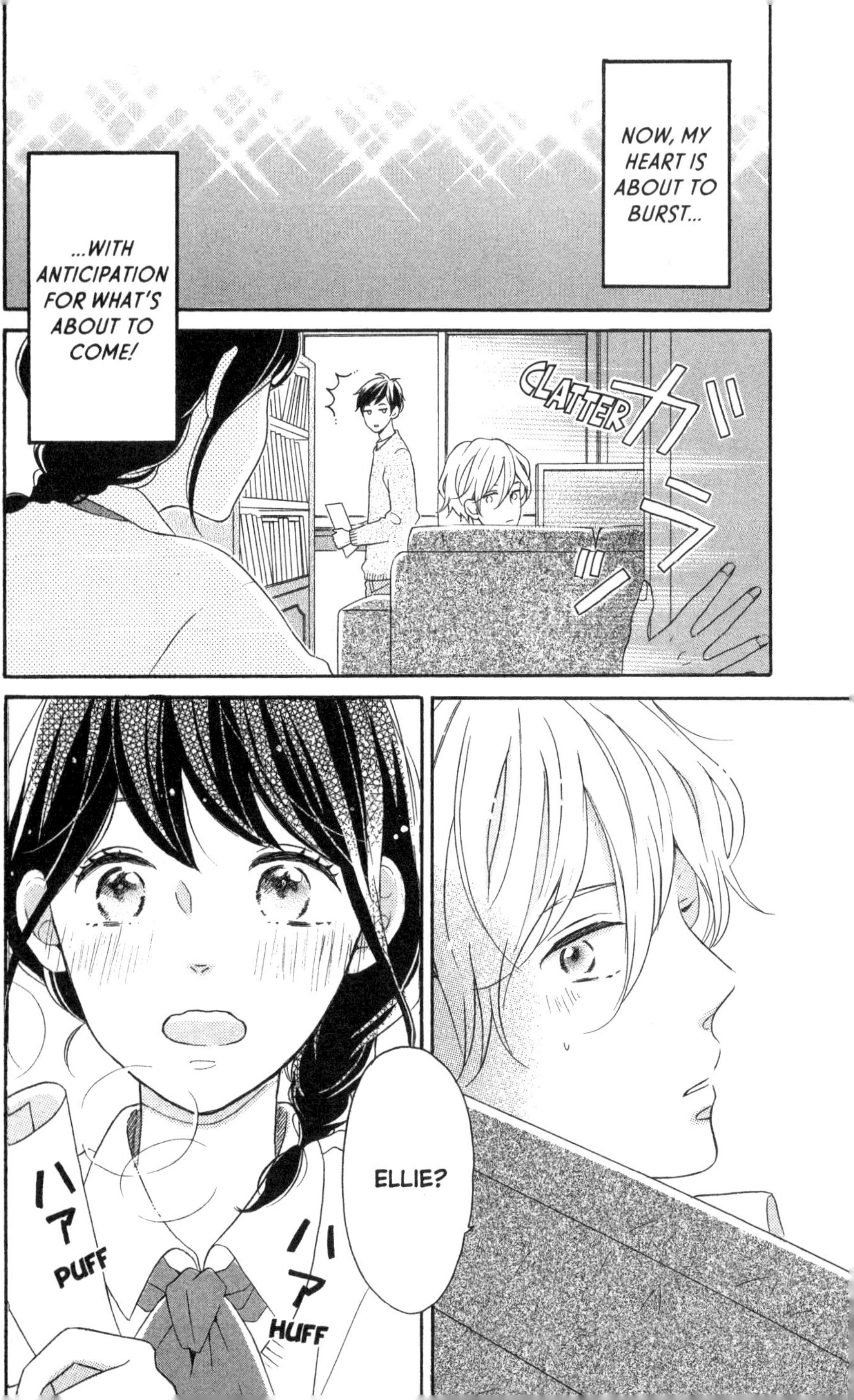
NOW, MY HEART IS ABOUT TO BURST...
...WITH ANTICIPATION FOR WHAT'S ABOUT TO COME!
ガラッ
CLATTER
ELLIE?
ハア
HUFF
ハア
PUFF

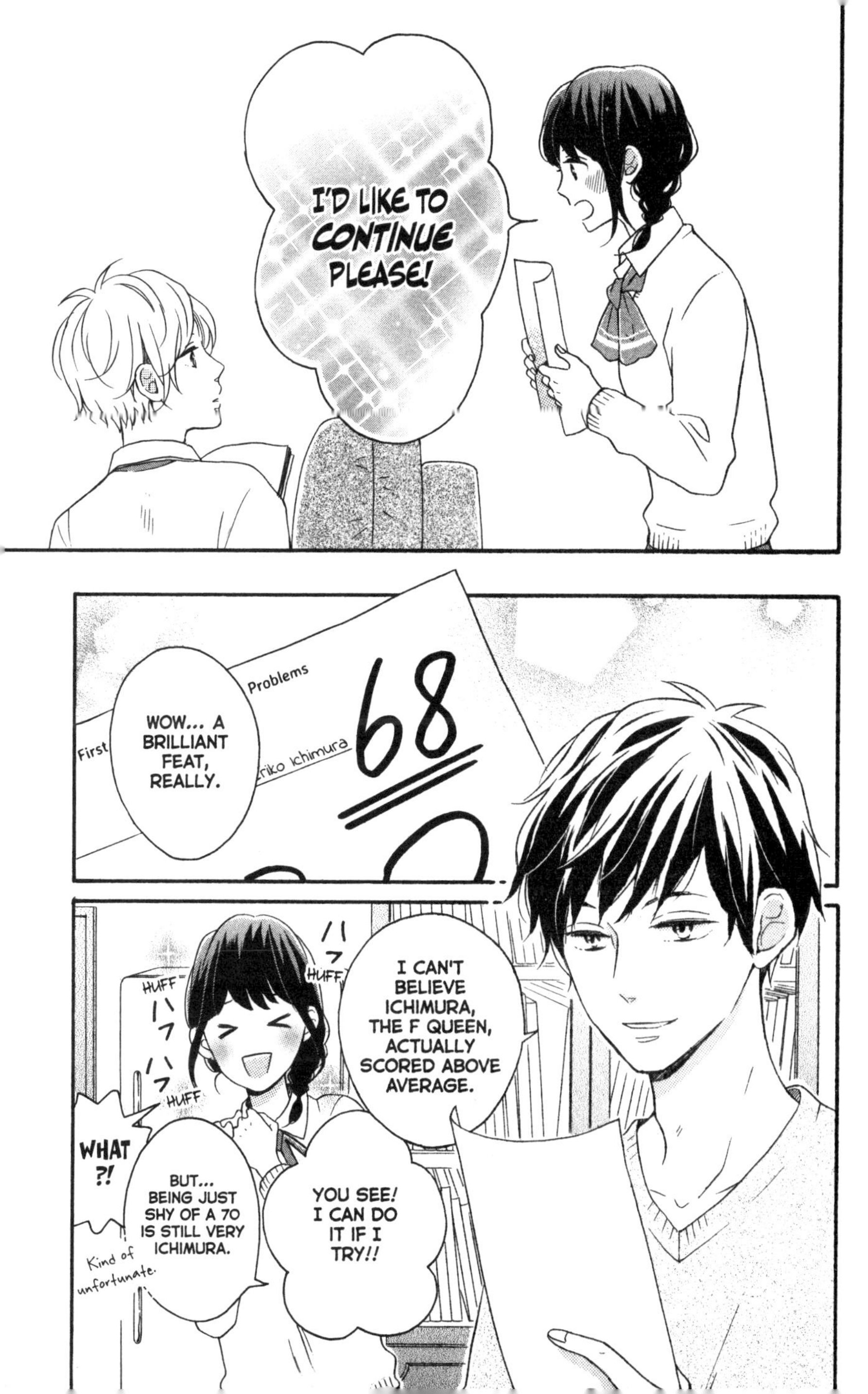
I'D LIKE TO CONTINUE PLEASE!
Problems
First
riko Ichimura
68
WOW... A BRILLIANT FEAT, REALLY.
I CAN'T BELIEVE ICHIMURA, THE F QUEEN, ACTUALLY SCORED ABOVE AVERAGE.
HUFF
HUFF
HUFF
YOU SEE! I CAN DO IT IF I TRY!!
WHAT?!
BUT... BEING JUST SHY OF A 70 IS STILL VERY ICHIMURA.
Kind of unfortunate.

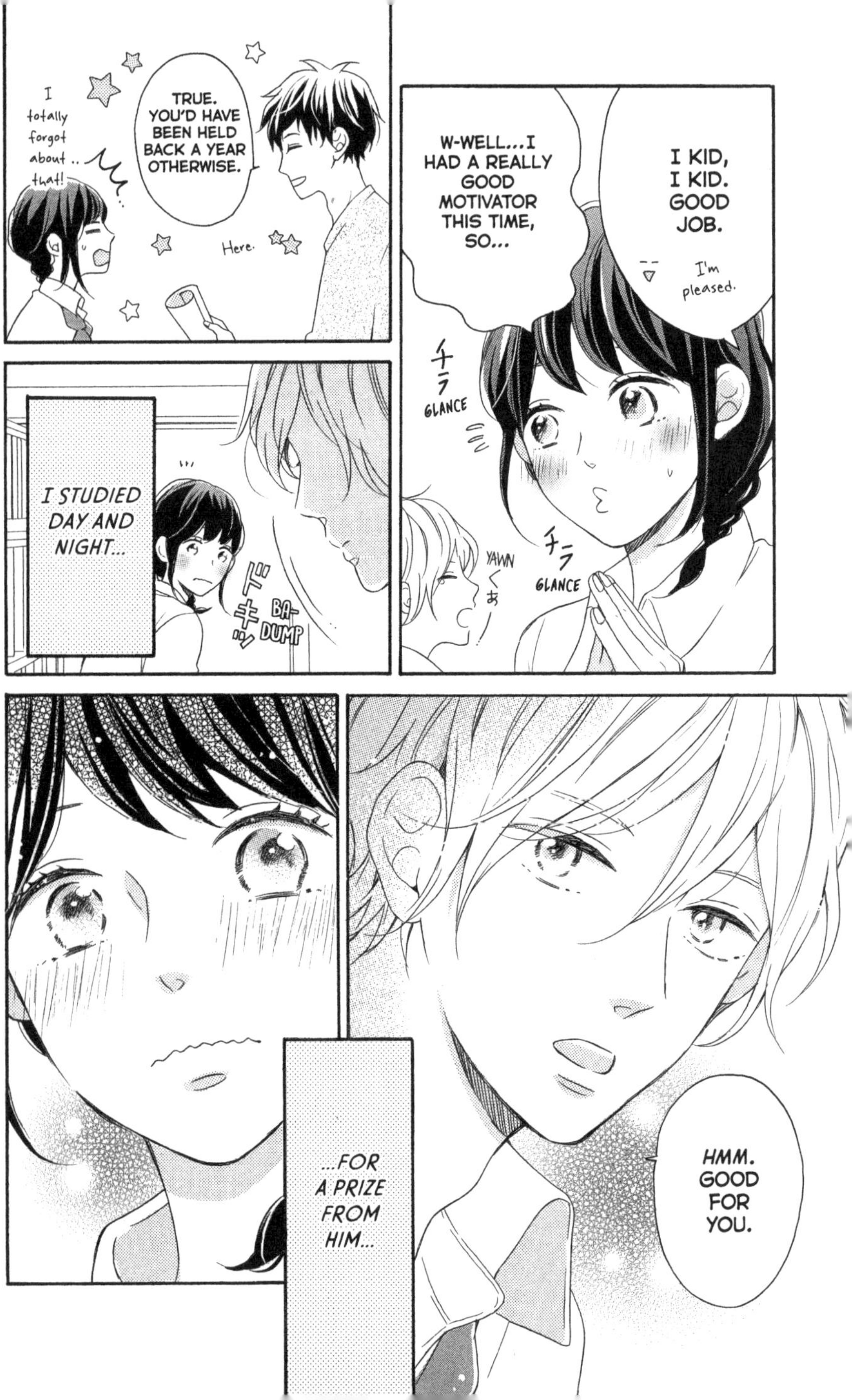
I totally forgot about.. that!
TRUE. YOU'D HAVE BEEN HELD BACK A YEAR OTHERWISE.
Here.
I KID, I KID. GOOD JOB.
I'm pleased.
W-WELL...I HAD A REALLY GOOD MOTIVATOR THIS TIME, SO...
チラ
GLANCE
チラ
GLANCE
YAWN
くぁ
I STUDIED DAY AND NIGHT...
ドキッ
BA-DUMP
HMM. GOOD FOR YOU.
...FOR A PRIZE FROM HIM...

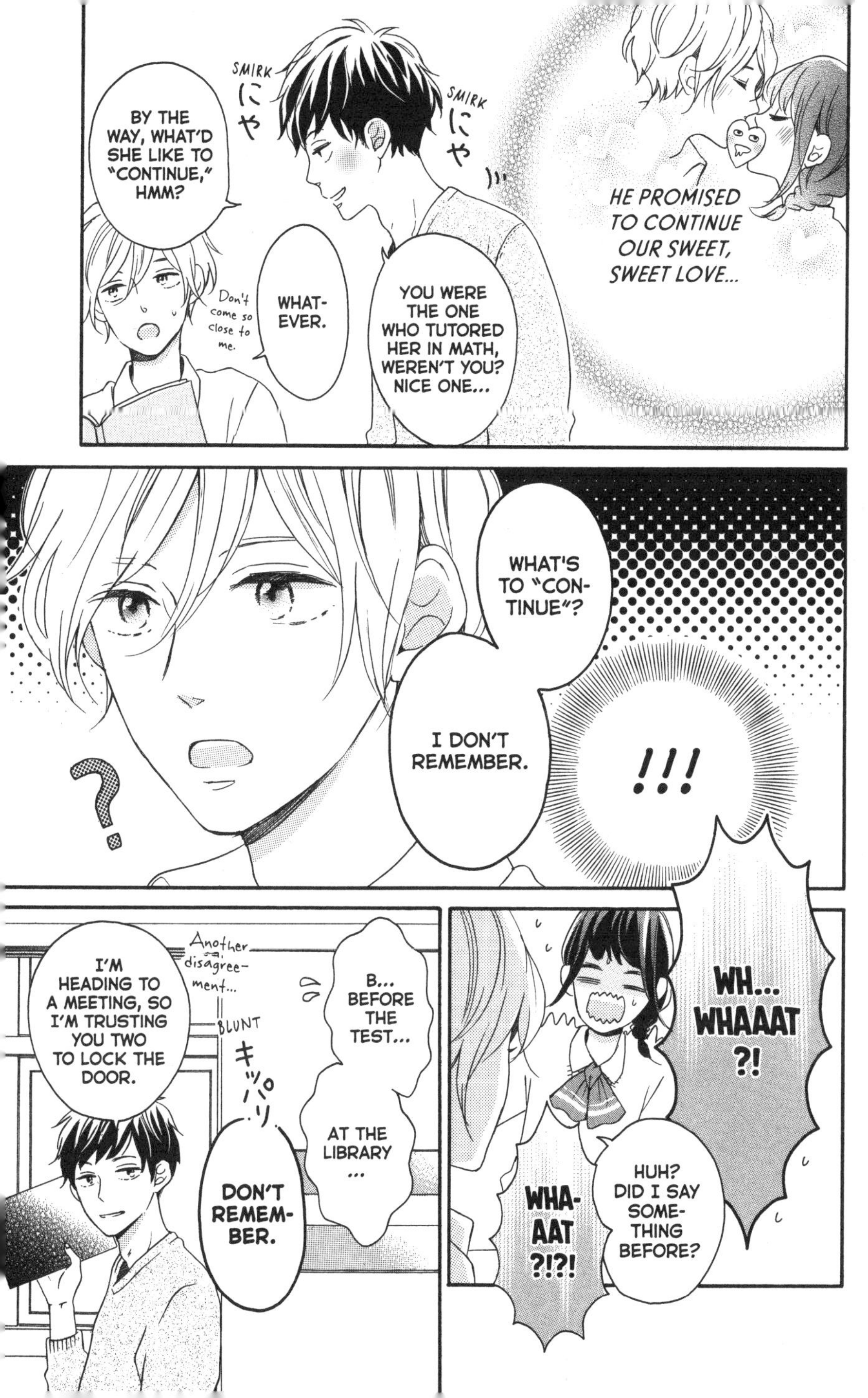
HE PROMISED TO CONTINUE OUR SWEET, SWEET LOVE...
SMIRK にや
YOU WERE THE ONE WHO TUTORED HER IN MATH, WEREN'T YOU? NICE ONE...
SMIRK にや
BY THE WAY, WHAT'D SHE LIKE TO "CONTINUE," HMM?
WHAT-EVER.
Don't come so close to me.
WHAT'S TO "CON-TINUE"?
I DON'T REMEMBER.
!!!
WH... WHAAAT?!
HUH? DID I SAY SOME-THING BEFORE?
WHA-AAT?!?!
B... BEFORE THE TEST...
AT THE LIBRARY...
BLUNT キッパリ
DON'T REMEM-BER.
Another disagree-ment...
I'M HEADING TO A MEETING, SO I'M TRUSTING YOU TWO TO LOCK THE DOOR.

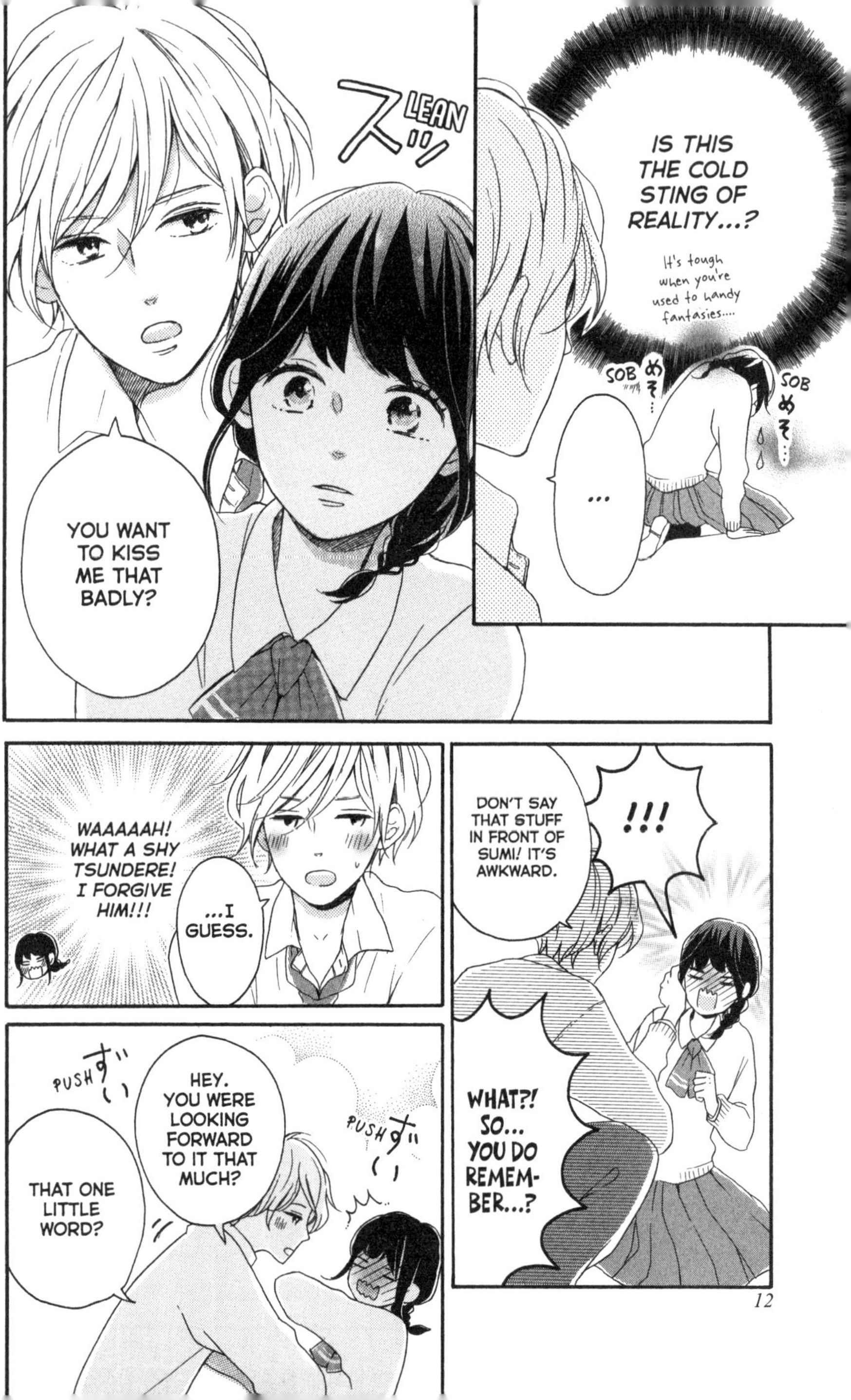
IS THIS THE COLD STING OF REALITY...?
It's tough when you're used to handy fantasies....
SOB めそ…
SOB めそ…
...
LEAN スッ
YOU WANT TO KISS ME THAT BADLY?
!!!
DON'T SAY THAT STUFF IN FRONT OF SUMI! IT'S AWKWARD.
WHAT?! SO... YOU DO REMEMBER...?
...I GUESS.
WAAAAAH! WHAT A SHY TSUNDERE! I FORGIVE HIM!!!
PUSH すい
HEY. YOU WERE LOOKING FORWARD TO IT THAT MUCH?
PUSH すい
THAT ONE LITTLE WORD?

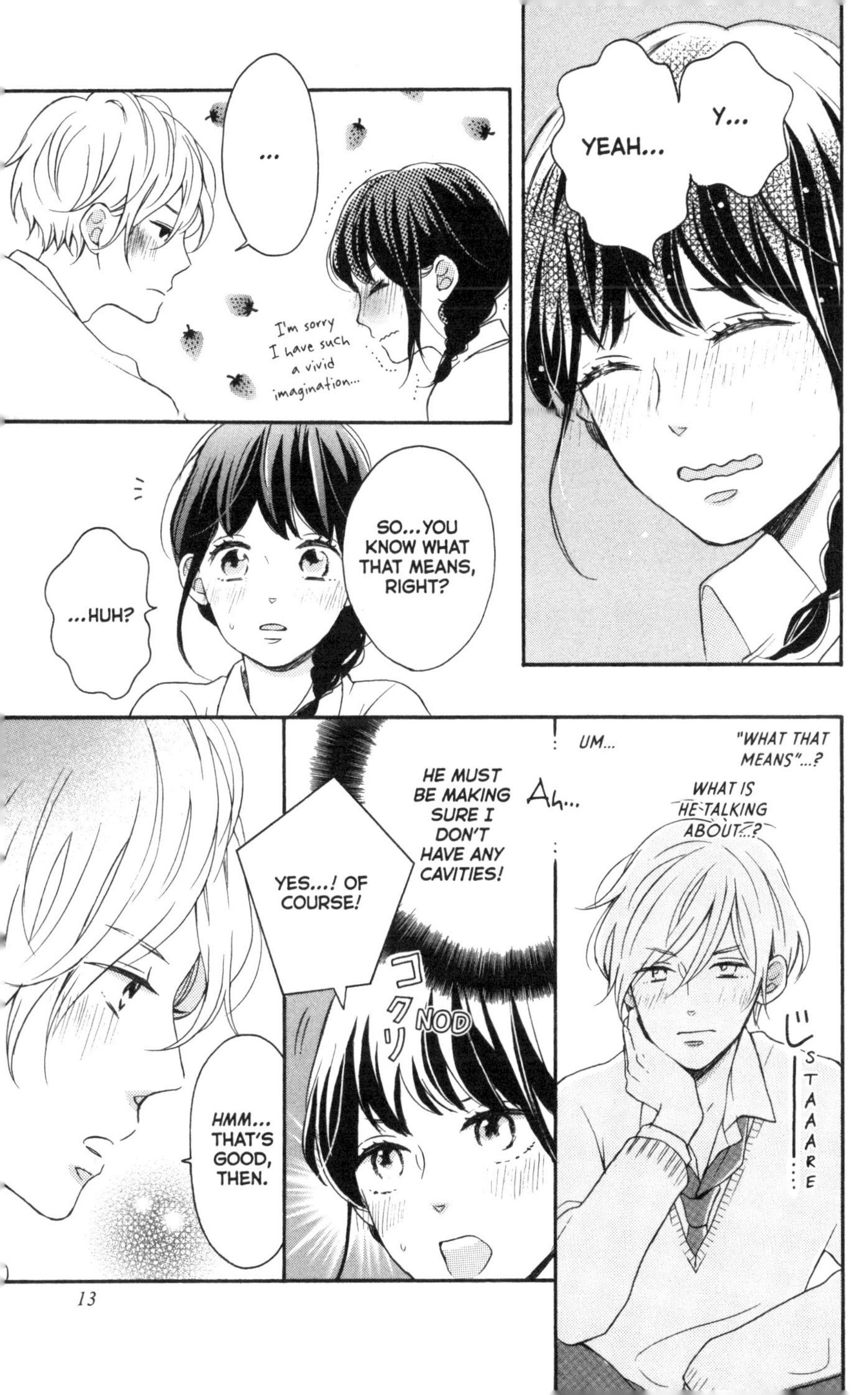
Y... YEAH...
...
I'm sorry I have such a vivid imagination...
SO...YOU KNOW WHAT THAT MEANS, RIGHT?
...HUH?
"WHAT THAT MEANS"...?
WHAT IS HE TALKING ABOUT...?
UM...
Ah...
STAAARE...
HE MUST BE MAKING SURE I DON'T HAVE ANY CAVITIES!
YES...! OF COURSE!
NOD
HMM... THAT'S GOOD, THEN.

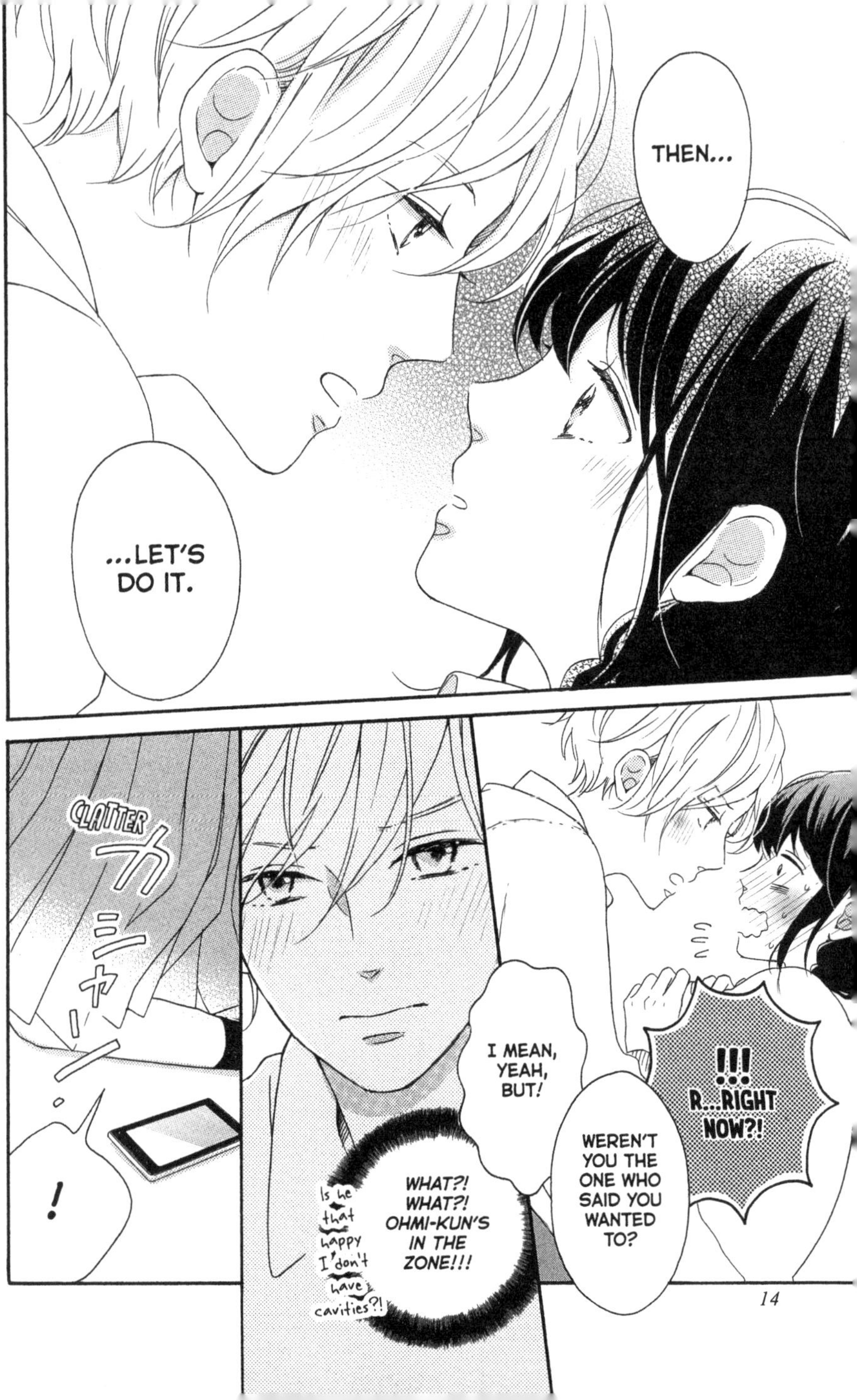
THEN...
...LET'S DO IT.
!!! R...RIGHT NOW?!
WEREN'T YOU THE ONE WHO SAID YOU WANTED TO?
I MEAN, YEAH, BUT!
WHAT?! WHAT?! OHMI-KUN'S IN THE ZONE!!!
Is he that happy I don't have cavities?!
CLATTER
!

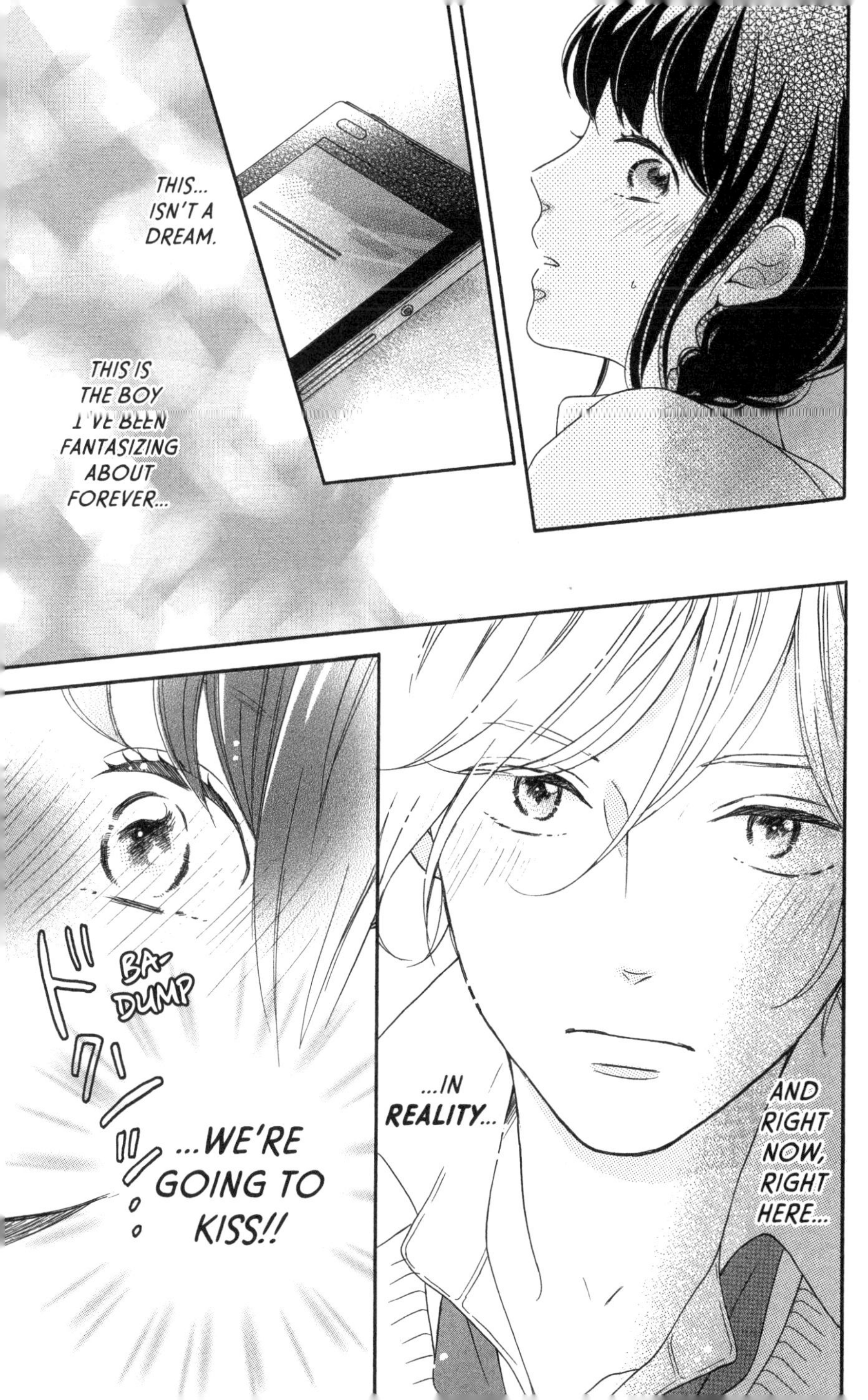
THIS... ISN'T A DREAM.
THIS IS THE BOY I'VE BEEN FANTASIZING ABOUT FOREVER...
AND RIGHT NOW, RIGHT HERE...
...IN REALITY...
BA-DUMP
...WE'RE GOING TO KISS!!

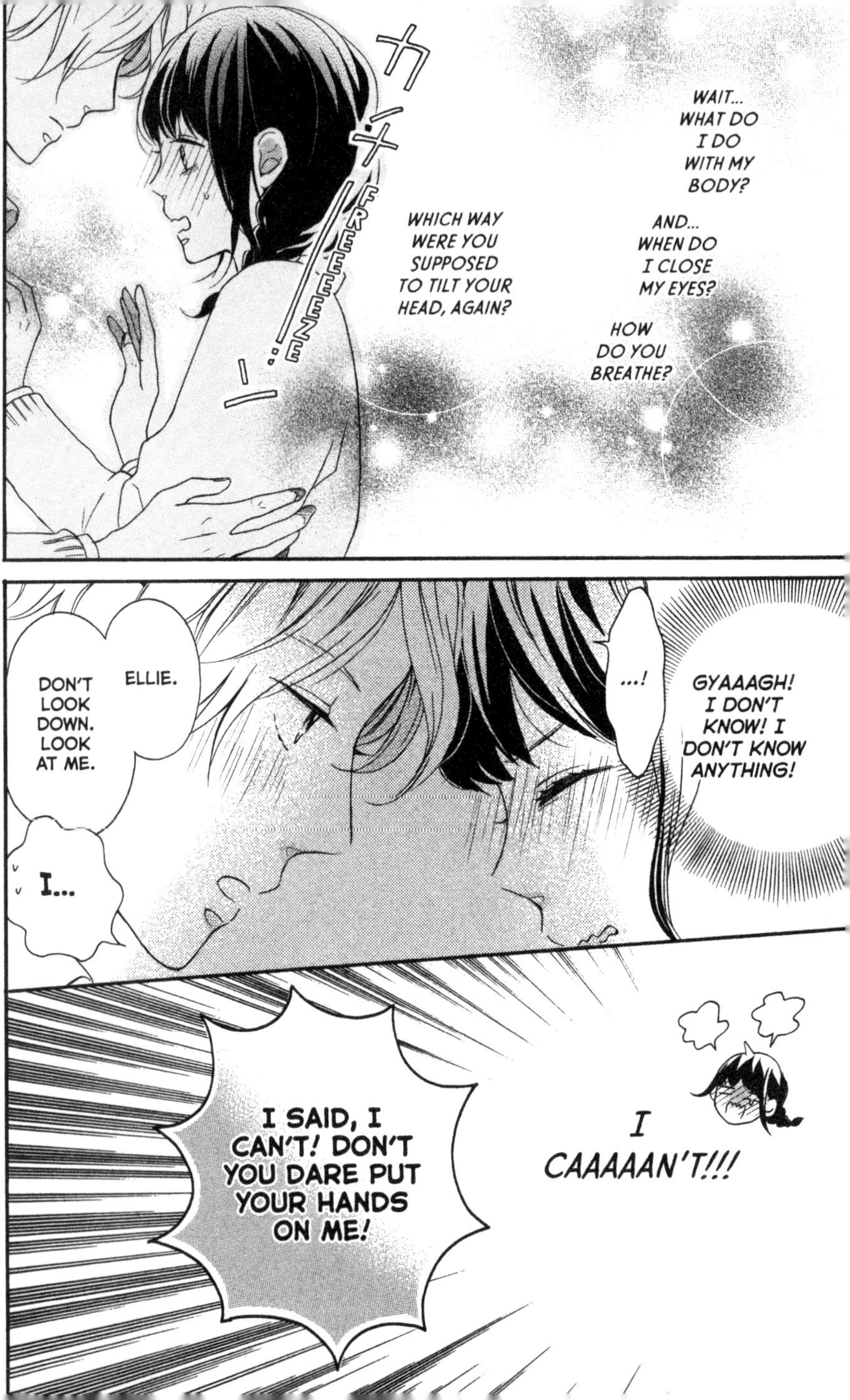
WAIT... WHAT DO I DO WITH MY BODY?
AND... WHEN DO I CLOSE MY EYES?
HOW DO YOU BREATHE?
WHICH WAY WERE YOU SUPPOSED TO TILT YOUR HEAD, AGAIN?
FREEEEZE..!
...!
GYAAAGH! I DON'T KNOW! I DON'T KNOW ANYTHING!
ELLIE.
DON'T LOOK DOWN. LOOK AT ME.
I...
I CAAAAAN'T!!!
I SAID, I CAN'T! DON'T YOU DARE PUT YOUR HANDS ON ME!

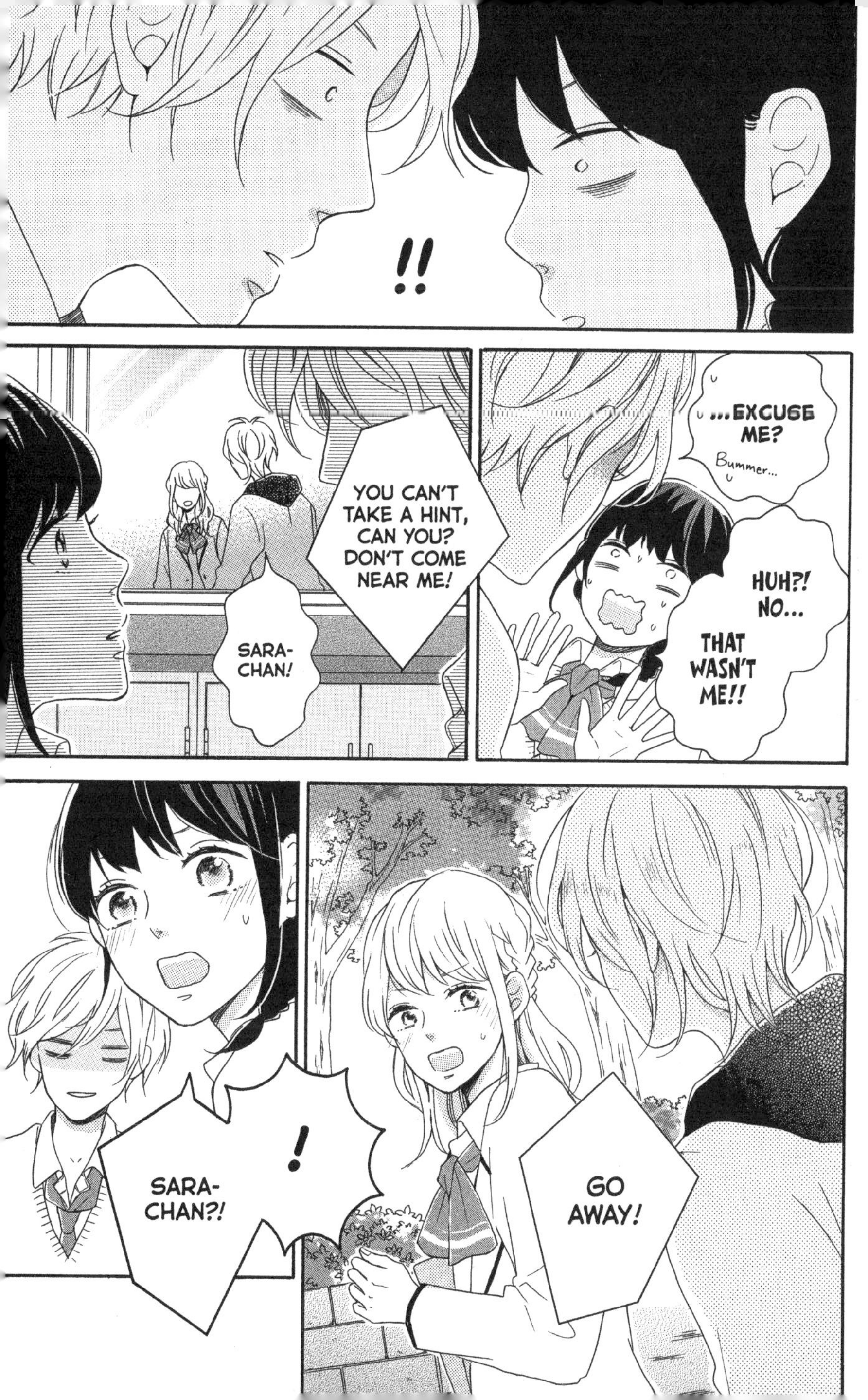
!!
...EXCUSE ME?
Bummer...
HUH?! NO...
THAT WASN'T ME!!
YOU CAN'T TAKE A HINT, CAN YOU? DON'T COME NEAR ME!
SARA-CHAN!
GO AWAY!
!
SARA-CHAN?!

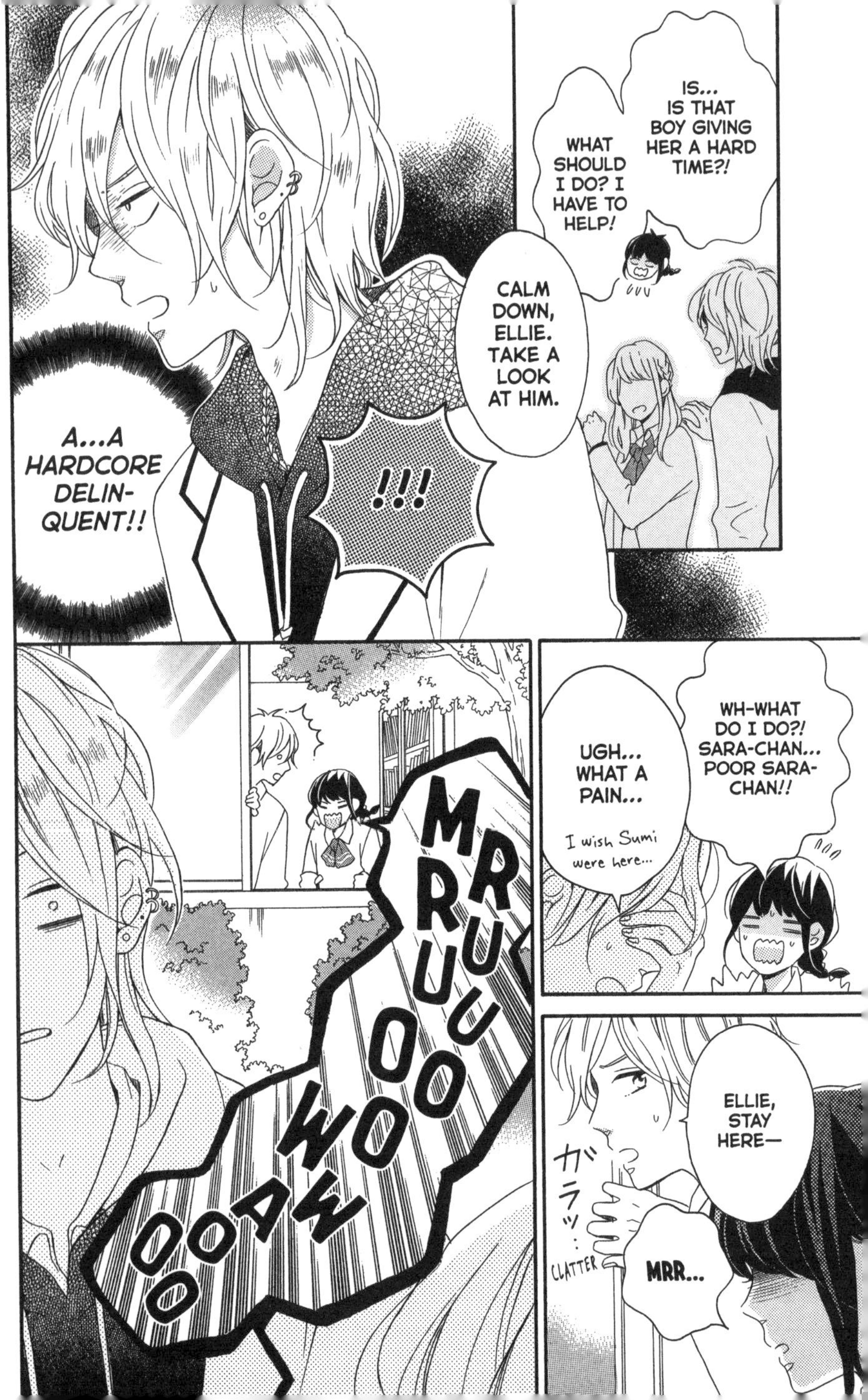

IS... IS THAT BOY GIVING HER A HARD TIME?!
WHAT SHOULD I DO? I HAVE TO HELP!
CALM DOWN, ELLIE. TAKE A LOOK AT HIM.
!!!
A...A HARDCORE DELIN-QUENT!!
WH-WHAT DO I DO?! SARA-CHAN... POOR SARA-CHAN!!
UGH... WHAT A PAIN...
I wish Sumi were here...
ELLIE, STAY HERE—
ガラッ
CLATTER
MRR...
MRRUUUOOOWOOOAWOOO

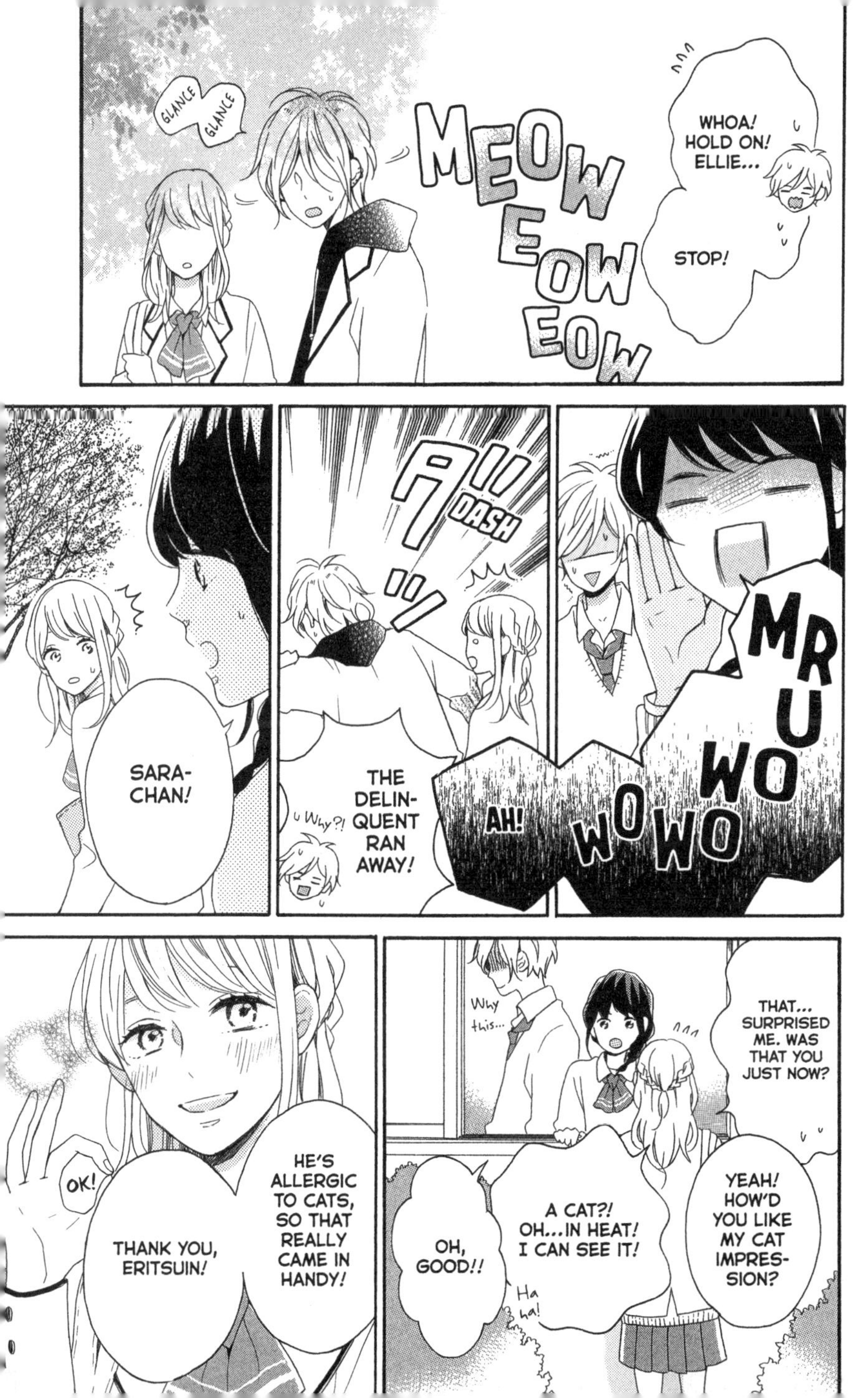
WHOA! HOLD ON! ELLIE...
STOP!
MEOW EOW EOW
GLANCE GLANCE
MRUWO WOWO
AH!
DASH
THE DELIN-QUENT RAN AWAY!
Why?!
SARA-CHAN!
THAT... SURPRISED ME. WAS THAT YOU JUST NOW?
YEAH! HOW'D YOU LIKE MY CAT IMPRES-SION?
A CAT?! OH...IN HEAT! I CAN SEE IT!
OH, GOOD!!
Ha ha!
Why this...
HE'S ALLERGIC TO CATS, SO THAT REALLY CAME IN HANDY!
THANK YOU, ERITSUIN!
OK!

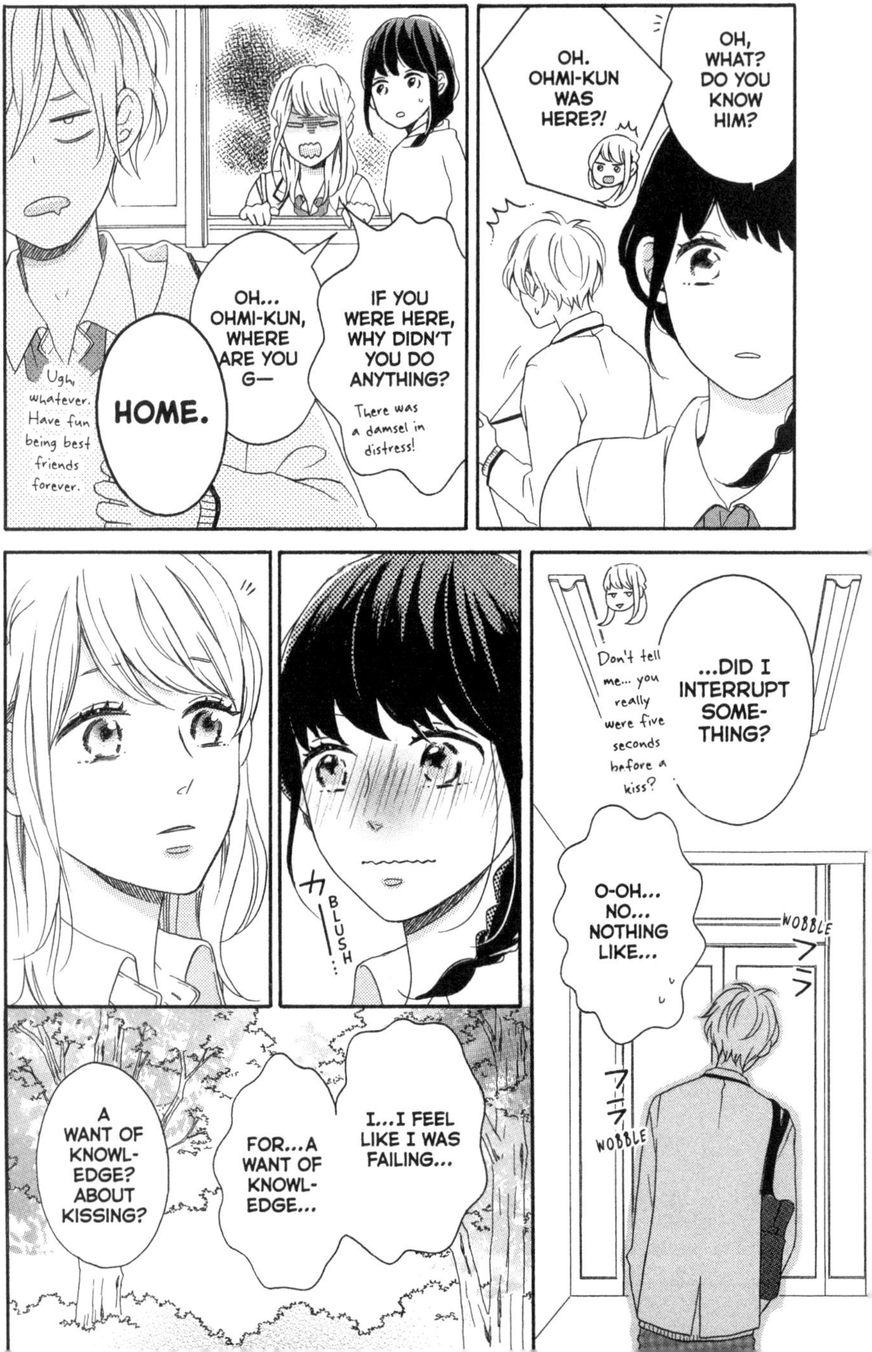
OH, WHAT? DO YOU KNOW HIM?
OH. OHMI-KUN WAS HERE?!
IF YOU WERE HERE, WHY DIDN'T YOU DO ANYTHING?
There was a damsel in distress!
OH... OHMI-KUN, WHERE ARE YOU G—
HOME.
Ugh, whatever. Have fun being best friends forever.
...DID I INTERRUPT SOME-THING?
Don't tell me... you really were five seconds before a kiss?
O-OH... NO... NOTHING LIKE...
WOBBLE
WOBBLE
BLUSH
I...I FEEL LIKE I WAS FAILING...
FOR...A WANT OF KNOWL-EDGE...
A WANT OF KNOWL-EDGE? ABOUT KISSING?

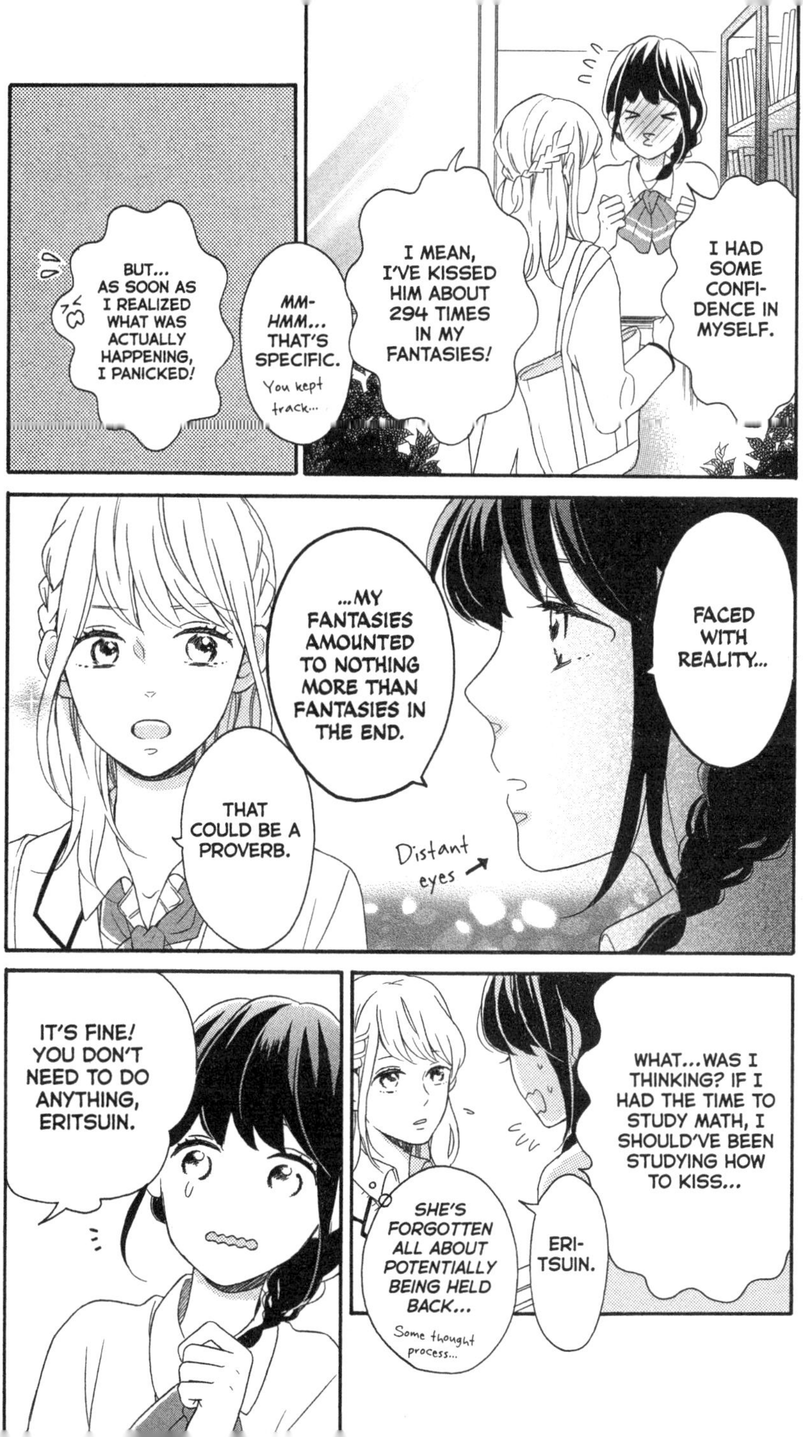

I HAD SOME CONFIDENCE IN MYSELF.
I MEAN, I'VE KISSED HIM ABOUT 294 TIMES IN MY FANTASIES!
MM-HMM... THAT'S SPECIFIC.
You kept track...
BUT... AS SOON AS I REALIZED WHAT WAS ACTUALLY HAPPENING, I PANICKED!
FACED WITH REALITY...
...MY FANTASIES AMOUNTED TO NOTHING MORE THAN FANTASIES IN THE END.
Distant eyes
THAT COULD BE A PROVERB.
WHAT...WAS I THINKING? IF I HAD THE TIME TO STUDY MATH, I SHOULD'VE BEEN STUDYING HOW TO KISS...
ERI-TSUIN.
SHE'S FORGOTTEN ALL ABOUT POTENTIALLY BEING HELD BACK...
Some thought process...
IT'S FINE! YOU DON'T NEED TO DO ANYTHING, ERITSUIN.

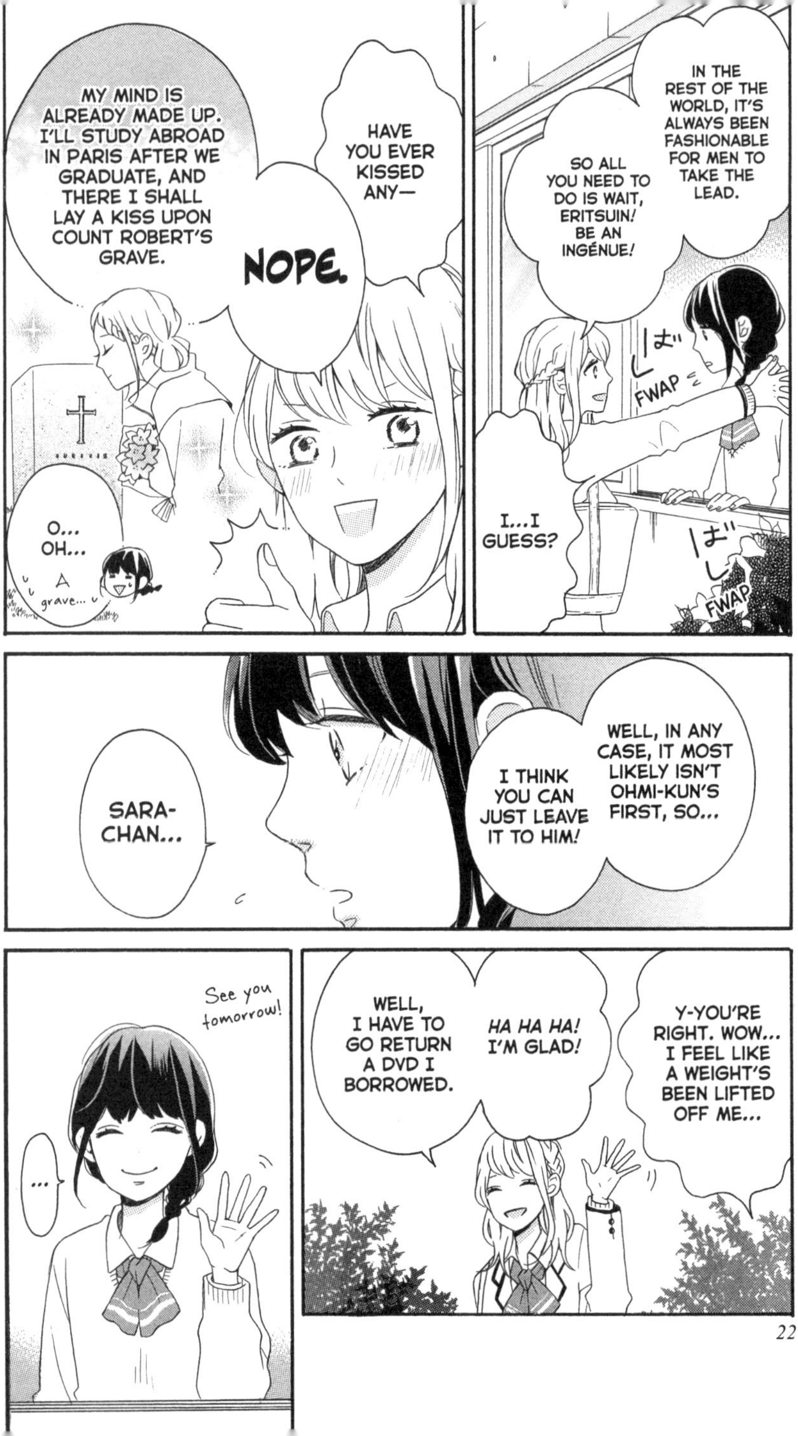
IN THE REST OF THE WORLD, IT'S ALWAYS BEEN FASHIONABLE FOR MEN TO TAKE THE LEAD.
SO ALL YOU NEED TO DO IS WAIT, ERITSUIN! BE AN INGÉNUE!
ばし FWAP
ばし FWAP
I...I GUESS?
HAVE YOU EVER KISSED ANY—
NOPE.
MY MIND IS ALREADY MADE UP. I'LL STUDY ABROAD IN PARIS AFTER WE GRADUATE, AND THERE I SHALL LAY A KISS UPON COUNT ROBERT'S GRAVE.
O... OH... A grave...
WELL, IN ANY CASE, IT MOST LIKELY ISN'T OHMI-KUN'S FIRST, SO...
I THINK YOU CAN JUST LEAVE IT TO HIM!
SARA-CHAN...
Y-YOU'RE RIGHT. WOW... I FEEL LIKE A WEIGHT'S BEEN LIFTED OFF ME...
HA HA HA! I'M GLAD!
WELL, I HAVE TO GO RETURN A DVD I BORROWED.
See you tomorrow!
...

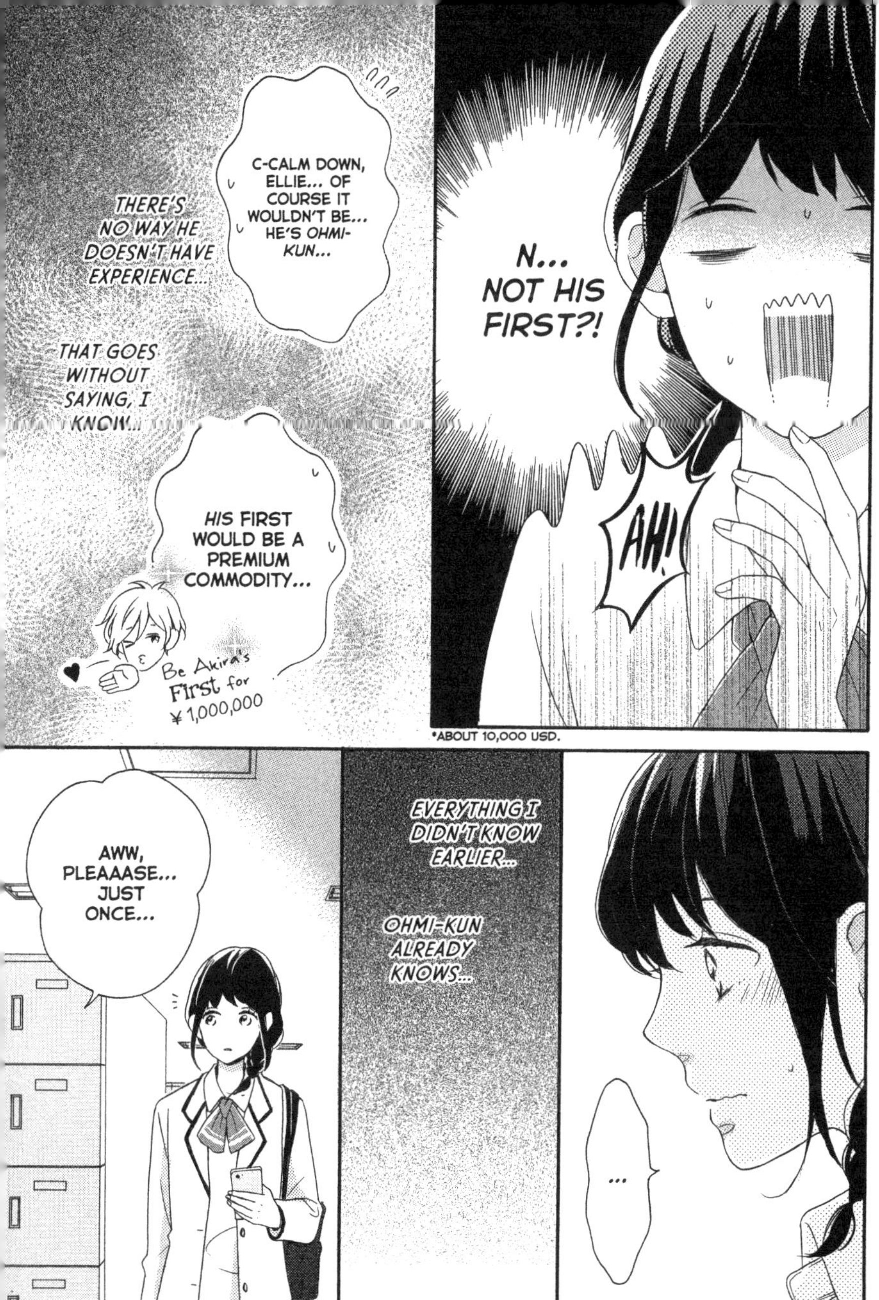
N... NOT HIS FIRST?!
AH!
C-CALM DOWN, ELLIE... OF COURSE IT WOULDN'T BE... HE'S OHMI-KUN...
THERE'S NO WAY HE DOESN'T HAVE EXPERIENCE...
THAT GOES WITHOUT SAYING, I KNOW...
HIS FIRST WOULD BE A PREMIUM COMMODITY...
Be Akira's First for ¥1,000,000
*ABOUT 10,000 USD.
...
EVERYTHING I DIDN'T KNOW EARLIER...
OHMI-KUN ALREADY KNOWS...
AWW, PLEAAASE... JUST ONCE...

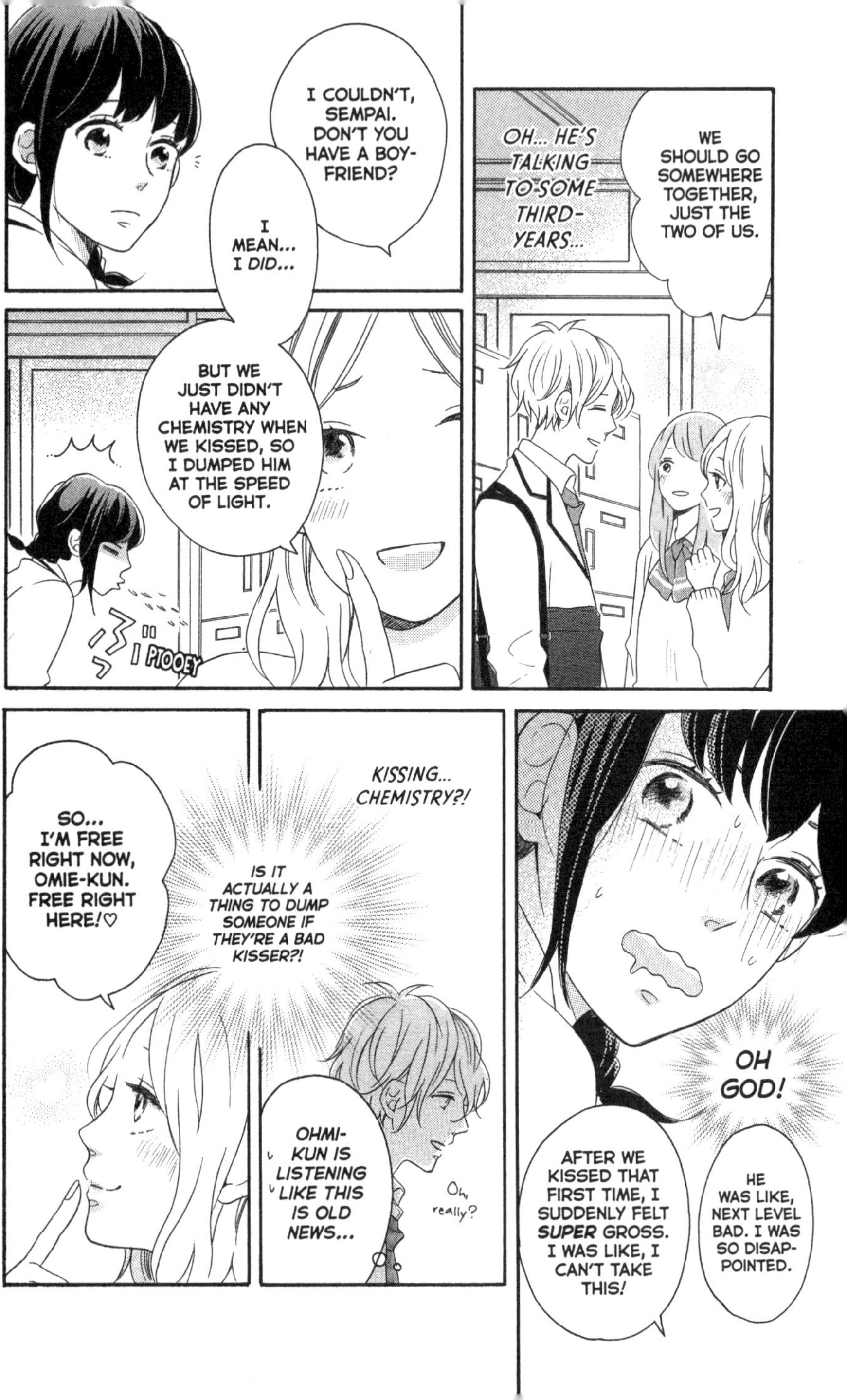
WE SHOULD GO SOMEWHERE TOGETHER, JUST THE TWO OF US.
OH... HE'S TALKING TO SOME THIRD-YEARS...
I COULDN'T, SEMPAI. DON'T YOU HAVE A BOY-FRIEND?
I MEAN... I DID...
BUT WE JUST DIDN'T HAVE ANY CHEMISTRY WHEN WE KISSED, SO I DUMPED HIM AT THE SPEED OF LIGHT.
PTOOEY
OH GOD!
HE WAS LIKE, NEXT LEVEL BAD. I WAS SO DISAP-POINTED.
AFTER WE KISSED THAT FIRST TIME, I SUDDENLY FELT SUPER GROSS. I WAS LIKE, I CAN'T TAKE THIS!
KISSING... CHEMISTRY?!
IS IT ACTUALLY A THING TO DUMP SOMEONE IF THEY'RE A BAD KISSER?!
Oh, really?
OHMI-KUN IS LISTENING LIKE THIS IS OLD NEWS...
SO... I'M FREE RIGHT NOW, OMIE-KUN. FREE RIGHT HERE!♡

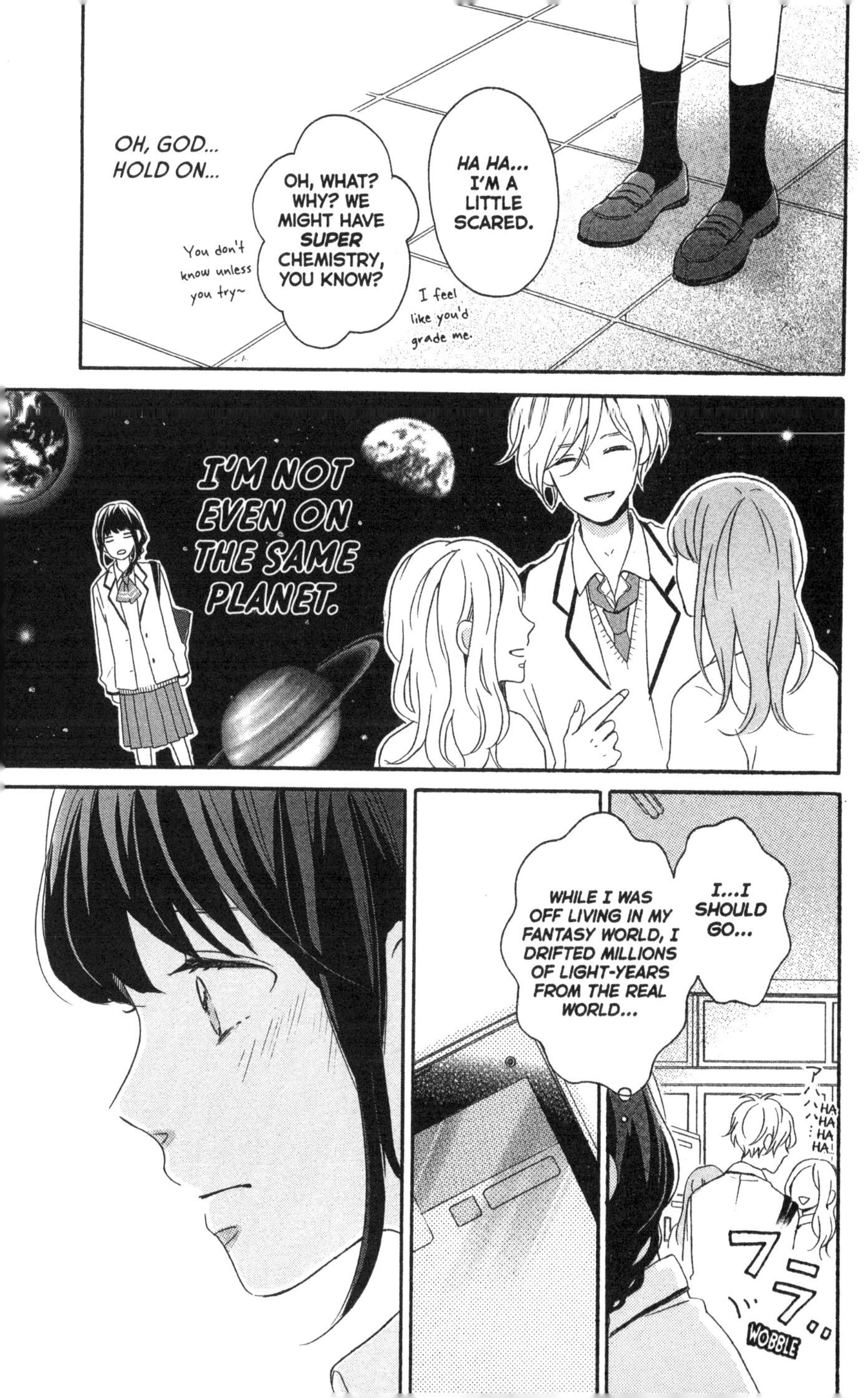
HA HA... I'M A LITTLE SCARED.
I feel like you'd grade me.
OH, WHAT? WHY? WE MIGHT HAVE **SUPER** CHEMISTRY, YOU KNOW?
You don't know unless you try~
OH, GOD... HOLD ON...
I'M NOT EVEN ON THE SAME PLANET.
I...I SHOULD GO...
HA HA HA HA!
WOBBLE
WHILE I WAS OFF LIVING IN MY FANTASY WORLD, I DRIFTED MILLIONS OF LIGHT-YEARS FROM THE REAL WORLD...

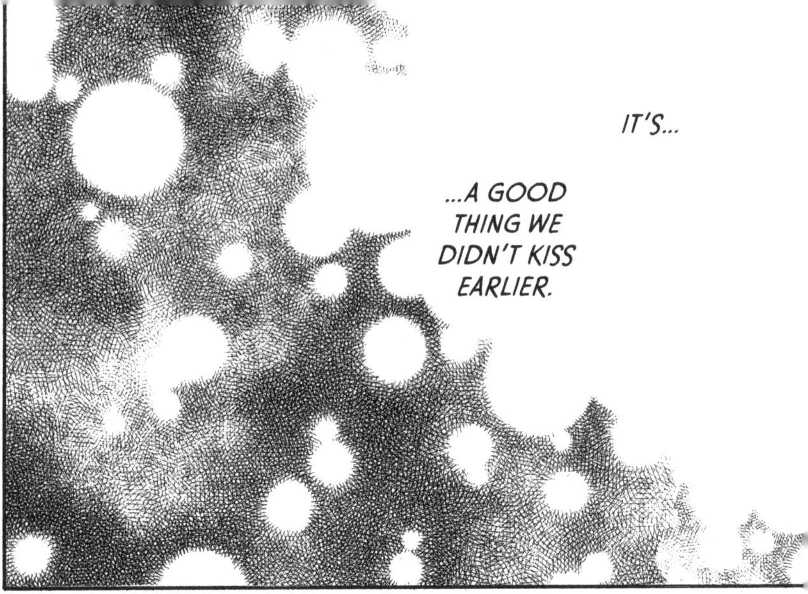
IT'S...
...A GOOD THING WE DIDN'T KISS EARLIER.

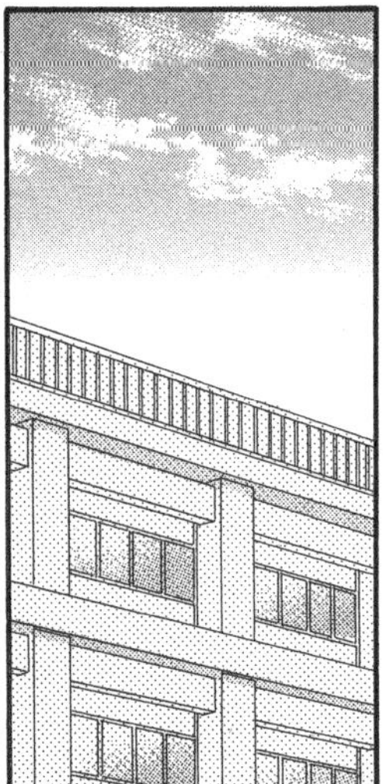

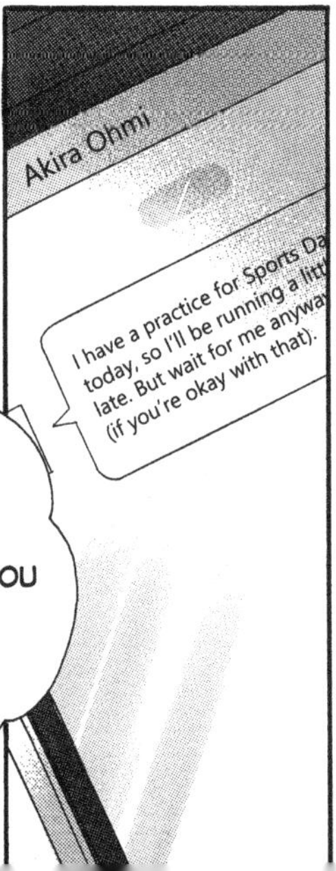
Akira Ohmi
I have a practice for Sports Da
today, so I'll be running a littl
late. But wait for me anyway
(if you're okay with that).

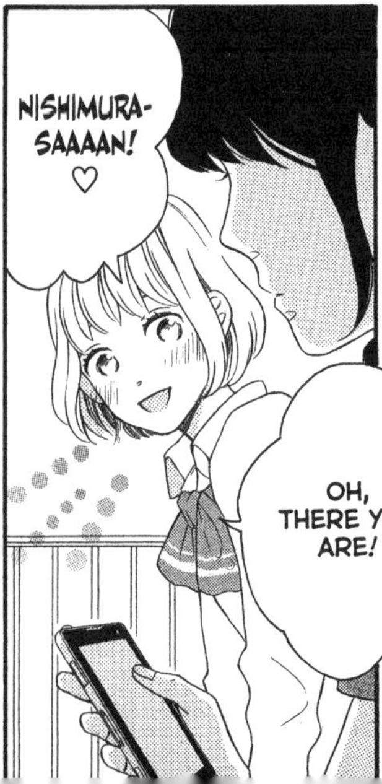
NISHIMURA-SAAAAN! ♡
OH, THERE YOU ARE!

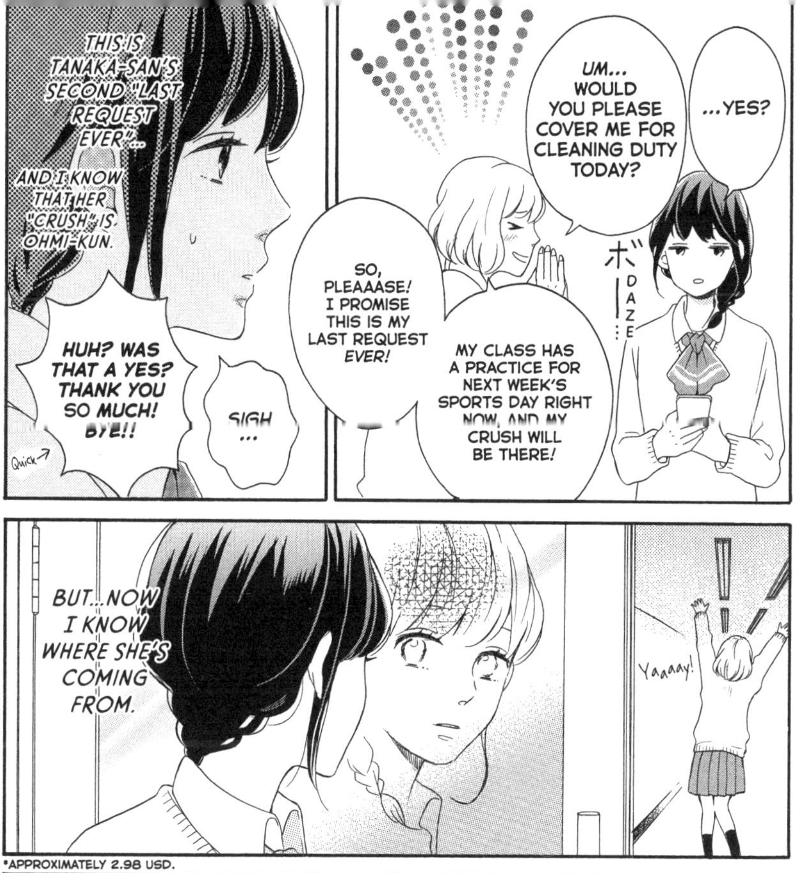
...YES?
UM... WOULD YOU PLEASE COVER ME FOR CLEANING DUTY TODAY?
ボ
DAZE
MY CLASS HAS A PRACTICE FOR NEXT WEEK'S SPORTS DAY RIGHT NOW, AND MY CRUSH WILL BE THERE!
SO, PLEAAASE! I PROMISE THIS IS MY LAST REQUEST *EVER!*
SIGH...
HUH? WAS THAT A YES? THANK YOU SO *MUCH!* BYE!!
Quick
THIS IS TANAKA-SAN'S SECOND "LAST REQUEST EVER"...
AND I KNOW THAT HER "CRUSH" IS OHMI-KUN.
Yaaaay!
BUT... NOW I KNOW WHERE SHE'S COMING FROM.

*APPROXIMATELY 2.98 USD.

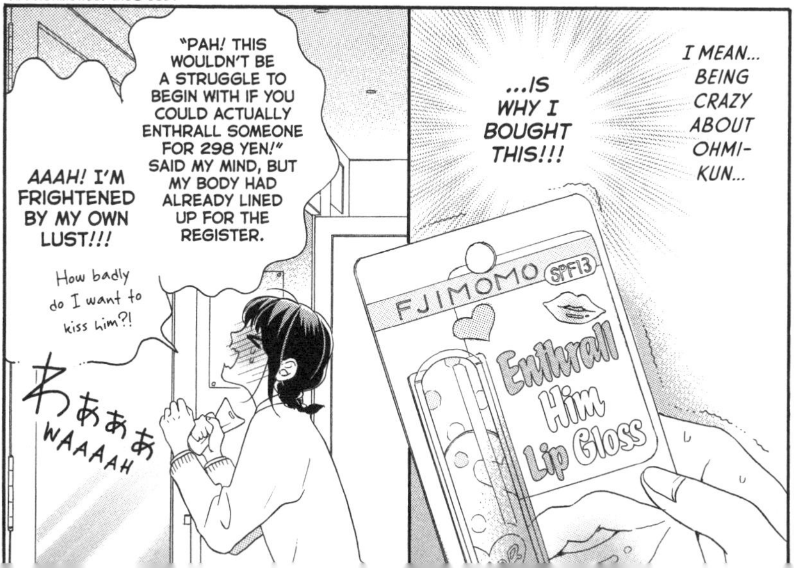
I MEAN... BEING CRAZY ABOUT OHMI-KUN...
...IS WHY I BOUGHT THIS!!!
FJIMOMO
SPF13
Enthrall Him Lip Gloss
"PAH! THIS WOULDN'T BE A STRUGGLE TO BEGIN WITH IF YOU COULD ACTUALLY ENTHRALL SOMEONE FOR 298 YEN!" SAID MY MIND, BUT MY BODY HAD ALREADY LINED UP FOR THE REGISTER.
AAAH! I'M FRIGHTENED BY MY OWN LUST!!!
How badly do I want to kiss him?!
わあああ
WAAAAAH

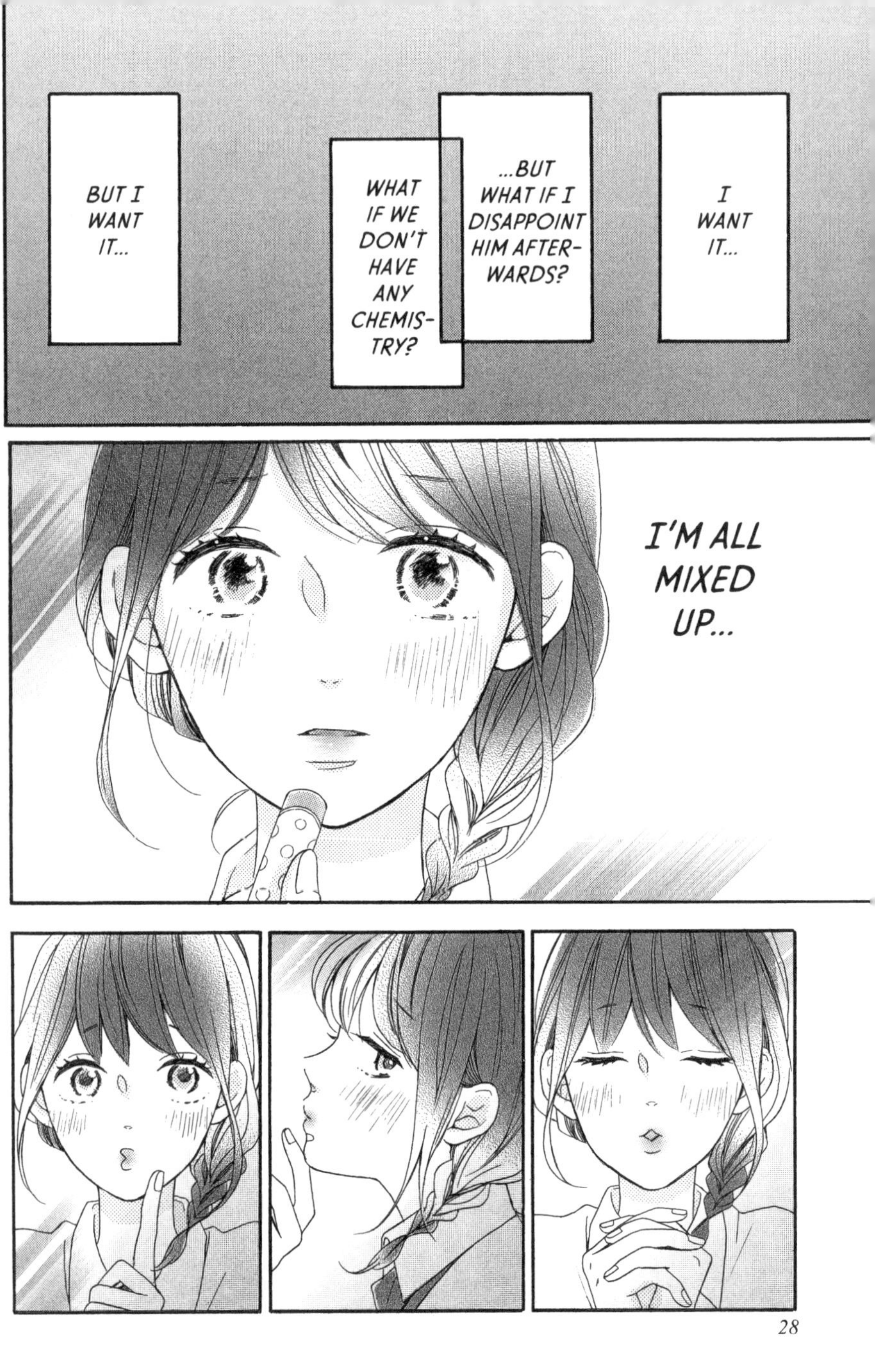
I WANT IT...
...BUT WHAT IF I DISAPPOINT HIM AFTER-WARDS?
WHAT IF WE DON'T HAVE ANY CHEMIS-TRY?
BUT I WANT IT...
I'M ALL MIXED UP...

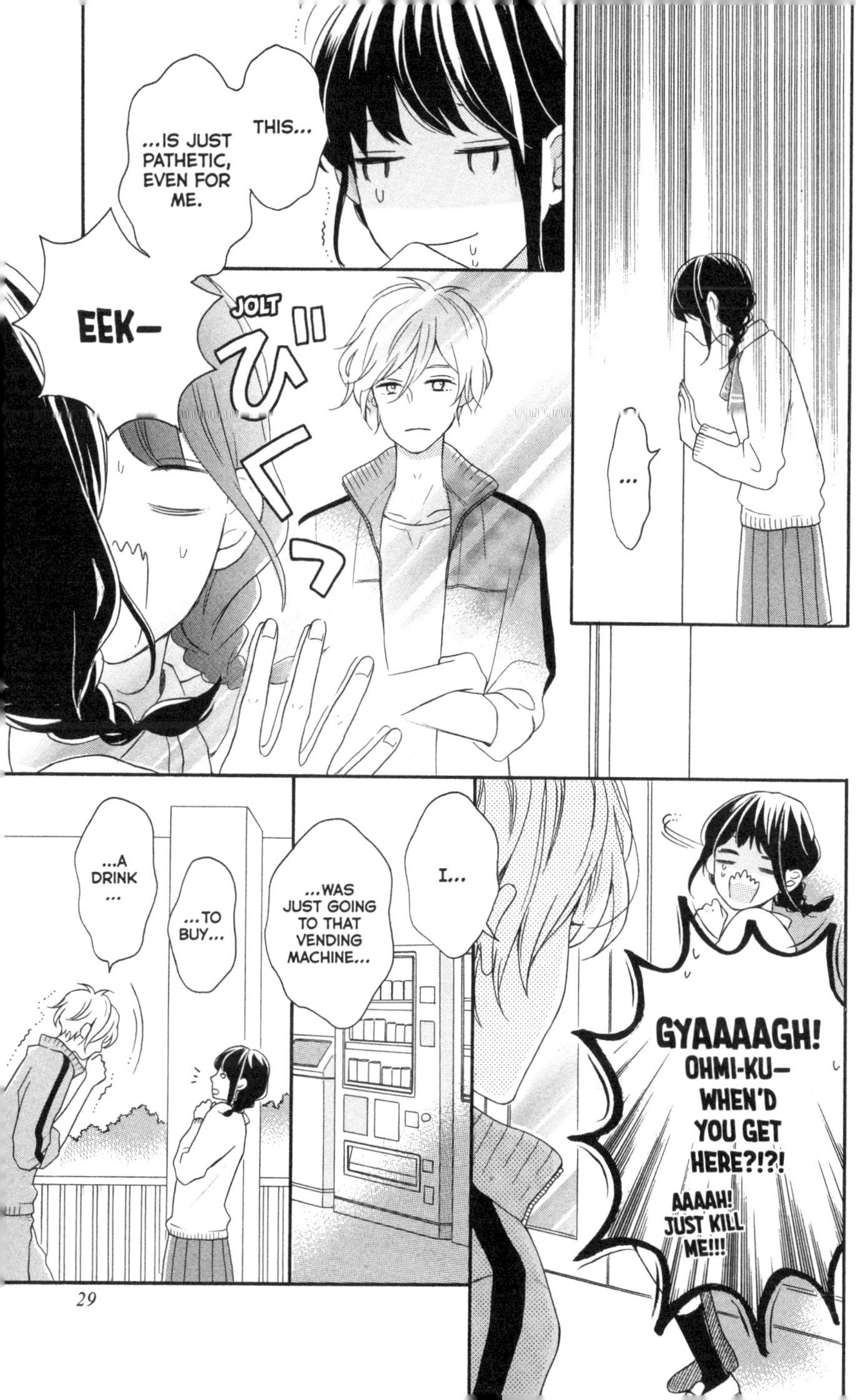
...
THIS...
...IS JUST PATHETIC, EVEN FOR ME.
JOLT
EEK—
GYAAAAGH! OHMI-KU— WHEN'D YOU GET HERE?!?!
AAAAH! JUST KILL ME!!!
I...
...WAS JUST GOING TO THAT VENDING MACHINE...
...A DRINK...
...TO BUY...

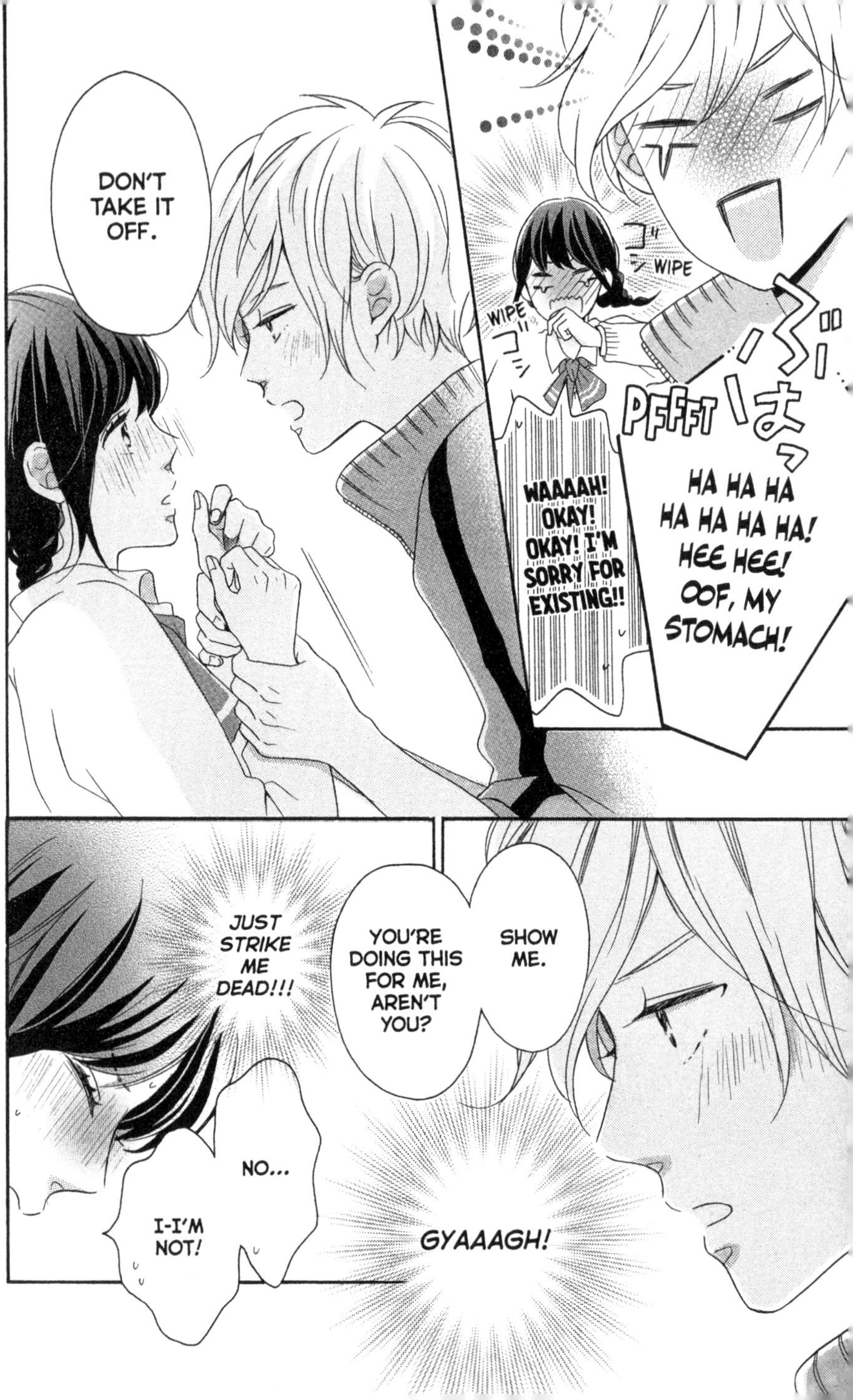

PFFFT
HA HA HA HA HA HA HA! HEE HEE! OOF, MY STOMACH!
WAAAAH! OKAY! OKAY! I'M SORRY FOR EXISTING!!
WIPE
WIPE
DON'T TAKE IT OFF.
SHOW ME.
YOU'RE DOING THIS FOR ME, AREN'T YOU?
JUST STRIKE ME DEAD!!!
NO...
I-I'M NOT!
GYAAAGH!

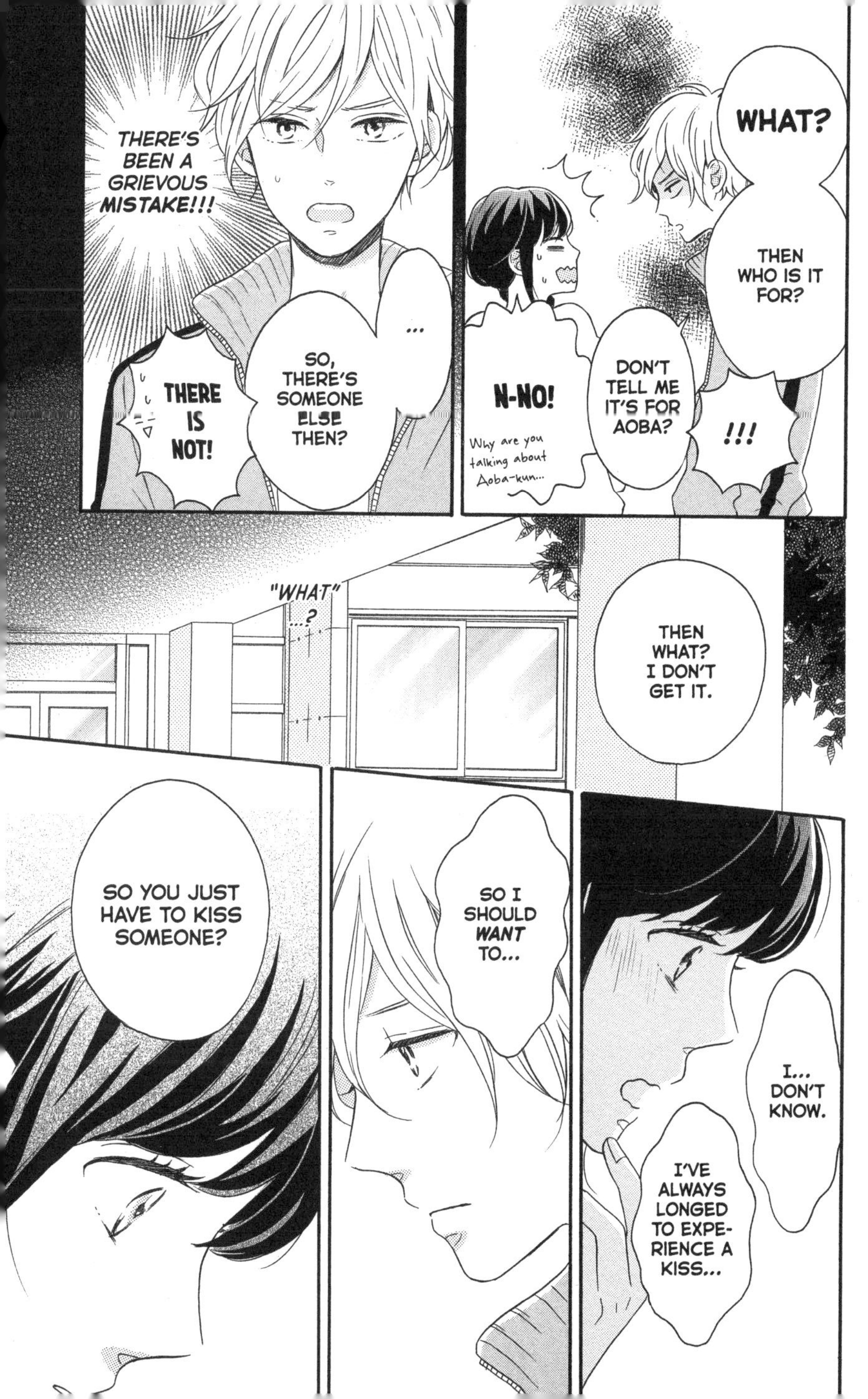
WHAT?
THEN WHO IS IT FOR?
DON'T TELL ME IT'S FOR AOBA?
!!!
N-NO!
Why are you talking about Aoba-kun...
...
SO, THERE'S SOMEONE ELSE THEN?
THERE IS NOT!
THERE'S BEEN A GRIEVOUS MISTAKE!!!
THEN WHAT? I DON'T GET IT.
"WHAT" ...?
I... DON'T KNOW.
I'VE ALWAYS LONGED TO EXPE-RIENCE A KISS...
SO I SHOULD WANT TO...
SO YOU JUST HAVE TO KISS SOMEONE?

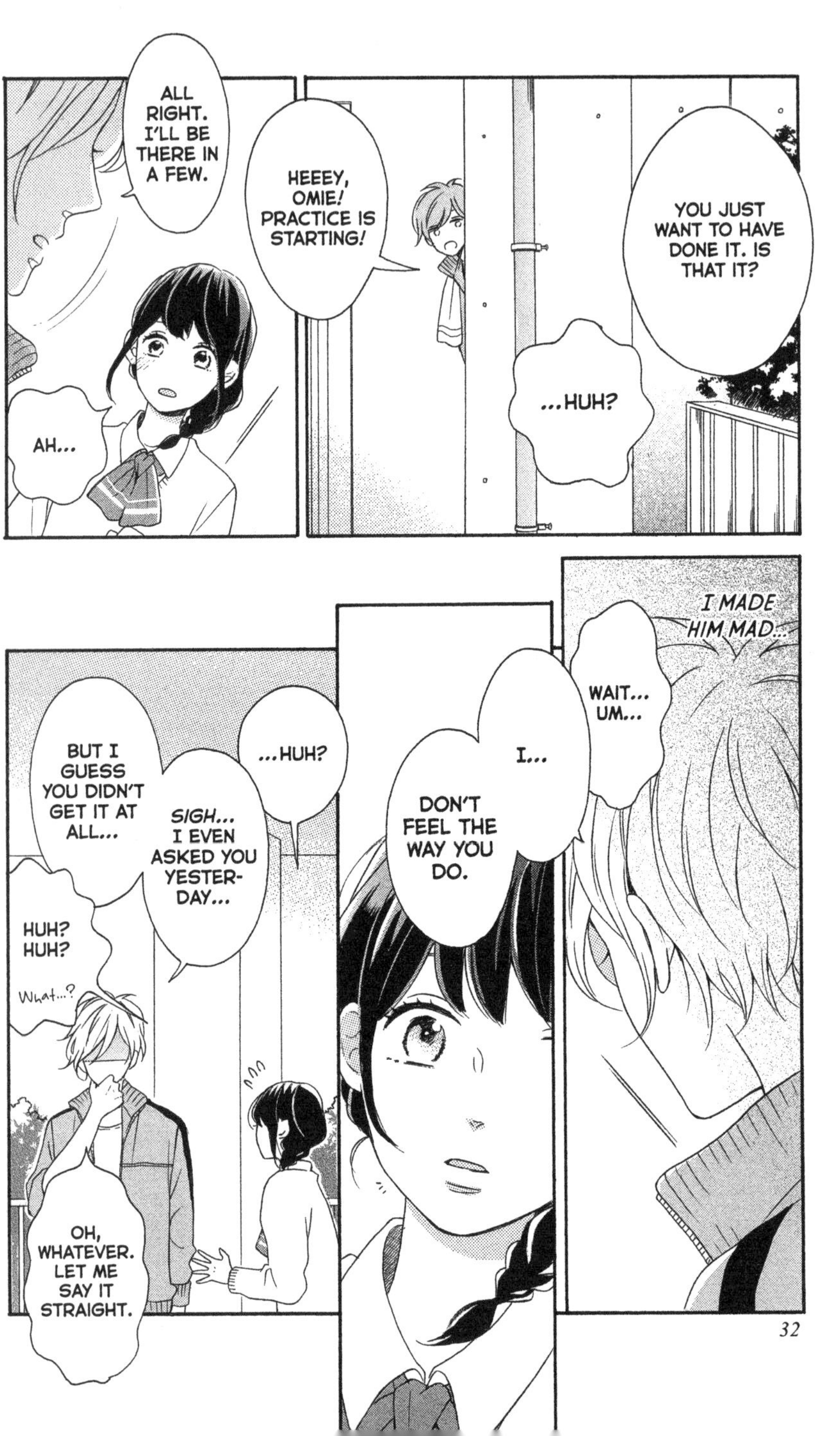
YOU JUST WANT TO HAVE DONE IT. IS THAT IT?
...HUH?
HEEEY, OMIE! PRACTICE IS STARTING!
ALL RIGHT. I'LL BE THERE IN A FEW.
AH...
I MADE HIM MAD...
WAIT... UM...
I...
DON'T FEEL THE WAY YOU DO.
...HUH?
SIGH... I EVEN ASKED YOU YESTER-DAY...
BUT I GUESS YOU DIDN'T GET IT AT ALL...
HUH? HUH?
What...?
OH, WHATEVER. LET ME SAY IT STRAIGHT.

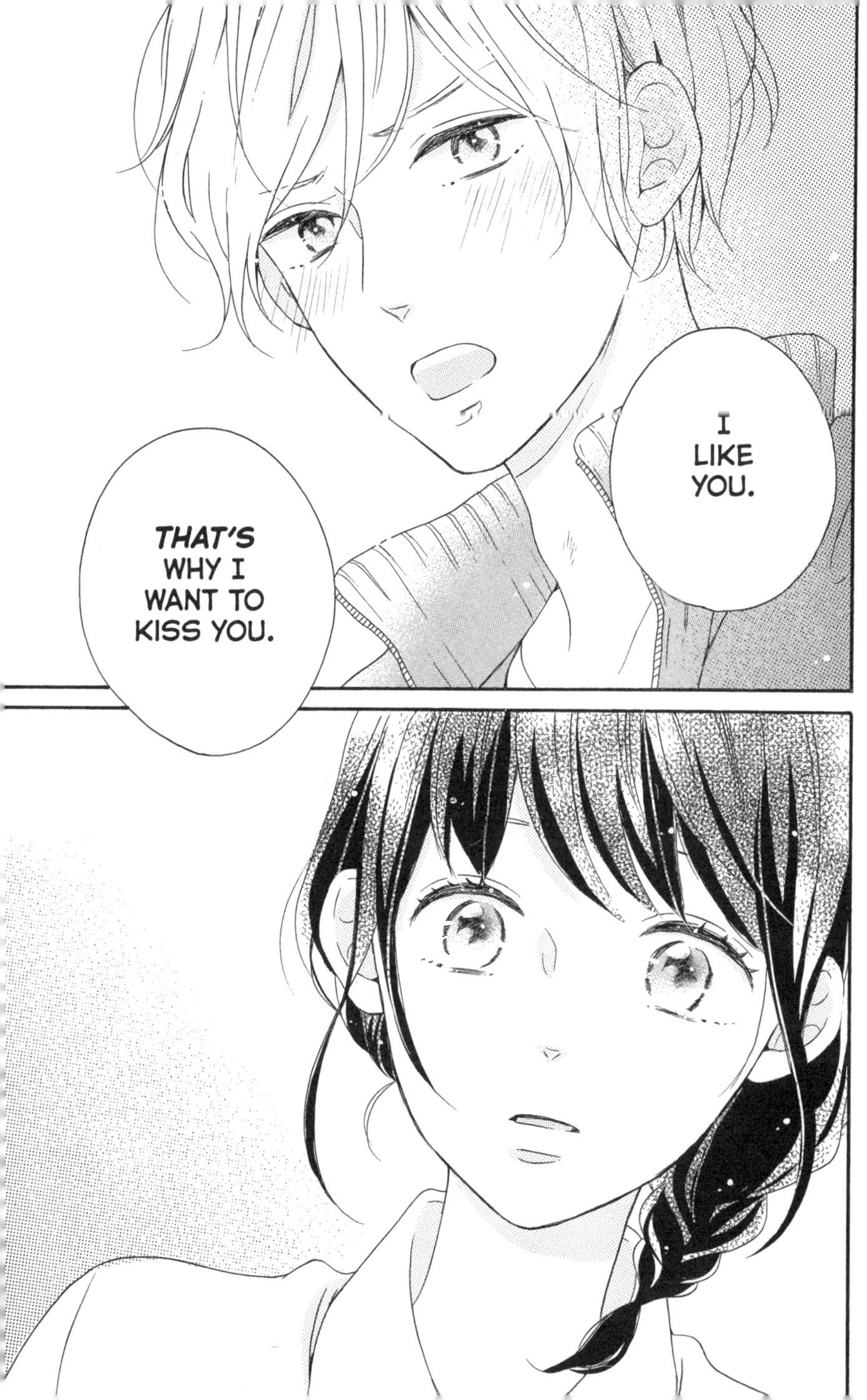
I LIKE YOU.
THAT'S WHY I WANT TO KISS YOU.

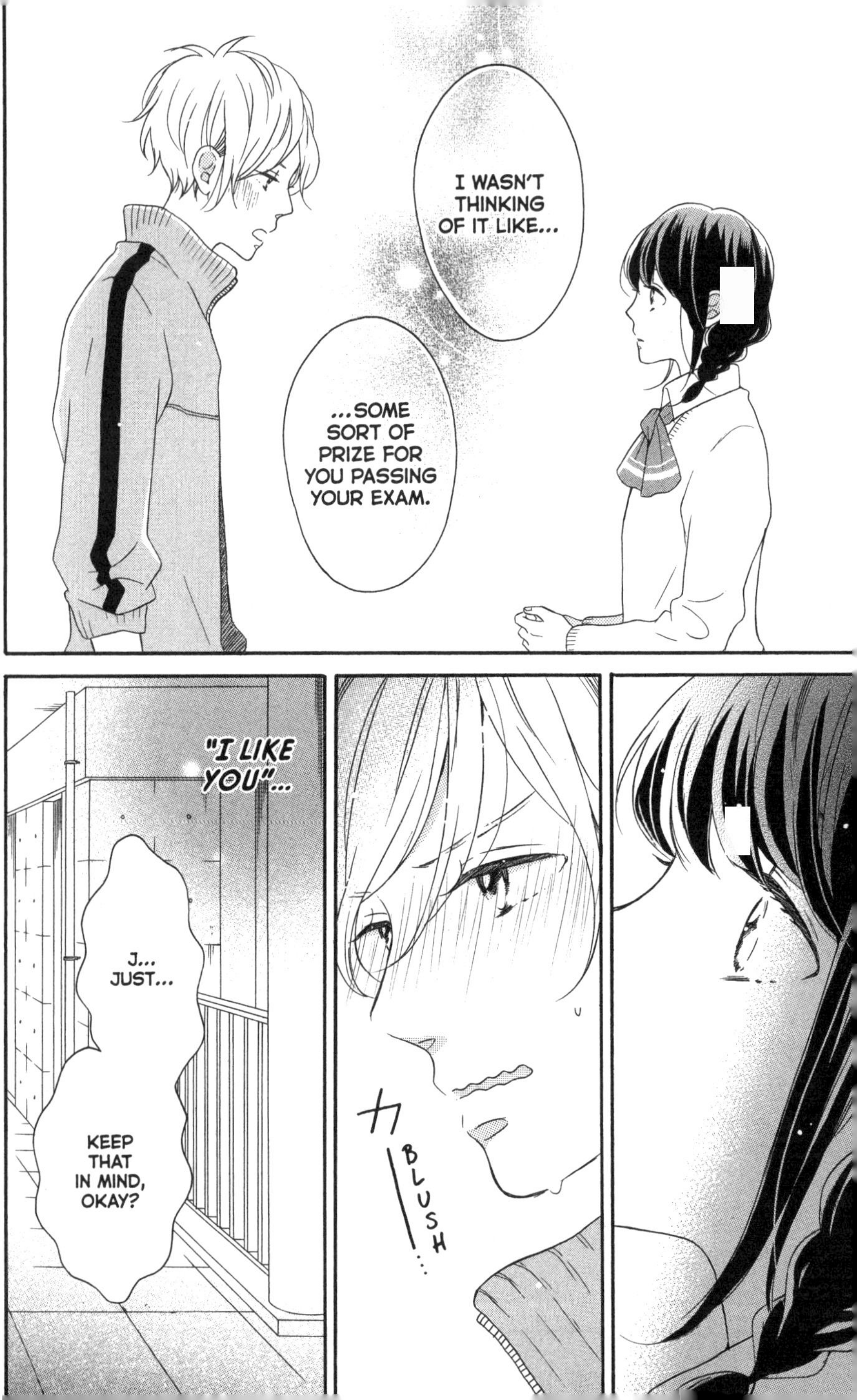
I WASN'T THINKING OF IT LIKE...
...SOME SORT OF PRIZE FOR YOU PASSING YOUR EXAM.
カ
BLUSH...
"I LIKE YOU"...
J... JUST...
KEEP THAT IN MIND, OKAY?

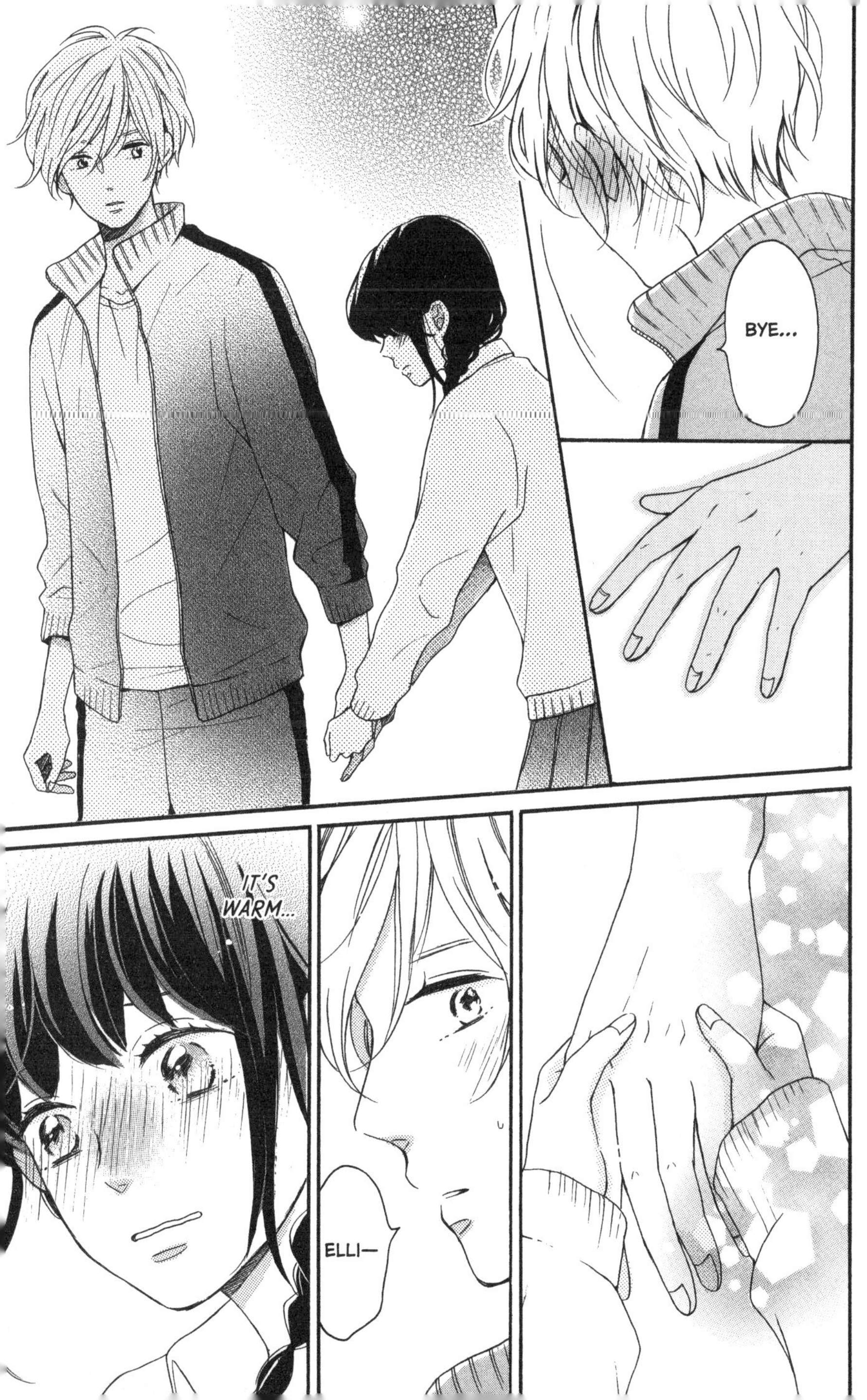
BYE...
ELLI—
IT'S WARM...

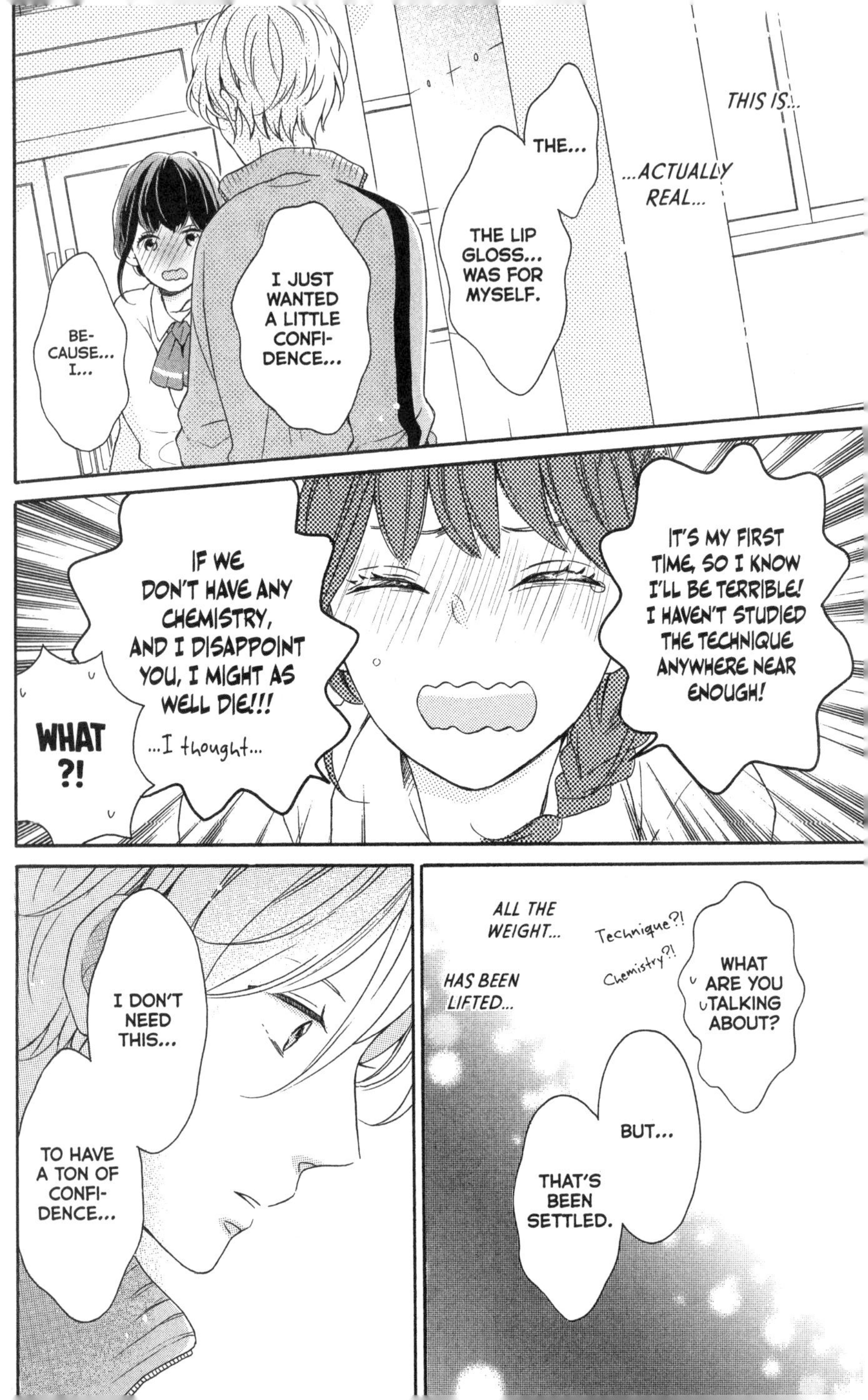

THIS IS...
...ACTUALLY REAL...
THE...
THE LIP GLOSS... WAS FOR MYSELF.
I JUST WANTED A LITTLE CONFIDENCE...
BECAUSE... I...
IT'S MY FIRST TIME, SO I KNOW I'LL BE TERRIBLE! I HAVEN'T STUDIED THE TECHNIQUE ANYWHERE NEAR ENOUGH!
IF WE DON'T HAVE ANY CHEMISTRY, AND I DISAPPOINT YOU, I MIGHT AS WELL DIE!!!
...I thought...
WHAT?!
WHAT ARE YOU TALKING ABOUT?
Technique?!
Chemistry?!
ALL THE WEIGHT...
HAS BEEN LIFTED...
BUT... THAT'S BEEN SETTLED.
I DON'T NEED THIS...
TO HAVE A TON OF CONFIDENCE...

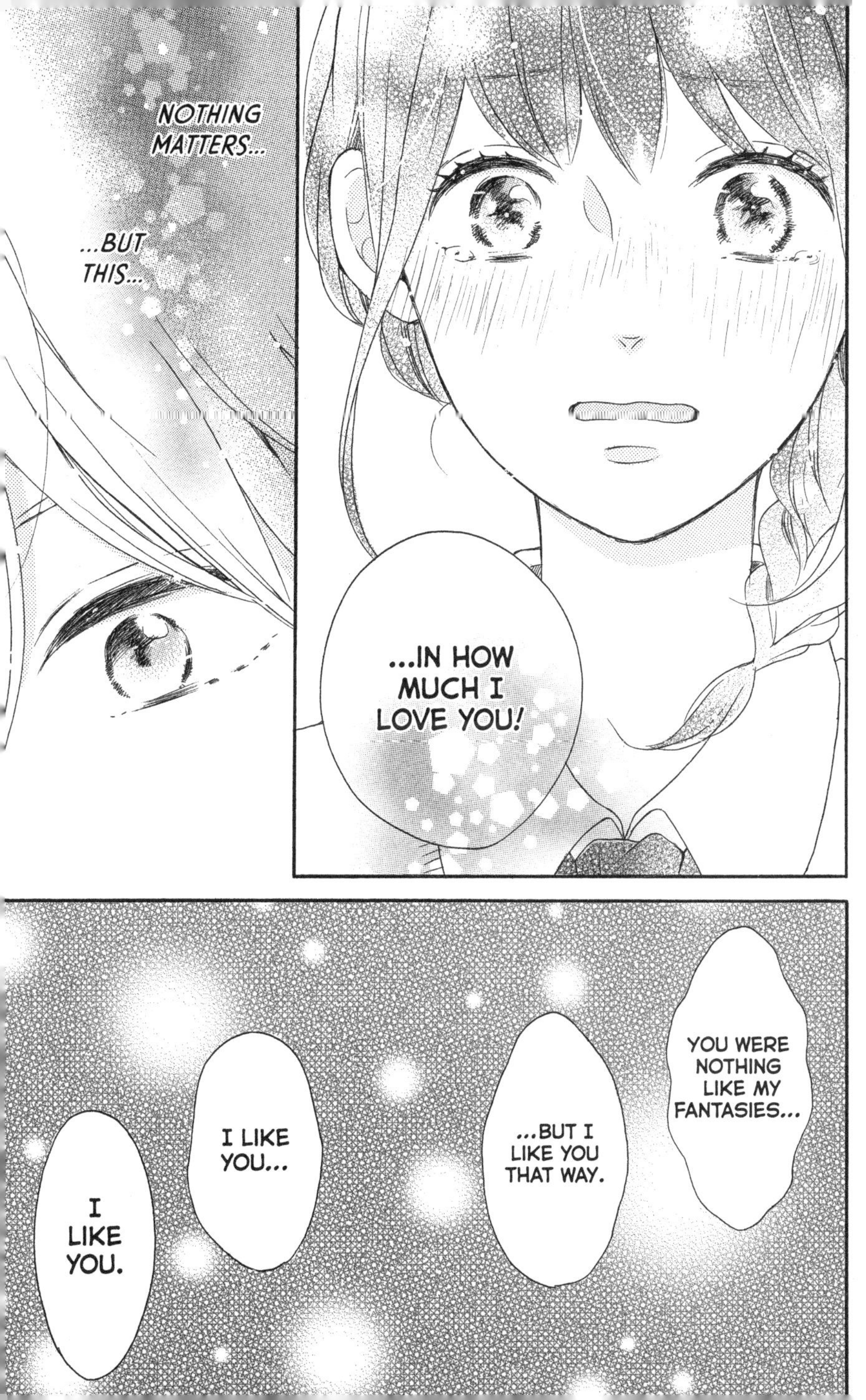
...IN HOW MUCH I LOVE YOU!
NOTHING MATTERS...
...BUT THIS...
YOU WERE NOTHING LIKE MY FANTASIES...
...BUT I LIKE YOU THAT WAY.
I LIKE YOU...
I LIKE YOU.

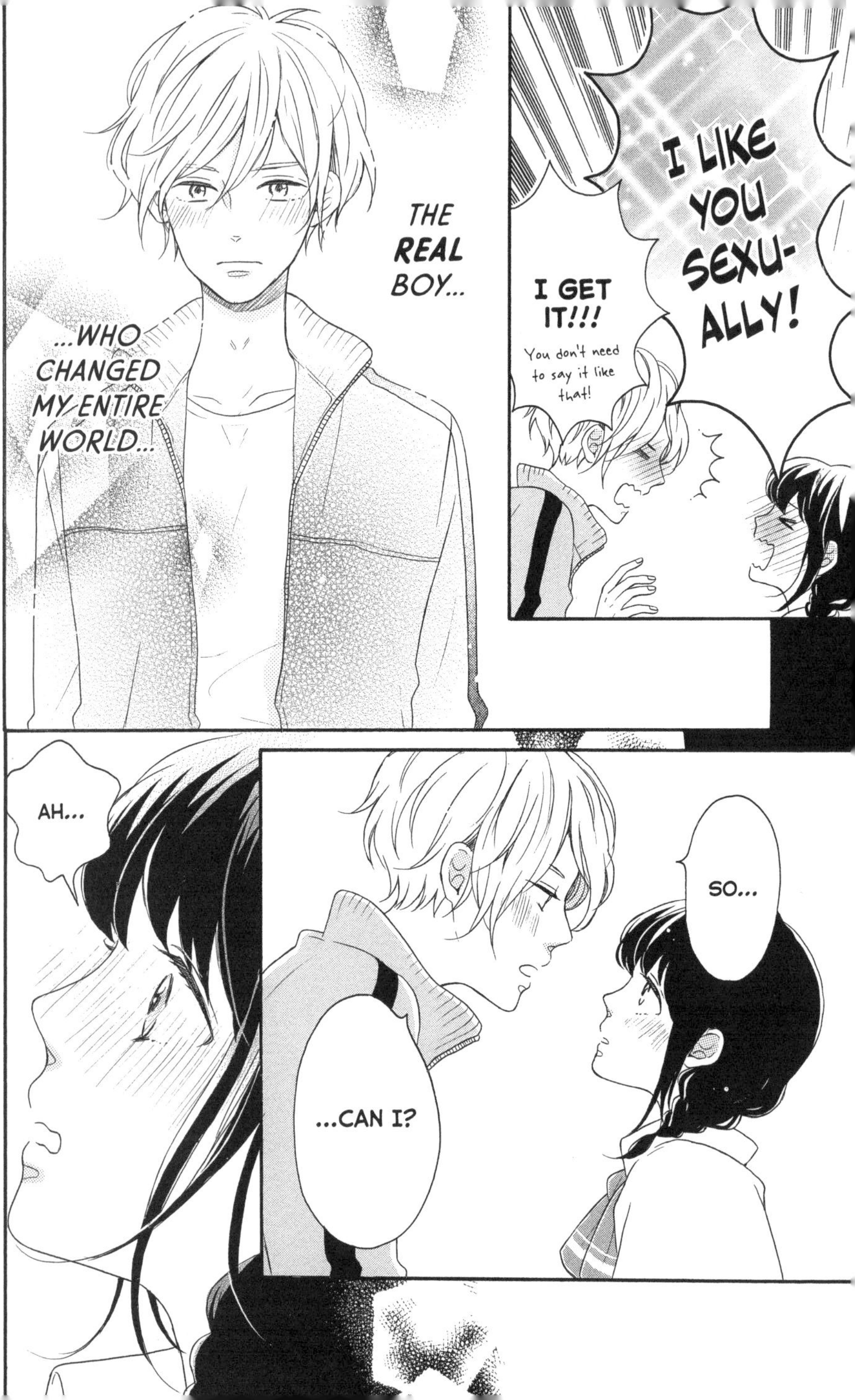
I LIKE YOU SEXU- ALLY!
I GET IT!!!
You don't need to say it like that!
THE REAL BOY...
...WHO CHANGED MY ENTIRE WORLD...
SO...
...CAN I?
AH...

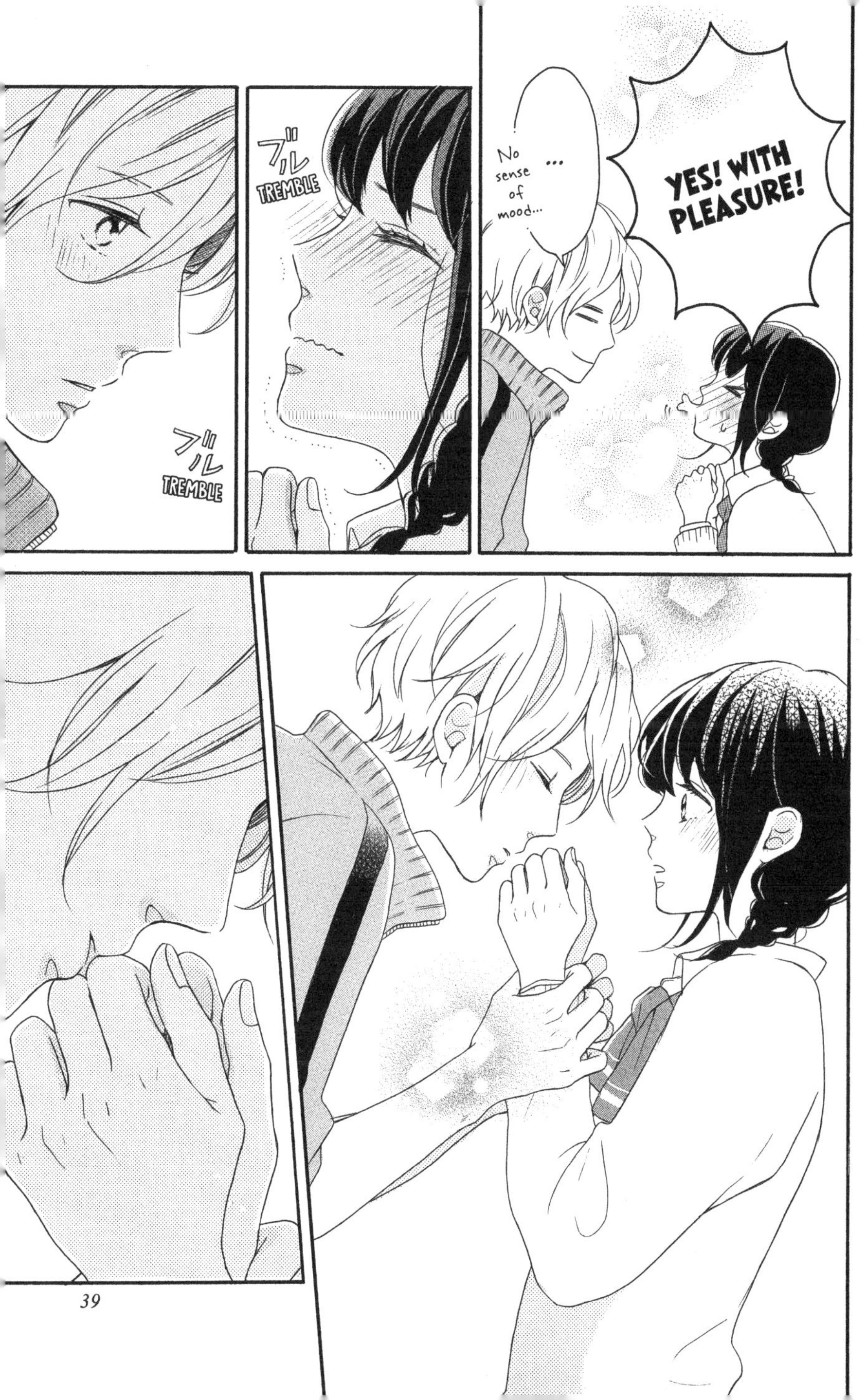
YES! WITH PLEASURE!
...
No sense of mood...
ブル
TREMBLE
ブル
TREMBLE

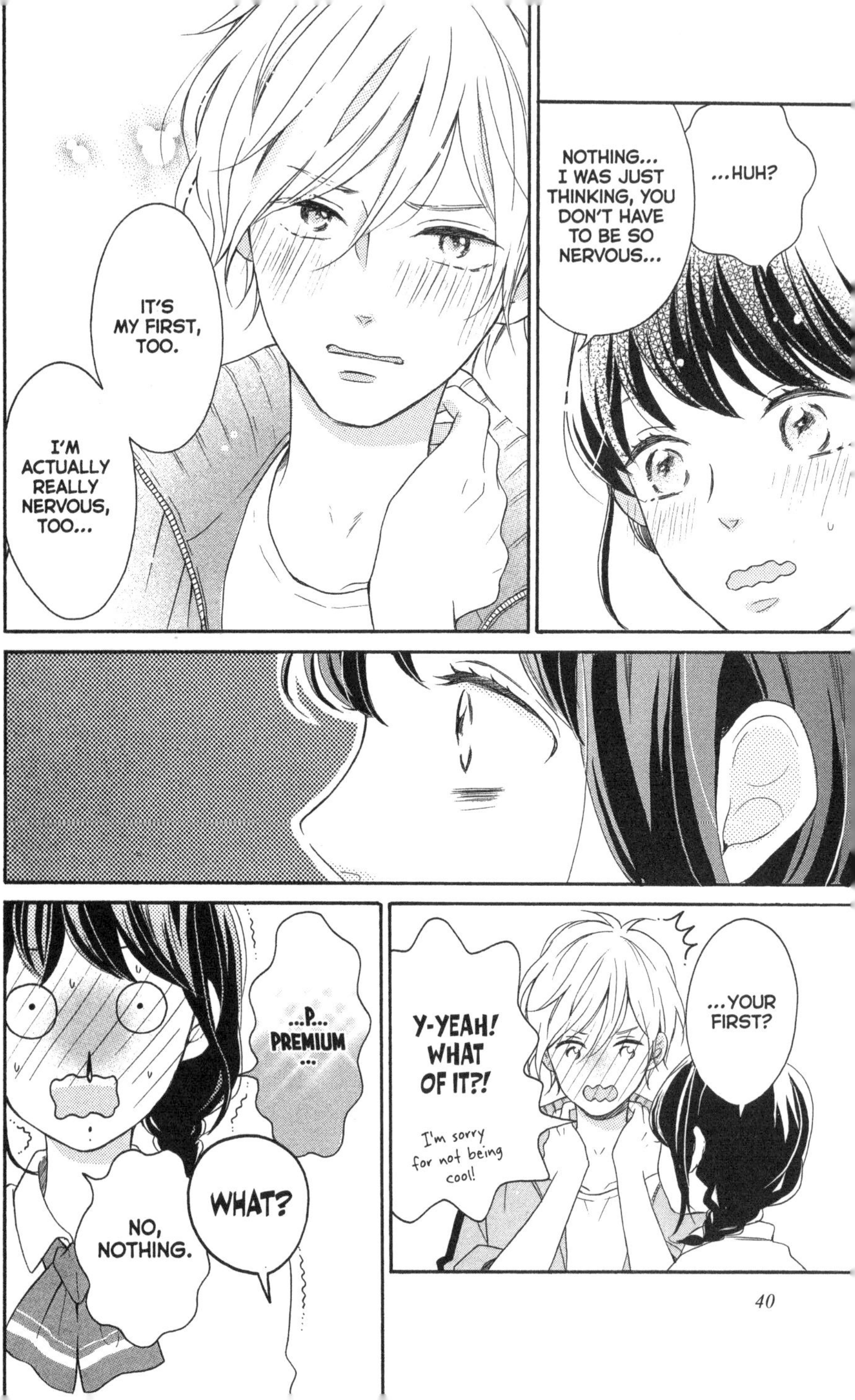
...HUH?
NOTHING... I WAS JUST THINKING, YOU DON'T HAVE TO BE SO NERVOUS...
IT'S MY FIRST, TOO.
I'M ACTUALLY REALLY NERVOUS, TOO...
...YOUR FIRST?
Y-YEAH! WHAT OF IT?!
I'm sorry for not being cool!
...P... PREMIUM...
WHAT?
NO, NOTHING.

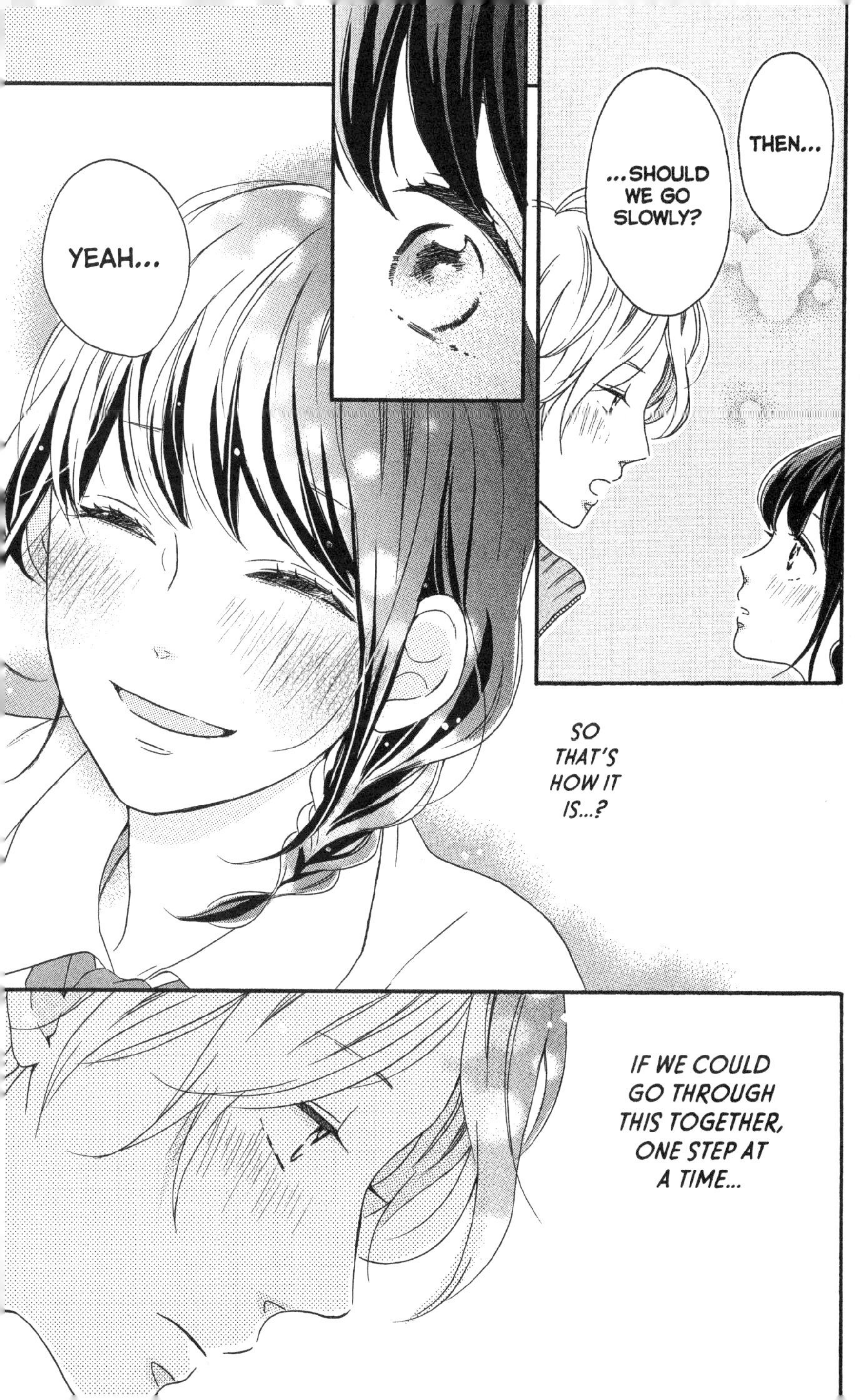
THEN...
...SHOULD WE GO SLOWLY?
YEAH...
SO THAT'S HOW IT IS...?
IF WE COULD GO THROUGH THIS TOGETHER, ONE STEP AT A TIME...

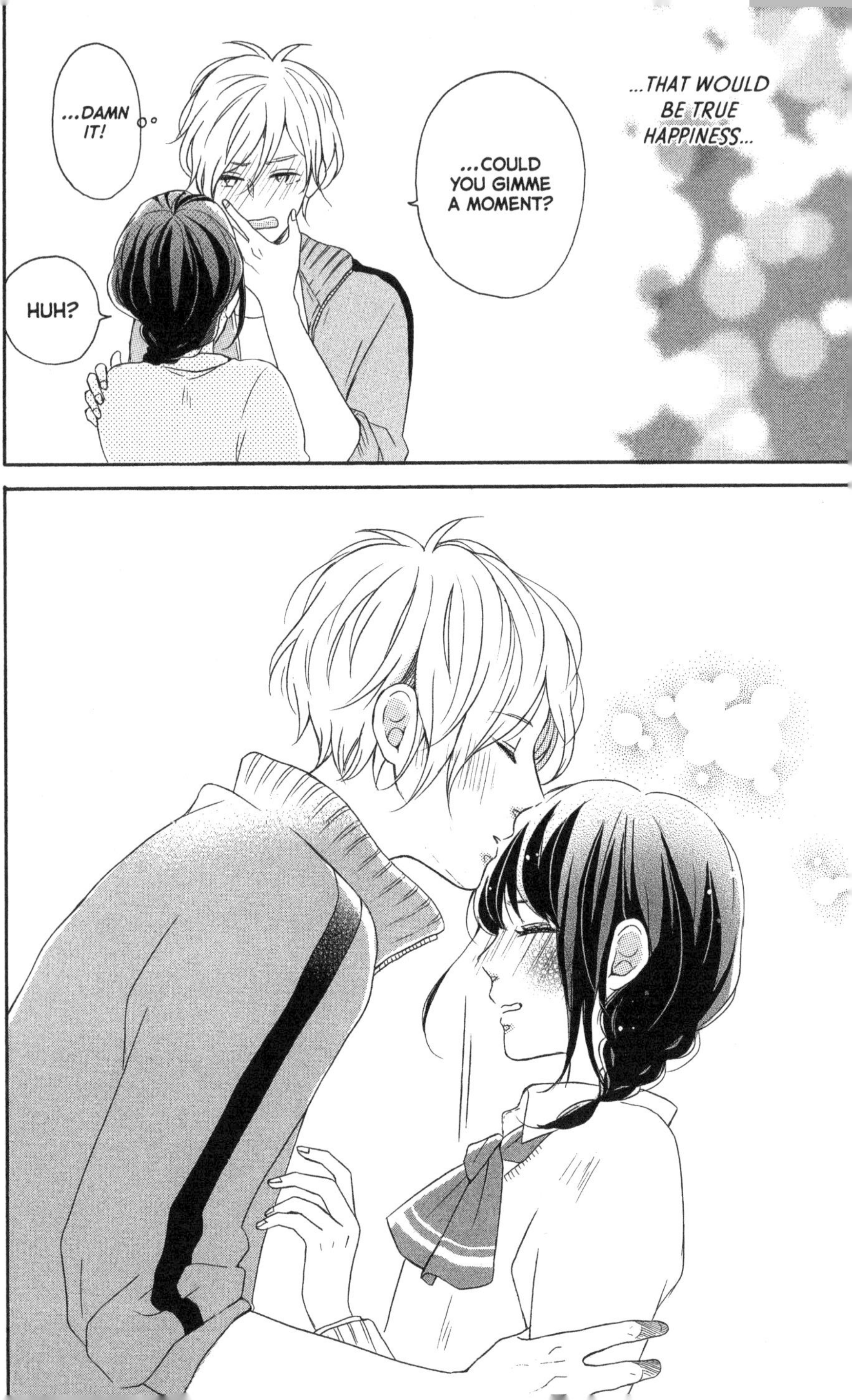
...THAT WOULD BE TRUE HAPPINESS...
...COULD YOU GIMME A MOMENT?
...DAMN IT!
HUH?

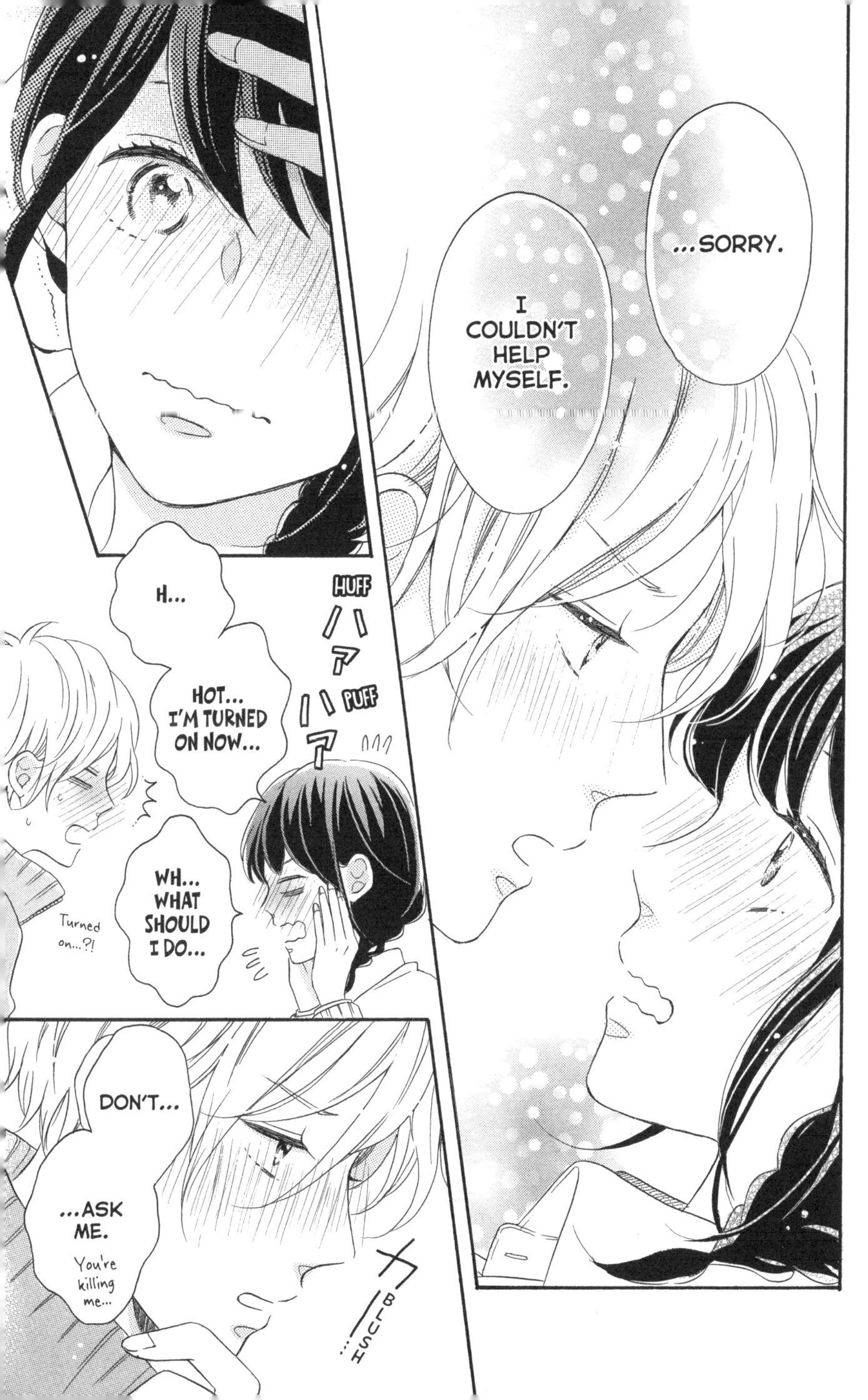
...SORRY.
I COULDN'T HELP MYSELF.
H...
HOT... I'M TURNED ON NOW...
HUFF
PUFF
WH... WHAT SHOULD I DO...
Turned on...?!
DON'T...
...ASK ME.
You're killing me...
BLUSH

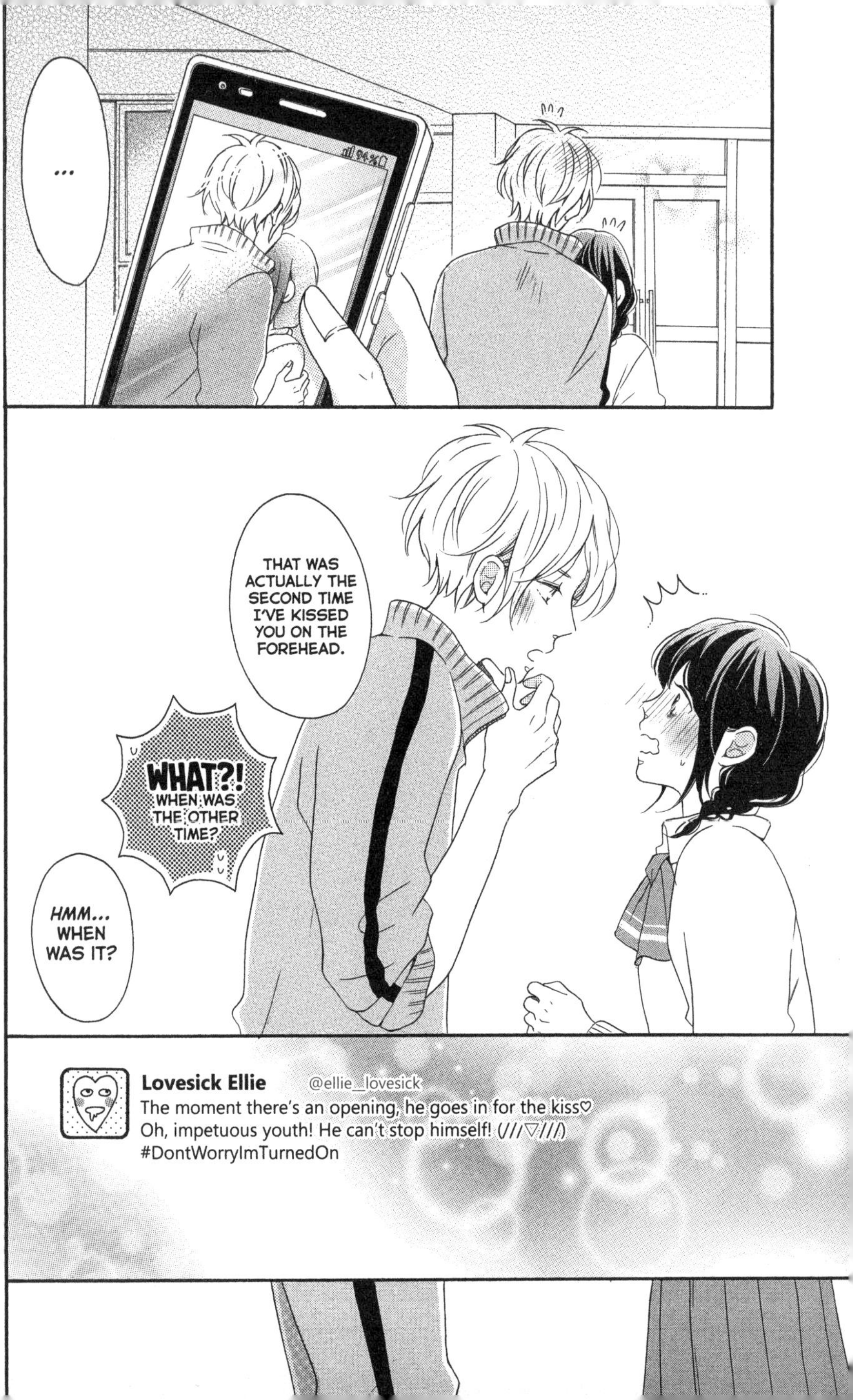
...
THAT WAS ACTUALLY THE SECOND TIME I'VE KISSED YOU ON THE FOREHEAD.
WHAT?! WHEN WAS THE OTHER TIME?
HMM... WHEN WAS IT?
Lovesick Ellie @ellie_lovesick
The moment there's an opening, he goes in for the kiss♡
Oh, impetuous youth! He can't stop himself! (///▽///)
#DontWorryImTurnedOn

10 #LosingOhmiKun

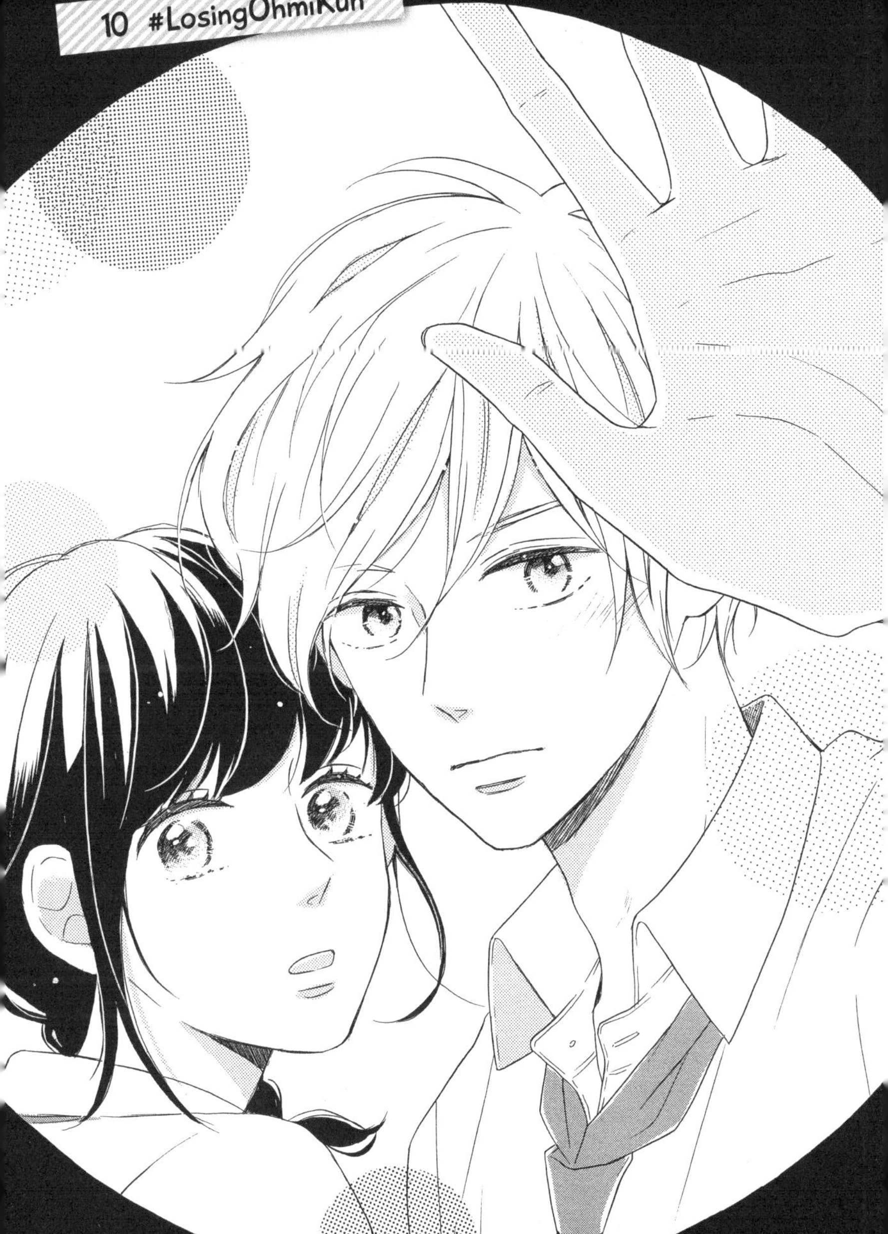

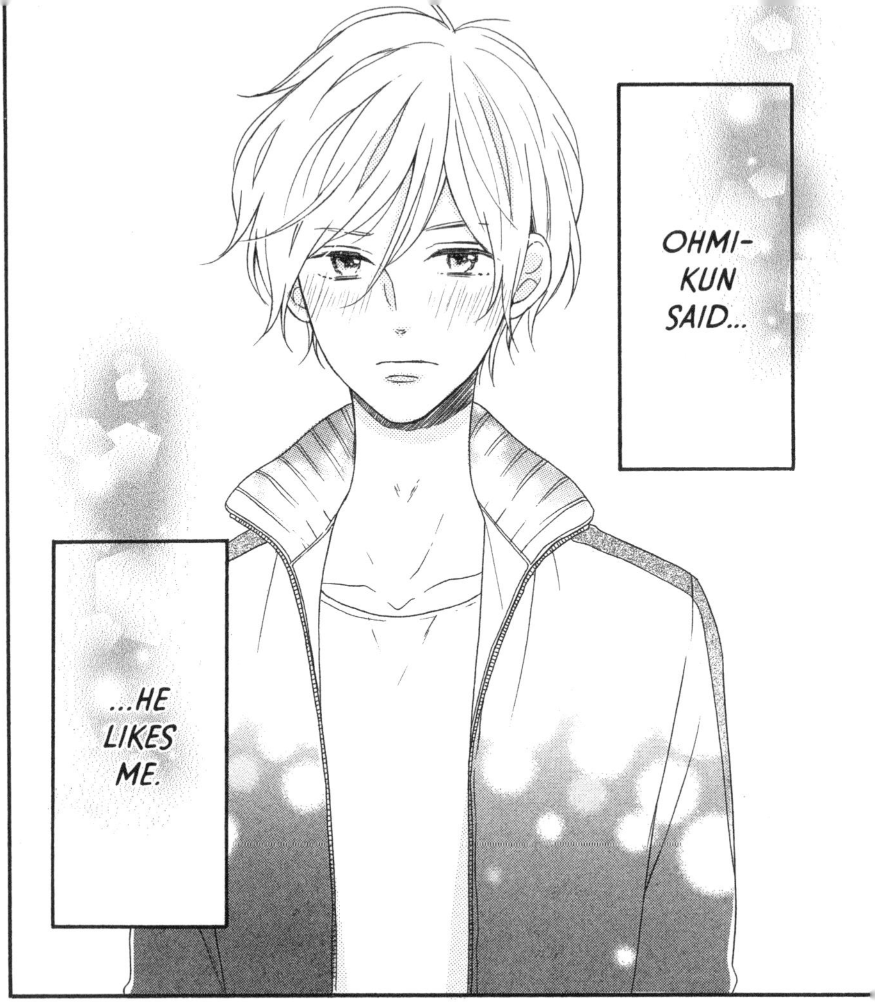
OHMI-KUN SAID...
...HE LIKES ME.

I have a habit of giving a myriad of nicknames to my friends in real life, but recently, I've begun noticing that this has crossed over into even my manga. Look at how many different things Ellie is called in here....

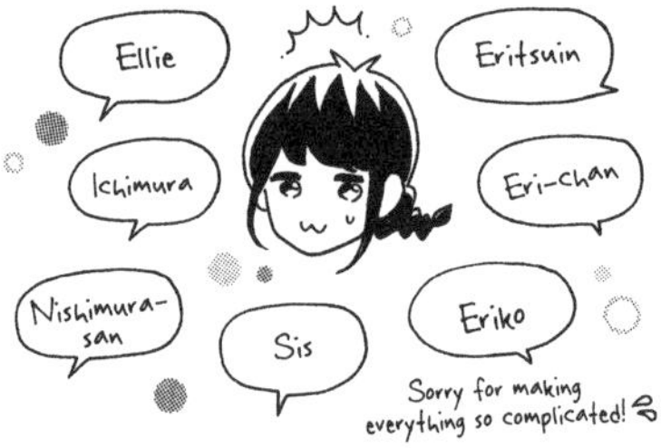
Ellie
Eritsuin
Ichimura
Eri-chan
Nishimura-san
Sis
Eriko
Sorry for making everything so complicated!

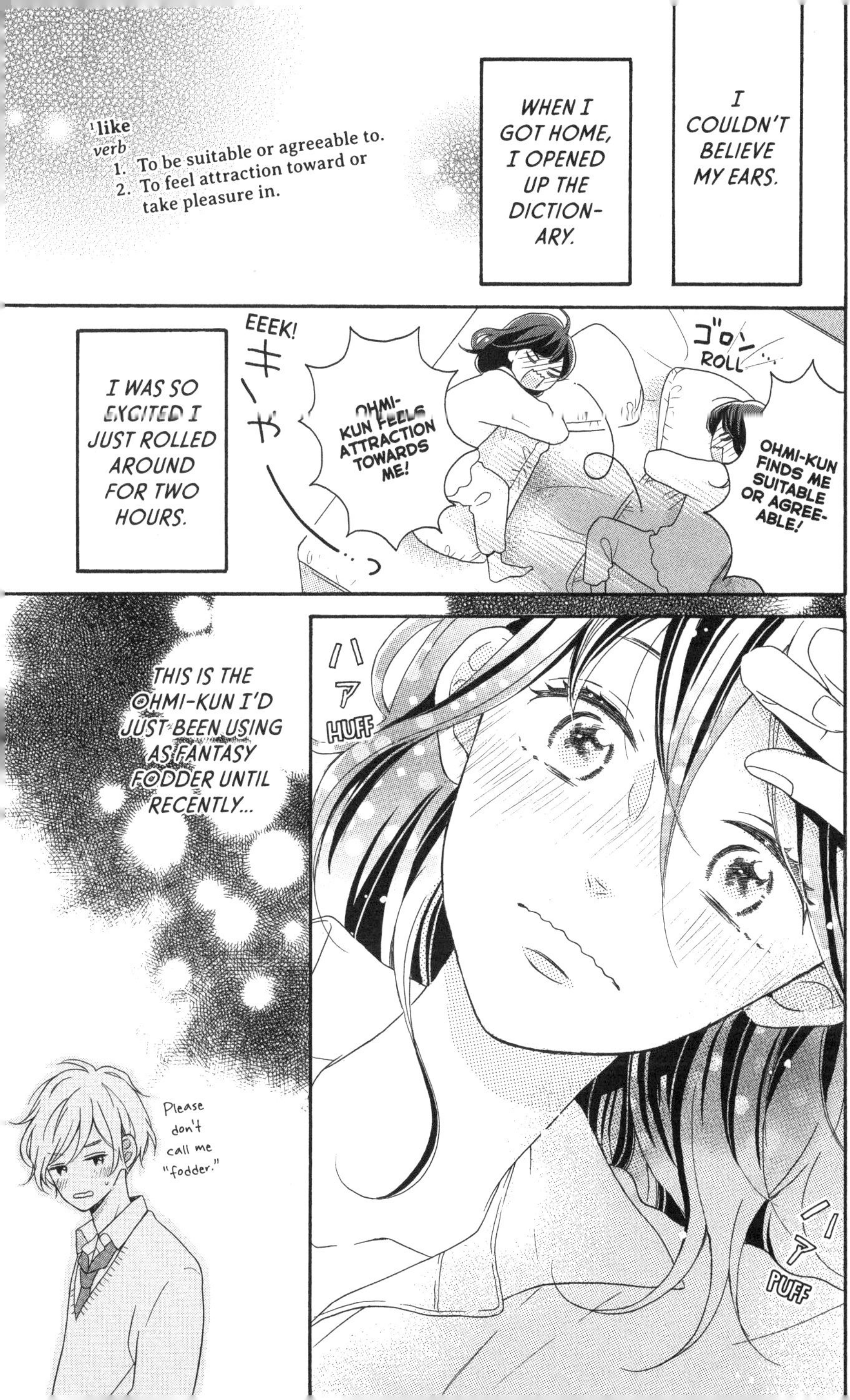

I COULDN'T BELIEVE MY EARS.
WHEN I GOT HOME, I OPENED UP THE DICTION-ARY.
[1]like
verb
1. To be suitable or agreeable to.
2. To feel attraction toward or take pleasure in.
ゴロン
ROLL
OHMI-KUN FINDS ME SUITABLE OR AGREE-ABLE!
OHMI-KUN FEELS ATTRACTION TOWARDS ME!
キャー
EEEK!
I WAS SO EXCITED I JUST ROLLED AROUND FOR TWO HOURS.
ハア
HUFF
ハア
PUFF
THIS IS THE OHMI-KUN I'D JUST BEEN USING AS FANTASY FODDER UNTIL RECENTLY...
Please don't call me "fodder."

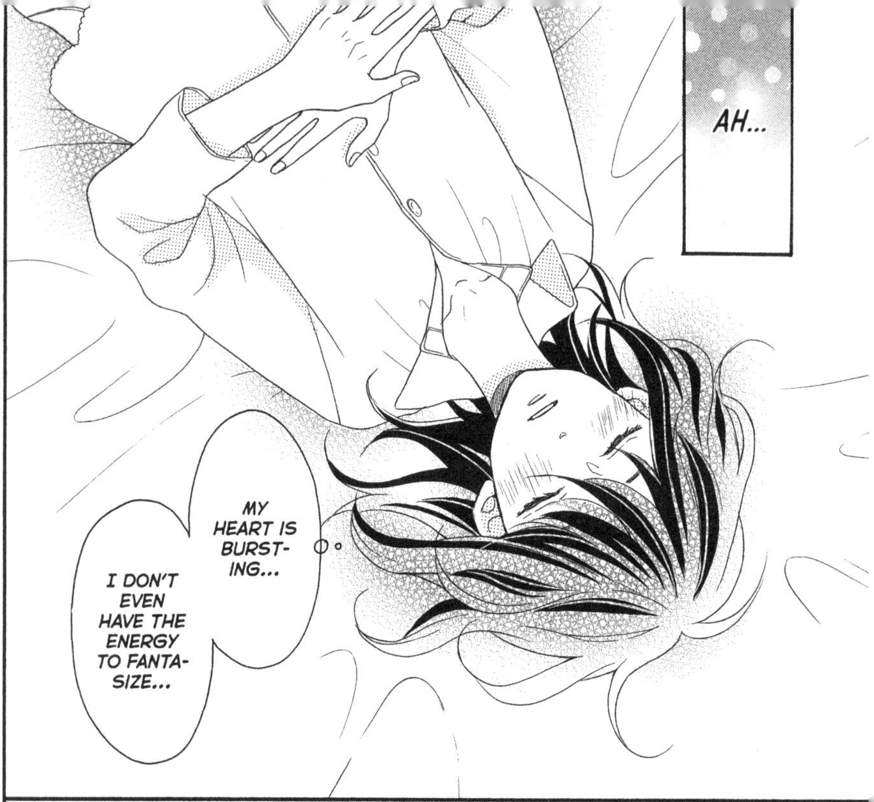
AH...
MY HEART IS BURST-ING...
I DON'T EVEN HAVE THE ENERGY TO FANTA-SIZE...
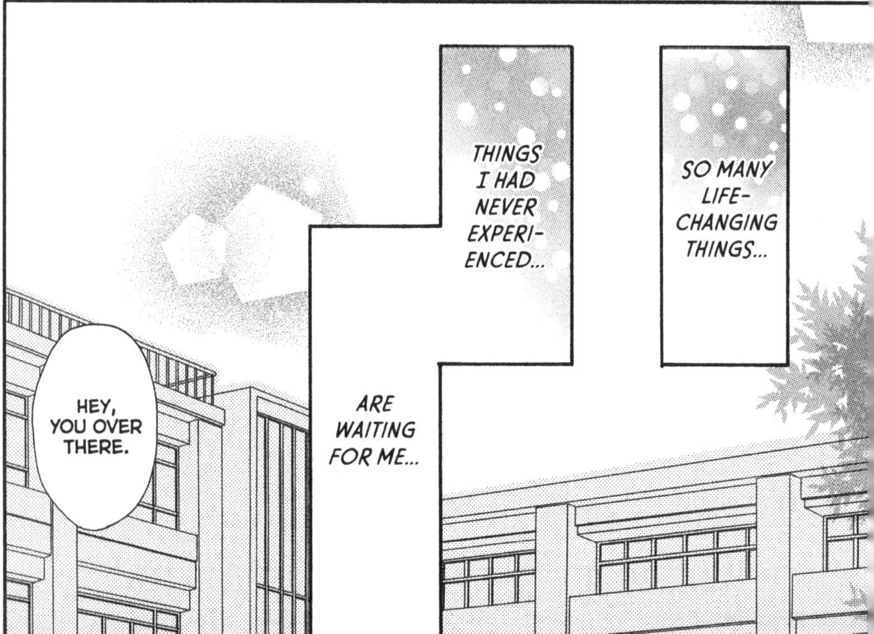
SO MANY LIFE-CHANGING THINGS...
THINGS I HAD NEVER EXPERI-ENCED...
ARE WAITING FOR ME...
HEY, YOU OVER THERE.

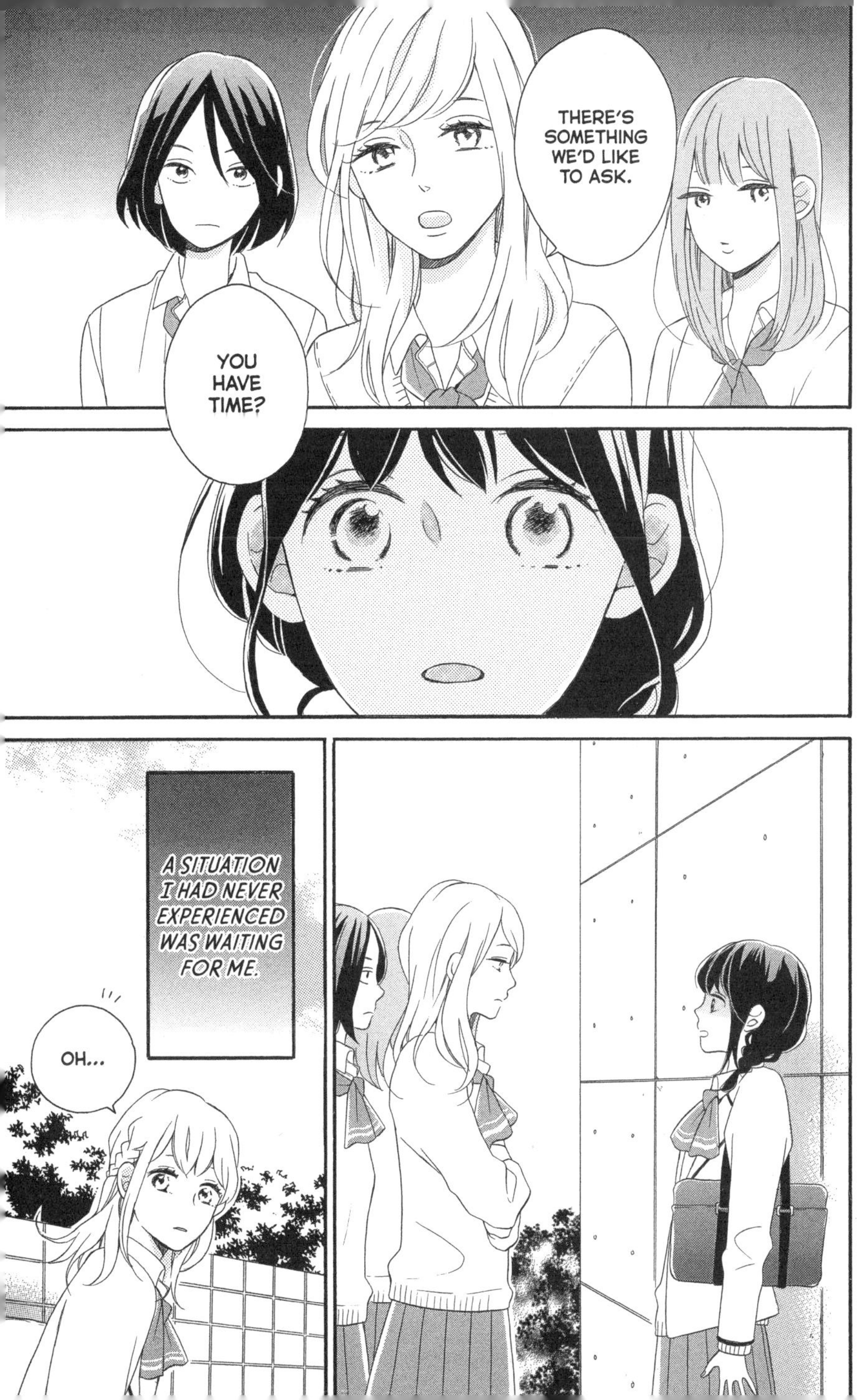
THERE'S SOMETHING WE'D LIKE TO ASK.
YOU HAVE TIME?
A SITUATION I HAD NEVER EXPERIENCED WAS WAITING FOR ME.
OH...

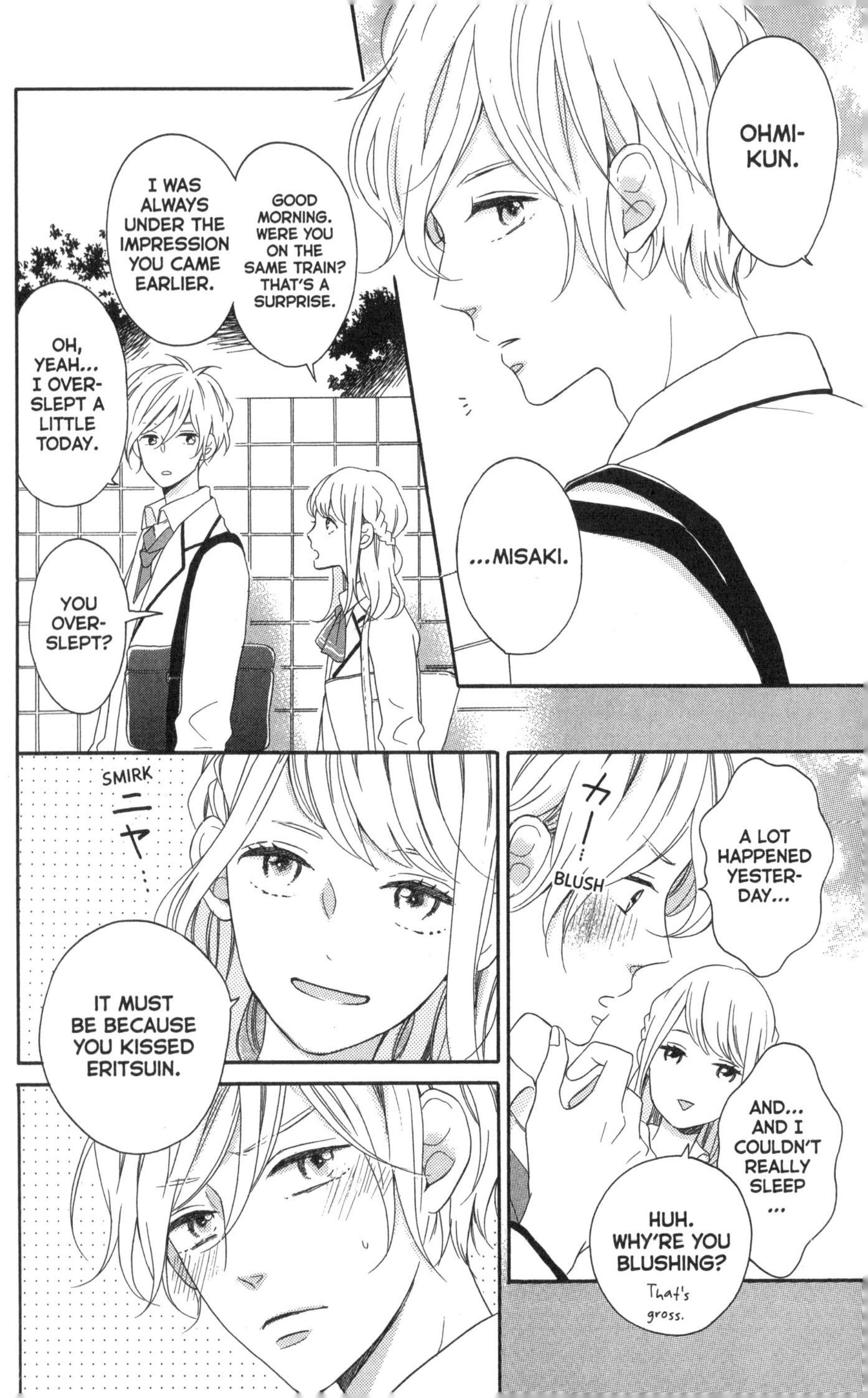
OHMI-KUN.
...MISAKI.
GOOD MORNING. WERE YOU ON THE SAME TRAIN? THAT'S A SURPRISE.
I WAS ALWAYS UNDER THE IMPRESSION YOU CAME EARLIER.
OH, YEAH... I OVER-SLEPT A LITTLE TODAY.
YOU OVER-SLEPT?
カー!
BLUSH
A LOT HAPPENED YESTER-DAY...
AND... AND I COULDN'T REALLY SLEEP...
HUH. WHY'RE YOU BLUSHING?
That's gross.
SMIRK
ニヤ…
IT MUST BE BECAUSE YOU KISSED ERITSUIN.

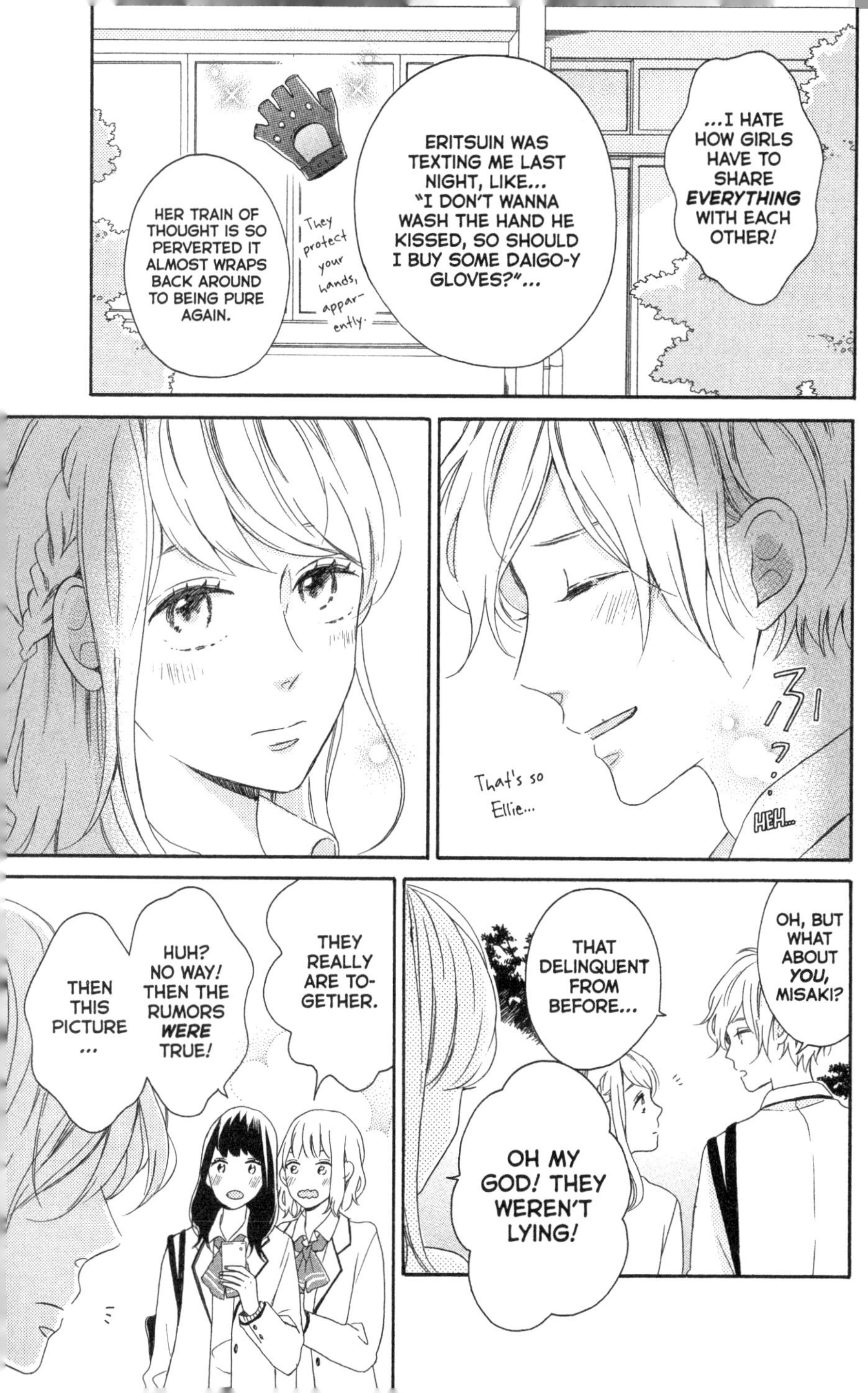
...I HATE HOW GIRLS HAVE TO SHARE *EVERYTHING* WITH EACH OTHER!
ERITSUIN WAS TEXTING ME LAST NIGHT, LIKE... "I DON'T WANNA WASH THE HAND HE KISSED, SO SHOULD I BUY SOME DAIGO-Y GLOVES?"...
They protect your hands, apparently.
HER TRAIN OF THOUGHT IS SO PERVERTED IT ALMOST WRAPS BACK AROUND TO BEING PURE AGAIN.
That's so Ellie...
HEH...
OH, BUT WHAT ABOUT *YOU*, MISAKI?
THAT DELINQUENT FROM BEFORE...
OH MY GOD! THEY WEREN'T LYING!
THEY REALLY ARE TO-GETHER.
HUH? NO WAY! THEN THE RUMORS *WERE* TRUE!
THEN THIS PICTURE ...

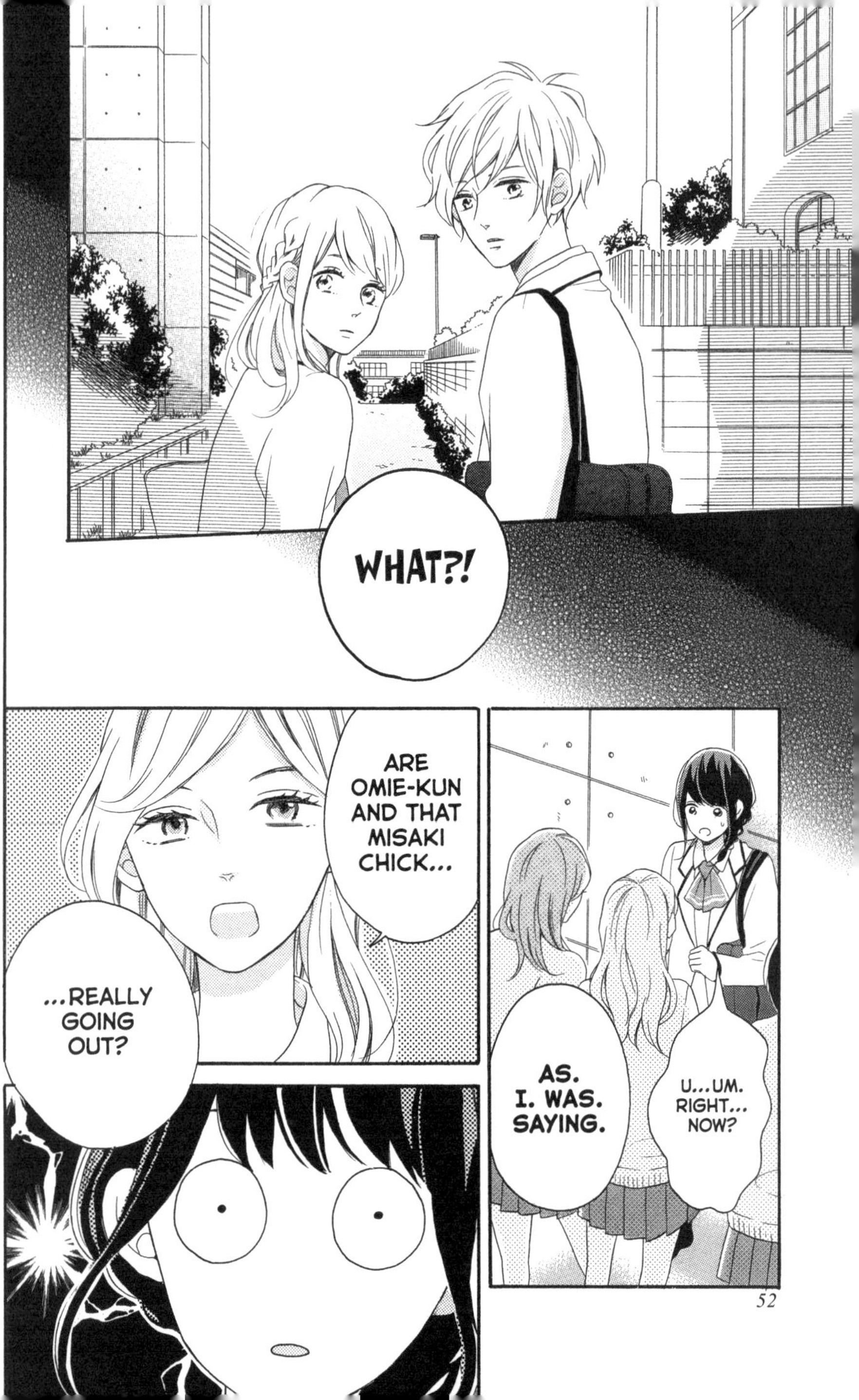
WHAT?!
U...UM. RIGHT... NOW?
AS. I. WAS. SAYING.
ARE OMIE-KUN AND THAT MISAKI CHICK...
...REALLY GOING OUT?

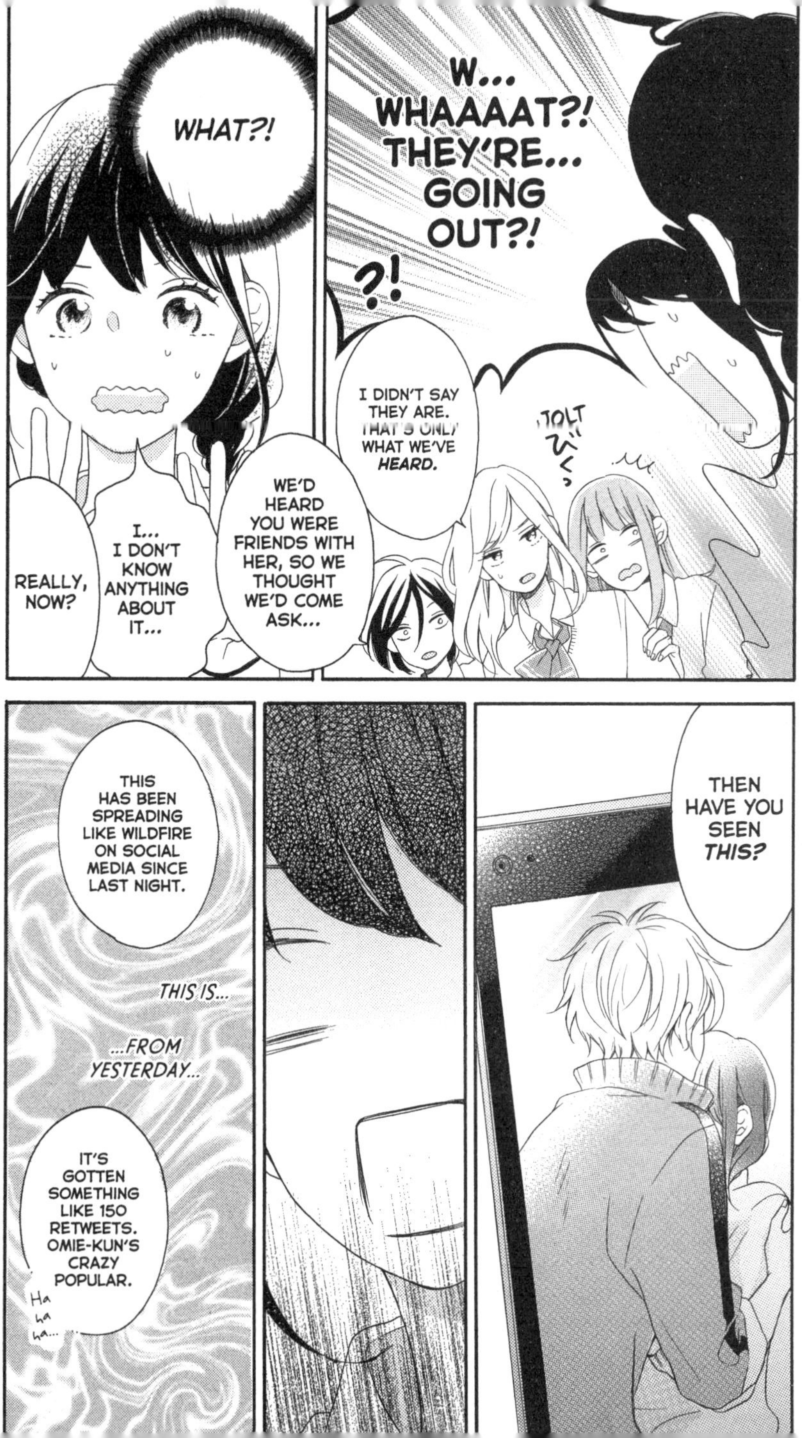

W... WHAAAAT?! THEY'RE... GOING OUT?!
?!
I DIDN'T SAY THEY ARE. THAT'S ONLY WHAT WE'VE *HEARD.*
JOLT
WHAT?!
WE'D HEARD YOU WERE FRIENDS WITH HER, SO WE THOUGHT WE'D COME ASK...
I... I DON'T KNOW ANYTHING ABOUT IT...
REALLY, NOW?
THEN HAVE YOU SEEN *THIS?*
THIS HAS BEEN SPREADING LIKE WILDFIRE ON SOCIAL MEDIA SINCE LAST NIGHT.
THIS IS...
...FROM YESTERDAY...
IT'S GOTTEN SOMETHING LIKE 150 RETWEETS. OMIE-KUN'S CRAZY POPULAR.
Ha ha ha...

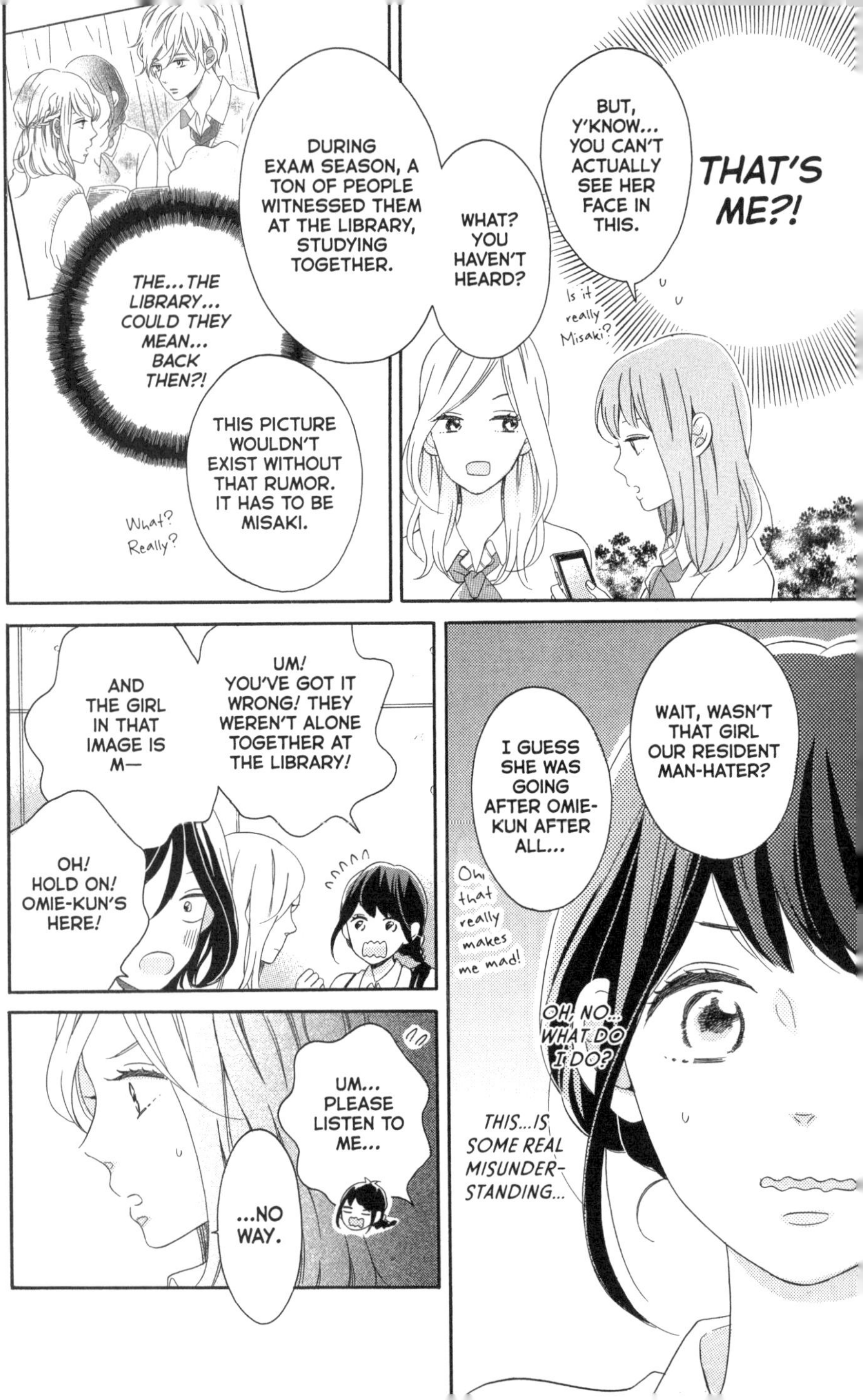
THAT'S ME?!
BUT, Y'KNOW... YOU CAN'T ACTUALLY SEE HER FACE IN THIS.
Is it really Misaki?
WHAT? YOU HAVEN'T HEARD?
DURING EXAM SEASON, A TON OF PEOPLE WITNESSED THEM AT THE LIBRARY, STUDYING TOGETHER.
THE...THE LIBRARY... COULD THEY MEAN... BACK THEN?!
THIS PICTURE WOULDN'T EXIST WITHOUT THAT RUMOR. IT HAS TO BE MISAKI.
What? Really?
WAIT, WASN'T THAT GIRL OUR RESIDENT MAN-HATER?
I GUESS SHE WAS GOING AFTER OMIE-KUN AFTER ALL...
Oh that really makes me mad!
OH, NO... WHAT DO I DO?
THIS...IS SOME REAL MISUNDERSTANDING...
UM! YOU'VE GOT IT WRONG! THEY WEREN'T ALONE TOGETHER AT THE LIBRARY!
AND THE GIRL IN THAT IMAGE IS M—
OH! HOLD ON! OMIE-KUN'S HERE!
UM... PLEASE LISTEN TO ME...
...NO WAY.

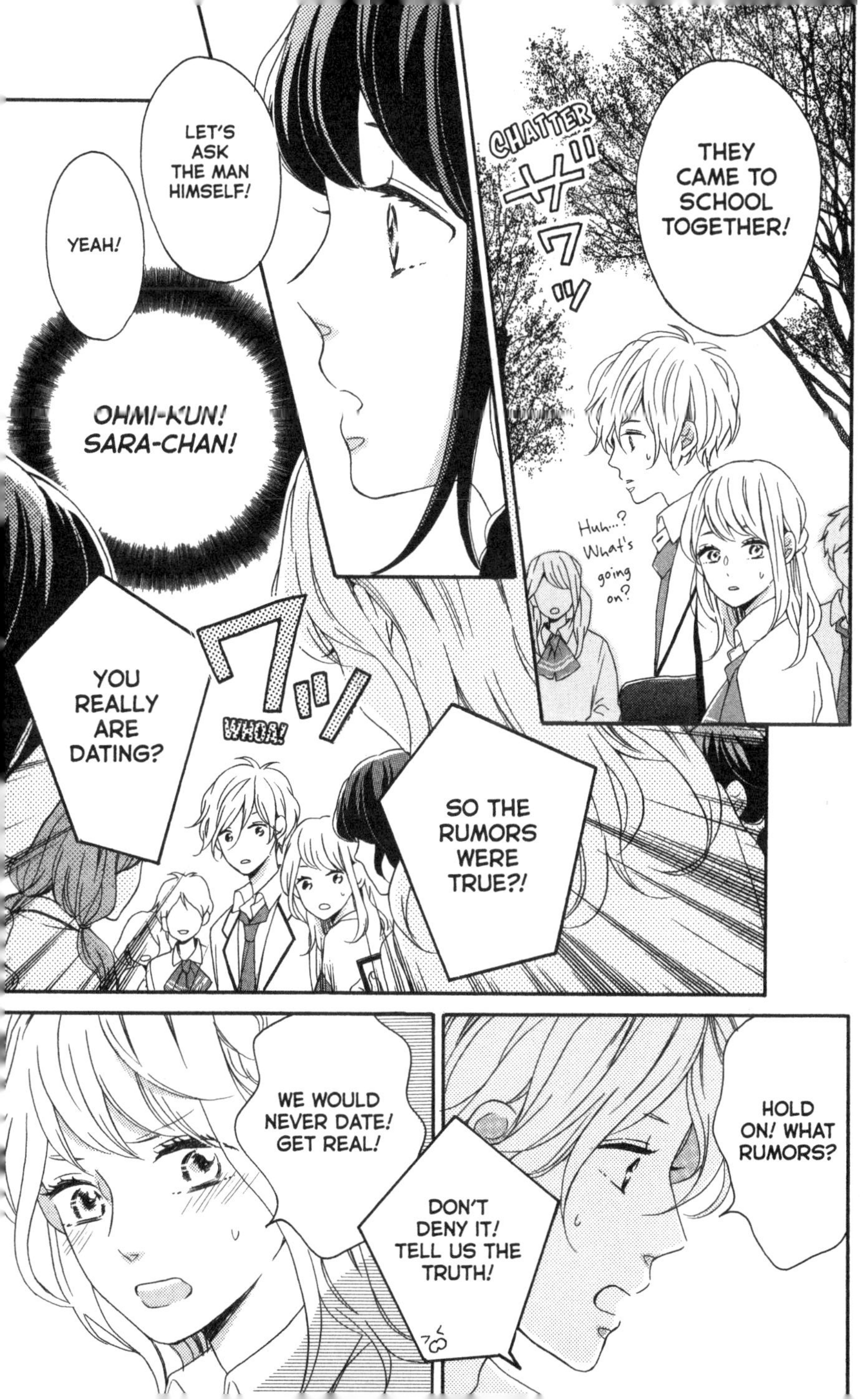
CHATTER
THEY CAME TO SCHOOL TOGETHER!
Huh...? What's going on?
LET'S ASK THE MAN HIMSELF!
YEAH!
OHMI-KUN! SARA-CHAN!
SO THE RUMORS WERE TRUE?!
WHOA!
YOU REALLY ARE DATING?
HOLD ON! WHAT RUMORS?
DON'T DENY IT! TELL US THE TRUTH!
WE WOULD NEVER DATE! GET REAL!

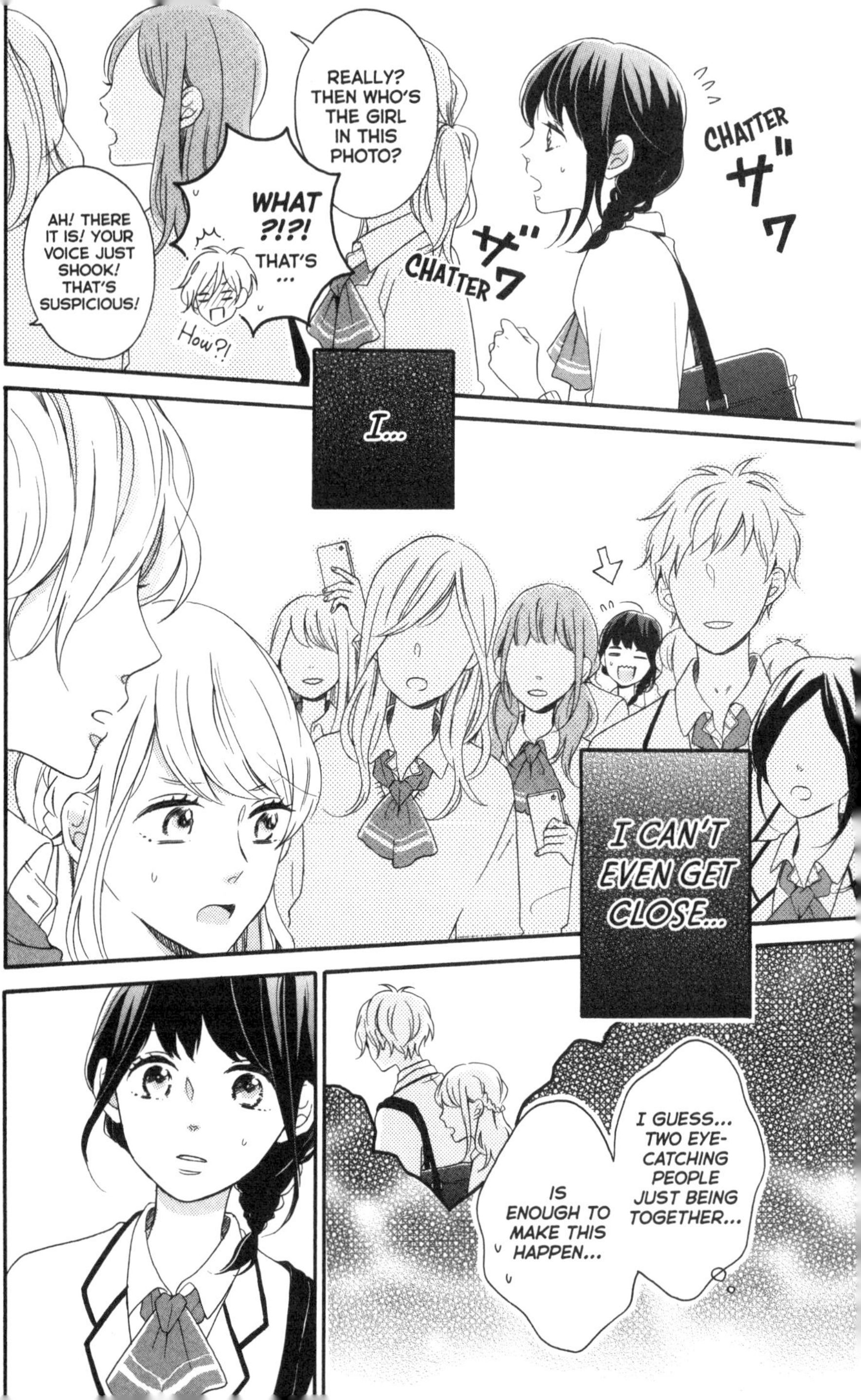
CHATTER ザワ
CHATTER ザワ
REALLY? THEN WHO'S THE GIRL IN THIS PHOTO?
WHAT ?!?! THAT'S ...
How?!
AH! THERE IT IS! YOUR VOICE JUST SHOOK! THAT'S SUSPICIOUS!
I...
I CAN'T EVEN GET CLOSE...
I GUESS... TWO EYE-CATCHING PEOPLE JUST BEING TOGETHER...
IS ENOUGH TO MAKE THIS HAPPEN...

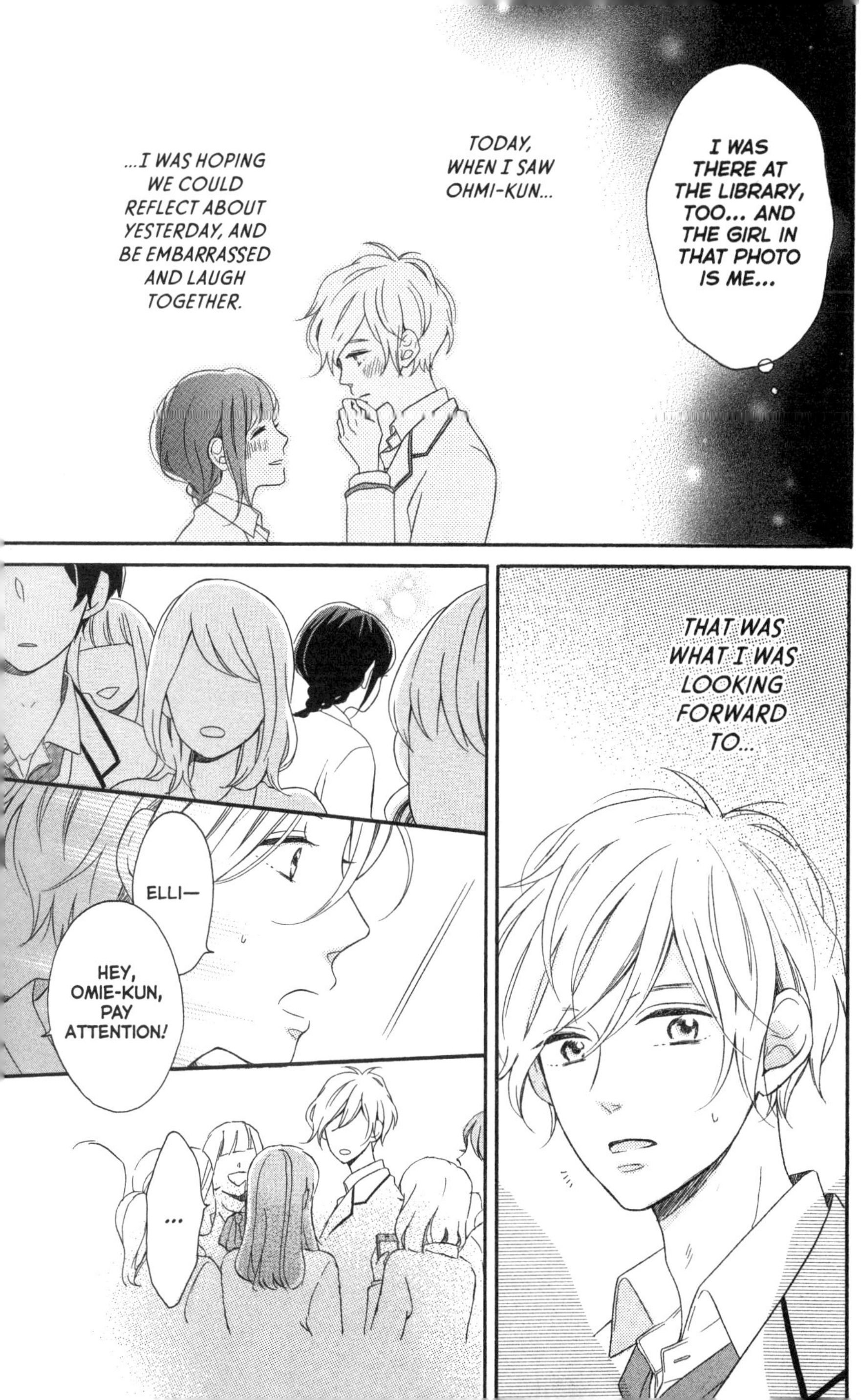
I WAS THERE AT THE LIBRARY, TOO... AND THE GIRL IN THAT PHOTO IS ME...
TODAY, WHEN I SAW OHMI-KUN...
...I WAS HOPING WE COULD REFLECT ABOUT YESTERDAY, AND BE EMBARRASSED AND LAUGH TOGETHER.
THAT WAS WHAT I WAS LOOKING FORWARD TO...
ELLI—
HEY, OMIE-KUN, PAY ATTENTION!
...

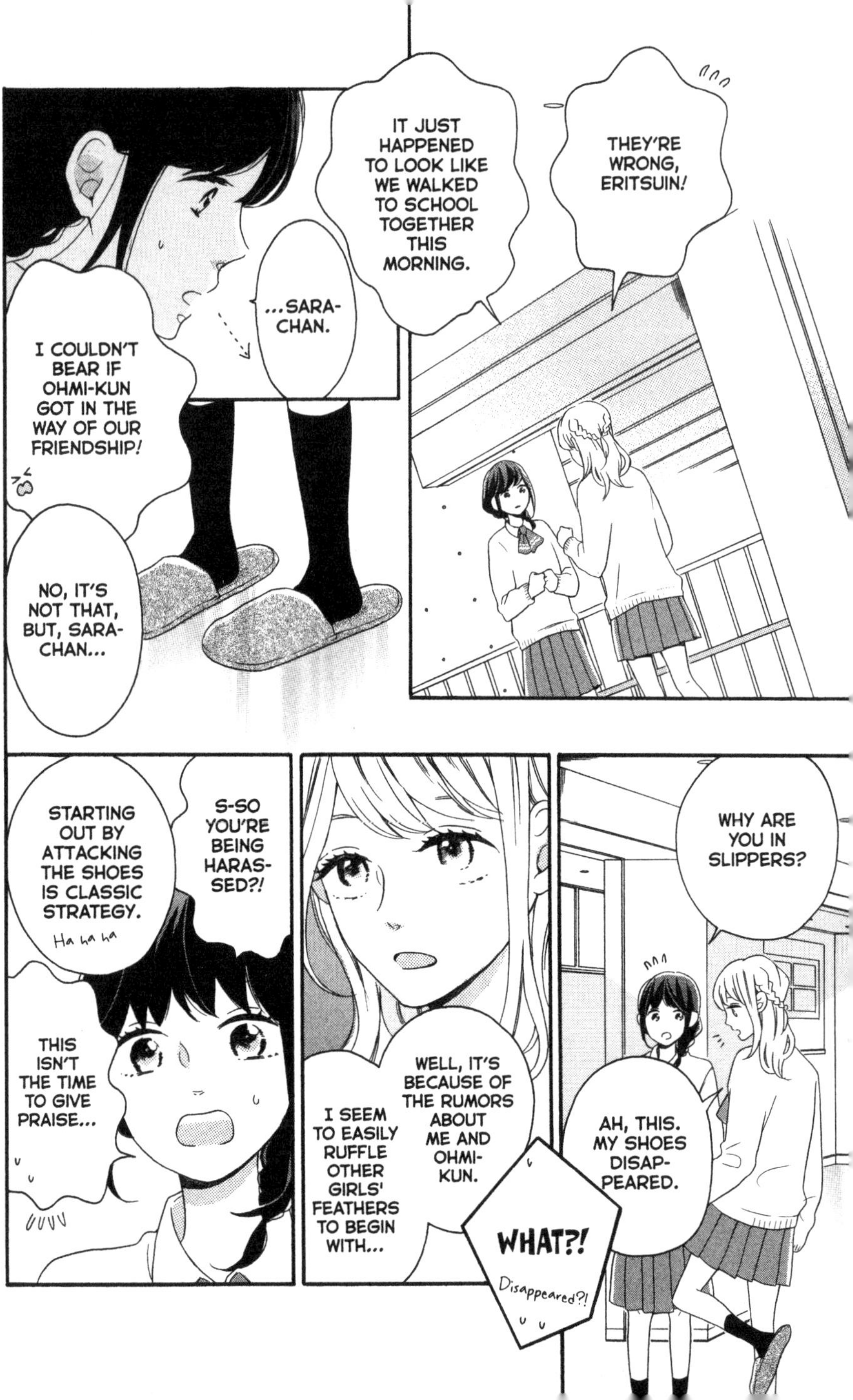
THEY'RE WRONG, ERITSUIN!
IT JUST HAPPENED TO LOOK LIKE WE WALKED TO SCHOOL TOGETHER THIS MORNING.
...SARA-CHAN.
I COULDN'T BEAR IF OHMI-KUN GOT IN THE WAY OF OUR FRIENDSHIP!
NO, IT'S NOT THAT, BUT, SARA-CHAN...
WHY ARE YOU IN SLIPPERS?
AH, THIS. MY SHOES DISAPPEARED.
WHAT?!
Disappeared?!
WELL, IT'S BECAUSE OF THE RUMORS ABOUT ME AND OHMI-KUN.
I SEEM TO EASILY RUFFLE OTHER GIRLS' FEATHERS TO BEGIN WITH...
S-SO YOU'RE BEING HARASSED?!
STARTING OUT BY ATTACKING THE SHOES IS CLASSIC STRATEGY.
Ha ha ha
THIS ISN'T THE TIME TO GIVE PRAISE...

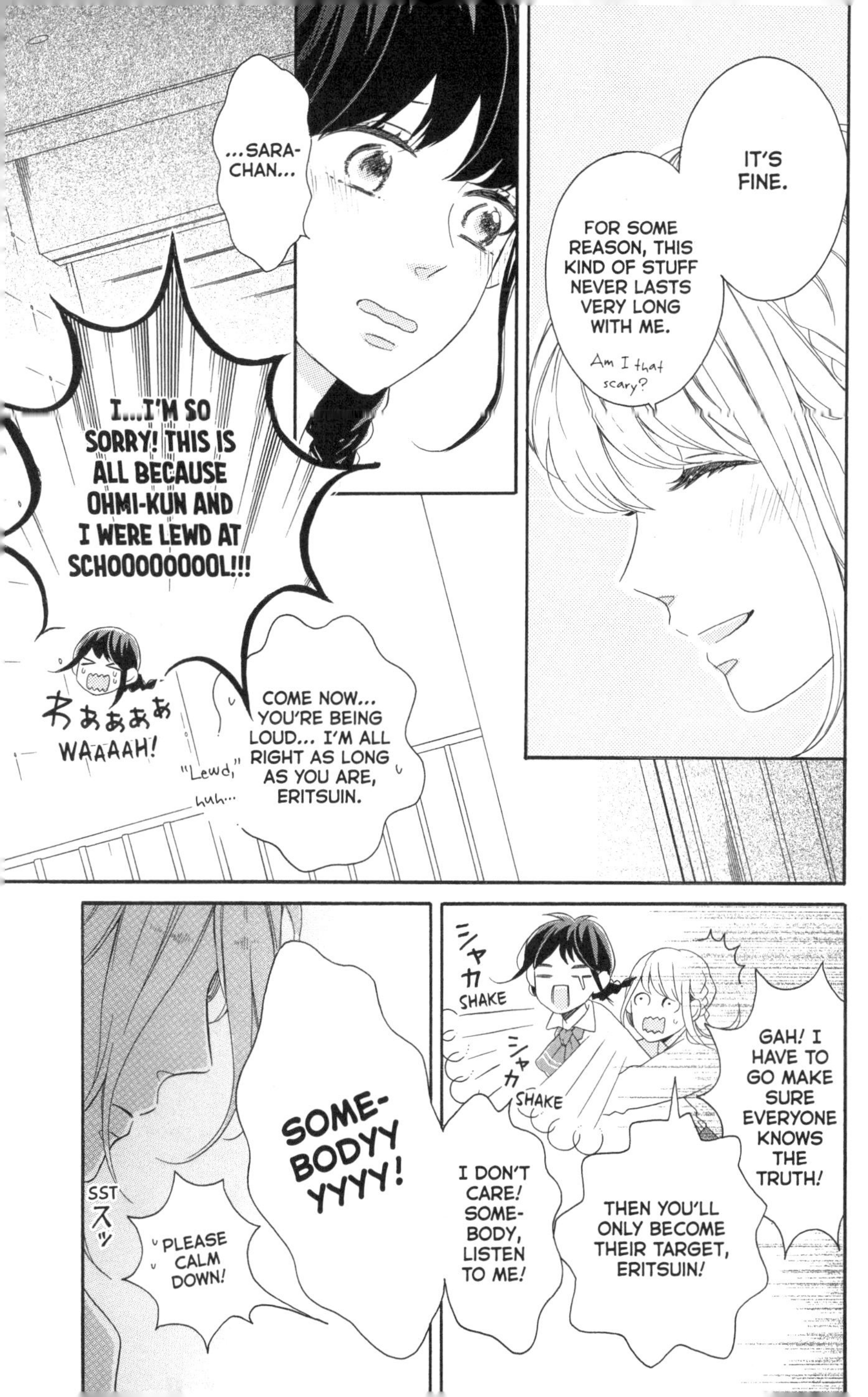
IT'S FINE.
FOR SOME REASON, THIS KIND OF STUFF NEVER LASTS VERY LONG WITH ME.
Am I that scary?
...SARA-CHAN...
I...I'M SO SORRY! THIS IS ALL BECAUSE OHMI-KUN AND I WERE LEWD AT SCHOOOOOOOOL!!!
わああああ
WAAAAH!
COME NOW... YOU'RE BEING LOUD... I'M ALL RIGHT AS LONG AS YOU ARE, ERITSUIN.
"Lewd," huh...
GAH! I HAVE TO GO MAKE SURE EVERYONE KNOWS THE TRUTH!
シャカ
SHAKE
シャカ
SHAKE
THEN YOU'LL ONLY BECOME THEIR TARGET, ERITSUIN!
I DON'T CARE! SOMEBODY, LISTEN TO ME!
SOMEBODYYYYY!
スッ
SST
PLEASE CALM DOWN!

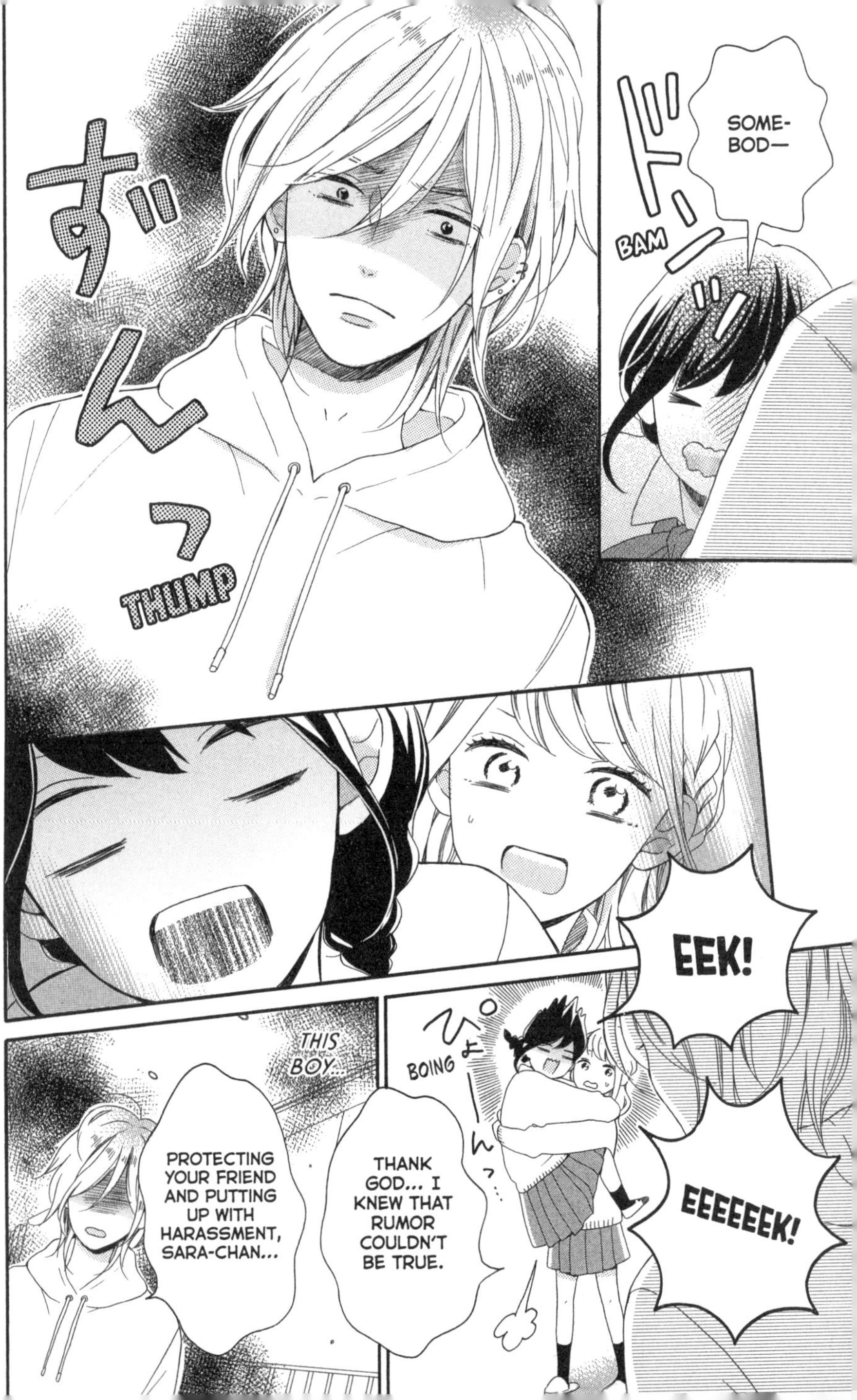
SOME-BOD—
BAM
THUMP
EEK!
BOING
ぴょーんっ…
THANK GOD... I KNEW THAT RUMOR COULDN'T BE TRUE.
EEEEEEK!
THIS BOY...
PROTECTING YOUR FRIEND AND PUTTING UP WITH HARASSMENT, SARA-CHAN...

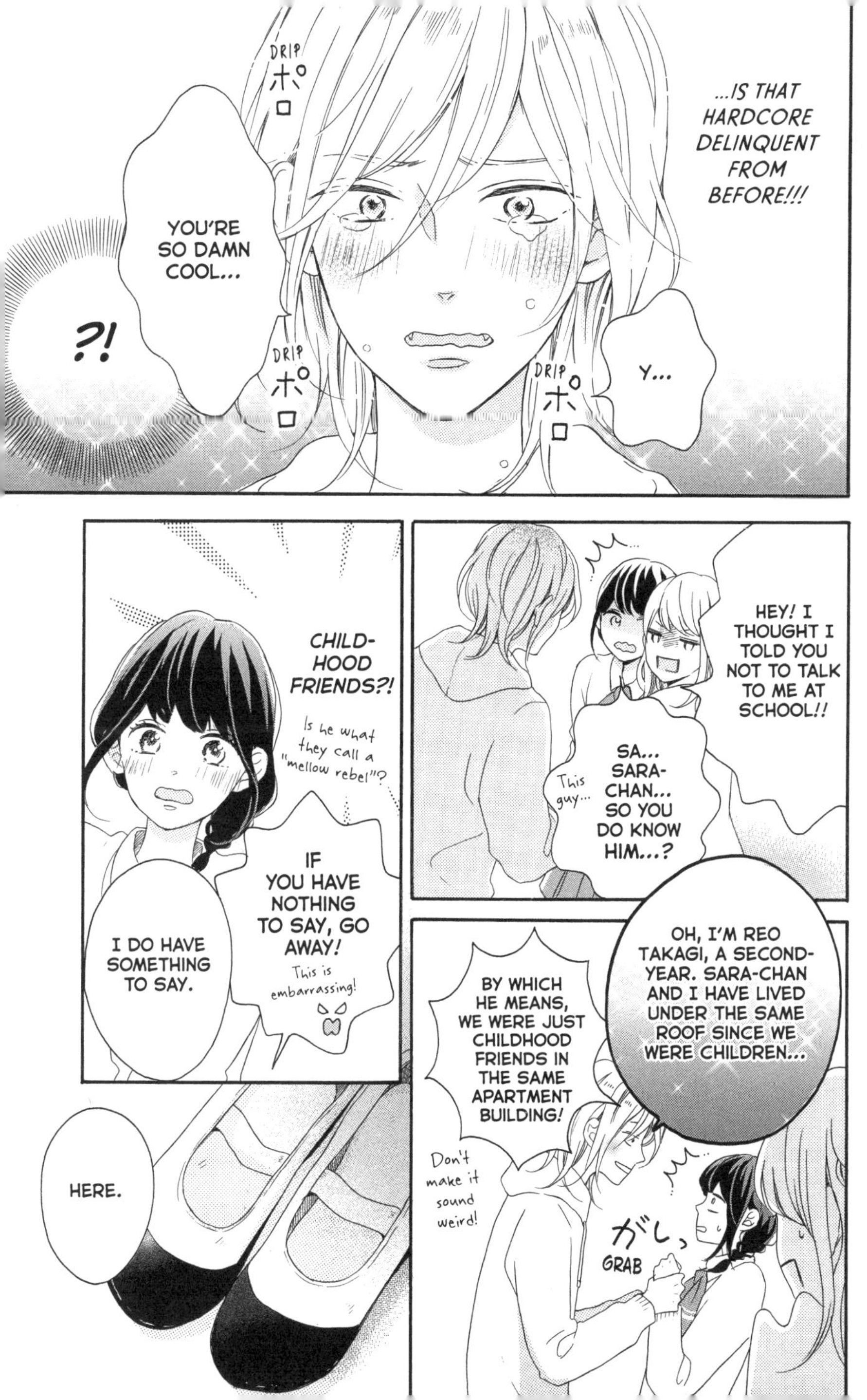
...IS THAT HARDCORE DELINQUENT FROM BEFORE!!!
DRIP ポロ
Y...
DRIP ポロ
DRIP ポロ
YOU'RE SO DAMN COOL...
?!
HEY! I THOUGHT I TOLD YOU NOT TO TALK TO ME AT SCHOOL!!
SA... SARA-CHAN... SO YOU DO KNOW HIM...?
This guy...
CHILD-HOOD FRIENDS?!
Is he what they call a "mellow rebel"?
IF YOU HAVE NOTHING TO SAY, GO AWAY!
This is embarrassing!
I DO HAVE SOMETHING TO SAY.
OH, I'M REO TAKAGI, A SECOND-YEAR. SARA-CHAN AND I HAVE LIVED UNDER THE SAME ROOF SINCE WE WERE CHILDREN...
BY WHICH HE MEANS, WE WERE JUST CHILDHOOD FRIENDS IN THE SAME APARTMENT BUILDING!
Don't make it sound weird!
ガしっ GRAB
HERE.

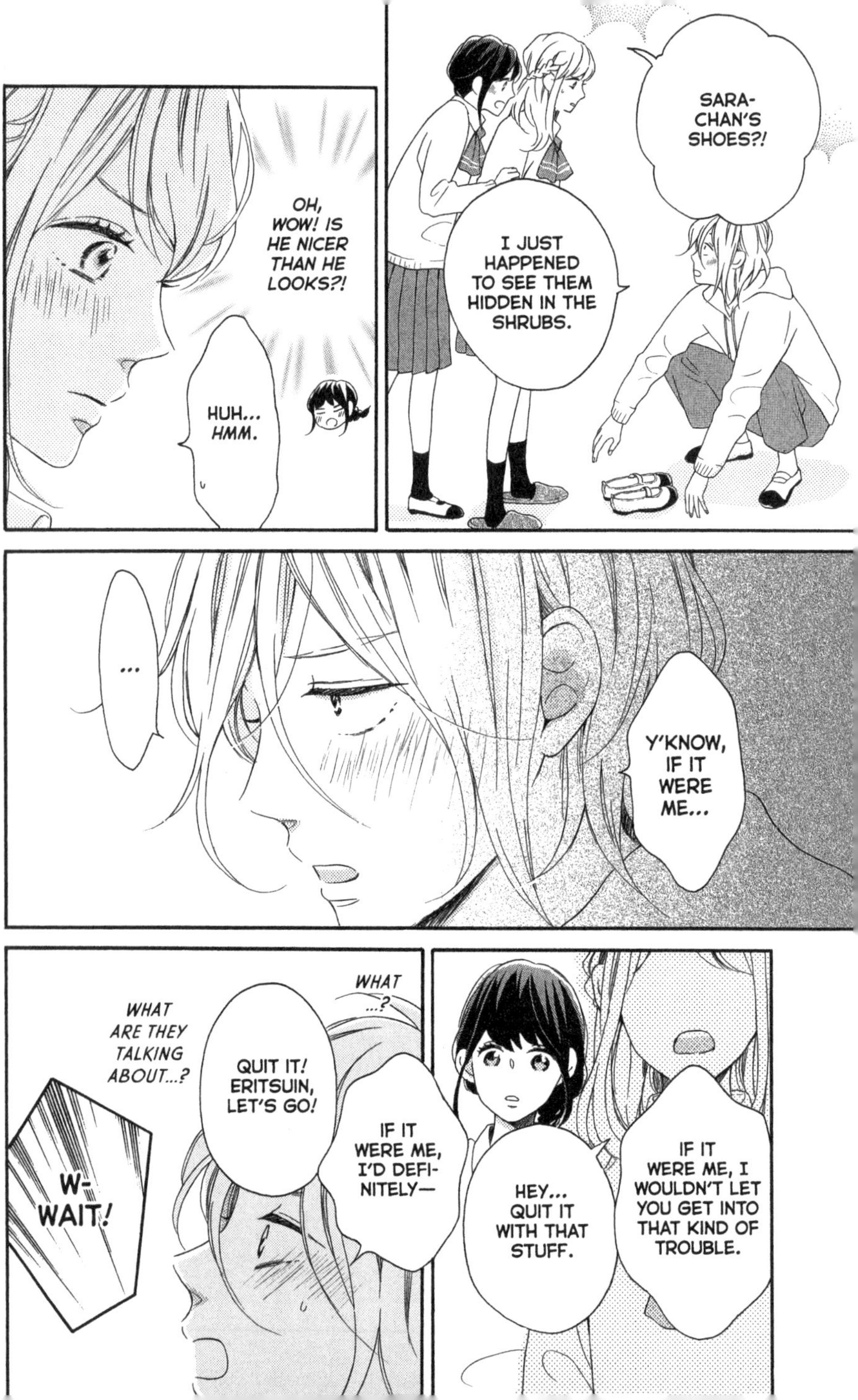
SARA-CHAN'S SHOES?!
I JUST HAPPENED TO SEE THEM HIDDEN IN THE SHRUBS.
OH, WOW! IS HE NICER THAN HE LOOKS?!
HUH... HMM.
Y'KNOW, IF IT WERE ME...
...
IF IT WERE ME, I WOULDN'T LET YOU GET INTO THAT KIND OF TROUBLE.
HEY... QUIT IT WITH THAT STUFF.
WHAT ...?
IF IT WERE ME, I'D DEFI-NITELY—
QUIT IT! ERITSUIN, LET'S GO!
WHAT ARE THEY TALKING ABOUT...?
W-WAIT!

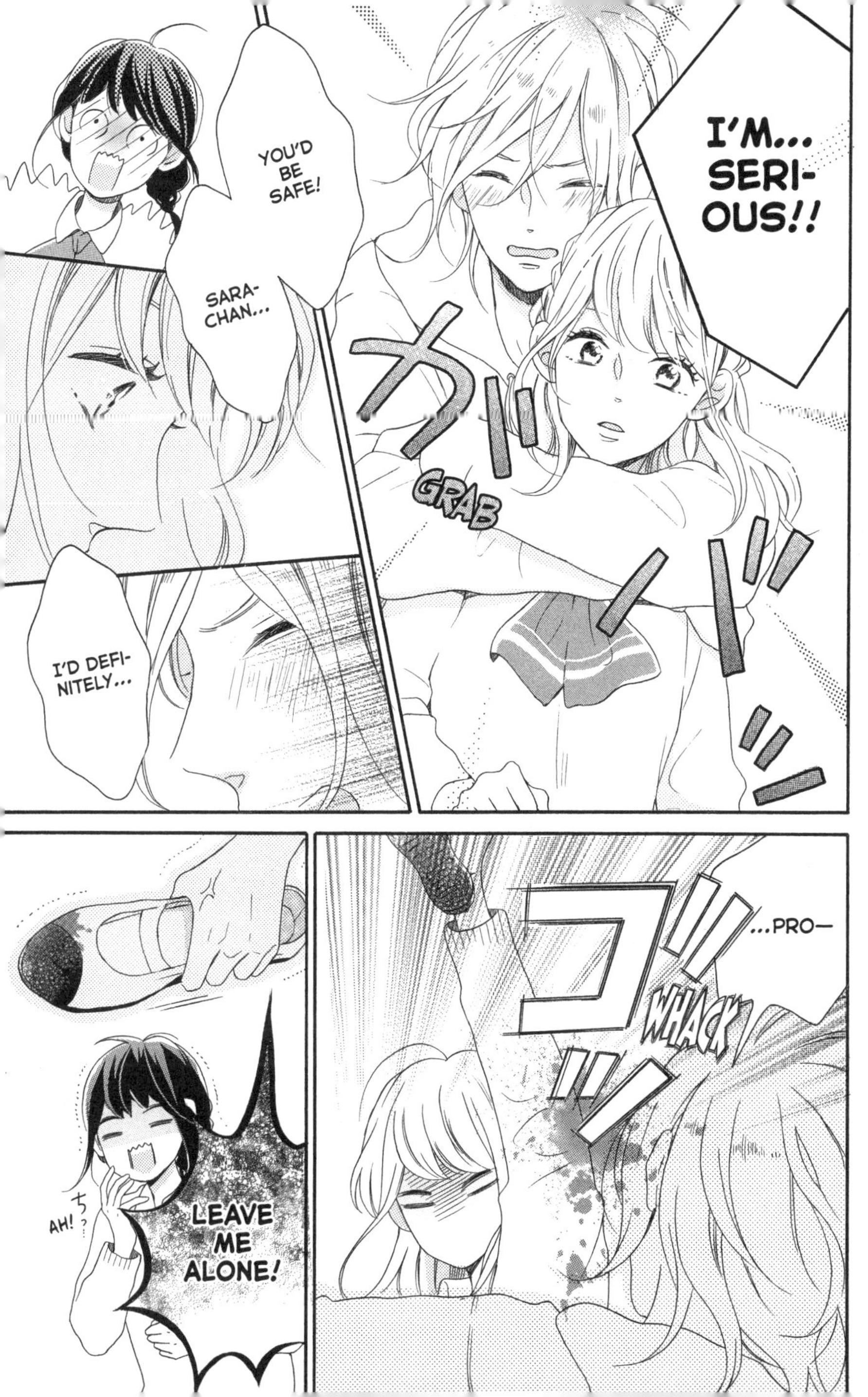
I'M... SERI-OUS!!
GRAB
YOU'D BE SAFE!
SARA-CHAN...
I'D DEFI-NITELY...
...PRO—
WHACK
LEAVE ME ALONE!
AH!

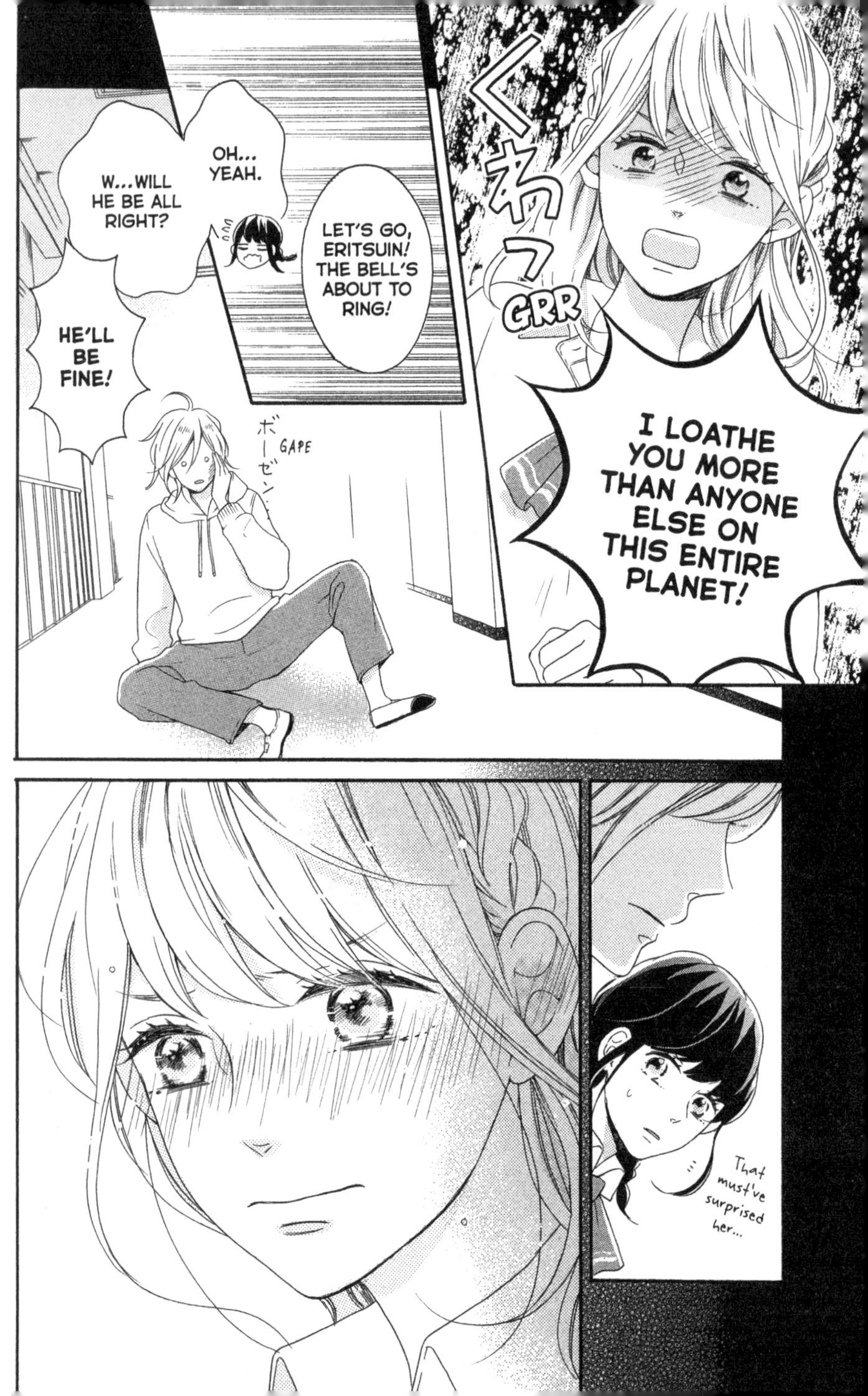
くわっ
GRR
I LOATHE YOU MORE THAN ANYONE ELSE ON THIS ENTIRE PLANET!
LET'S GO, ERITSUIN! THE BELL'S ABOUT TO RING!
OH... YEAH.
W...WILL HE BE ALL RIGHT?
HE'LL BE FINE!
ボーゼン…
GAPE
That must've surprised her...

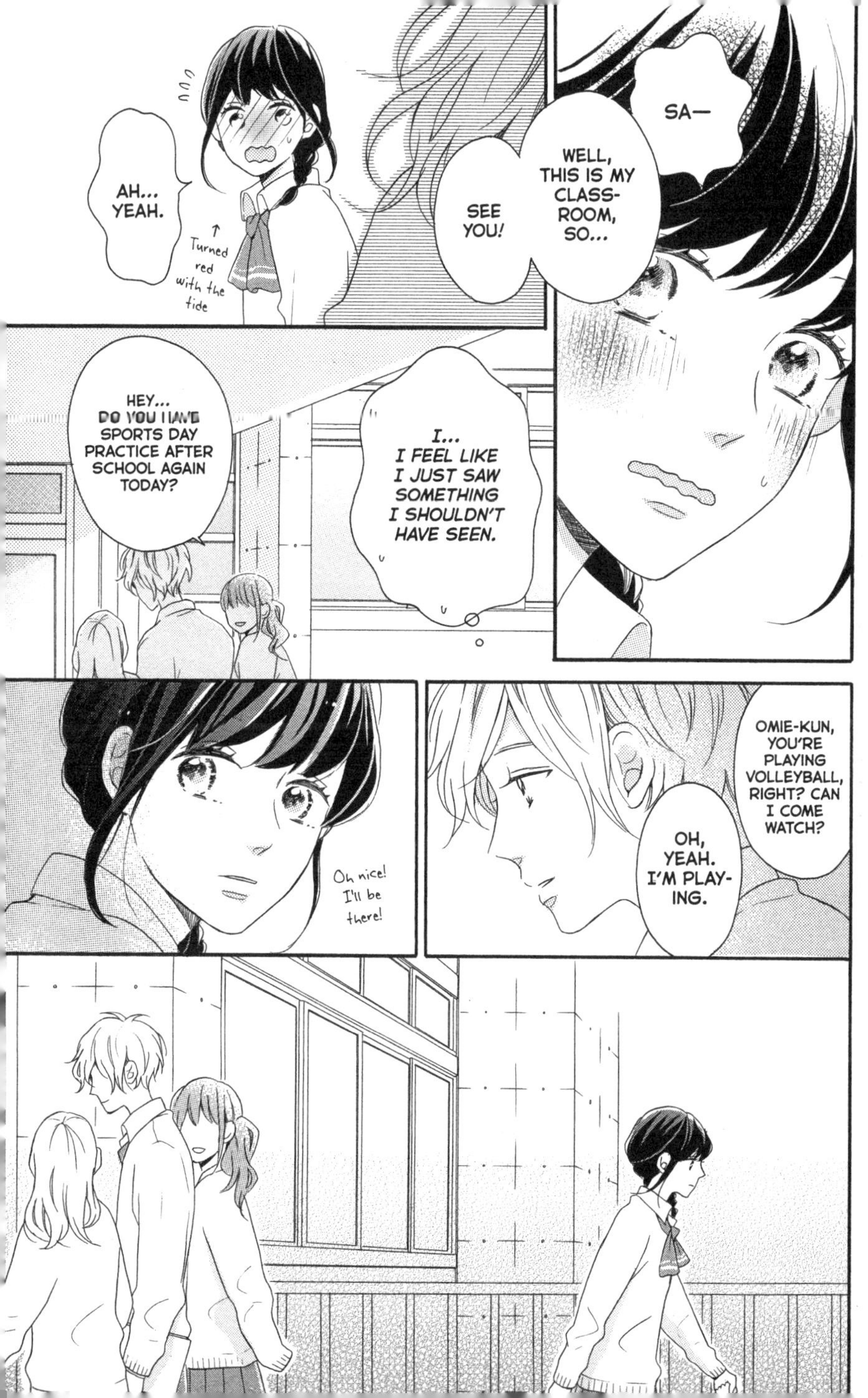
SA—
WELL, THIS IS MY CLASSROOM, SO...
SEE YOU!
AH... YEAH.
Turned red with the tide
I... I FEEL LIKE I JUST SAW SOMETHING I SHOULDN'T HAVE SEEN.
HEY... DO YOU HAVE SPORTS DAY PRACTICE AFTER SCHOOL AGAIN TODAY?
OMIE-KUN, YOU'RE PLAYING VOLLEYBALL, RIGHT? CAN I COME WATCH?
OH, YEAH. I'M PLAYING.
Oh nice! I'll be there!

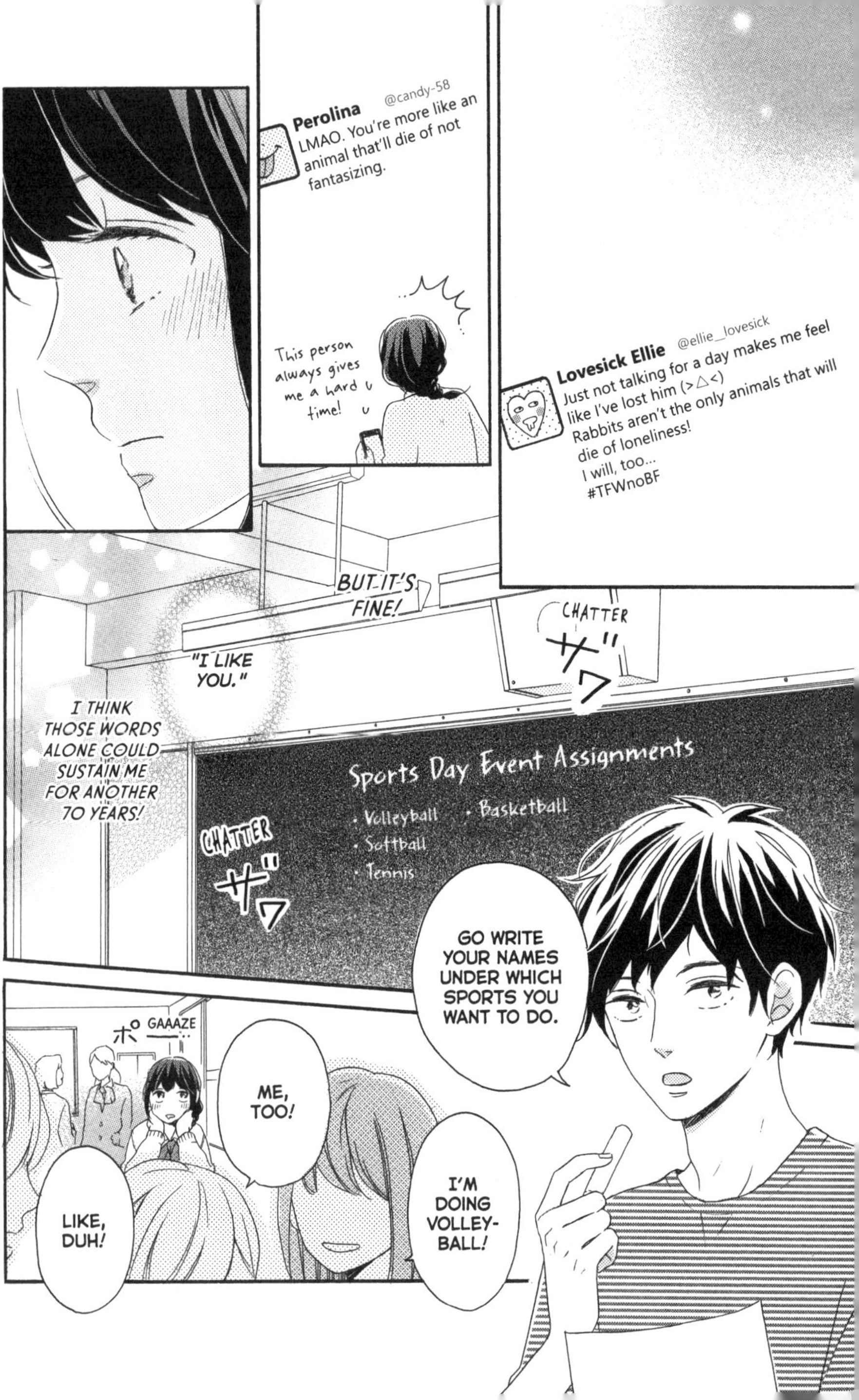

Lovesick Ellie @ellie_lovesick
Just not talking for a day makes me feel like I've lost him (>△<) Rabbits aren't the only animals that will die of loneliness! I will, too... #TFWnoBF
Perolina @candy-58
LMAO. You're more like an animal that'll die of not fantasizing.
This person always gives me a hard time!
BUT IT'S FINE!
"I LIKE YOU."
I THINK THOSE WORDS ALONE COULD SUSTAIN ME FOR ANOTHER 70 YEARS!
CHATTER
ザワ
Sports Day Event Assignments
· Volleyball
· Basketball
· Softball
· Tennis
CHATTER
ザワ
GO WRITE YOUR NAMES UNDER WHICH SPORTS YOU WANT TO DO.
I'M DOING VOLLEY-BALL!
ME, TOO!
LIKE, DUH!
GAAAZE
ポー

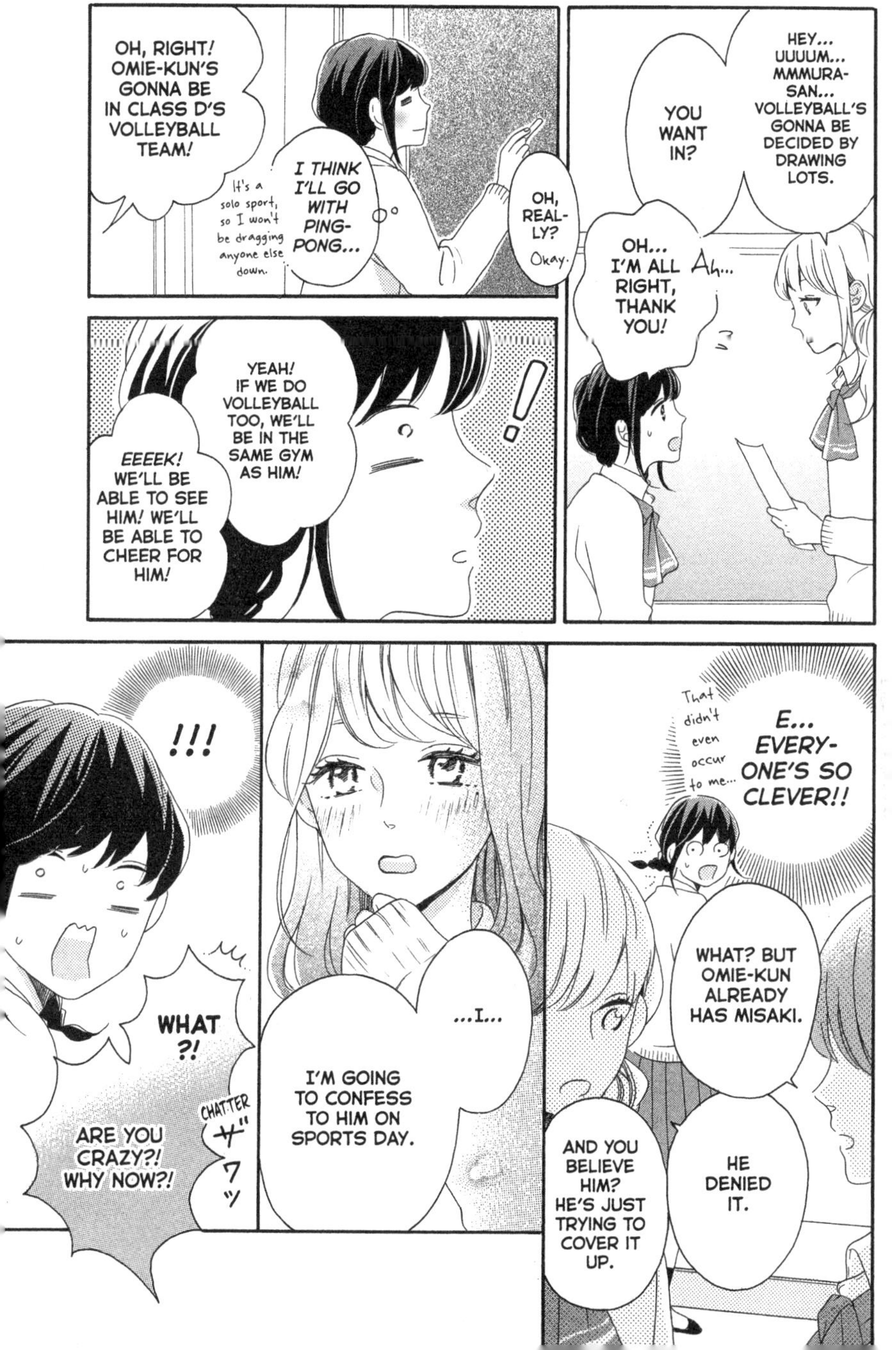
HEY... UUUUM... MMMURA-SAN... VOLLEYBALL'S GONNA BE DECIDED BY DRAWING LOTS.
YOU WANT IN?
OH... I'M ALL RIGHT, THANK YOU!
Ah...
I THINK I'LL GO WITH PING-PONG...
It's a solo sport, so I won't be dragging anyone else down.
OH, REALLY? Okay.
OH, RIGHT! OMIE-KUN'S GONNA BE IN CLASS D'S VOLLEYBALL TEAM!
YEAH! IF WE DO VOLLEYBALL TOO, WE'LL BE IN THE SAME GYM AS HIM!
EEEEK! WE'LL BE ABLE TO SEE HIM! WE'LL BE ABLE TO CHEER FOR HIM!
E... EVERY-ONE'S SO CLEVER!!
That didn't even occur to me...
WHAT? BUT OMIE-KUN ALREADY HAS MISAKI.
HE DENIED IT.
AND YOU BELIEVE HIM? HE'S JUST TRYING TO COVER IT UP.
...I...
I'M GOING TO CONFESS TO HIM ON SPORTS DAY.
!!!
WHAT?!
CHATTER ザワッ
ARE YOU CRAZY?! WHY NOW?!

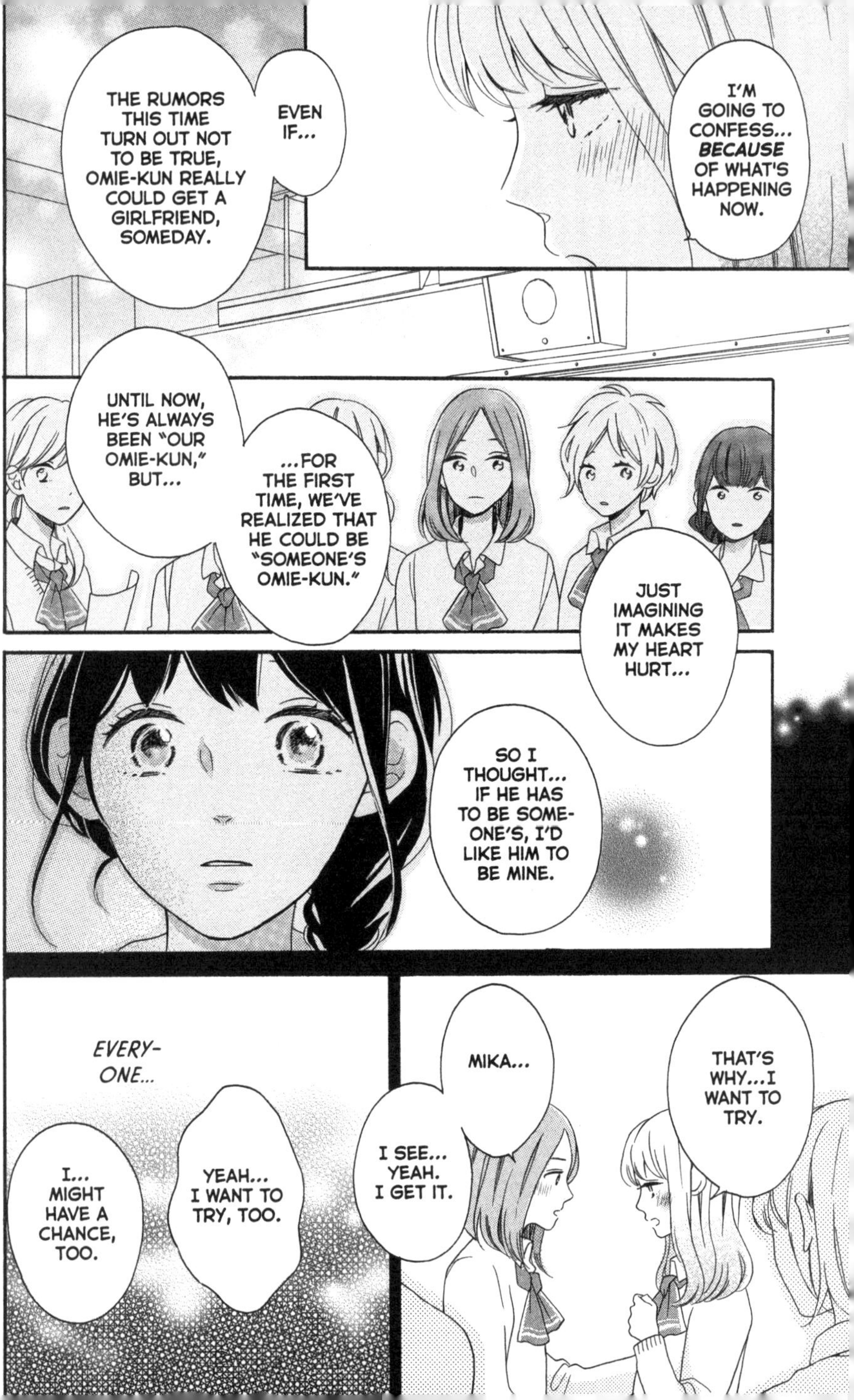
I'M GOING TO CONFESS... *BECAUSE* OF WHAT'S HAPPENING NOW.
EVEN IF...
THE RUMORS THIS TIME TURN OUT NOT TO BE TRUE, OMIE-KUN REALLY COULD GET A GIRLFRIEND, SOMEDAY.
UNTIL NOW, HE'S ALWAYS BEEN "OUR OMIE-KUN," BUT...
...FOR THE FIRST TIME, WE'VE REALIZED THAT HE COULD BE "SOMEONE'S OMIE-KUN."
JUST IMAGINING IT MAKES MY HEART HURT...
SO I THOUGHT... IF HE HAS TO BE SOME-ONE'S, I'D LIKE HIM TO BE MINE.
THAT'S WHY...I WANT TO TRY.
MIKA...
I SEE... YEAH. I GET IT.
EVERY-ONE...
YEAH... I WANT TO TRY, TOO.
I... MIGHT HAVE A CHANCE, TOO.

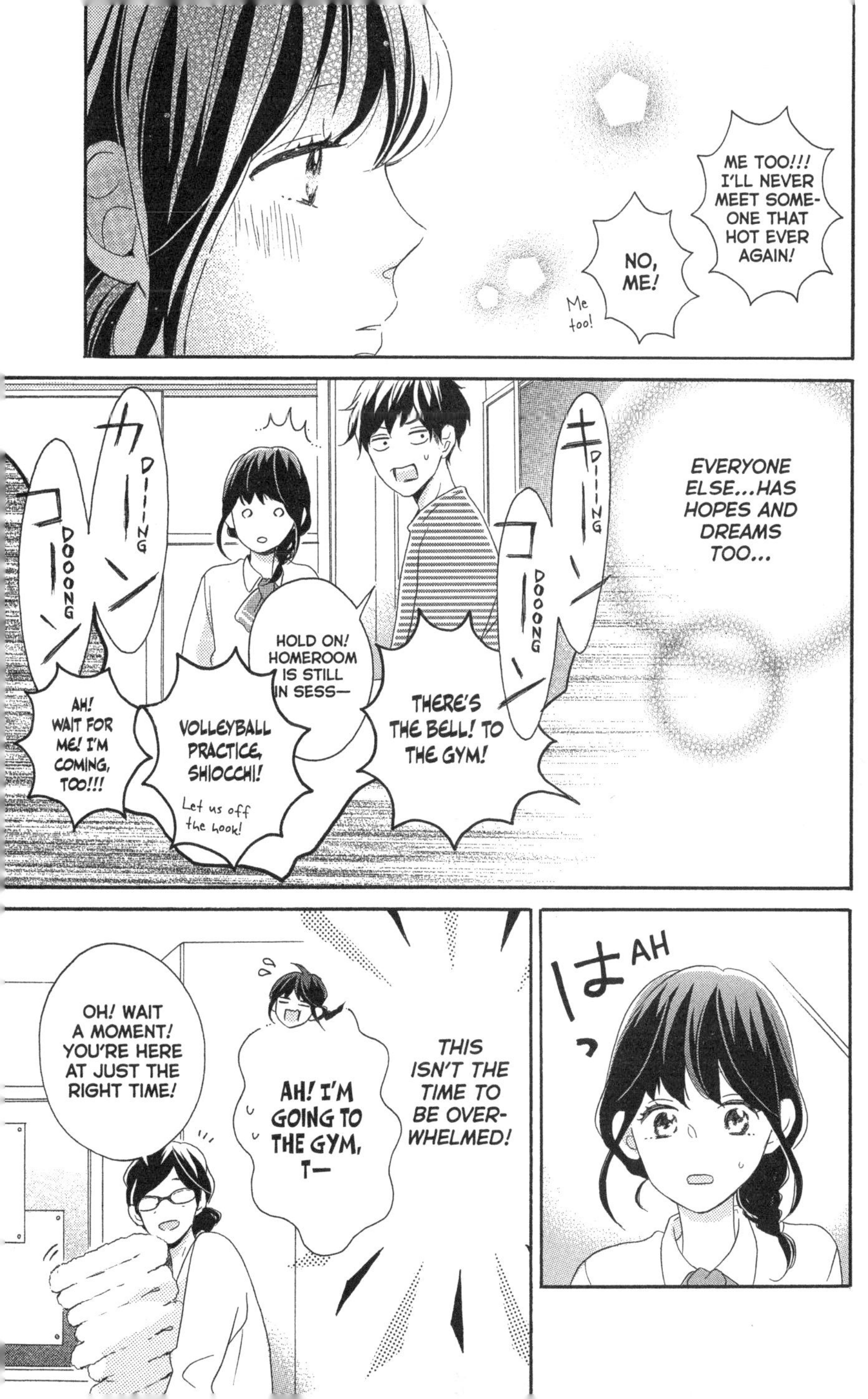
ME TOO!!! I'LL NEVER MEET SOME-ONE THAT HOT EVER AGAIN!
NO, ME!
Me too!
EVERYONE ELSE...HAS HOPES AND DREAMS TOO...
キーンコーン DIIING DOOONG
THERE'S THE BELL! TO THE GYM!
HOLD ON! HOMEROOM IS STILL IN SESS—
カーンコーン DIIING DOOONG
VOLLEYBALL PRACTICE, SHIOCCHI!
Let us off the hook!
AH! WAIT FOR ME! I'M COMING, TOO!!!
はっ AH
THIS ISN'T THE TIME TO BE OVER-WHELMED!
AH! I'M GOING TO THE GYM, T—
OH! WAIT A MOMENT! YOU'RE HERE AT JUST THE RIGHT TIME!

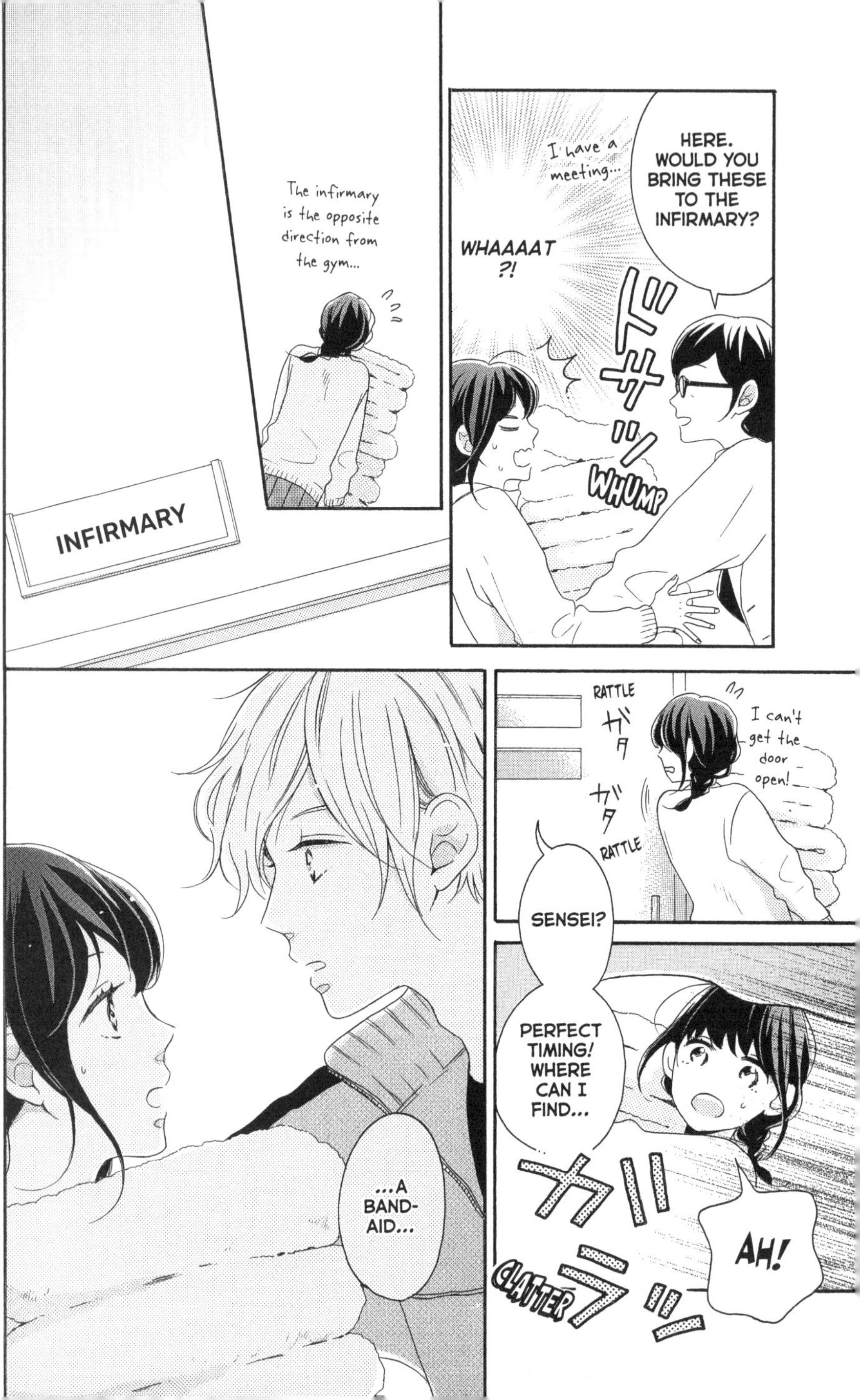
HERE. WOULD YOU BRING THESE TO THE INFIRMARY?
I have a meeting...
WHAAAAT?!
WHUMP
The infirmary is the opposite direction from the gym...
INFIRMARY
RATTLE
RATTLE
I can't get the door open!
SENSEI?
PERFECT TIMING! WHERE CAN I FIND...
CLATTER
AH!
...A BAND-AID...

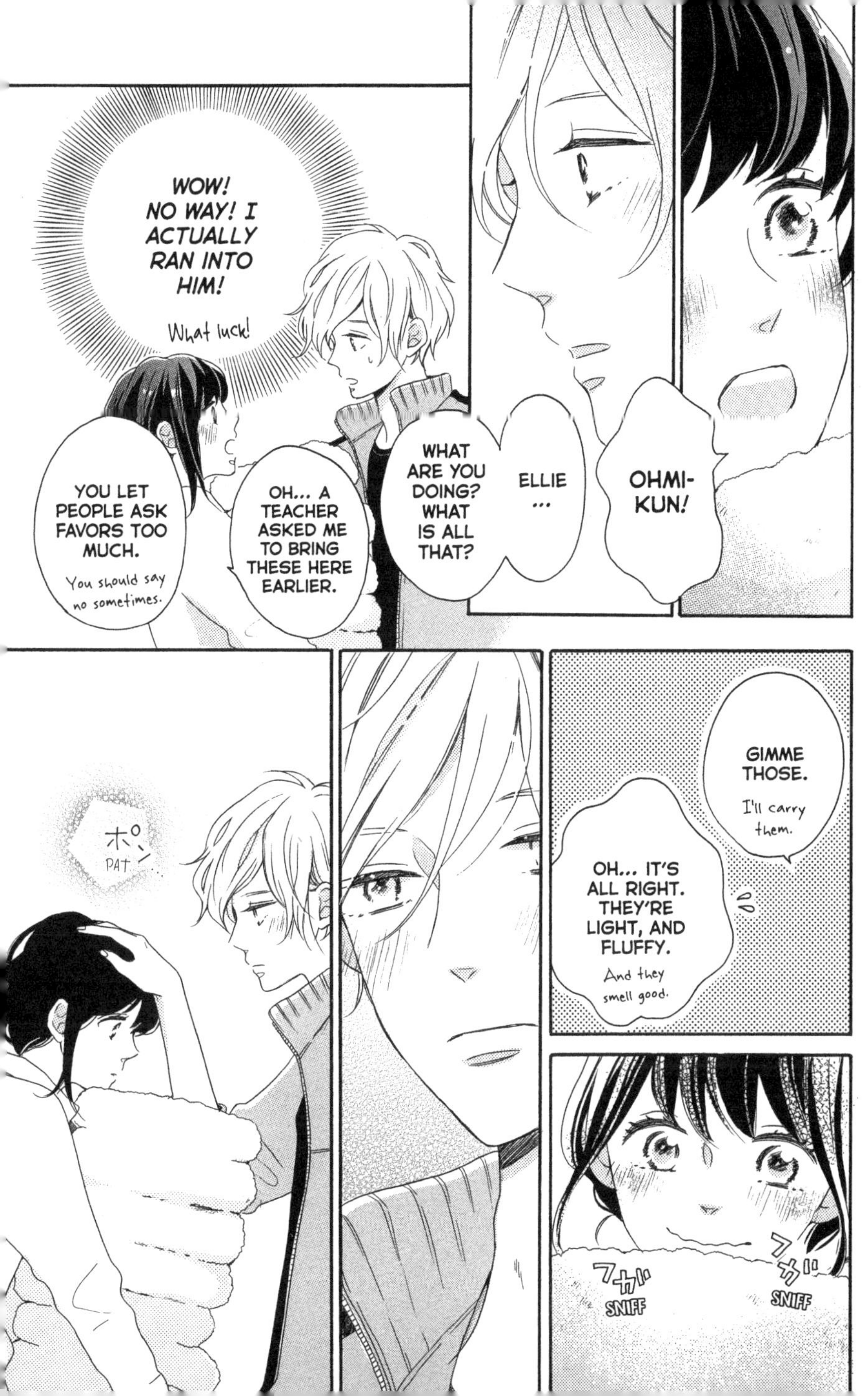
OHMI-KUN!
ELLIE ...
WHAT ARE YOU DOING? WHAT IS ALL THAT?
WOW! NO WAY! I ACTUALLY RAN INTO HIM!
What luck!
OH... A TEACHER ASKED ME TO BRING THESE HERE EARLIER.
YOU LET PEOPLE ASK FAVORS TOO MUCH.
You should say no sometimes.
GIMME THOSE.
I'll carry them.
OH... IT'S ALL RIGHT. THEY'RE LIGHT, AND FLUFFY.
And they smell good.
フガ
SNIFF
フガ
SNIFF
ポン
PAT

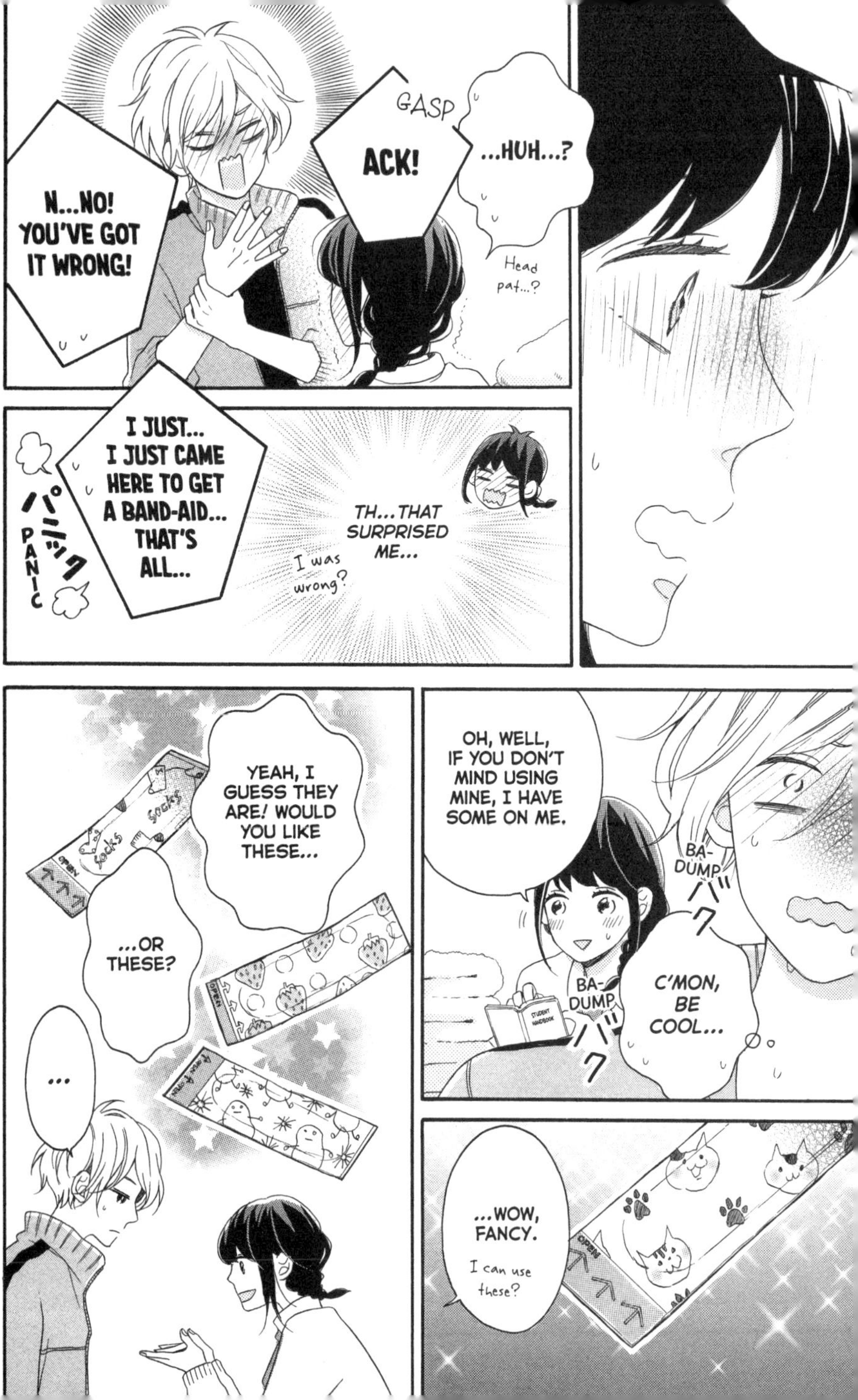

...HUH...?
GASP
ACK!
Head pat...?
N...NO! YOU'VE GOT IT WRONG!
TH...THAT SURPRISED ME...
I was wrong?
I JUST... I JUST CAME HERE TO GET A BAND-AID... THAT'S ALL...
パニック
PANIC
OH, WELL, IF YOU DON'T MIND USING MINE, I HAVE SOME ON ME.
BA-DUMP
バク
C'MON, BE COOL...
BA-DUMP
バク
STUDENT HANDBOOK
...WOW, FANCY.
I can use these?
YEAH, I GUESS THEY ARE! WOULD YOU LIKE THESE...
socks
...OR THESE?
...

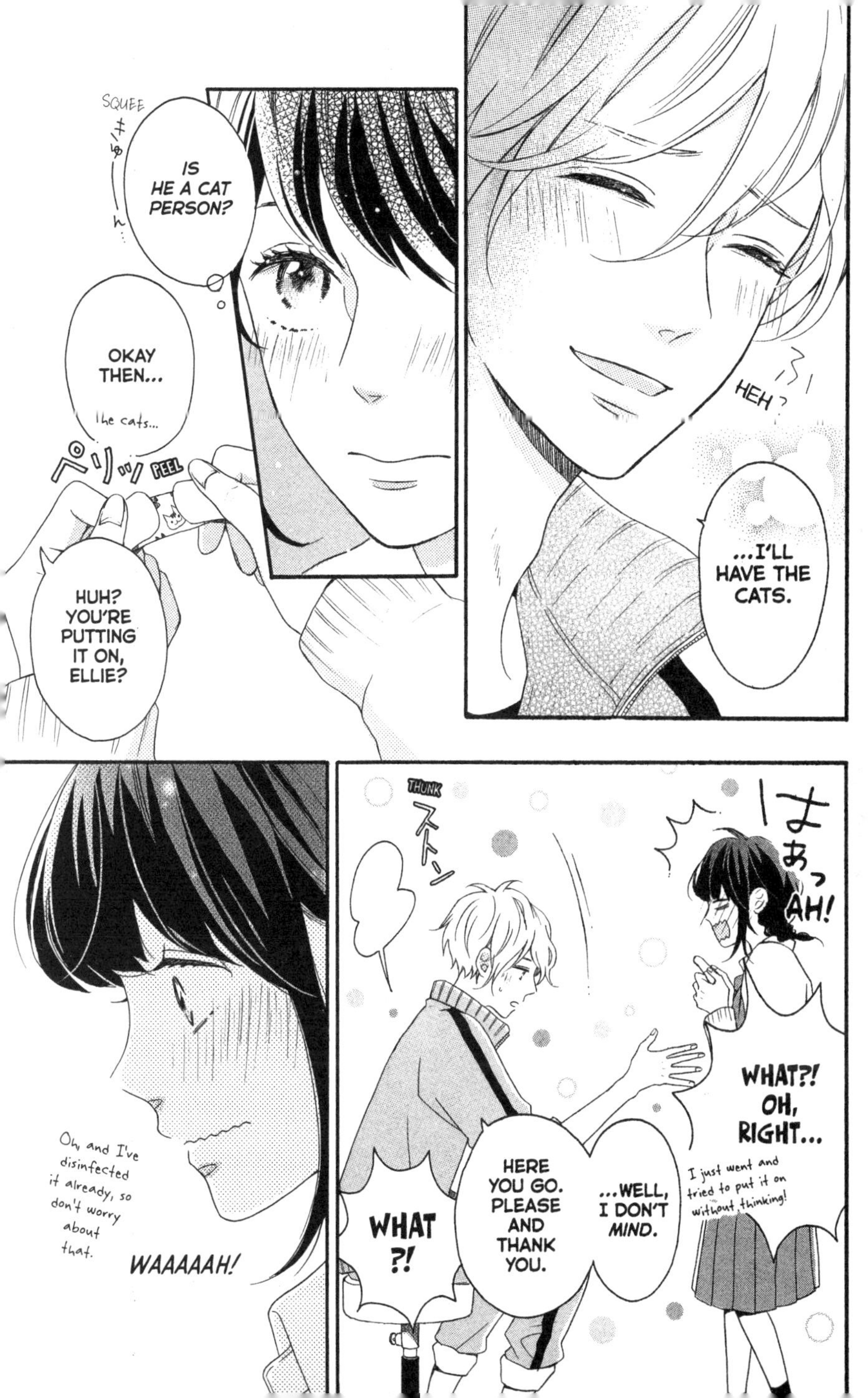
HEH
...I'LL HAVE THE CATS.
SQUEE
IS HE A CAT PERSON?
OKAY THEN...
The cats...
PEEL
HUH? YOU'RE PUTTING IT ON, ELLIE?
AH!
WHAT?! OH, RIGHT...
I just went and tried to put it on without thinking!
...WELL, I DON'T MIND.
HERE YOU GO. PLEASE AND THANK YOU.
THUNK
WHAT?!
WAAAAAH!
Oh, and I've disinfected it already, so don't worry about that.

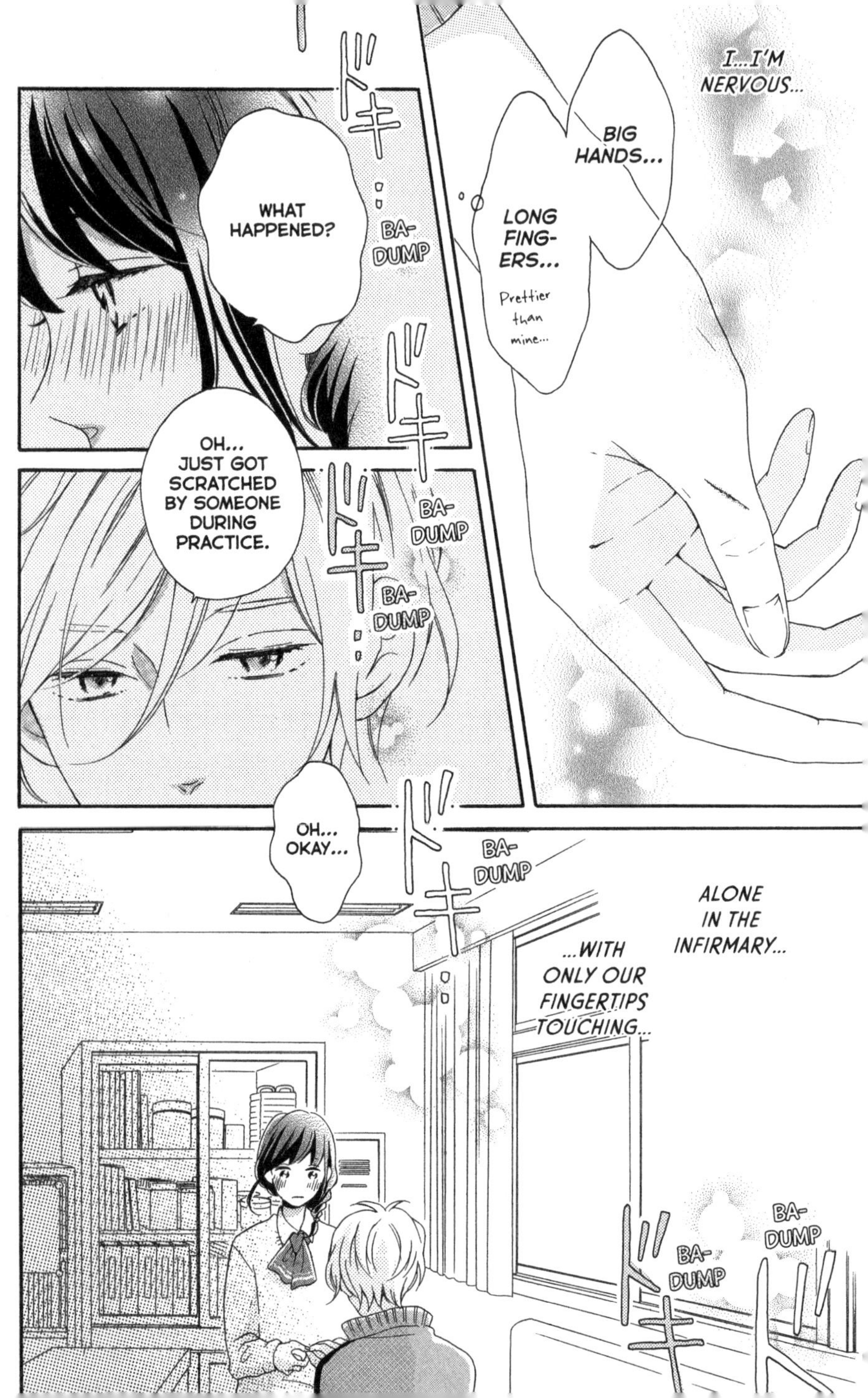
I...I'M NERVOUS...
BIG HANDS...
LONG FING-ERS...
Prettier than mine...
WHAT HAPPENED?
ドキ
BA-DUMP
ドキ
OH... JUST GOT SCRATCHED BY SOMEONE DURING PRACTICE.
BA-DUMP
ドキ
BA-DUMP
OH... OKAY...
ドキ
BA-DUMP
ALONE IN THE INFIRMARY...
...WITH ONLY OUR FINGERTIPS TOUCHING...
BA-DUMP
ドキ
BA-DUMP
ドキ

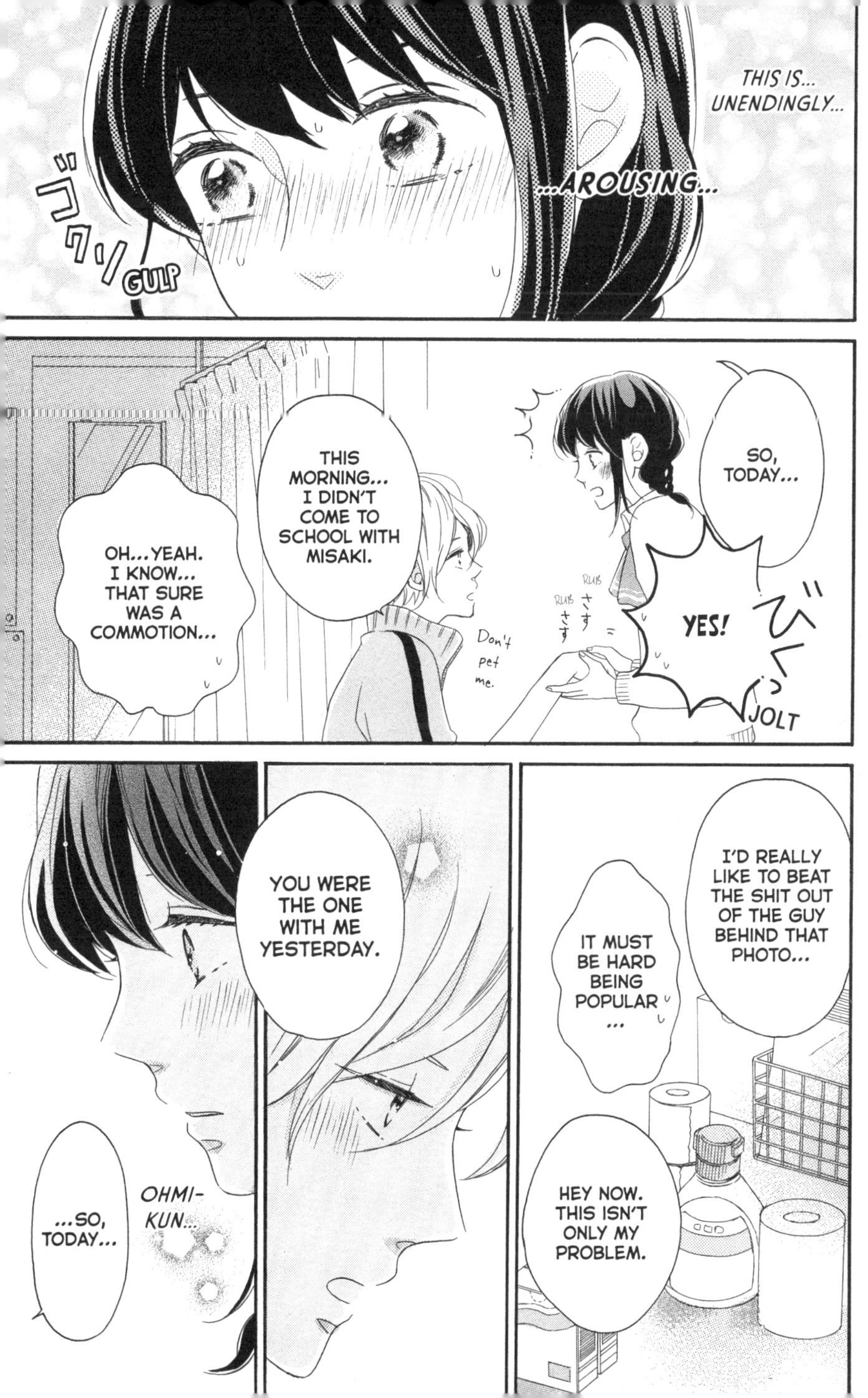
THIS IS... UNENDINGLY...
...AROUSING...
ゴクッ
GULP
SO, TODAY...
YES!
びくっ
JOLT
RUB さす
RUB さす
Don't pet me.
THIS MORNING... I DIDN'T COME TO SCHOOL WITH MISAKI.
OH...YEAH. I KNOW... THAT SURE WAS A COMMOTION...
I'D REALLY LIKE TO BEAT THE SHIT OUT OF THE GUY BEHIND THAT PHOTO...
IT MUST BE HARD BEING POPULAR...
HEY NOW. THIS ISN'T ONLY MY PROBLEM.
YOU WERE THE ONE WITH ME YESTERDAY.
OHMI-KUN...
...SO, TODAY...

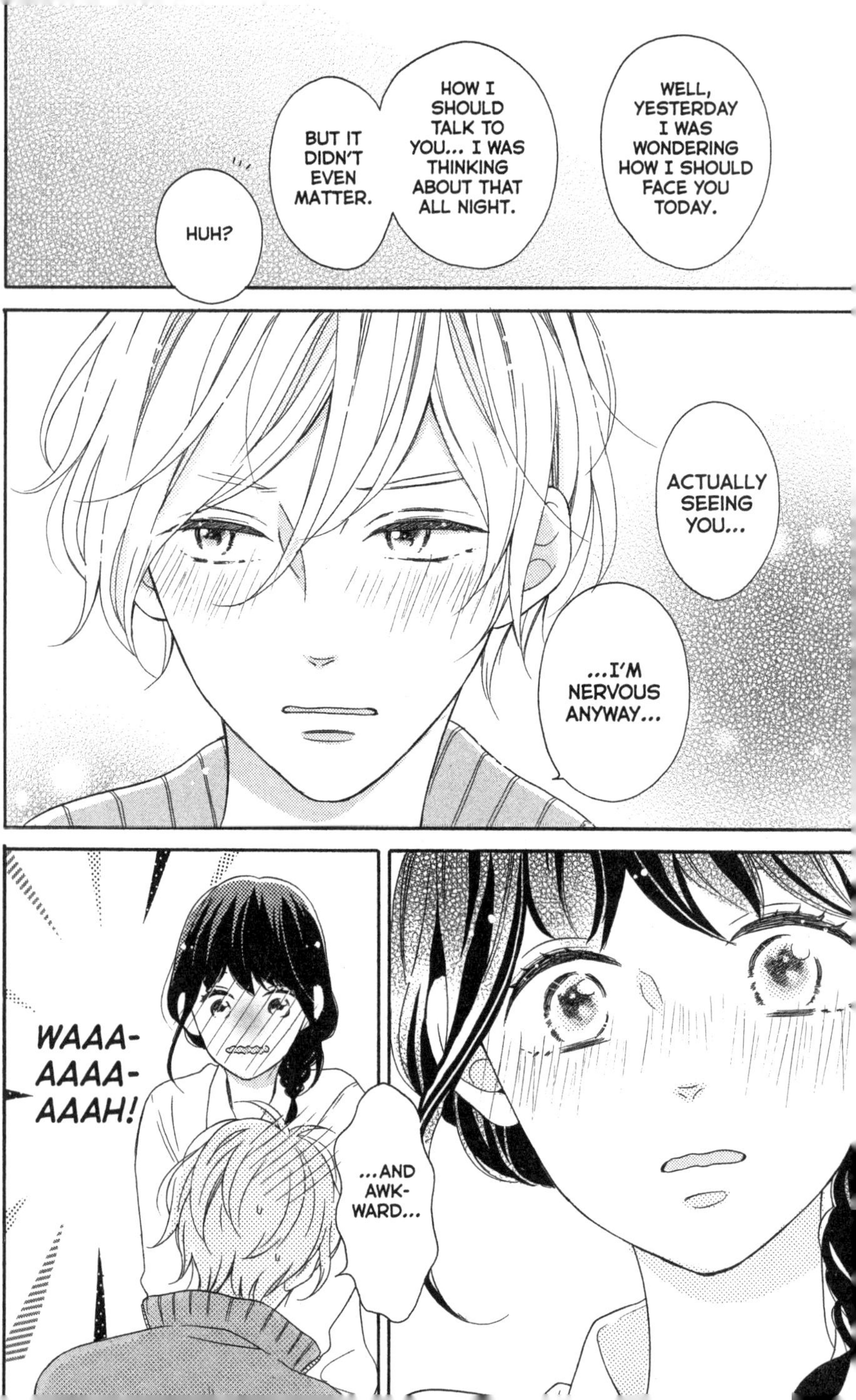
WELL, YESTERDAY I WAS WONDERING HOW I SHOULD FACE YOU TODAY.
HOW I SHOULD TALK TO YOU... I WAS THINKING ABOUT THAT ALL NIGHT.
BUT IT DIDN'T EVEN MATTER.
HUH?
ACTUALLY SEEING YOU...
...I'M NERVOUS ANYWAY...
...AND AWK-WARD...
WAAA-AAAA-AAAH!

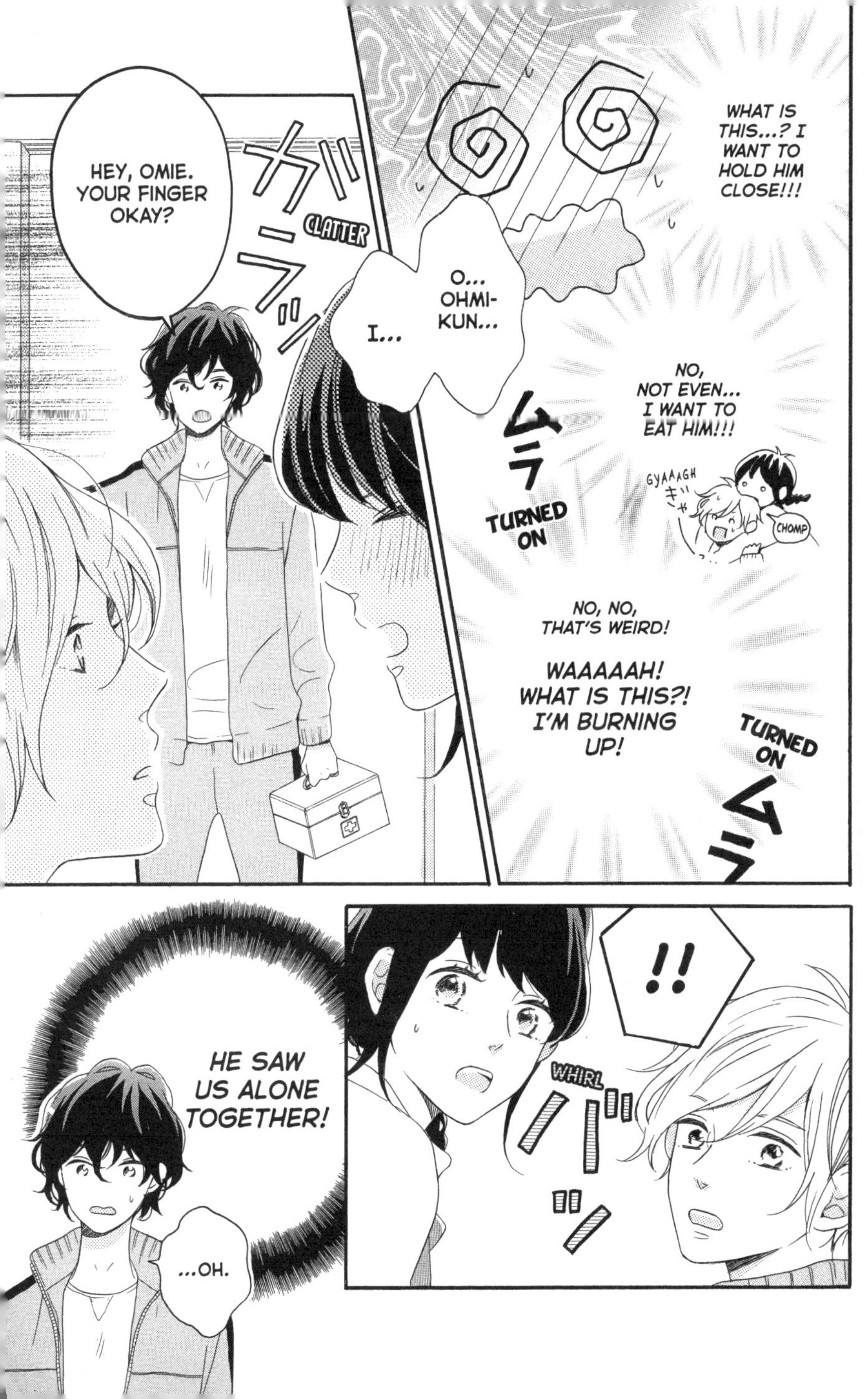
WHAT IS THIS...? I WANT TO HOLD HIM CLOSE!!!
O... OHMI-KUN... I...
NO, NOT EVEN... I WANT TO EAT HIM!!!
GYAAAGH
CHOMP
TURNED ON
NO, NO, THAT'S WEIRD!
WAAAAAH! WHAT IS THIS?! I'M BURNING UP!
TURNED ON
CLATTER
HEY, OMIE. YOUR FINGER OKAY?
!!
WHIRL
HE SAW US ALONE TOGETHER!
...OH.

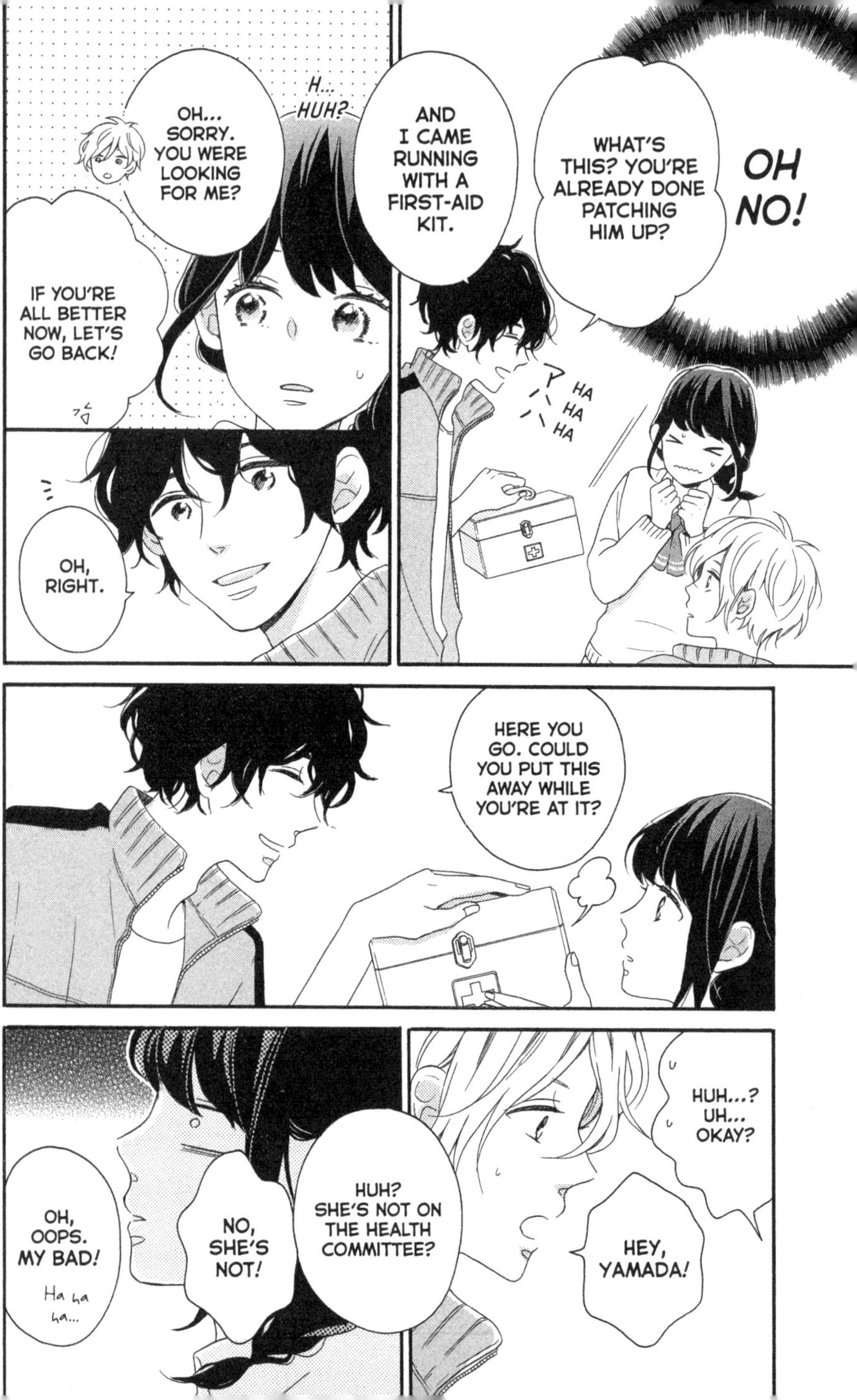
OH NO!
WHAT'S THIS? YOU'RE ALREADY DONE PATCHING HIM UP?
AND I CAME RUNNING WITH A FIRST-AID KIT.
HA HA HA
H... HUH?
OH... SORRY. YOU WERE LOOKING FOR ME?
IF YOU'RE ALL BETTER NOW, LET'S GO BACK!
OH, RIGHT.
HERE YOU GO. COULD YOU PUT THIS AWAY WHILE YOU'RE AT IT?
HUH...? UH... OKAY?
HEY, YAMADA!
HUH? SHE'S NOT ON THE HEALTH COMMITTEE?
NO, SHE'S NOT!
OH, OOPS. MY BAD!
Ha ha ha...

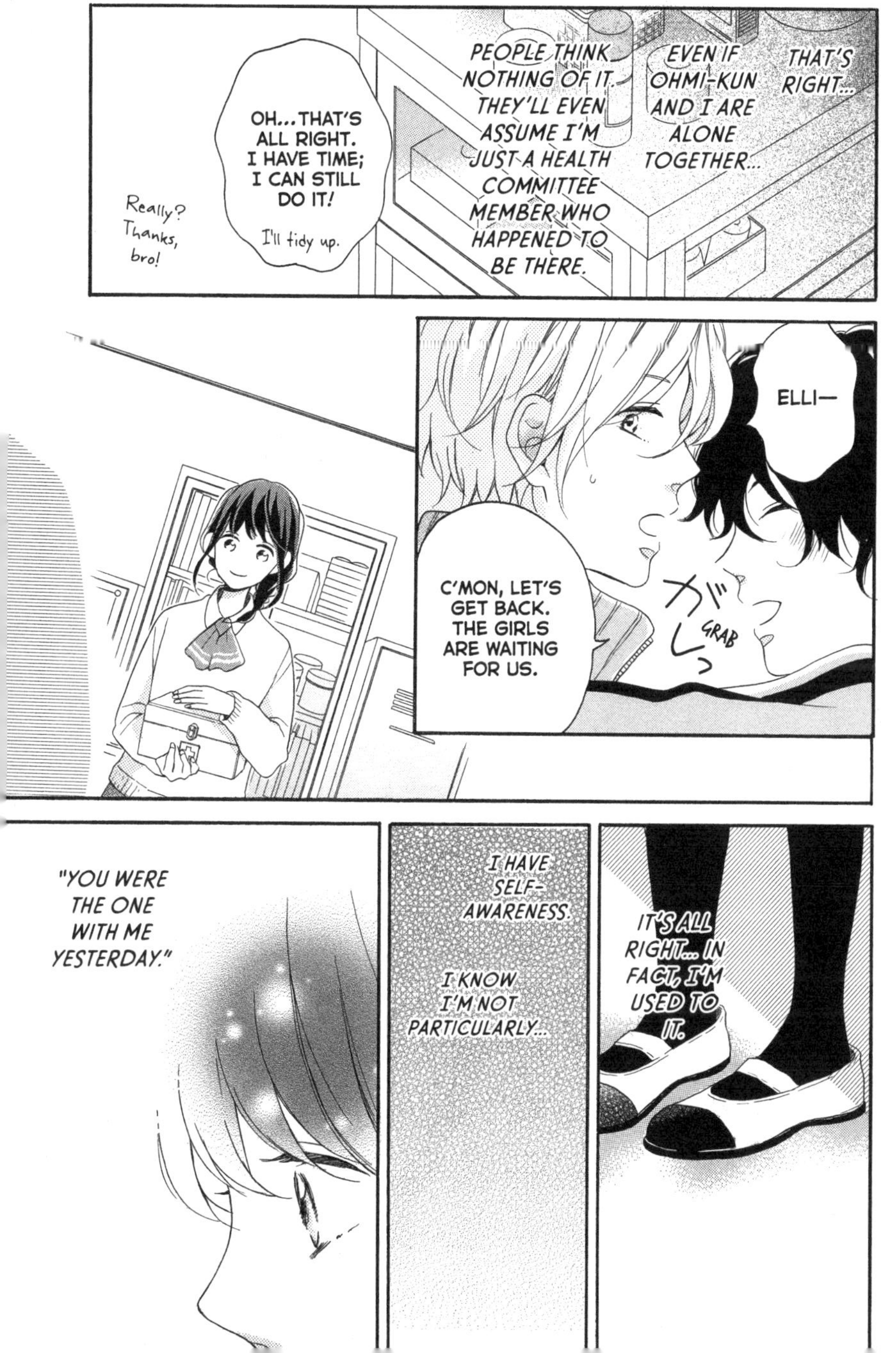

THAT'S RIGHT...
EVEN IF OHMI-KUN AND I ARE ALONE TOGETHER...
PEOPLE THINK NOTHING OF IT. THEY'LL EVEN ASSUME I'M JUST A HEALTH COMMITTEE MEMBER WHO HAPPENED TO BE THERE.
OH...THAT'S ALL RIGHT. I HAVE TIME; I CAN STILL DO IT!
I'll tidy up.
Really? Thanks, bro!
ELLI—
GRAB
C'MON, LET'S GET BACK. THE GIRLS ARE WAITING FOR US.
IT'S ALL RIGHT... IN FACT, I'M USED TO IT.
I HAVE SELF-AWARENESS.
I KNOW I'M NOT PARTICULARLY...
"YOU WERE THE ONE WITH ME YESTERDAY."

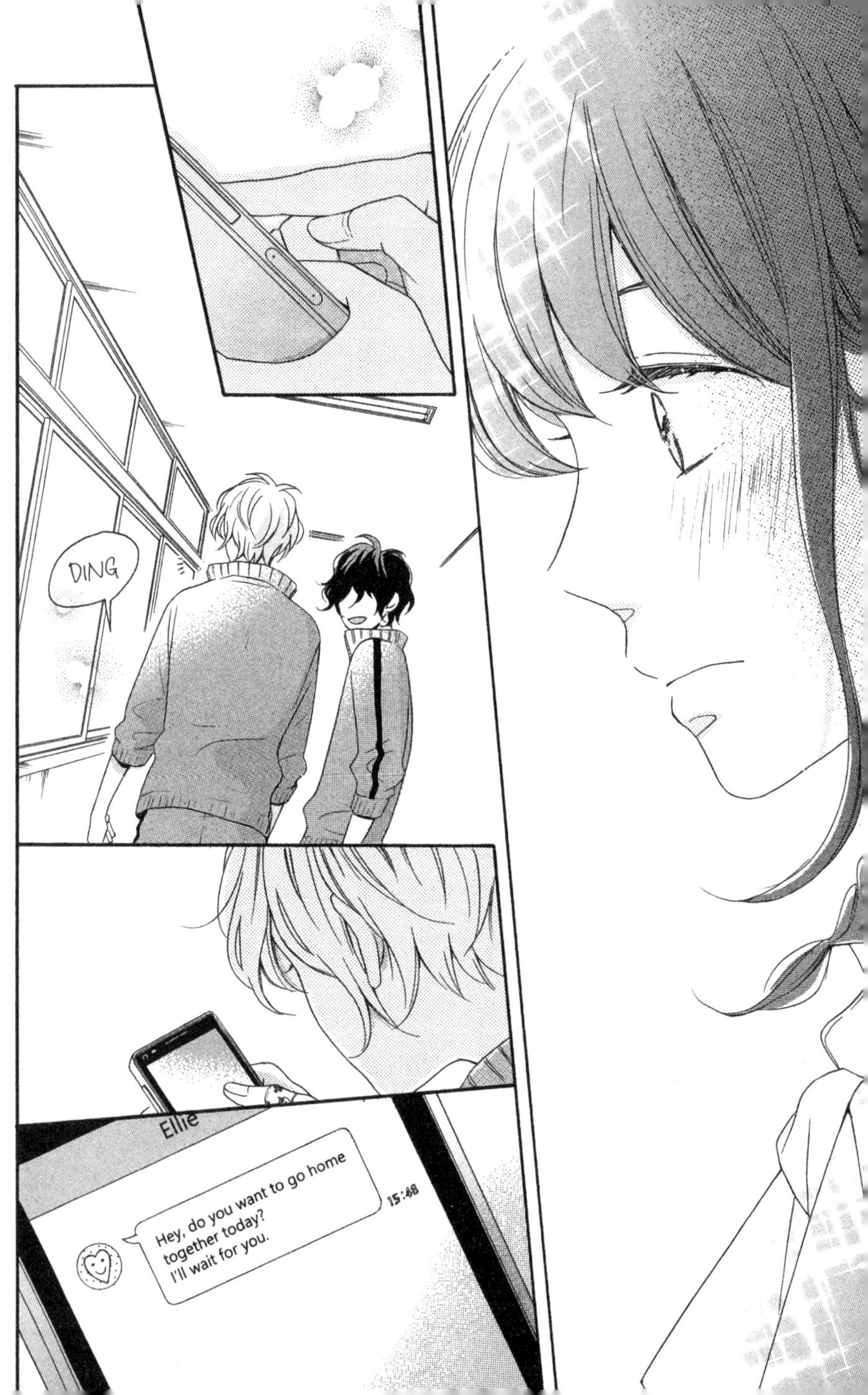
DING
Ellie
Hey, do you want to go home together today? I'll wait for you.
15:48

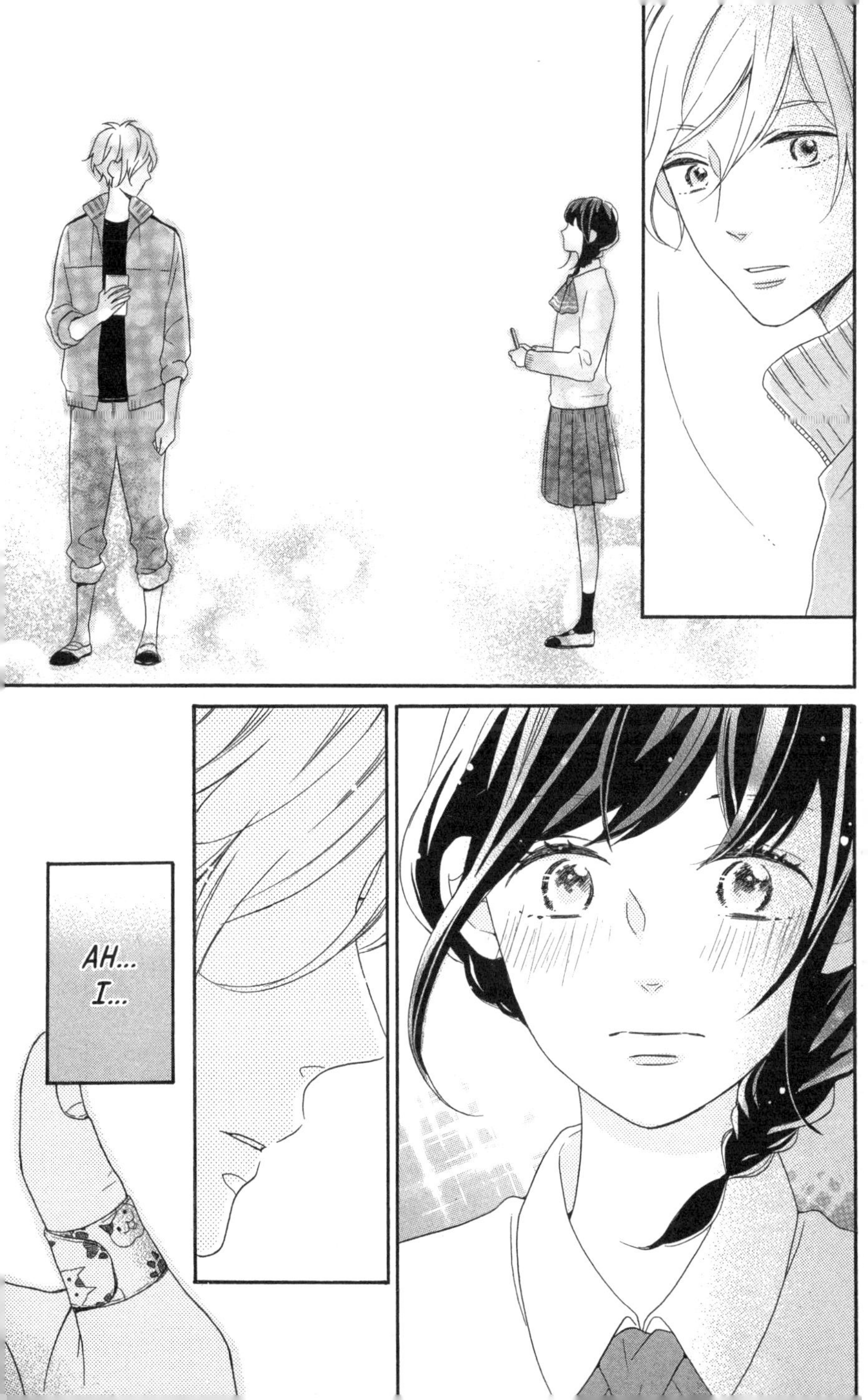
AH...
I...

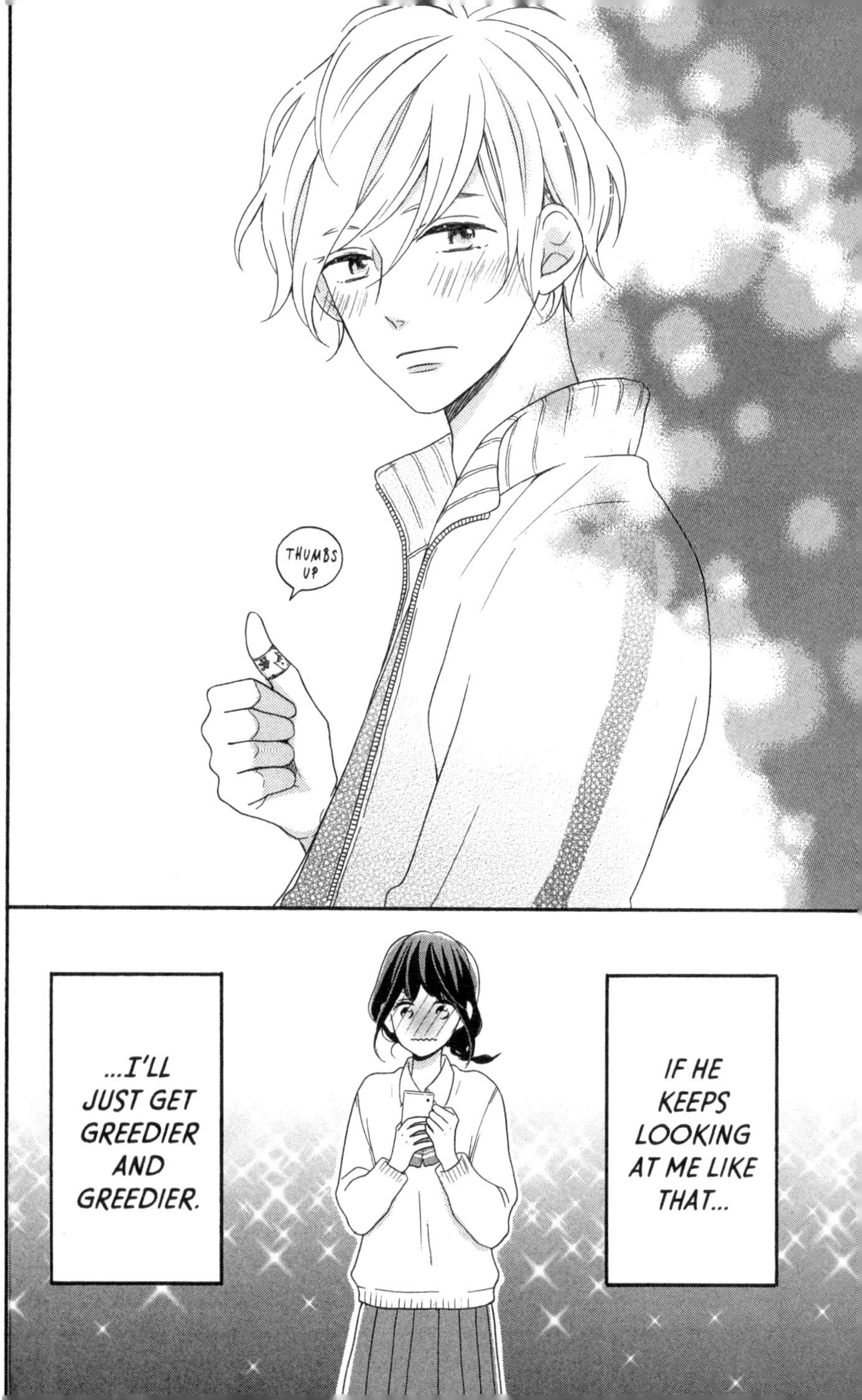
THUMBS UP
IF HE KEEPS LOOKING AT ME LIKE THAT...
...I'LL JUST GET GREEDIER AND GREEDIER.

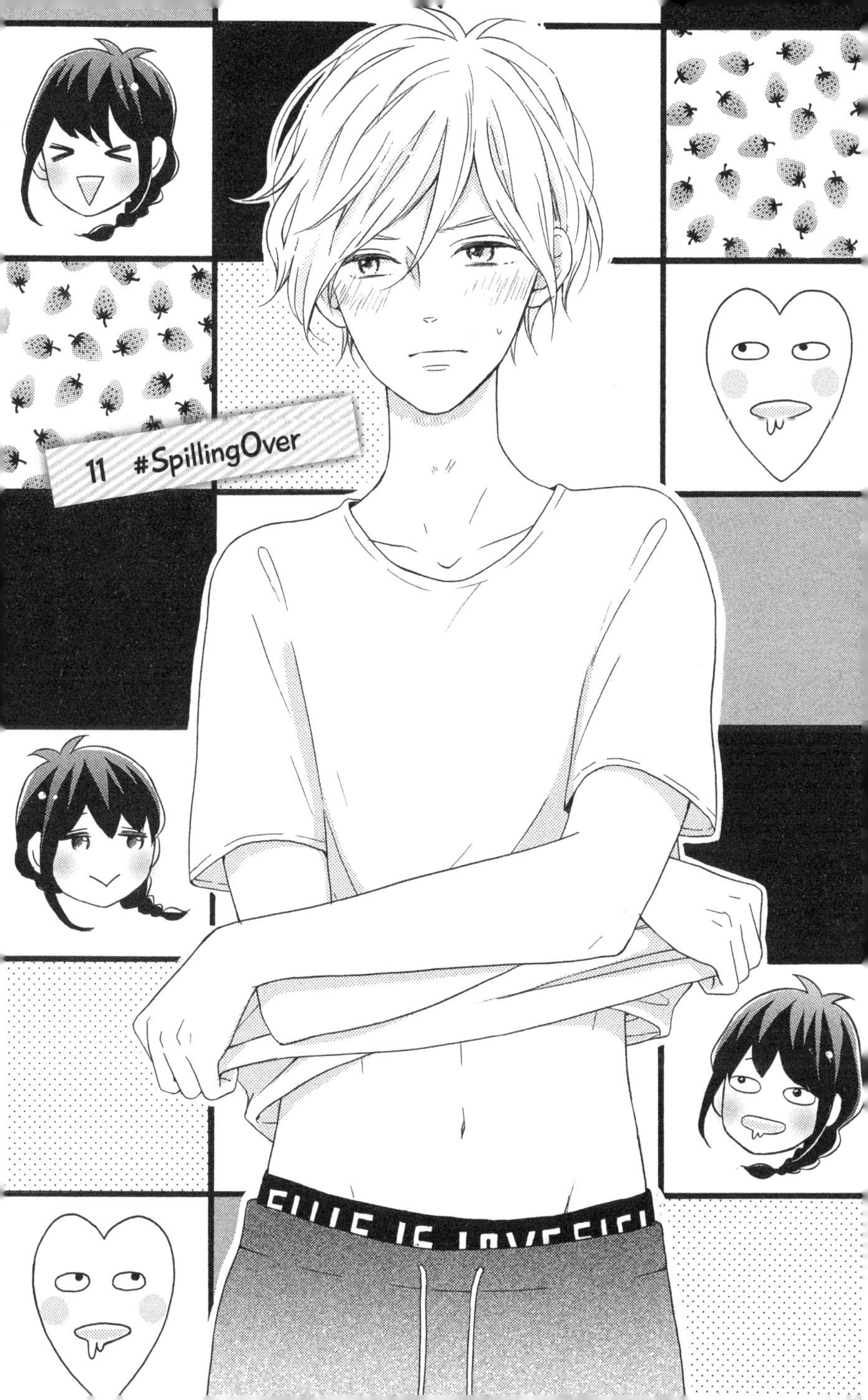
11 #SpillingOver

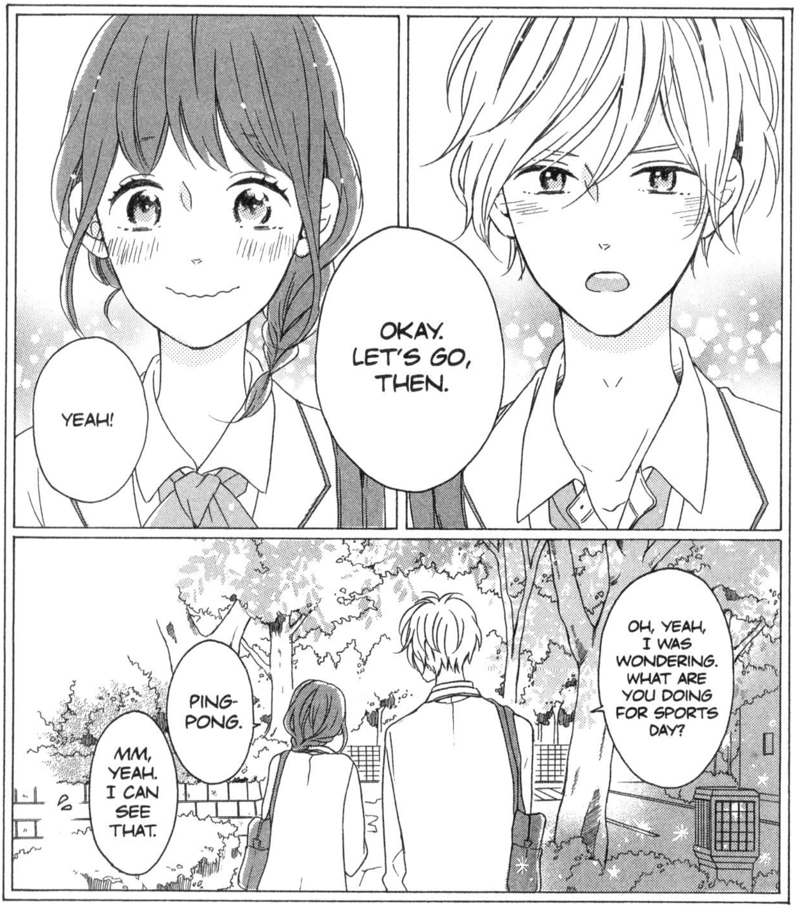
OKAY. LET'S GO, THEN.
YEAH!
OH, YEAH, I WAS WONDERING. WHAT ARE YOU DOING FOR SPORTS DAY?
PING-PONG.
MM, YEAH. I CAN SEE THAT.

The tweets that show up around the middle of chapter 11 are actually the winning submissions of the "Ellie's Dreams Come True Campaign" Twitter campaign! (Fans submitted their own Omie-related fantasies by actually tweeting on their own accounts. It was a fun campaign, but also difficult to run...in many ways... Thanks so much for all the submissions!)

My hat is off to fantasizing girls all across the country, for their brilliant work behind all those exciting, perverted masterpieces! Ellie's going to have to work hard not to lose!

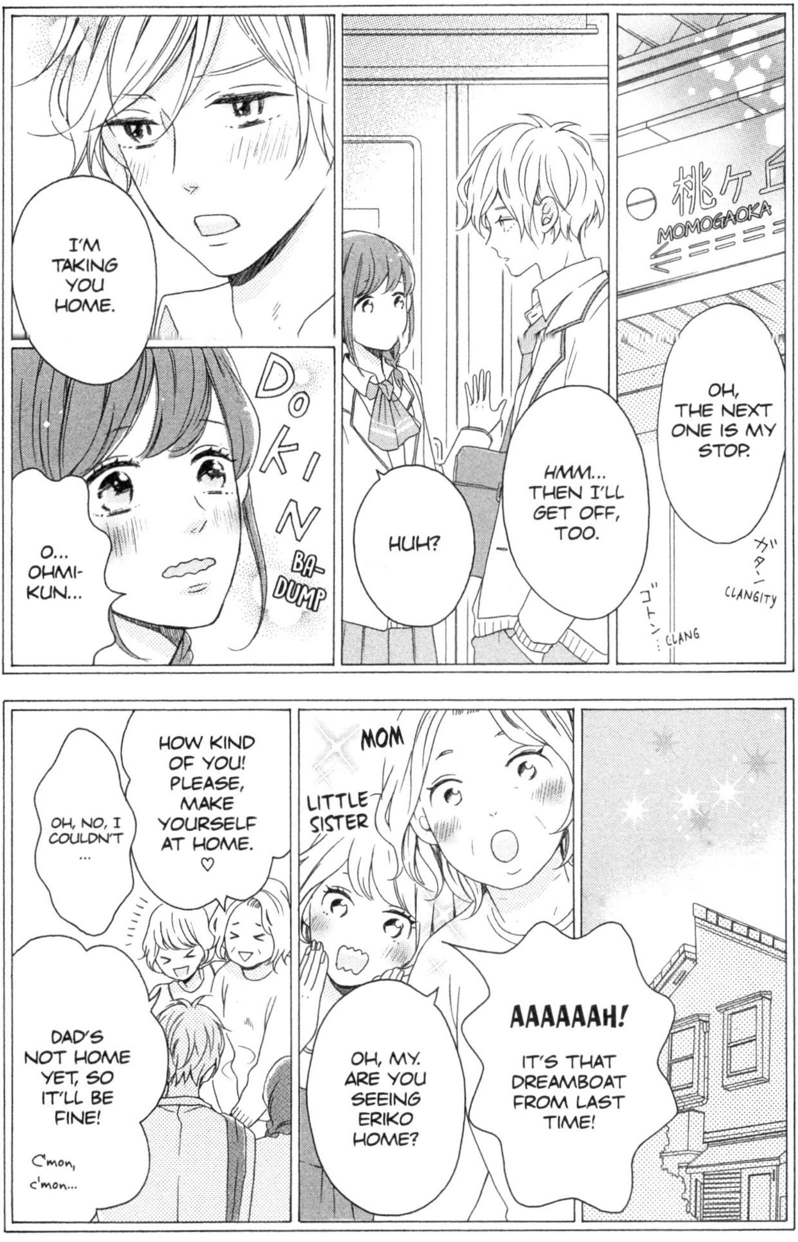

桃ヶ丘
MOMOGAOKA
OH, THE NEXT ONE IS MY STOP.
ガタン
CLANGITY
ゴトン…
CLANG
HMM... THEN I'LL GET OFF, TOO.
HUH?
I'M TAKING YOU HOME.
DOKIN
BA-DUMP
O... OHMI-KUN...
MOM
LITTLE SISTER
AAAAAAH! IT'S THAT DREAMBOAT FROM LAST TIME!
OH, MY. ARE YOU SEEING ERIKO HOME?
HOW KIND OF YOU! PLEASE, MAKE YOURSELF AT HOME. ♡
OH, NO, I COULDN'T ...
DAD'S NOT HOME YET, SO IT'LL BE FINE!
C'mon, c'mon...

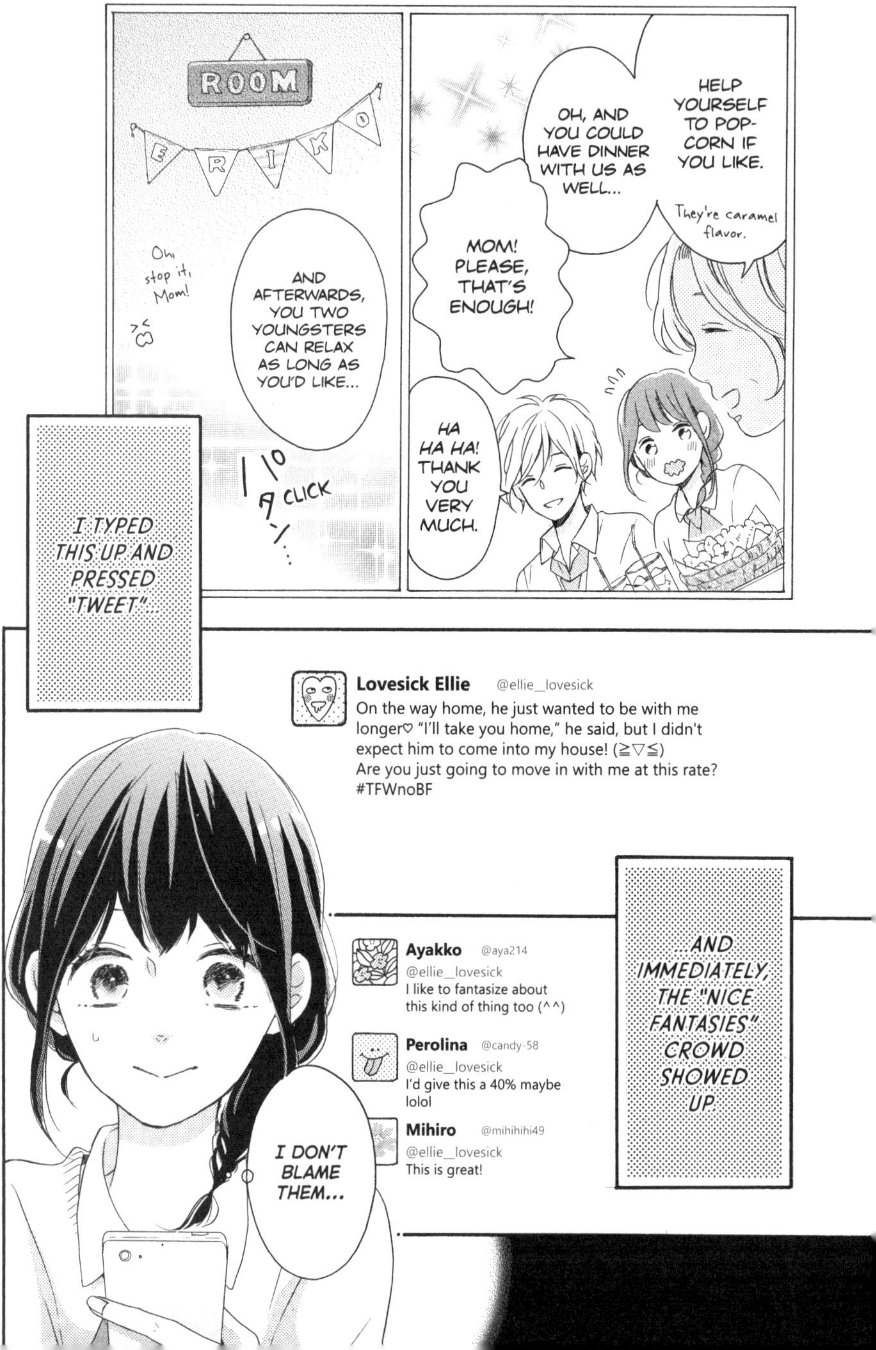
HELP YOURSELF TO POPCORN IF YOU LIKE.
They're caramel flavor.
OH, AND YOU COULD HAVE DINNER WITH US AS WELL...
MOM! PLEASE, THAT'S ENOUGH!
HA HA HA! THANK YOU VERY MUCH.
ROOM
ERIKO
AND AFTERWARDS, YOU TWO YOUNGSTERS CAN RELAX AS LONG AS YOU'D LIKE...
Oh, stop it, Mom!
CLICK
I TYPED THIS UP AND PRESSED "TWEET"...
Lovesick Ellie @ellie__lovesick
On the way home, he just wanted to be with me longer♡ "I'll take you home," he said, but I didn't expect him to come into my house! (≧▽≦)
Are you just going to move in with me at this rate? #TFWnoBF
...AND IMMEDIATELY, THE "NICE FANTASIES" CROWD SHOWED UP
Ayakko @aya214
@ellie__lovesick
I like to fantasize about this kind of thing too (^^)
Perolina @candy-58
@ellie__lovesick
I'd give this a 40% maybe lolol
Mihiro @mihihihi49
@ellie__lovesick
This is great!
I DON'T BLAME THEM...

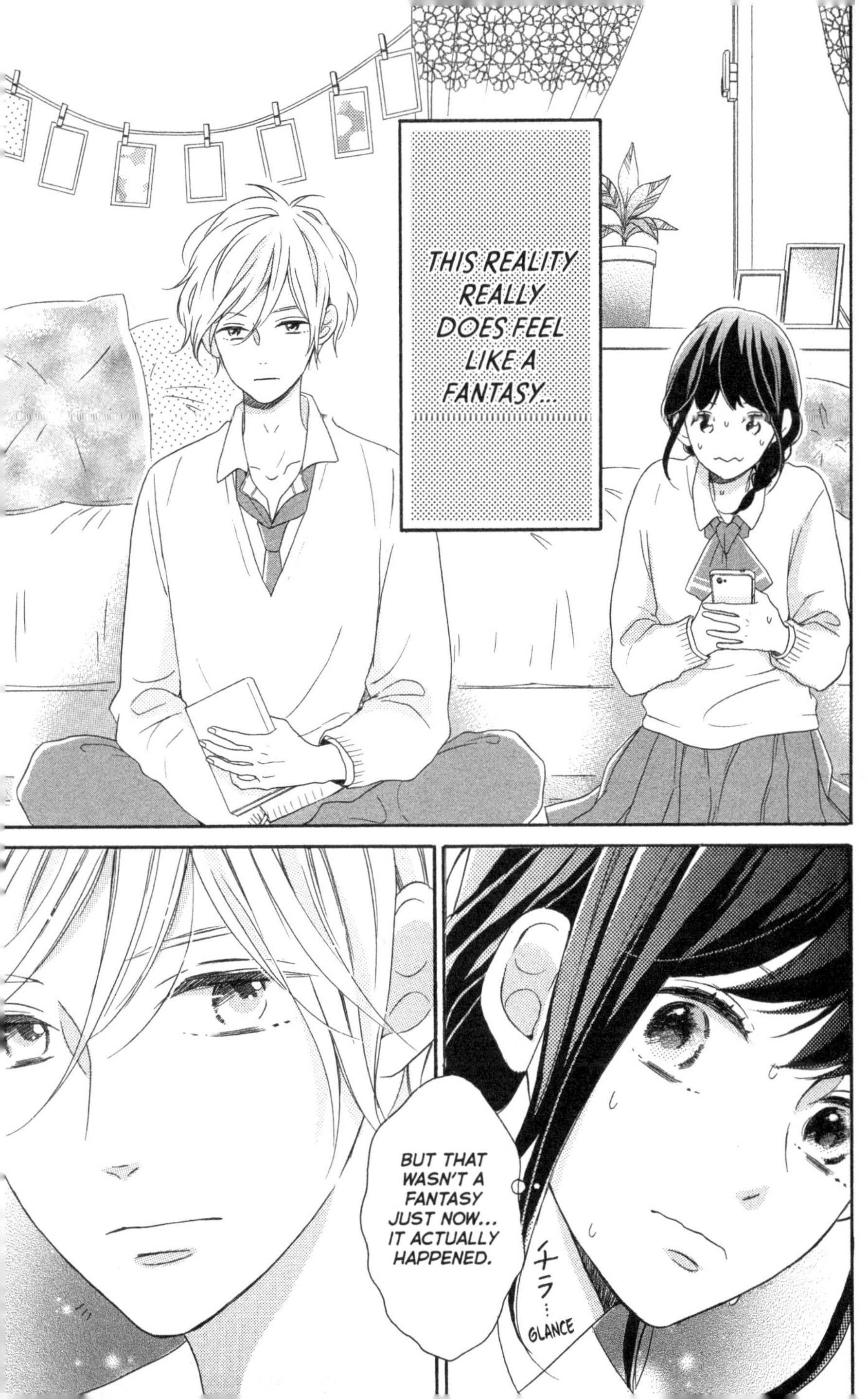
THIS REALITY REALLY DOES FEEL LIKE A FANTASY...
BUT THAT WASN'T A FANTASY JUST NOW... IT ACTUALLY HAPPENED.
チラ… GLANCE

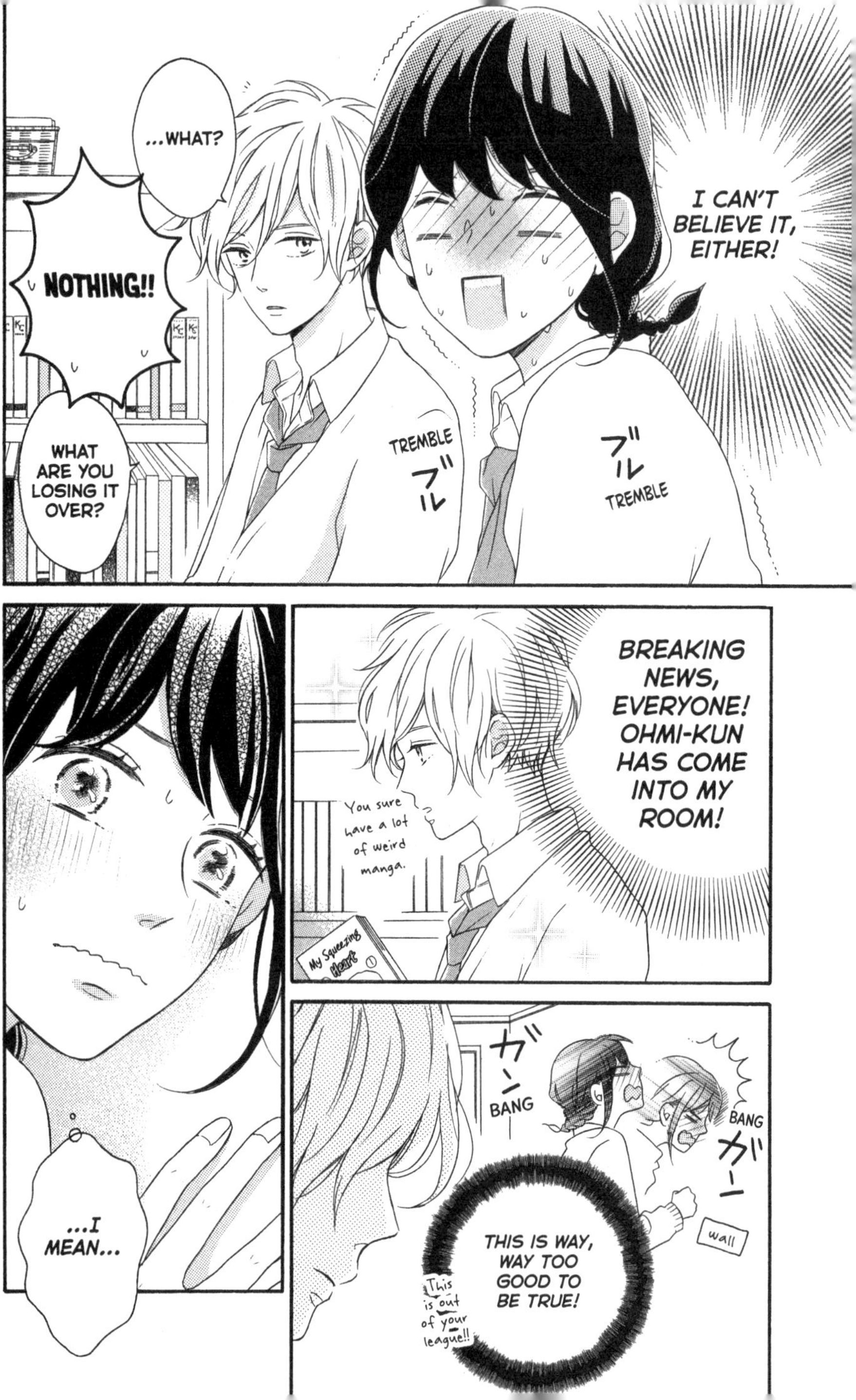
I CAN'T BELIEVE IT, EITHER!
...WHAT?
NOTHING!!
ブル
TREMBLE
TREMBLE
ブル
WHAT ARE YOU LOSING IT OVER?
BREAKING NEWS, EVERYONE! OHMI-KUN HAS COME INTO MY ROOM!
You sure have a lot of weird manga.
My Squeezing Heart 1
BANG
ガーン
ガーン
BANG
wall
THIS IS WAY, WAY TOO GOOD TO BE TRUE!
This is out of your league!!
...I MEAN...

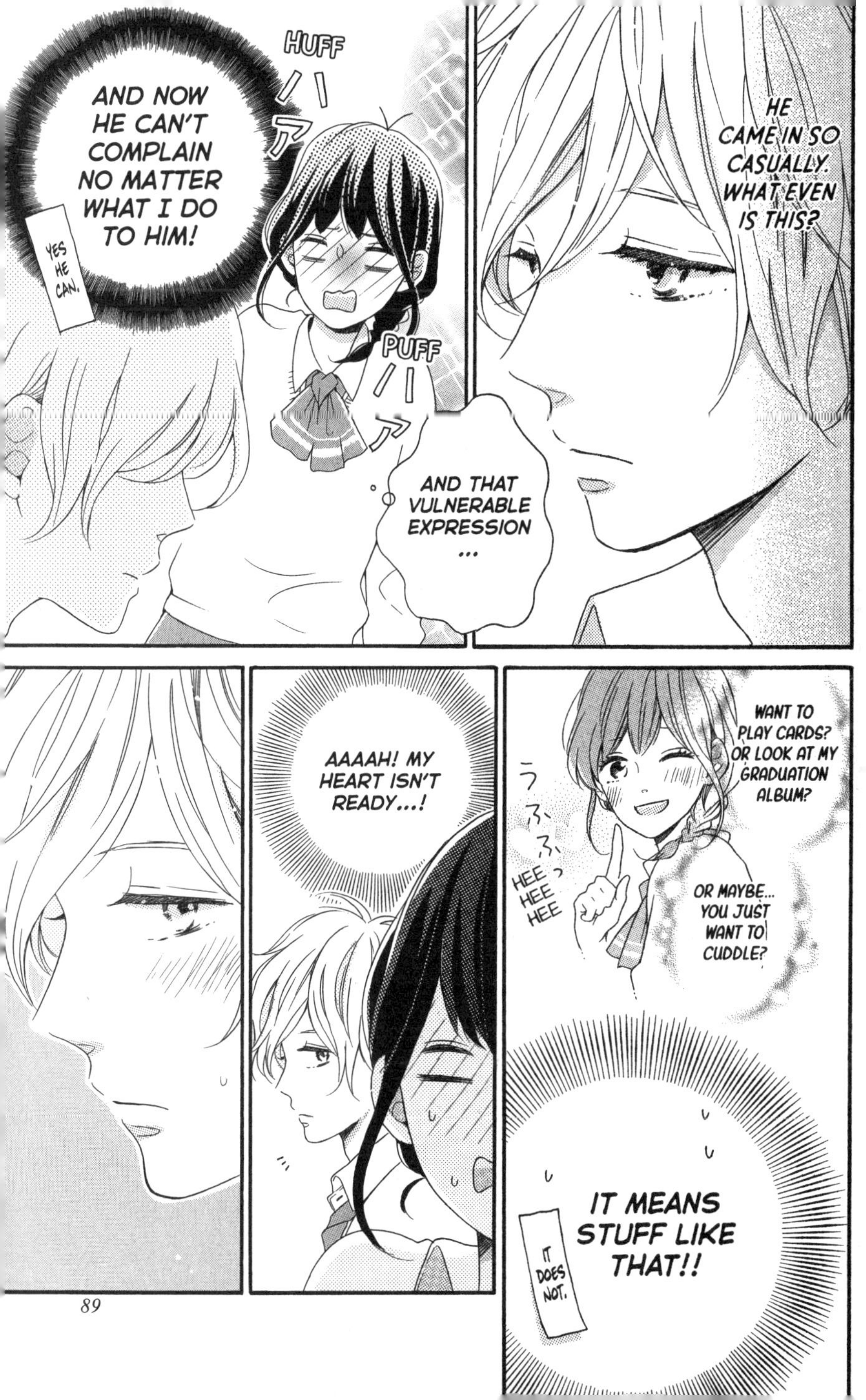
HE CAME IN SO CASUALLY. WHAT EVEN IS THIS?
AND THAT VULNERABLE EXPRESSION ...
HUFF
ハァ
AND NOW HE CAN'T COMPLAIN NO MATTER WHAT I DO TO HIM!
YES HE CAN.
PUFF
ハァ
WANT TO PLAY CARDS? OR LOOK AT MY GRADUATION ALBUM?
うふふっ
HEE HEE HEE
OR MAYBE... YOU JUST WANT TO CUDDLE?
IT MEANS STUFF LIKE THAT!!
IT DOES NOT.
AAAAH! MY HEART ISN'T READY...!

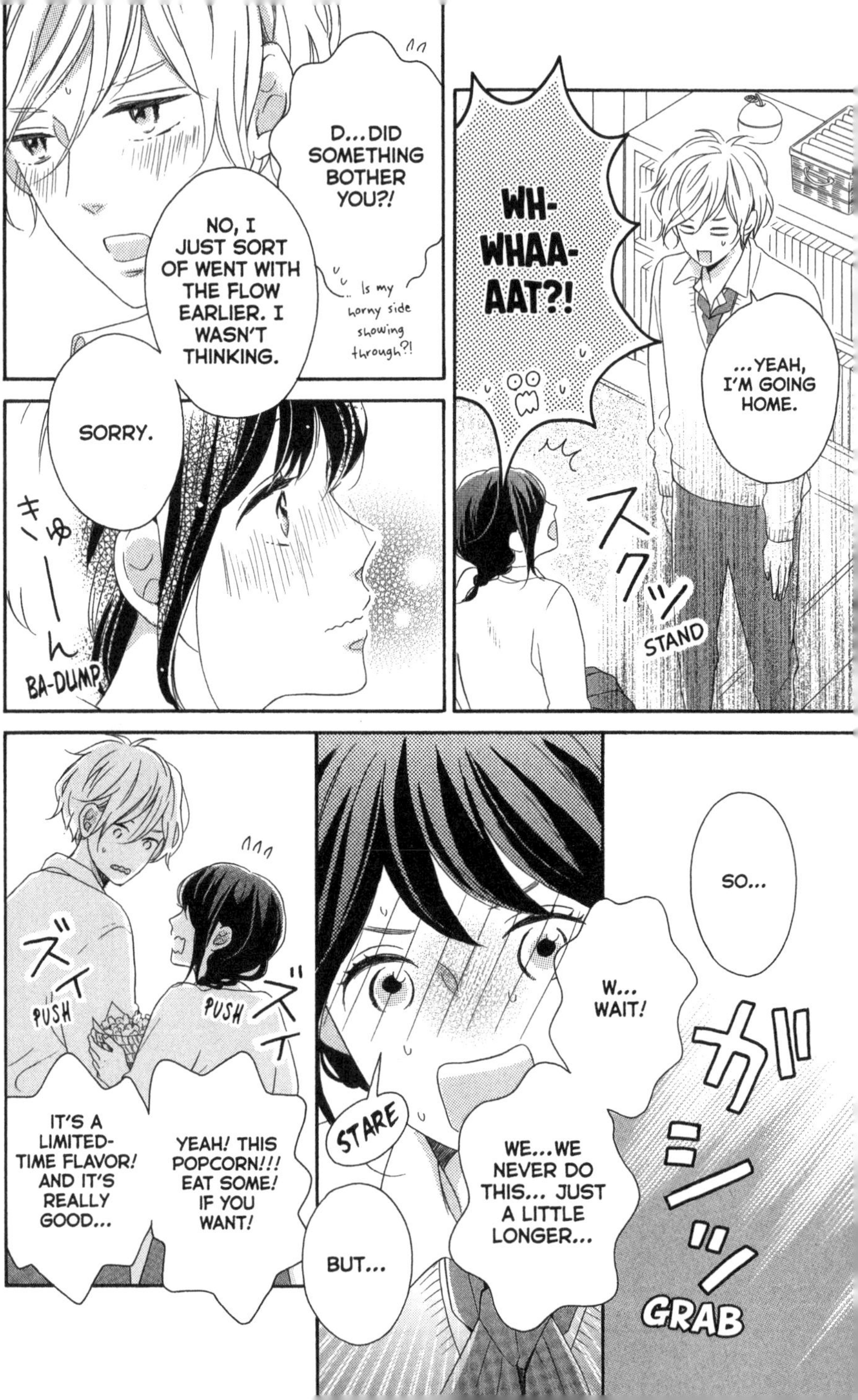
...YEAH, I'M GOING HOME.
WH-WHAAA-AAT?!
スクッ
STAND
D...DID SOMETHING BOTHER YOU?!
Is my horny side showing through?!
NO, I JUST SORT OF WENT WITH THE FLOW EARLIER. I WASN'T THINKING.
SORRY.
きゅーん
BA-DUMP
SO...
W... WAIT!
ガシッ
GRAB
WE...WE NEVER DO THIS... JUST A LITTLE LONGER...
BUT...
STARE
ズイ
PUSH
YEAH! THIS POPCORN!!! EAT SOME! IF YOU WANT!
ズイ
PUSH
IT'S A LIMITED-TIME FLAVOR! AND IT'S REALLY GOOD...

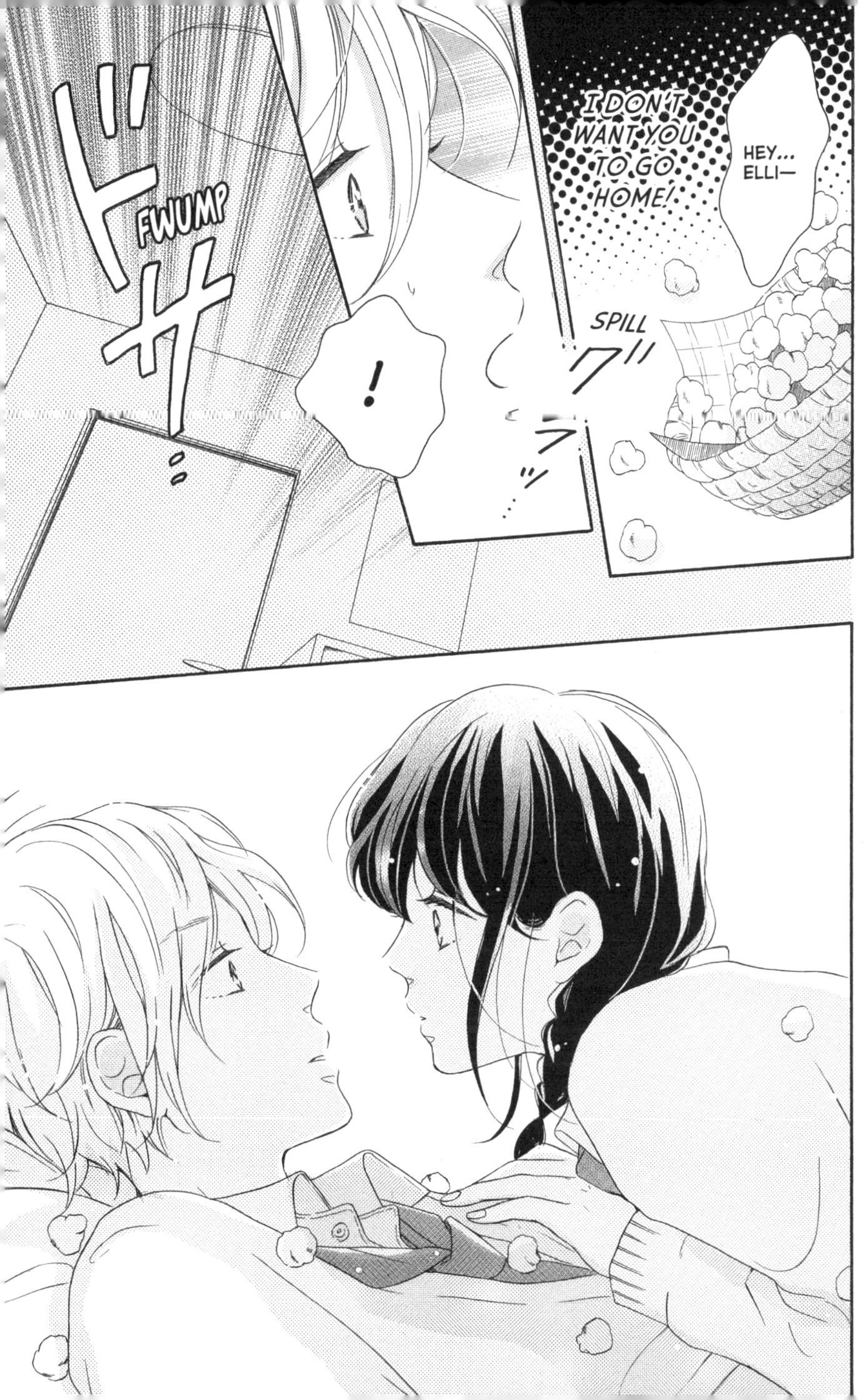
HEY... ELLI—
I DON'T WANT YOU TO GO HOME!
SPILL
!
FWUMP

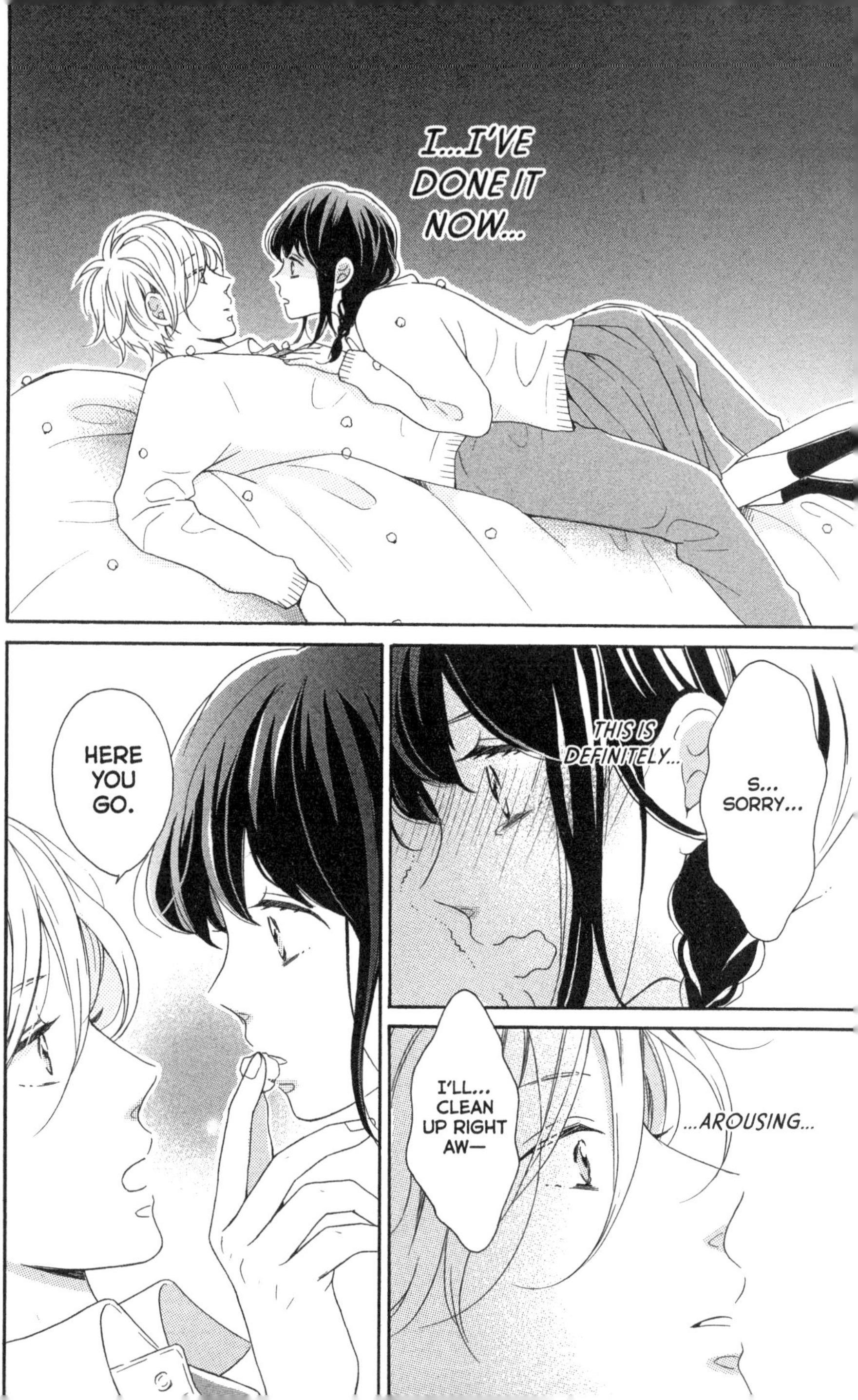
I...I'VE DONE IT NOW...
S... SORRY...
THIS IS DEFINITELY...
...AROUSING...
I'LL... CLEAN UP RIGHT AW—
HERE YOU GO.

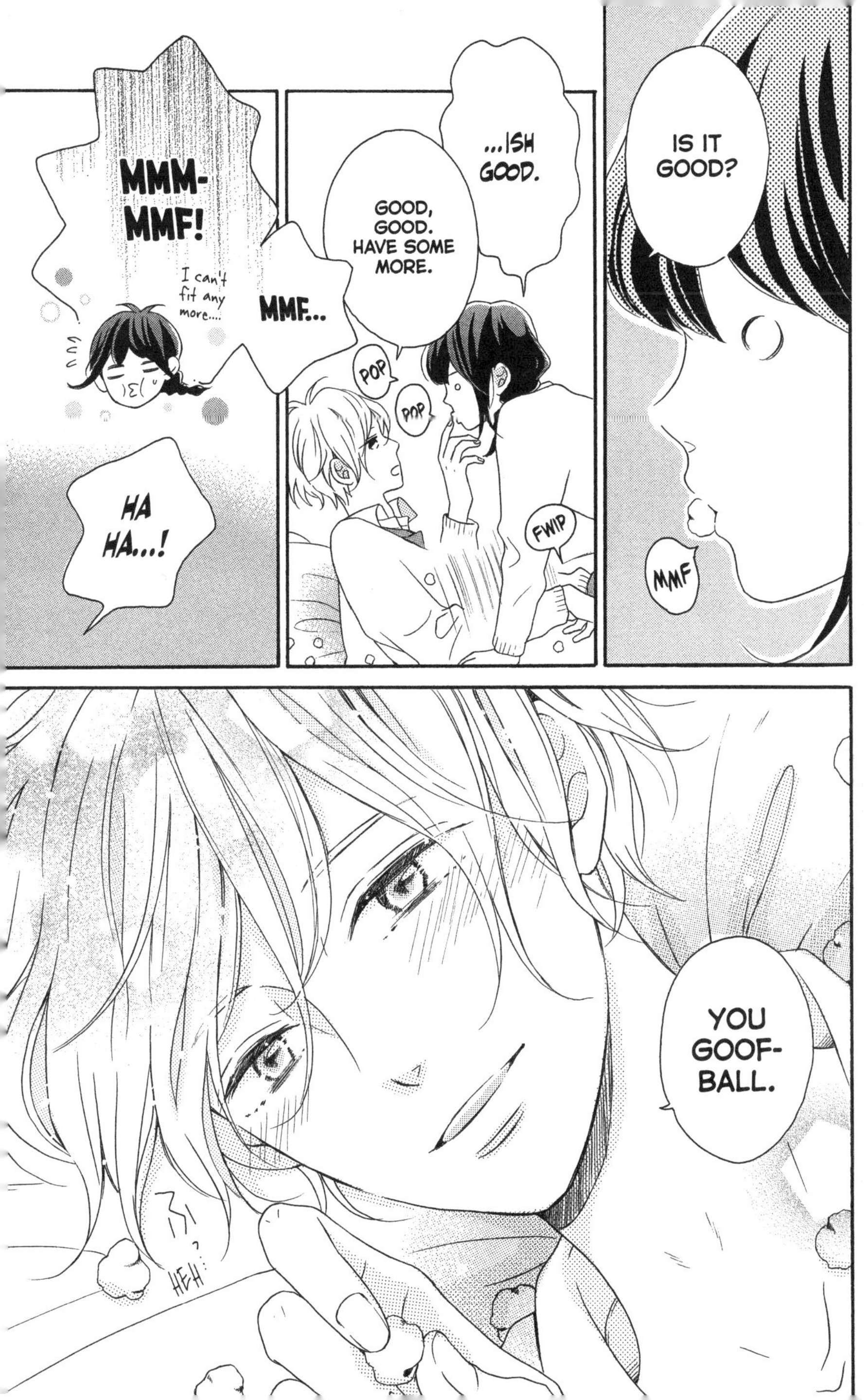
IS IT GOOD?
MMF
...ISH GOOD.
GOOD, GOOD. HAVE SOME MORE.
POP
POP
FWIP
MMM-MMF!
MMF...
I can't fit any more....
HA HA...!
YOU GOOF-BALL.
HEH

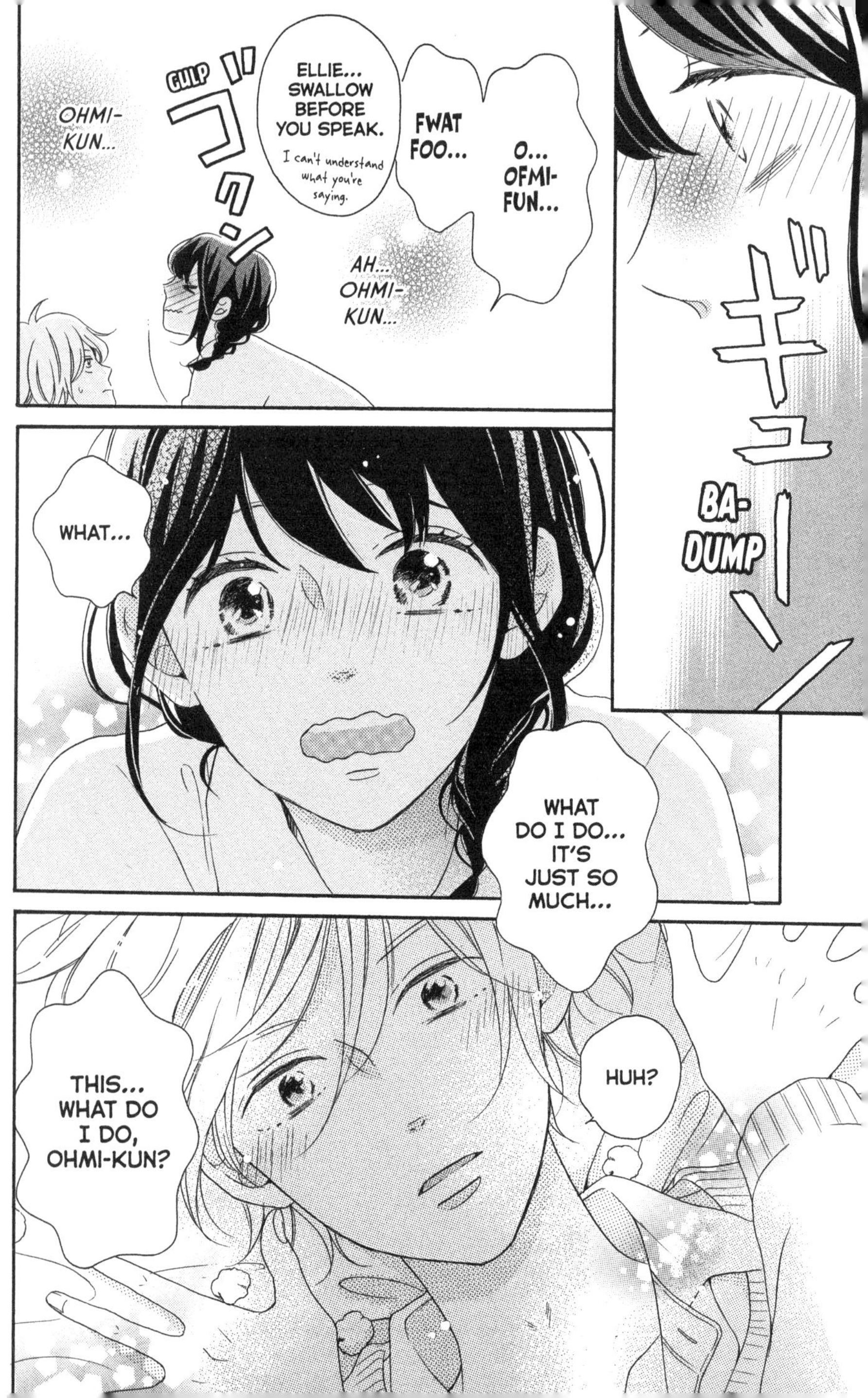
BA-DUMP
AH... OHMI-KUN...
O... OFMI-FUN...
FWAT FOO...
ELLIE... SWALLOW BEFORE YOU SPEAK.
I can't understand what you're saying.
GULP
OHMI-KUN...
WHAT...
WHAT DO I DO... IT'S JUST SO MUCH...
HUH?
THIS... WHAT DO I DO, OHMI-KUN?

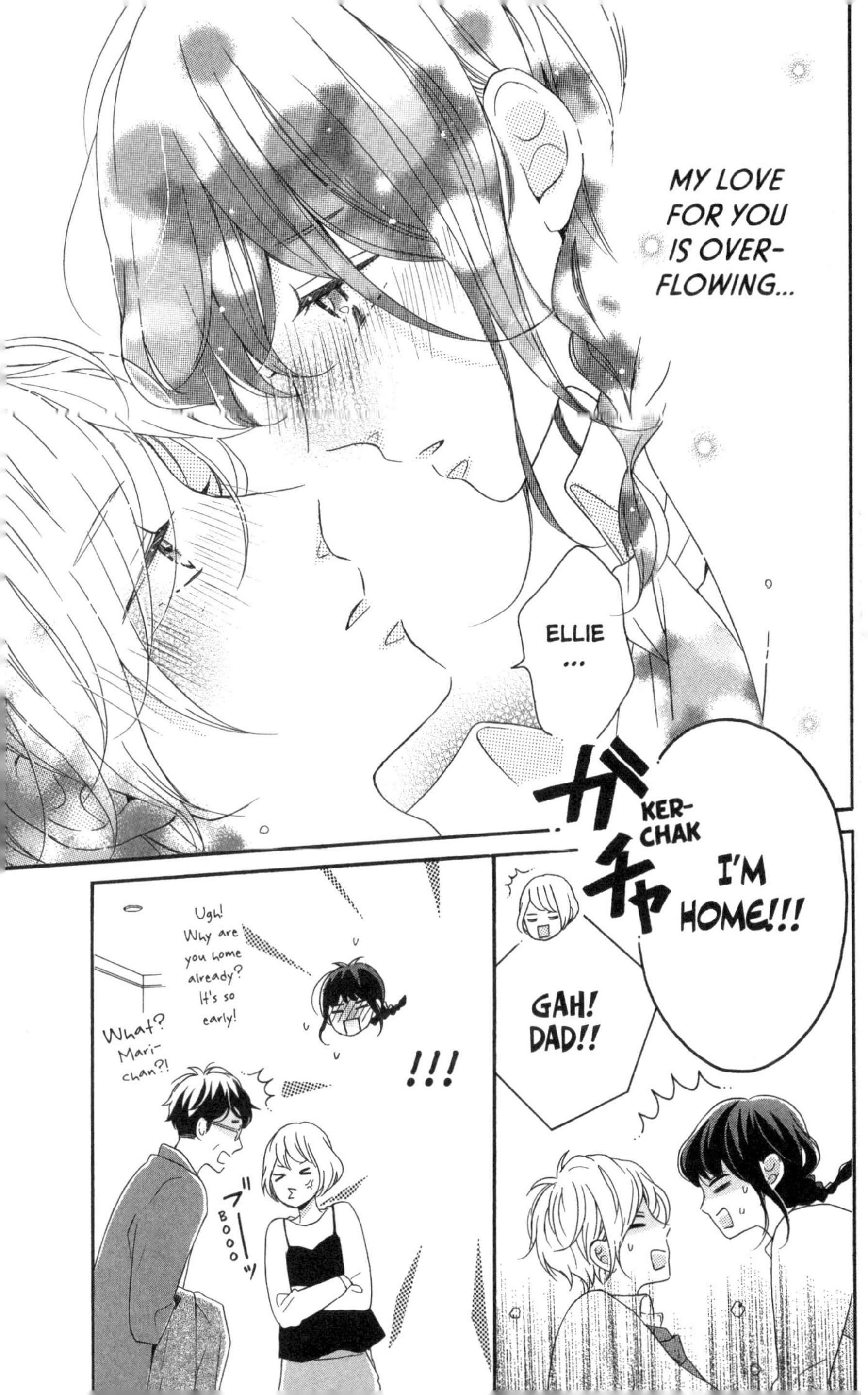
MY LOVE FOR YOU IS OVER-FLOWING...
ELLIE...
ガチャ
KER-CHAK
I'M HOME!!!
GAH! DAD!!
!!!
Ugh! Why are you home already? It's so early!
What? Mari-chan?!
ブーッ
BOOO

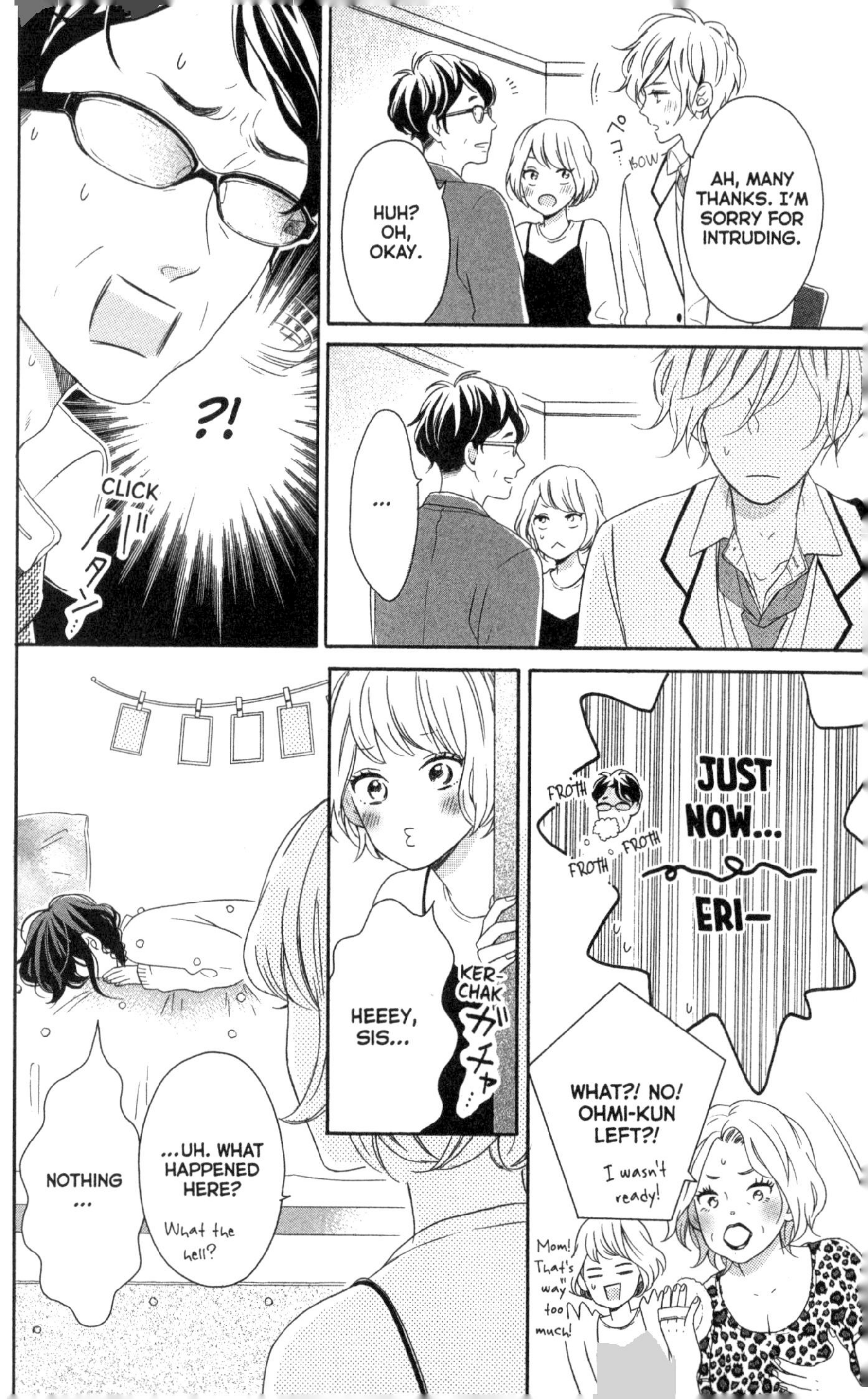
BOW
AH, MANY THANKS. I'M SORRY FOR INTRUDING.
HUH? OH, OKAY.
...
?!
CLICK
JUST NOW... ERI-
FROTH
FROTH
FROTH
WHAT?! NO! OHMI-KUN LEFT?!
I wasn't ready!
Mom! That's way too much!
KER-CHAK
HEEEY, SIS...
...UH. WHAT HAPPENED HERE?
What the hell?
NOTHING...

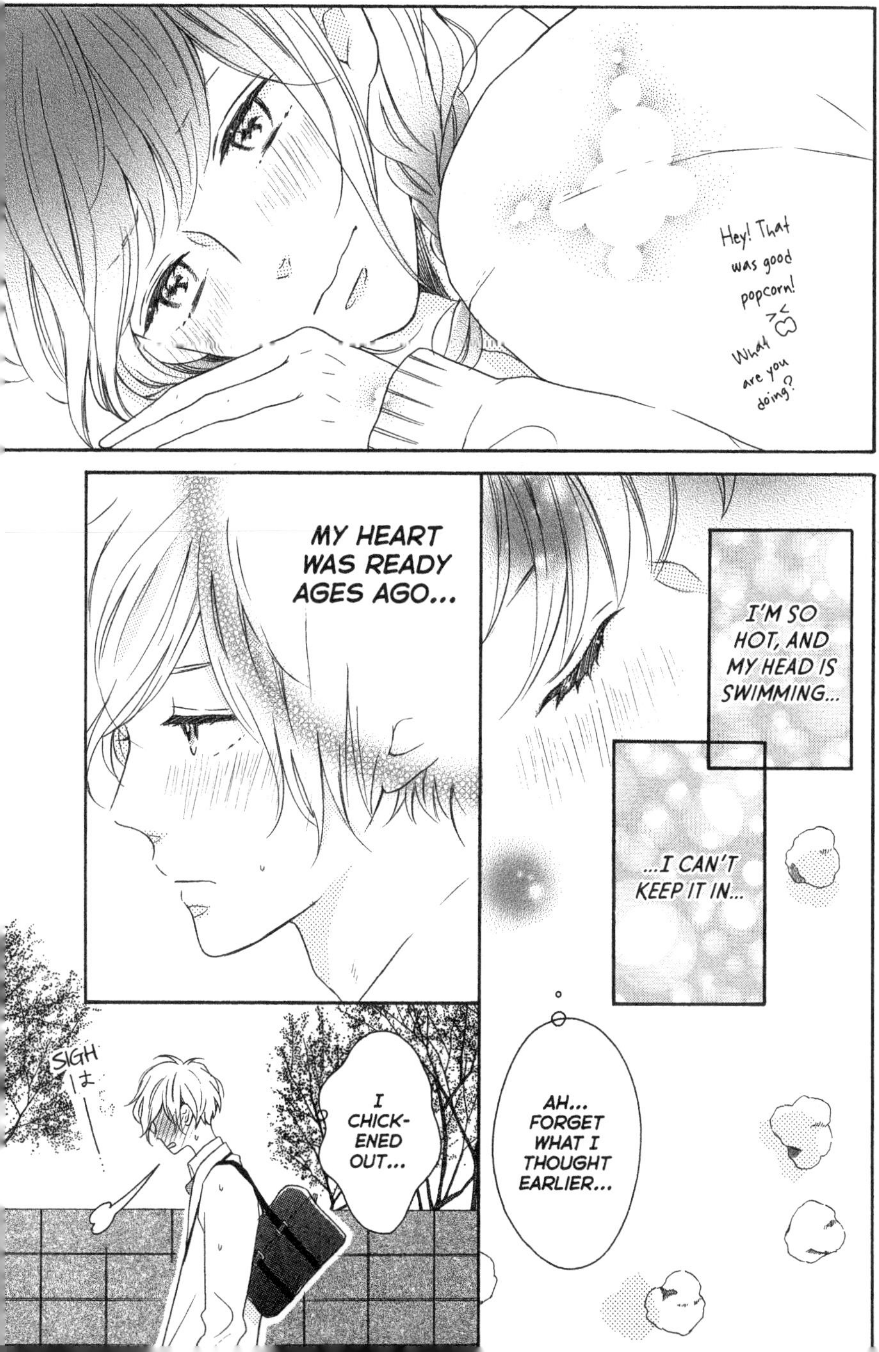
Hey! That was good popcorn! >< What are you doing?
I'M SO HOT, AND MY HEAD IS SWIMMING...
...I CAN'T KEEP IT IN...
AH... FORGET WHAT I THOUGHT EARLIER...
MY HEART WAS READY AGES AGO...
SIGH
は
I CHICK-ENED OUT...

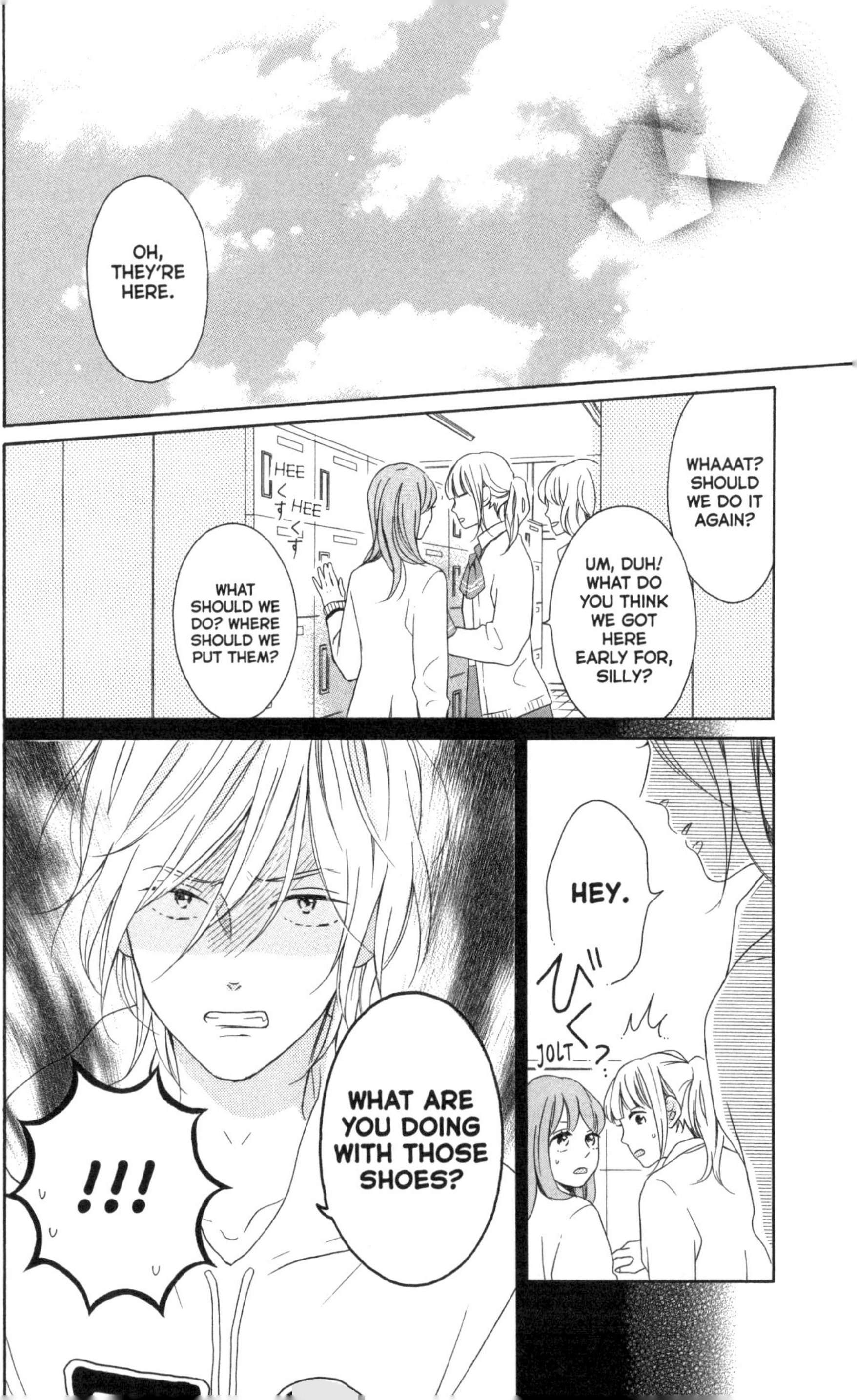
OH, THEY'RE HERE.
WHAAAT? SHOULD WE DO IT AGAIN?
UM, DUH! WHAT DO YOU THINK WE GOT HERE EARLY FOR, SILLY?
HEE HEE
WHAT SHOULD WE DO? WHERE SHOULD WE PUT THEM?
HEY.
JOLT
?
WHAT ARE YOU DOING WITH THOSE SHOES?
!!!

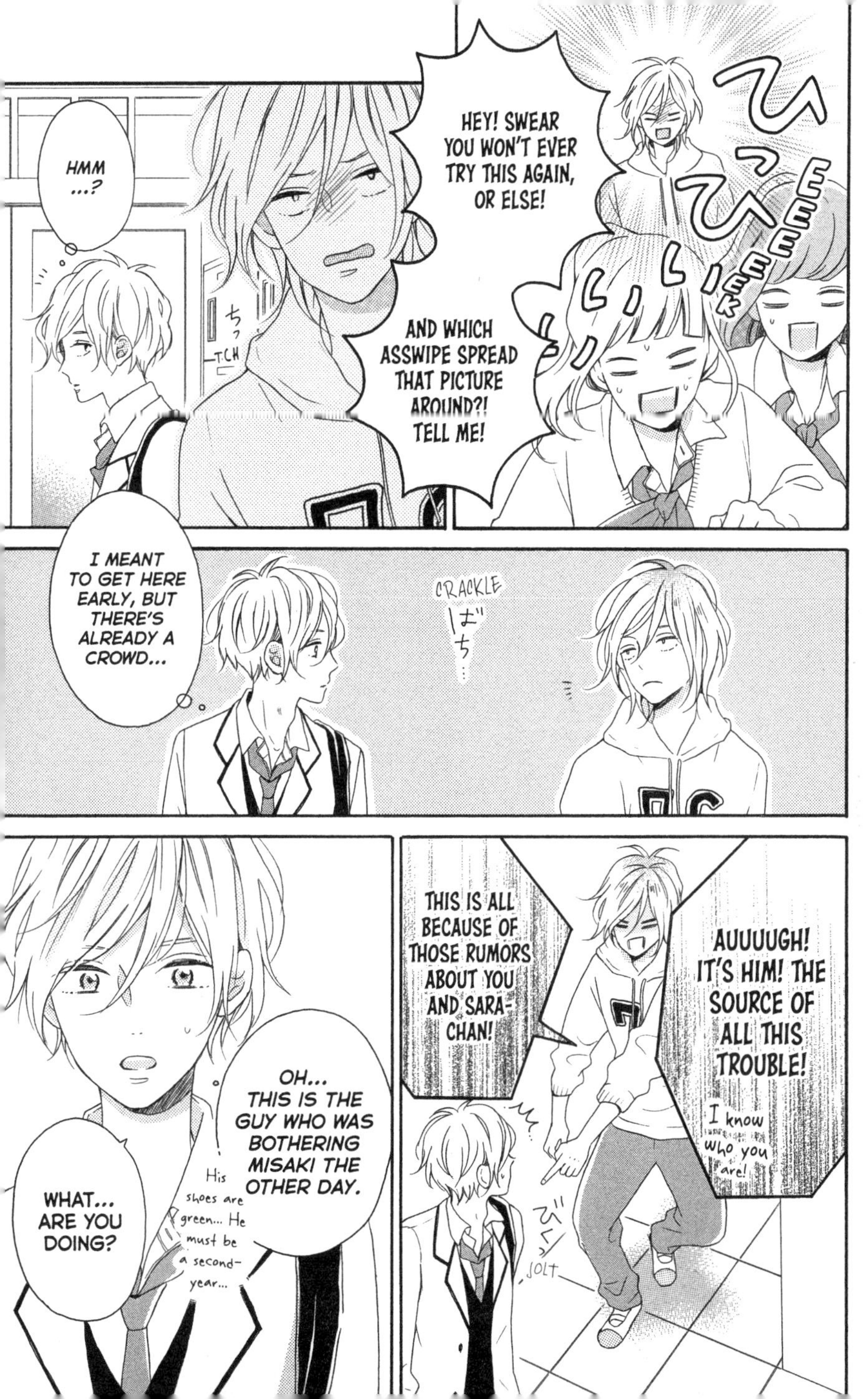
HEY! SWEAR YOU WON'T EVER TRY THIS AGAIN, OR ELSE!
EEEEEEK
AND WHICH ASSWIPE SPREAD THAT PICTURE AROUND?! TELL ME!
HMM ...?
TCH
I MEANT TO GET HERE EARLY, BUT THERE'S ALREADY A CROWD...
CRACKLE
AUUUUGH! IT'S HIM! THE SOURCE OF ALL THIS TROUBLE!
I know who you are!
THIS IS ALL BECAUSE OF THOSE RUMORS ABOUT YOU AND SARA-CHAN!
JOLT
OH... THIS IS THE GUY WHO WAS BOTHERING MISAKI THE OTHER DAY.
His shoes are green... He must be a second-year...
WHAT... ARE YOU DOING?

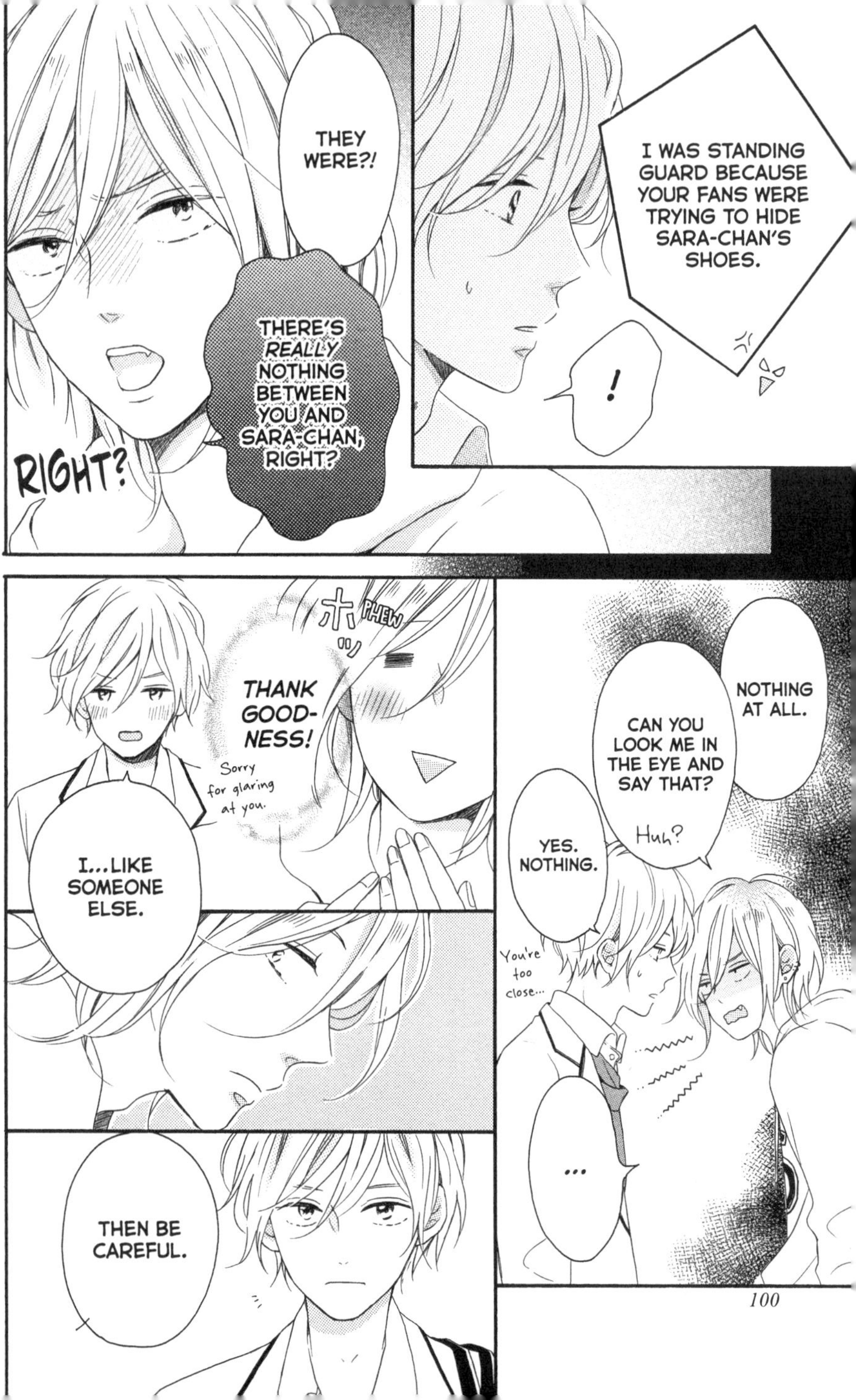
I WAS STANDING GUARD BECAUSE YOUR FANS WERE TRYING TO HIDE SARA-CHAN'S SHOES.
!
THEY WERE?!
THERE'S REALLY NOTHING BETWEEN YOU AND SARA-CHAN, RIGHT?
RIGHT?
NOTHING AT ALL.
CAN YOU LOOK ME IN THE EYE AND SAY THAT?
Huh?
YES. NOTHING.
You're too close...
...
ホッ
PHEW
THANK GOODNESS!
Sorry for glaring at you.
I...LIKE SOMEONE ELSE.
THEN BE CAREFUL.

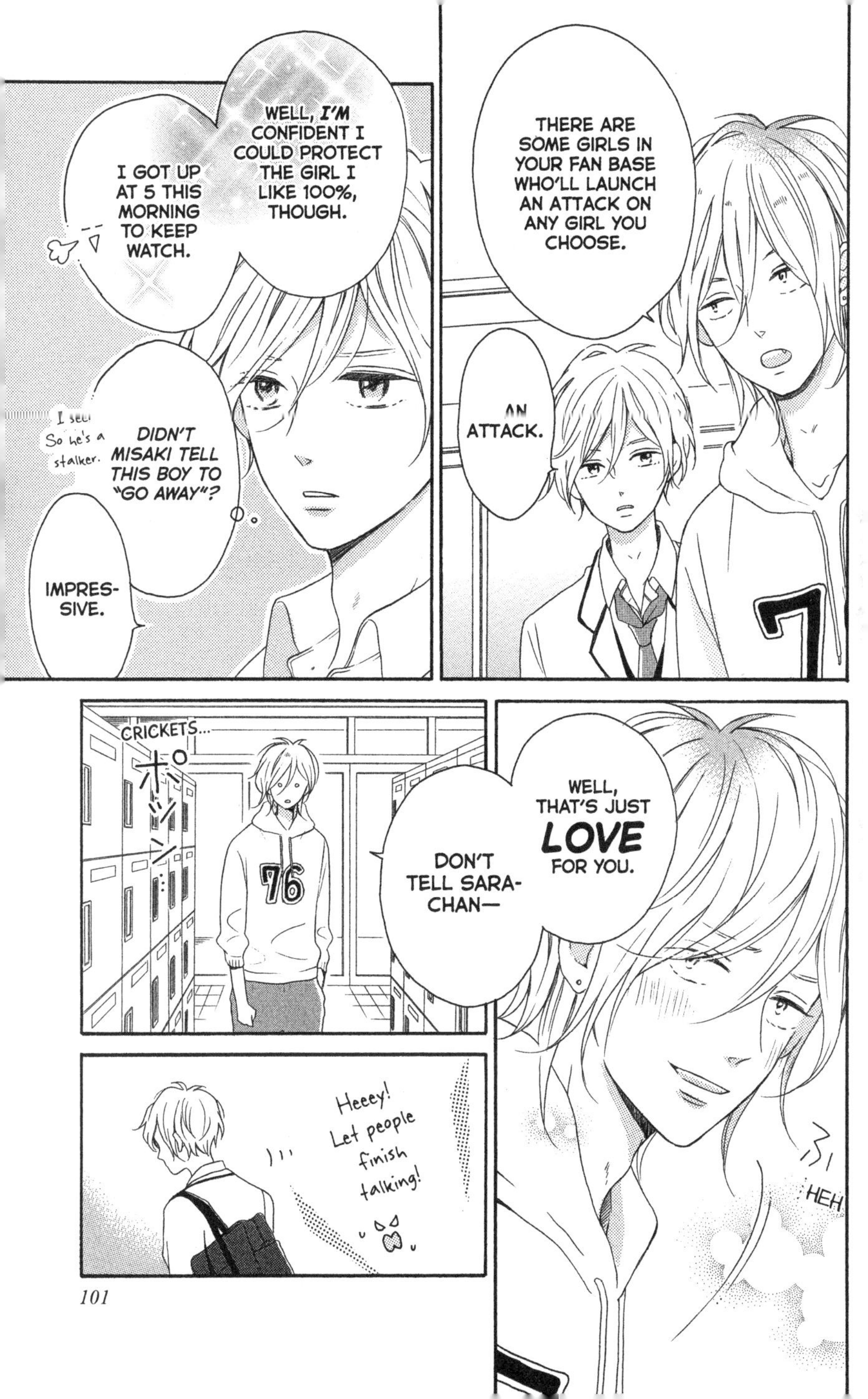

THERE ARE SOME GIRLS IN YOUR FAN BASE WHO'LL LAUNCH AN ATTACK ON ANY GIRL YOU CHOOSE.
AN ATTACK.
WELL, I'M CONFIDENT I COULD PROTECT THE GIRL I LIKE 100%, THOUGH.
I GOT UP AT 5 THIS MORNING TO KEEP WATCH.
I see! So he's a stalker.
DIDN'T MISAKI TELL THIS BOY TO "GO AWAY"?
IMPRESSIVE.
WELL, THAT'S JUST LOVE FOR YOU.
HEH
CRICKETS...
DON'T TELL SARA-CHAN—
Heeey! Let people finish talking!

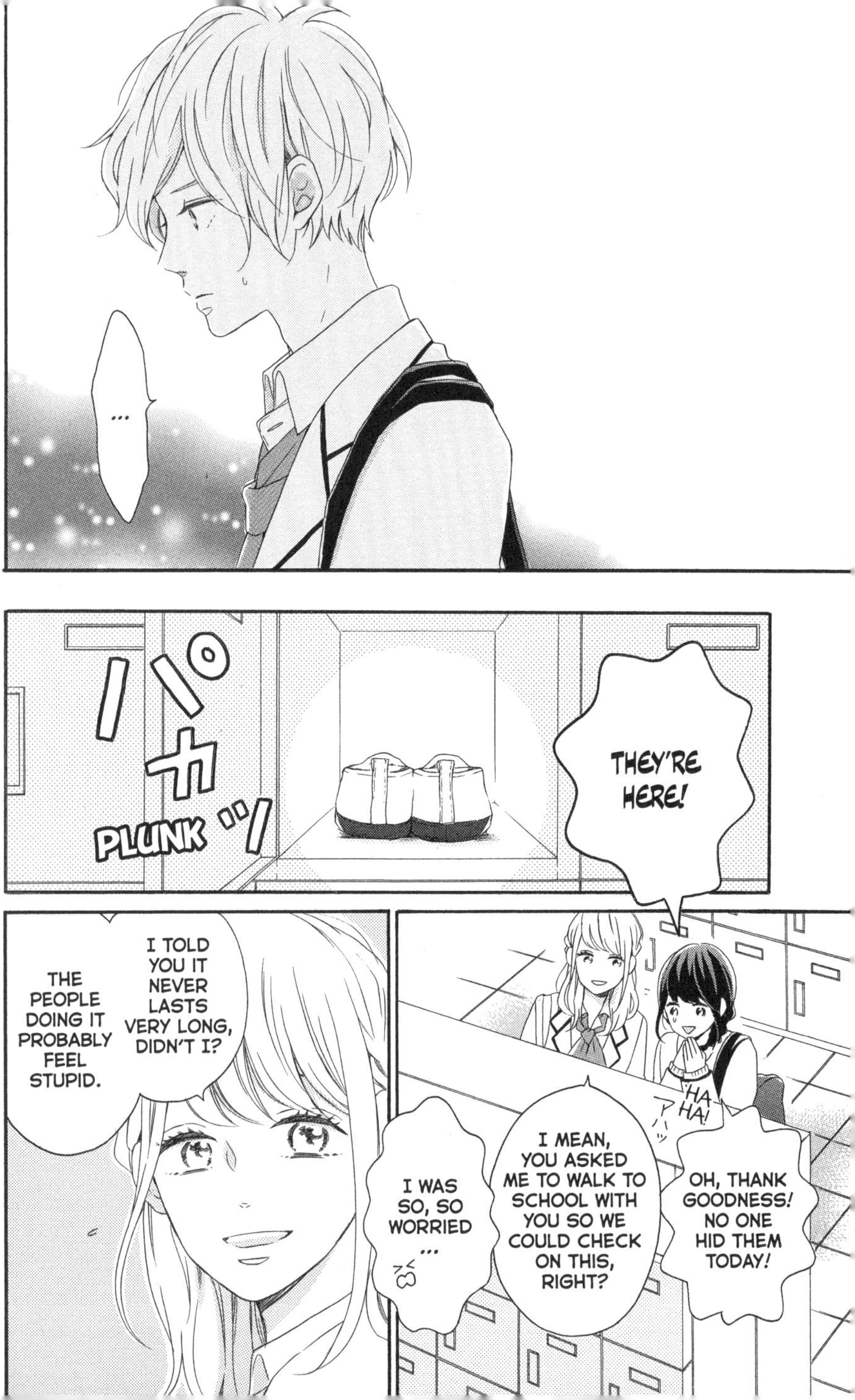
...
THEY'RE HERE!
パカッ
PLUNK
OH, THANK GOODNESS! NO ONE HID THEM TODAY!
HA HA!
I MEAN, YOU ASKED ME TO WALK TO SCHOOL WITH YOU SO WE COULD CHECK ON THIS, RIGHT?
I WAS SO, SO WORRIED...
I TOLD YOU IT NEVER LASTS VERY LONG, DIDN'T I?
THE PEOPLE DOING IT PROBABLY FEEL STUPID.

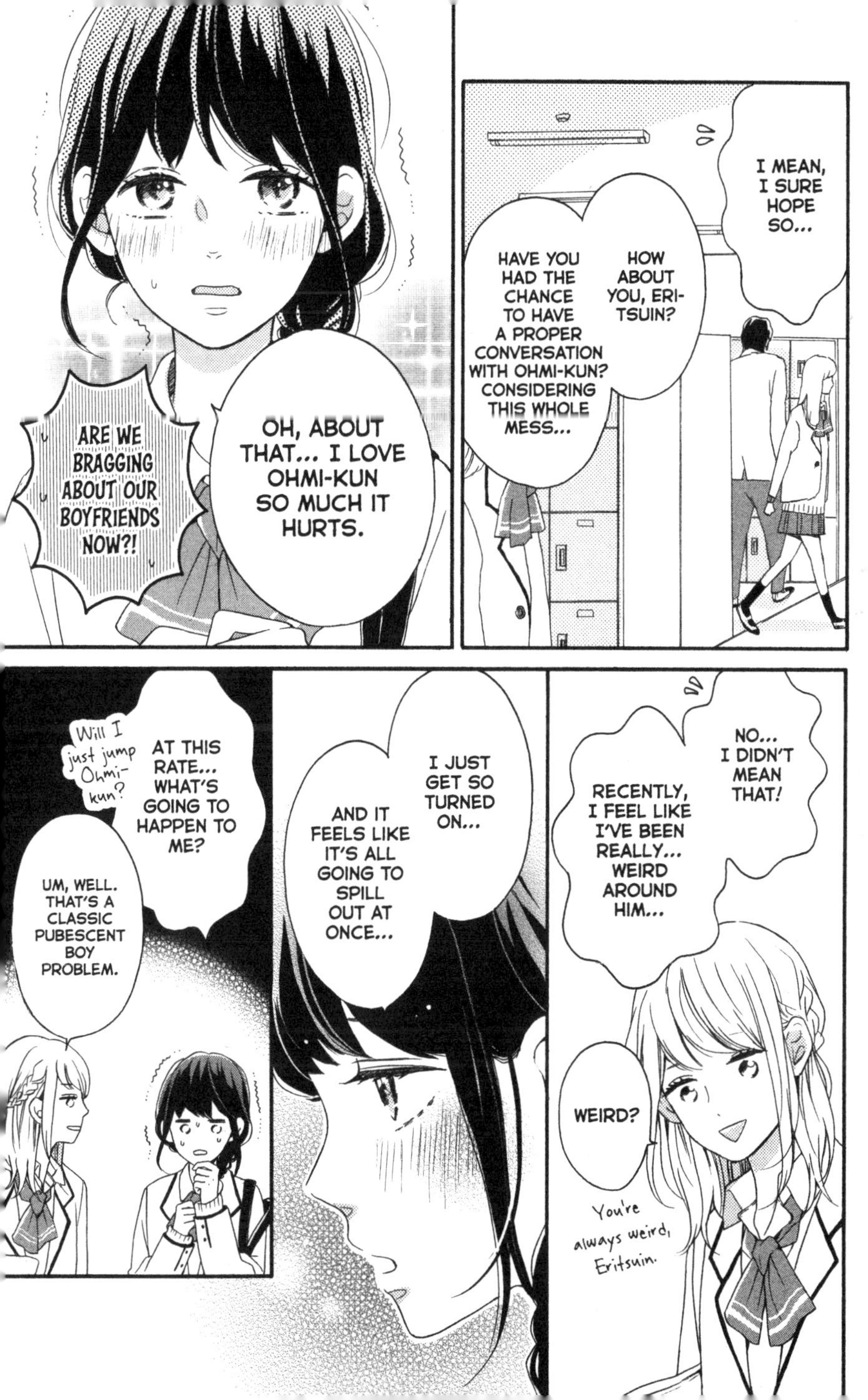
I MEAN, I SURE HOPE SO...
HOW ABOUT YOU, ERI-TSUIN?
HAVE YOU HAD THE CHANCE TO HAVE A PROPER CONVERSATION WITH OHMI-KUN? CONSIDERING THIS WHOLE MESS...
OH, ABOUT THAT... I LOVE OHMI-KUN SO MUCH IT HURTS.
ARE WE BRAGGING ABOUT OUR BOYFRIENDS NOW?!
NO... I DIDN'T MEAN THAT!
RECENTLY, I FEEL LIKE I'VE BEEN REALLY... WEIRD AROUND HIM...
WEIRD?
You're always weird, Eritsuin.
I JUST GET SO TURNED ON...
AND IT FEELS LIKE IT'S ALL GOING TO SPILL OUT AT ONCE...
AT THIS RATE... WHAT'S GOING TO HAPPEN TO ME?
Will I just jump Ohmi-kun?
UM, WELL. THAT'S A CLASSIC PUBESCENT BOY PROBLEM.

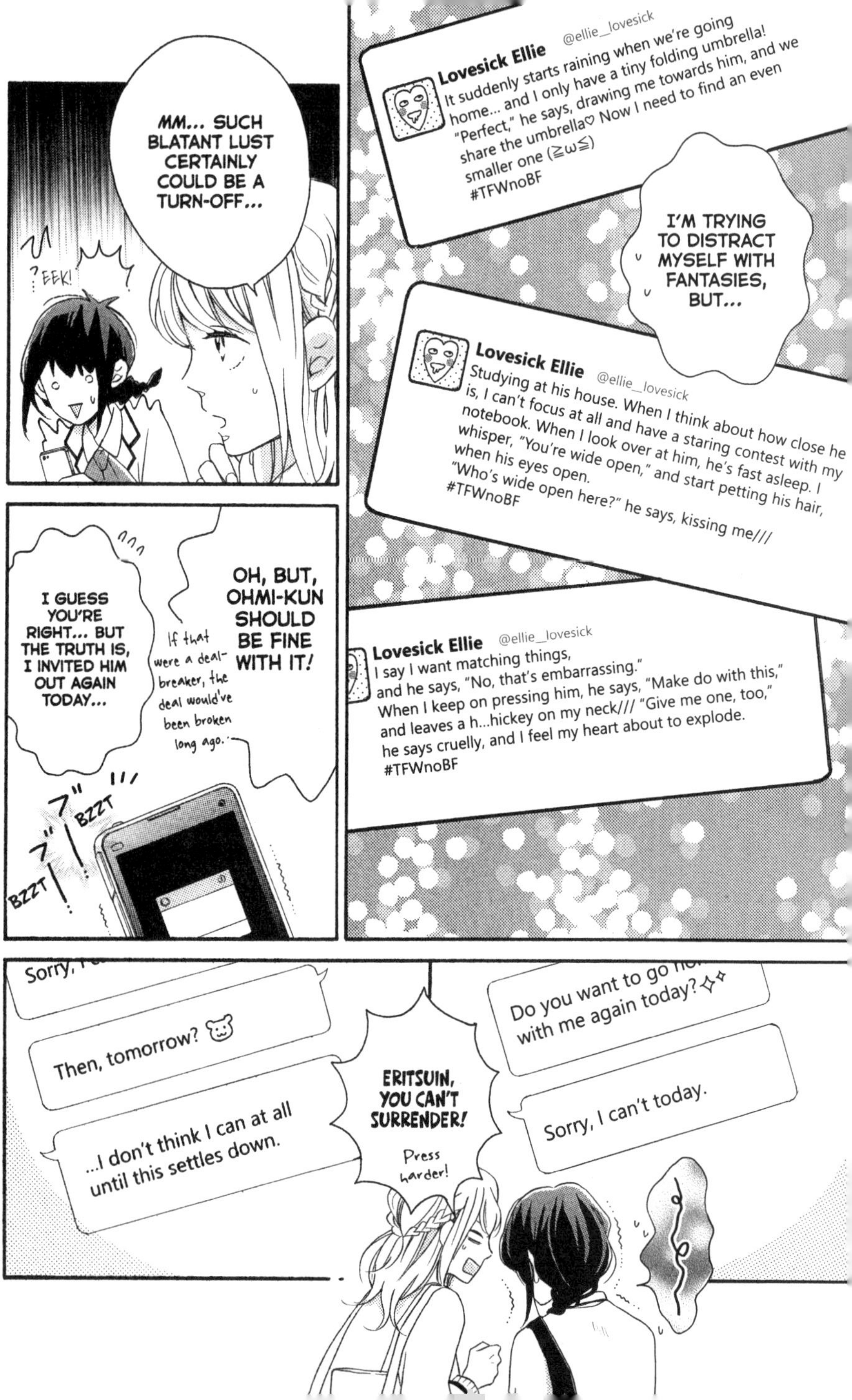
Lovesick Ellie @ellie__lovesick
It suddenly starts raining when we're going home... and I only have a tiny folding umbrella! "Perfect," he says, drawing me towards him, and we share the umbrella♡ Now I need to find an even smaller one (≧ω≦)
#TFWnoBF
I'M TRYING TO DISTRACT MYSELF WITH FANTASIES, BUT...
Lovesick Ellie @ellie__lovesick
Studying at his house. When I think about how close he is, I can't focus at all and have a staring contest with my notebook. When I look over at him, he's fast asleep. I whisper, "You're wide open," and start petting his hair, when his eyes open.
"Who's wide open here?" he says, kissing me///
#TFWnoBF
Lovesick Ellie @ellie__lovesick
I say I want matching things,
and he says, "No, that's embarrassing." "Make do with this,"
When I keep on pressing him, he says, "Give me one, too,"
and leaves a h...hickey on my neck///
he says cruelly, and I feel my heart about to explode.
#TFWnoBF
MM... SUCH BLATANT LUST CERTAINLY COULD BE A TURN-OFF...
EEK!
OH, BUT, OHMI-KUN SHOULD BE FINE WITH IT!
If that were a deal-breaker, the deal would've been broken long ago.
I GUESS YOU'RE RIGHT... BUT THE TRUTH IS, I INVITED HIM OUT AGAIN TODAY...
BZZT
BZZT
Do you want to go ho
with me again today?
Sorry, I can't today.
ERITSUIN, YOU CAN'T SURRENDER!
Press harder!
Sorry,
Then, tomorrow?
...I don't think I can at all until this settles down.

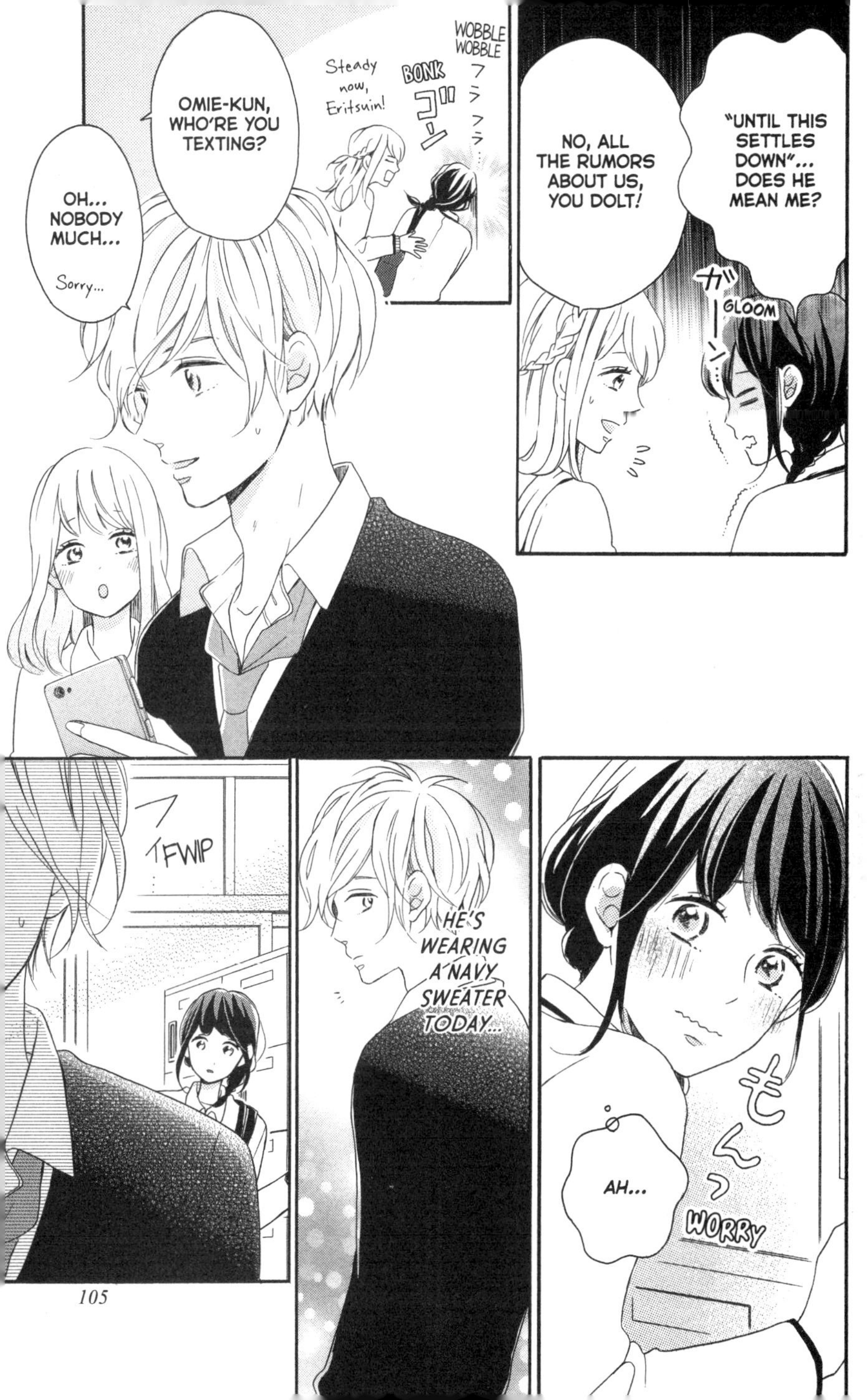
"UNTIL THIS SETTLES DOWN"... DOES HE MEAN ME?
NO, ALL THE RUMORS ABOUT US, YOU DOLT!
GLOOM
WOBBLE WOBBLE
BONK
Steady now, Eritsuin!
OMIE-KUN, WHO'RE YOU TEXTING?
OH... NOBODY MUCH...
Sorry...
AH...
WORRY
HE'S WEARING A NAVY SWEATER TODAY...
FWIP

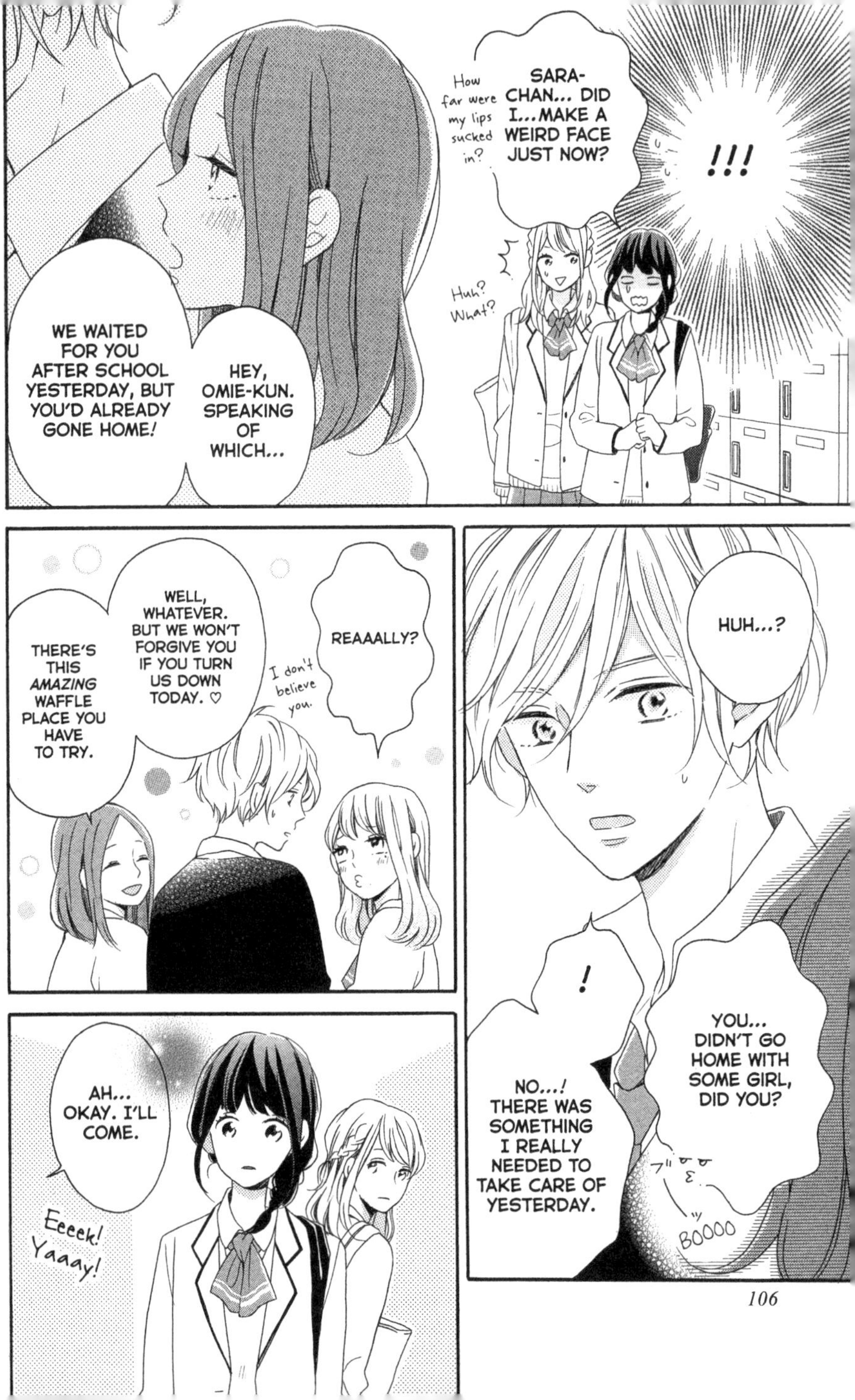
!!!
SARA-CHAN... DID I...MAKE A WEIRD FACE JUST NOW?
How far were my lips sucked in?
Huh? What?
HEY, OMIE-KUN. SPEAKING OF WHICH...
WE WAITED FOR YOU AFTER SCHOOL YESTERDAY, BUT YOU'D ALREADY GONE HOME!
HUH...?
YOU... DIDN'T GO HOME WITH SOME GIRL, DID YOU?
BOOOO
!
NO...! THERE WAS SOMETHING I REALLY NEEDED TO TAKE CARE OF YESTERDAY.
REAAALLY?
I don't believe you.
WELL, WHATEVER. BUT WE WON'T FORGIVE YOU IF YOU TURN US DOWN TODAY. ♡
THERE'S THIS *AMAZING* WAFFLE PLACE YOU HAVE TO TRY.
AH... OKAY. I'LL COME.
Eeeek! Yaaay!

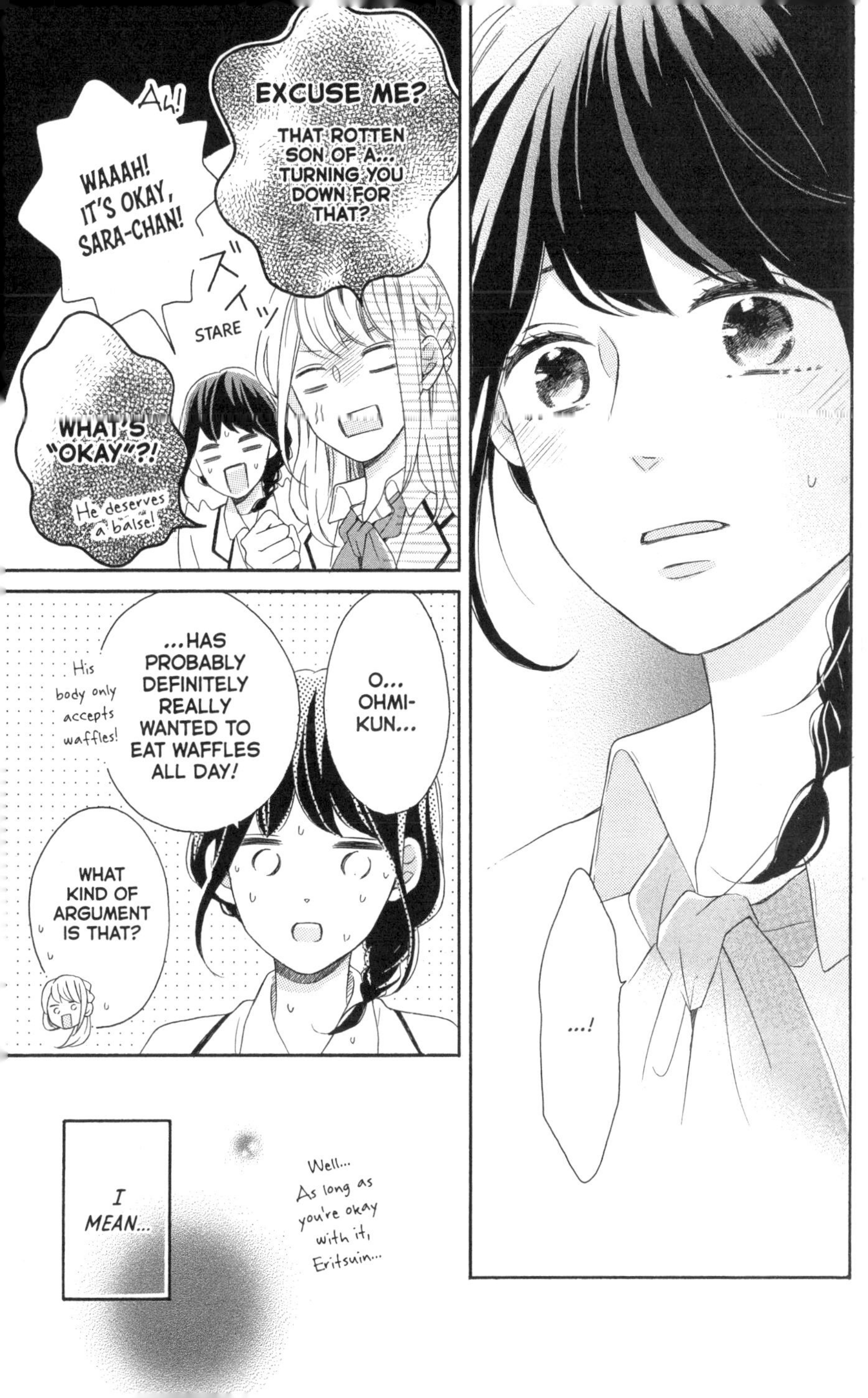
...!
EXCUSE ME?
THAT ROTTEN SON OF A... TURNING YOU DOWN FOR THAT?
Ah!
WAAAH! IT'S OKAY, SARA-CHAN!
ズイッ
STARE
WHAT'S "OKAY"?!
He deserves a balse!
O... OHMI-KUN...
...HAS PROBABLY DEFINITELY REALLY WANTED TO EAT WAFFLES ALL DAY!
His body only accepts waffles!
WHAT KIND OF ARGUMENT IS THAT?
Well... As long as you're okay with it, Eritsuin...
I MEAN...

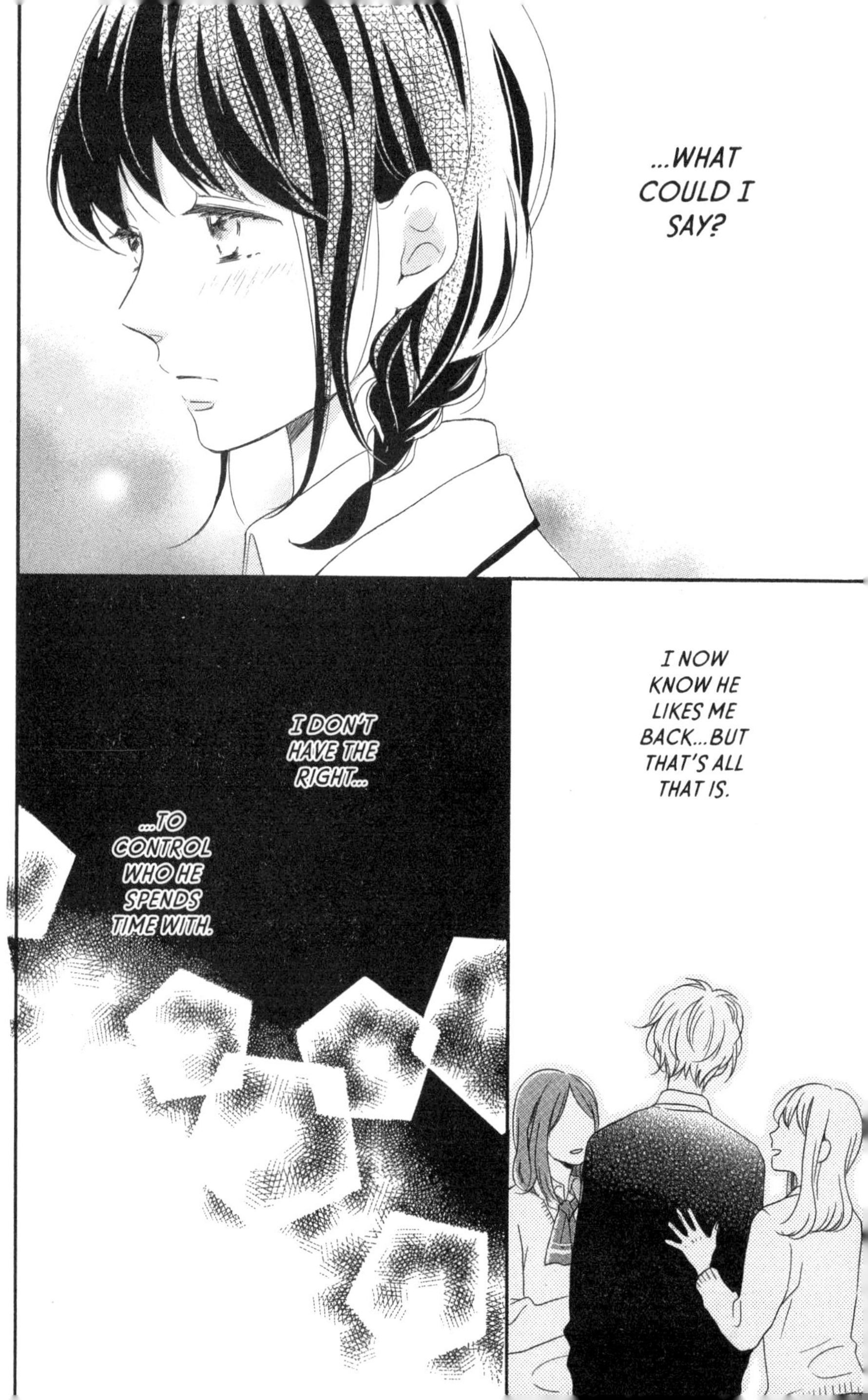
...WHAT COULD I SAY?
I NOW KNOW HE LIKES ME BACK...BUT THAT'S ALL THAT IS.
I DON'T HAVE THE RIGHT...
...TO CONTROL WHO HE SPENDS TIME WITH.

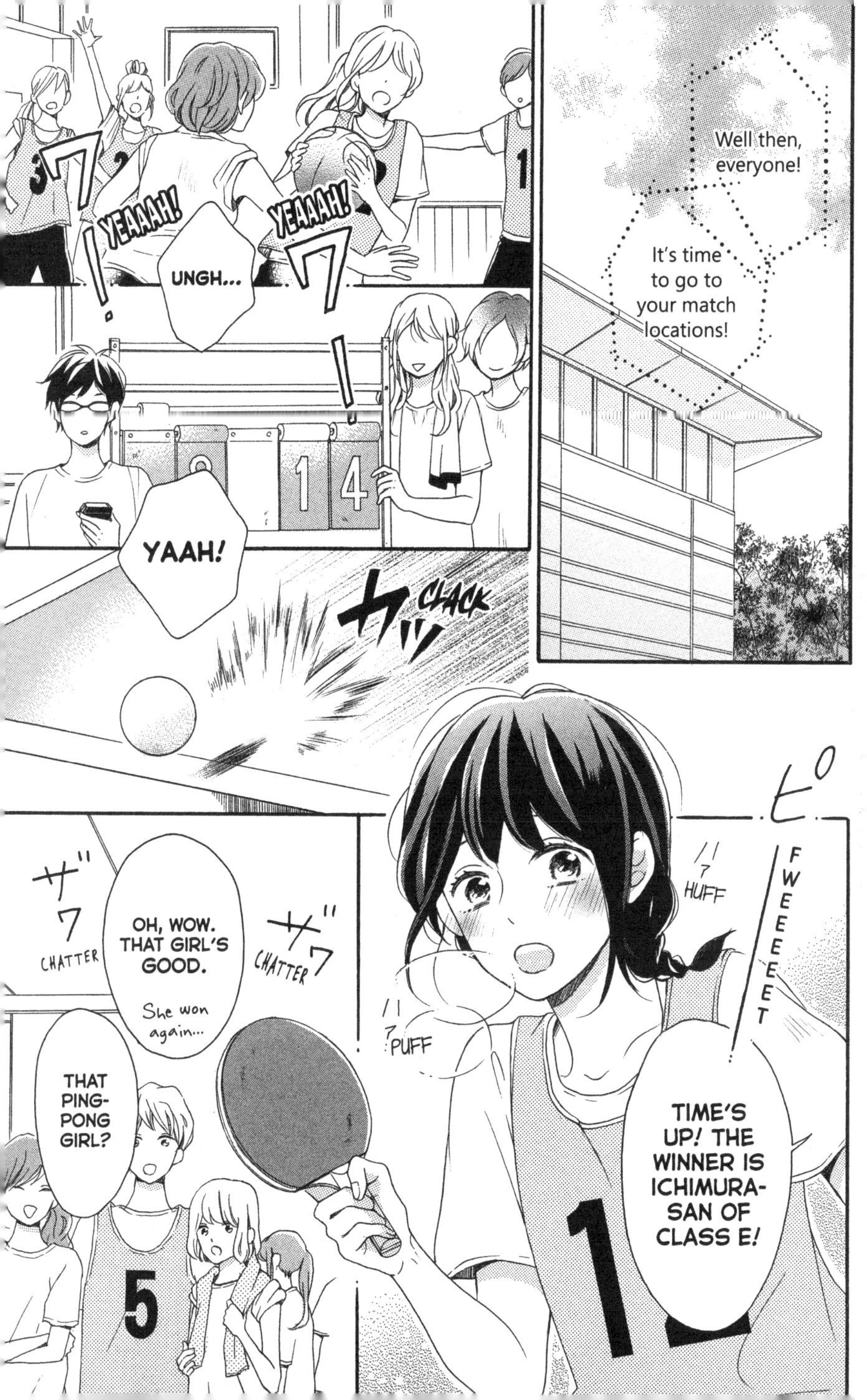
Well then, everyone!
It's time to go to your match locations!
YEAAAH!
UNGH...
YEAAAH!
YAAH!
CLACK
FWEEEEEEET
TIME'S UP! THE WINNER IS ICHIMURA-SAN OF CLASS E!
HUFF
PUFF
CHATTER
OH, WOW. THAT GIRL'S GOOD.
She won again...
CHATTER
THAT PING-PONG GIRL?

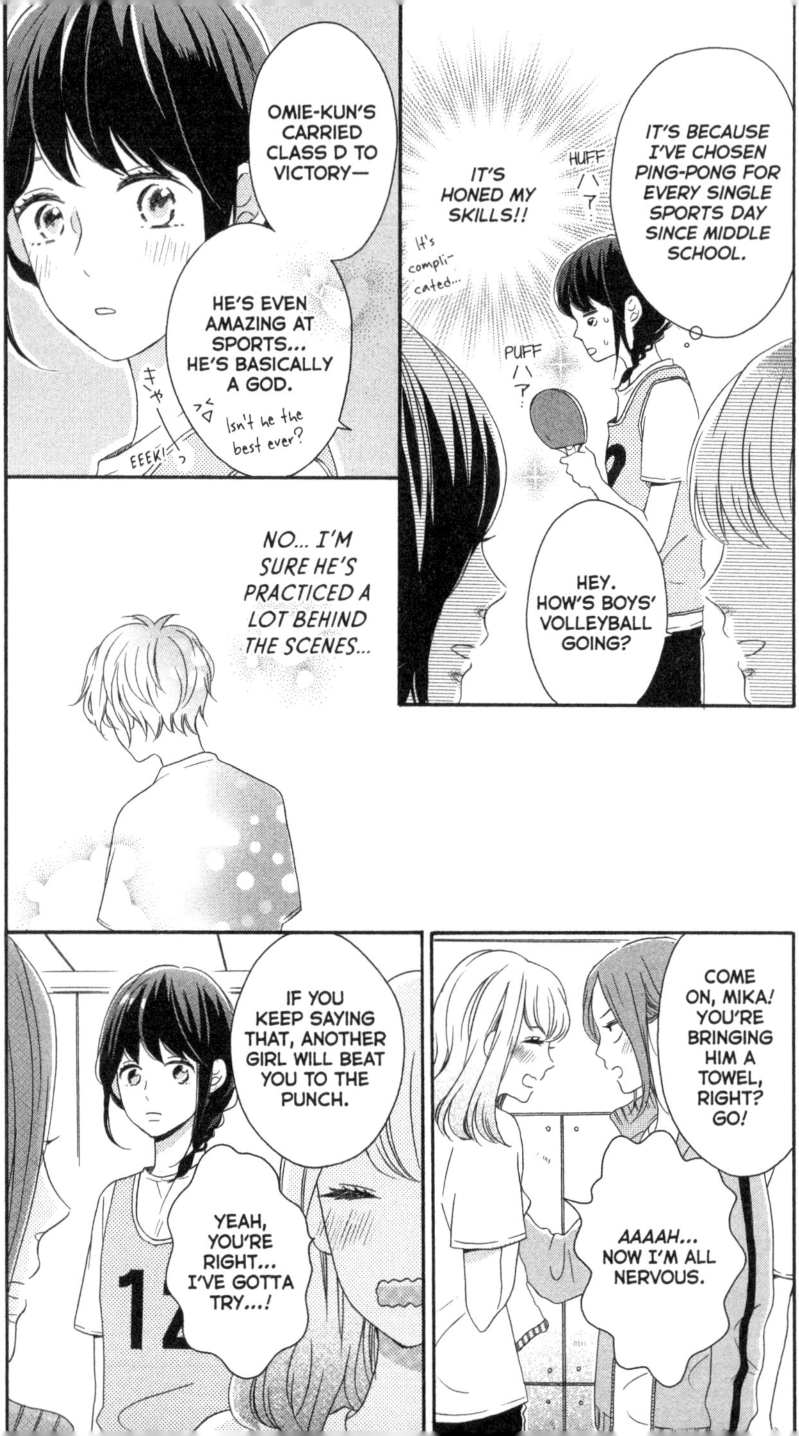
IT'S BECAUSE I'VE CHOSEN PING-PONG FOR EVERY SINGLE SPORTS DAY SINCE MIDDLE SCHOOL.
HUFF
IT'S HONED MY SKILLS!!
It's complicated...
PUFF
HEY. HOW'S BOYS' VOLLEYBALL GOING?
OMIE-KUN'S CARRIED CLASS D TO VICTORY—
HE'S EVEN AMAZING AT SPORTS... HE'S BASICALLY A GOD.
Isn't he the best ever?
EEEK!
NO... I'M SURE HE'S PRACTICED A LOT BEHIND THE SCENES...
COME ON, MIKA! YOU'RE BRINGING HIM A TOWEL, RIGHT? GO!
AAAAH... NOW I'M ALL NERVOUS.
IF YOU KEEP SAYING THAT, ANOTHER GIRL WILL BEAT YOU TO THE PUNCH.
YEAH, YOU'RE RIGHT... I'VE GOTTA TRY...!

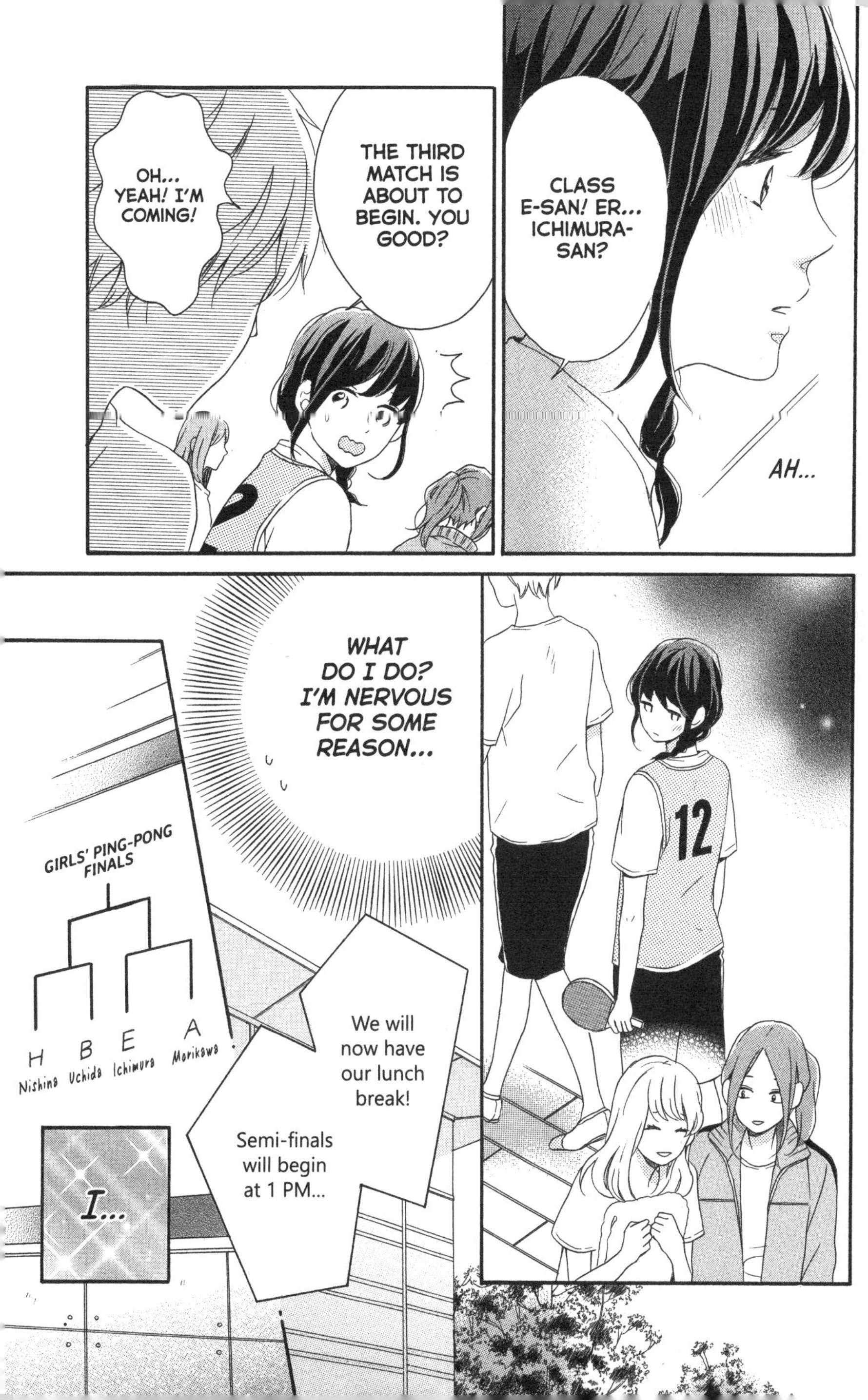
CLASS E-SAN! ER... ICHIMURA-SAN?
AH...
THE THIRD MATCH IS ABOUT TO BEGIN. YOU GOOD?
OH... YEAH! I'M COMING!
WHAT DO I DO? I'M NERVOUS FOR SOME REASON...
GIRLS' PING-PONG FINALS
H B E A
Nishina Uchida Ichimura Morikawa
We will now have our lunch break!
Semi-finals will begin at 1 PM...
I...

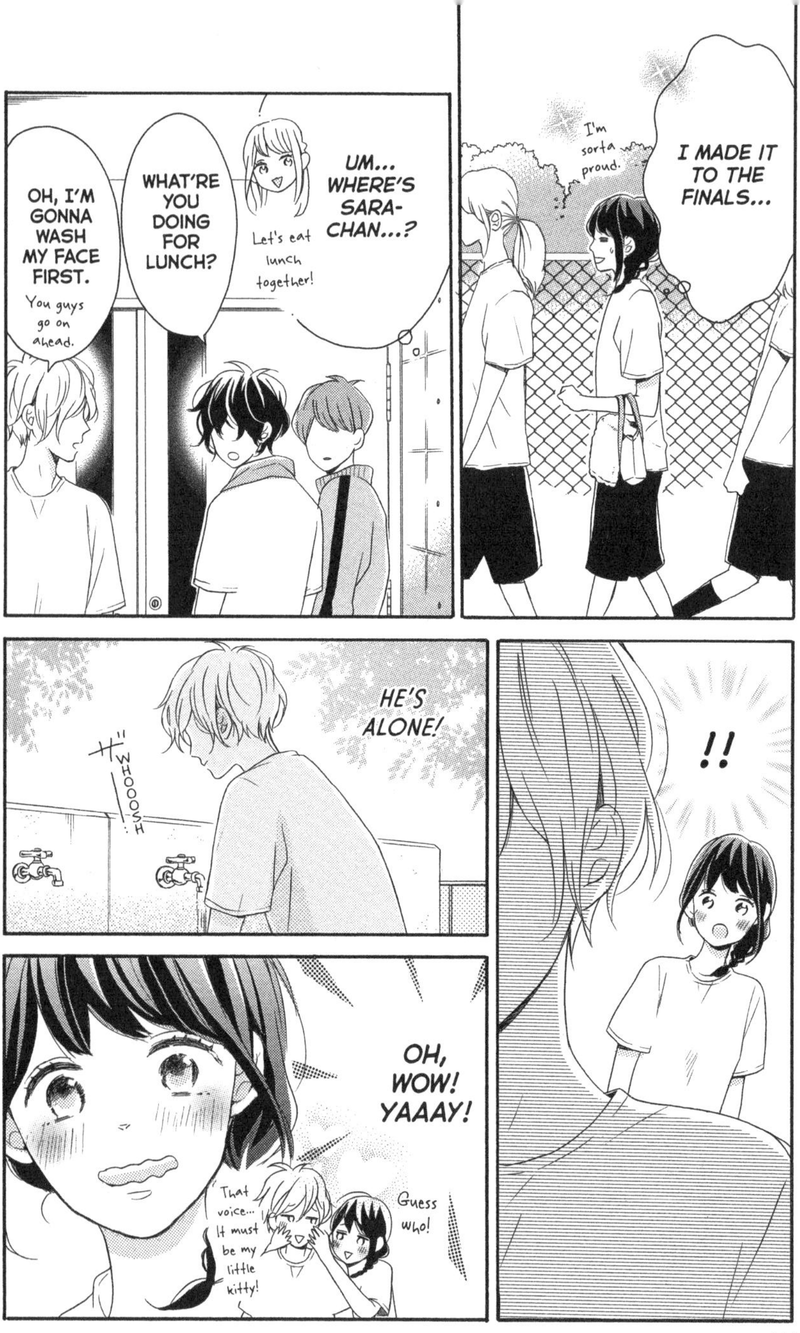
I MADE IT TO THE FINALS...
I'm sorta proud.
UM... WHERE'S SARA-CHAN...?
Let's eat lunch together!
WHAT'RE YOU DOING FOR LUNCH?
OH, I'M GONNA WASH MY FACE FIRST.
You guys go on ahead.
!!
HE'S ALONE!
WHOOOSH
OH, WOW! YAAAY!
Guess who!
That voice... It must be my little kitty!

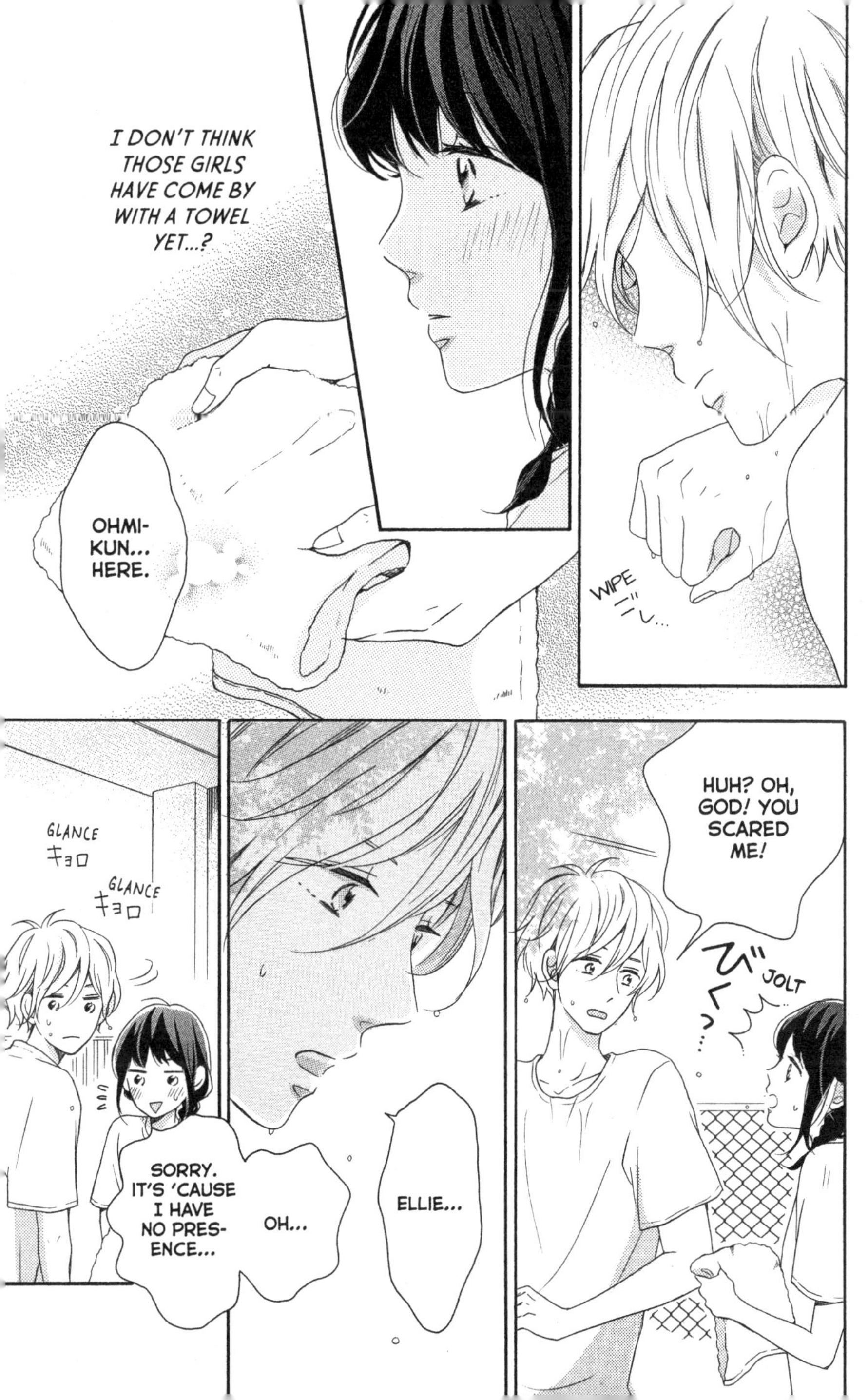
WIPE
ゴシ…
I DON'T THINK THOSE GIRLS HAVE COME BY WITH A TOWEL YET...?
OHMI-KUN... HERE.
HUH? OH, GOD! YOU SCARED ME!
JOLT
ビクッ…
ELLIE...
GLANCE
キョロ
GLANCE
キョロ
OH...
SORRY. IT'S 'CAUSE I HAVE NO PRESENCE...

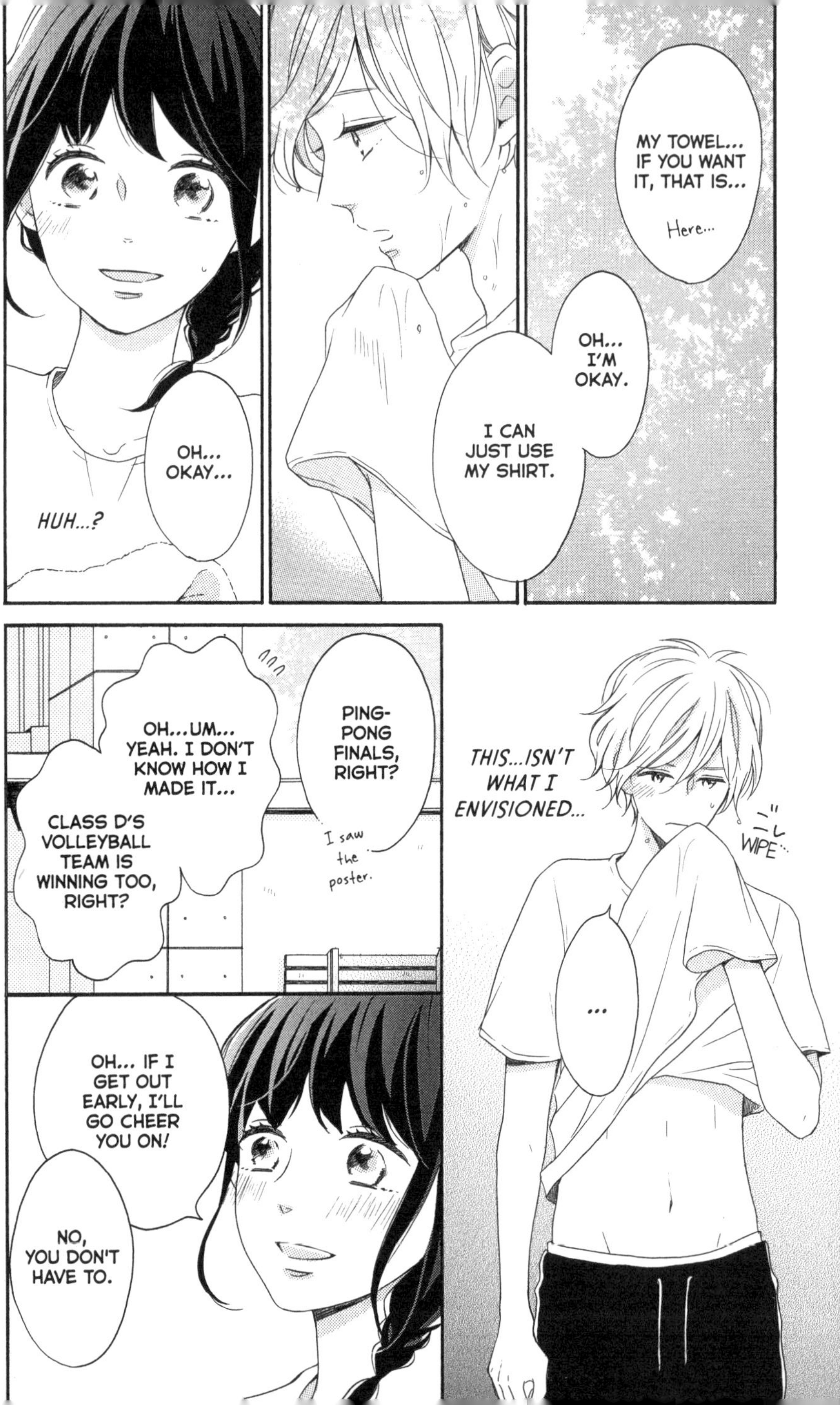
MY TOWEL... IF YOU WANT IT, THAT IS...
Here...
OH... I'M OKAY.
I CAN JUST USE MY SHIRT.
OH... OKAY...
HUH...?
THIS...ISN'T WHAT I ENVISIONED...
WIPE...
...
PING-PONG FINALS, RIGHT?
I saw the poster.
OH...UM... YEAH. I DON'T KNOW HOW I MADE IT...
CLASS D'S VOLLEYBALL TEAM IS WINNING TOO, RIGHT?
OH... IF I GET OUT EARLY, I'LL GO CHEER YOU ON!
NO, YOU DON'T HAVE TO.

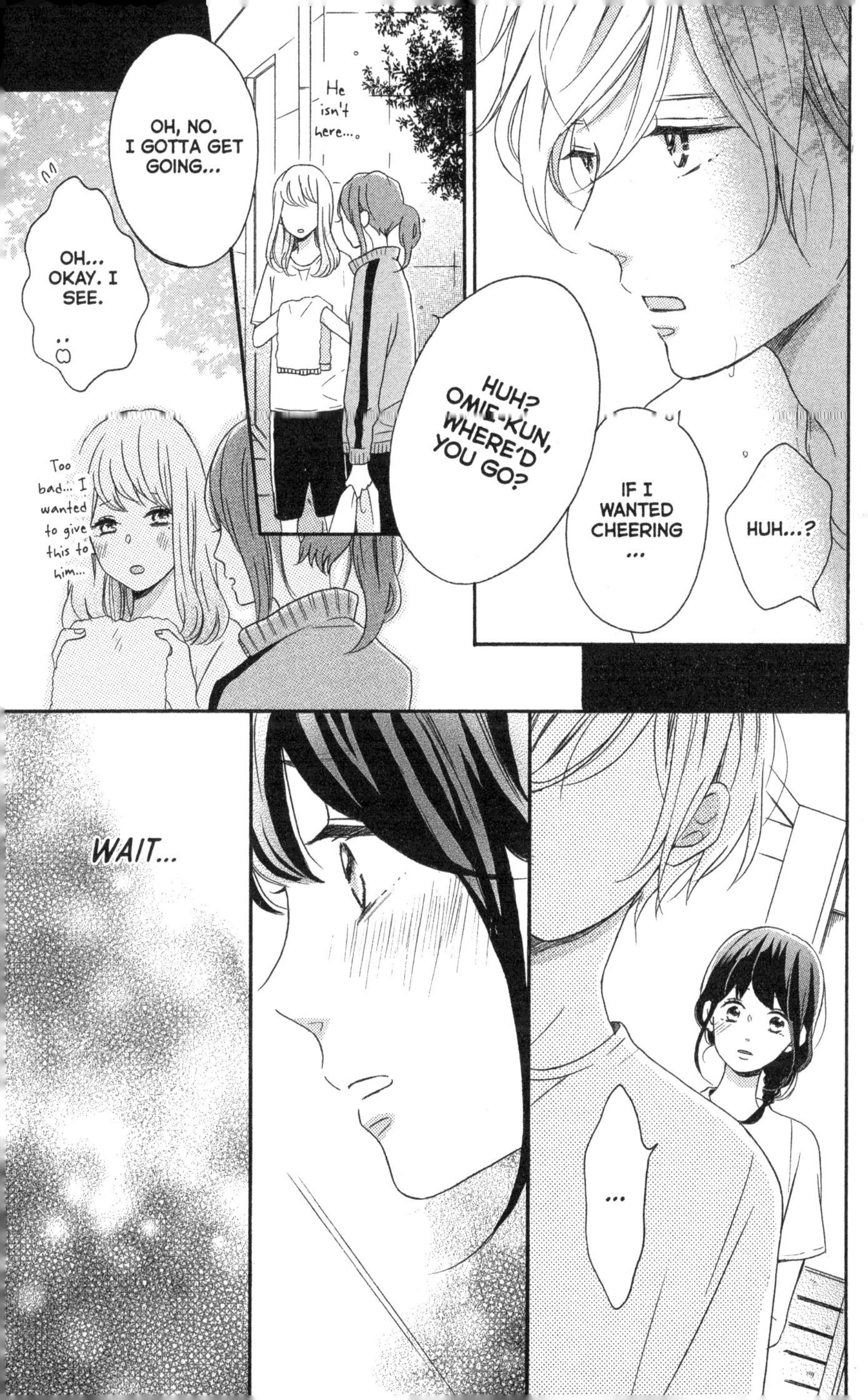
HUH...?
IF I WANTED CHEERING ...
HUH? OMIE-KUN, WHERE'D YOU GO?
He isn't here...
OH, NO. I GOTTA GET GOING...
OH... OKAY. I SEE.
Too bad... I wanted to give this to him...
...
WAIT...

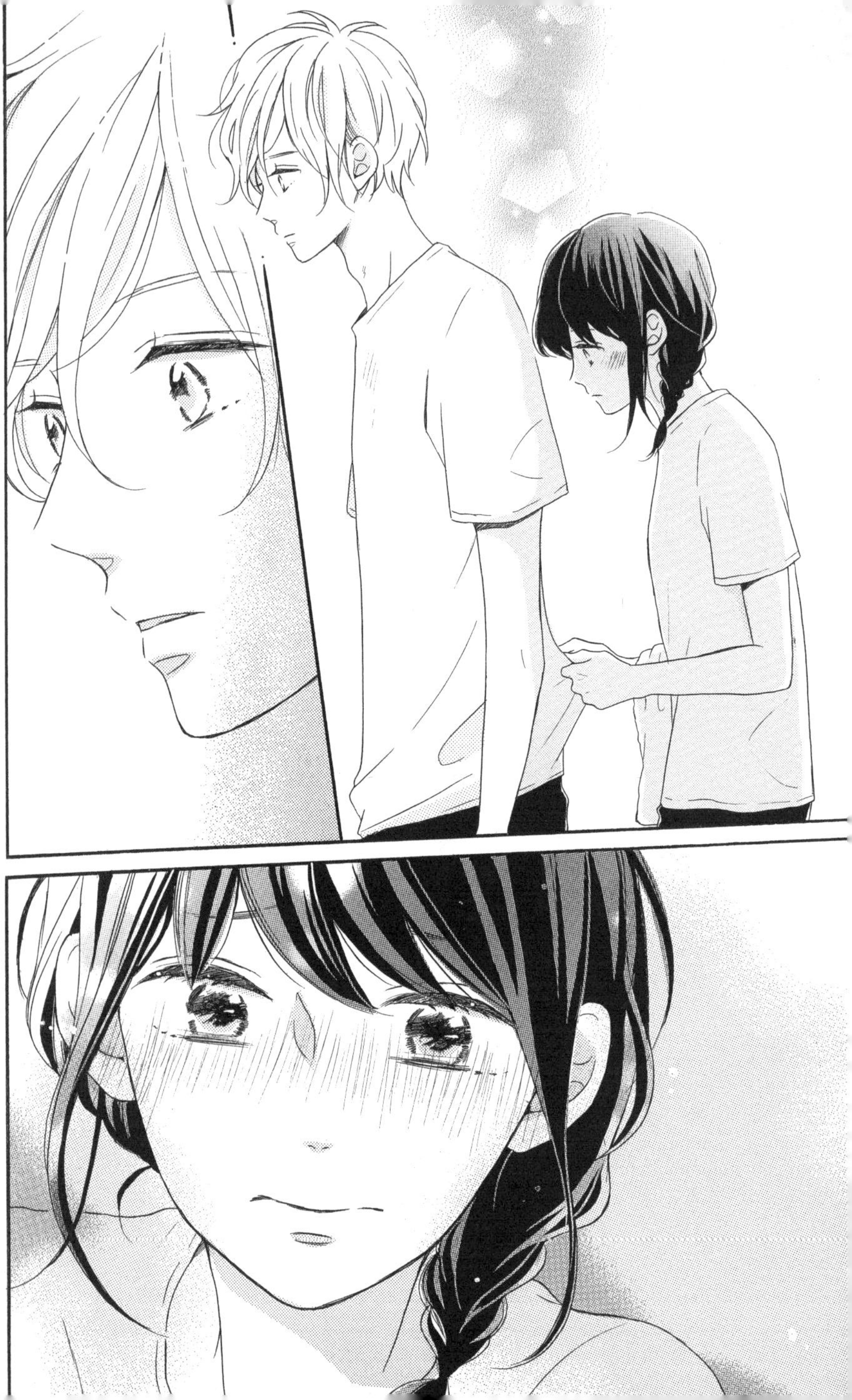
!

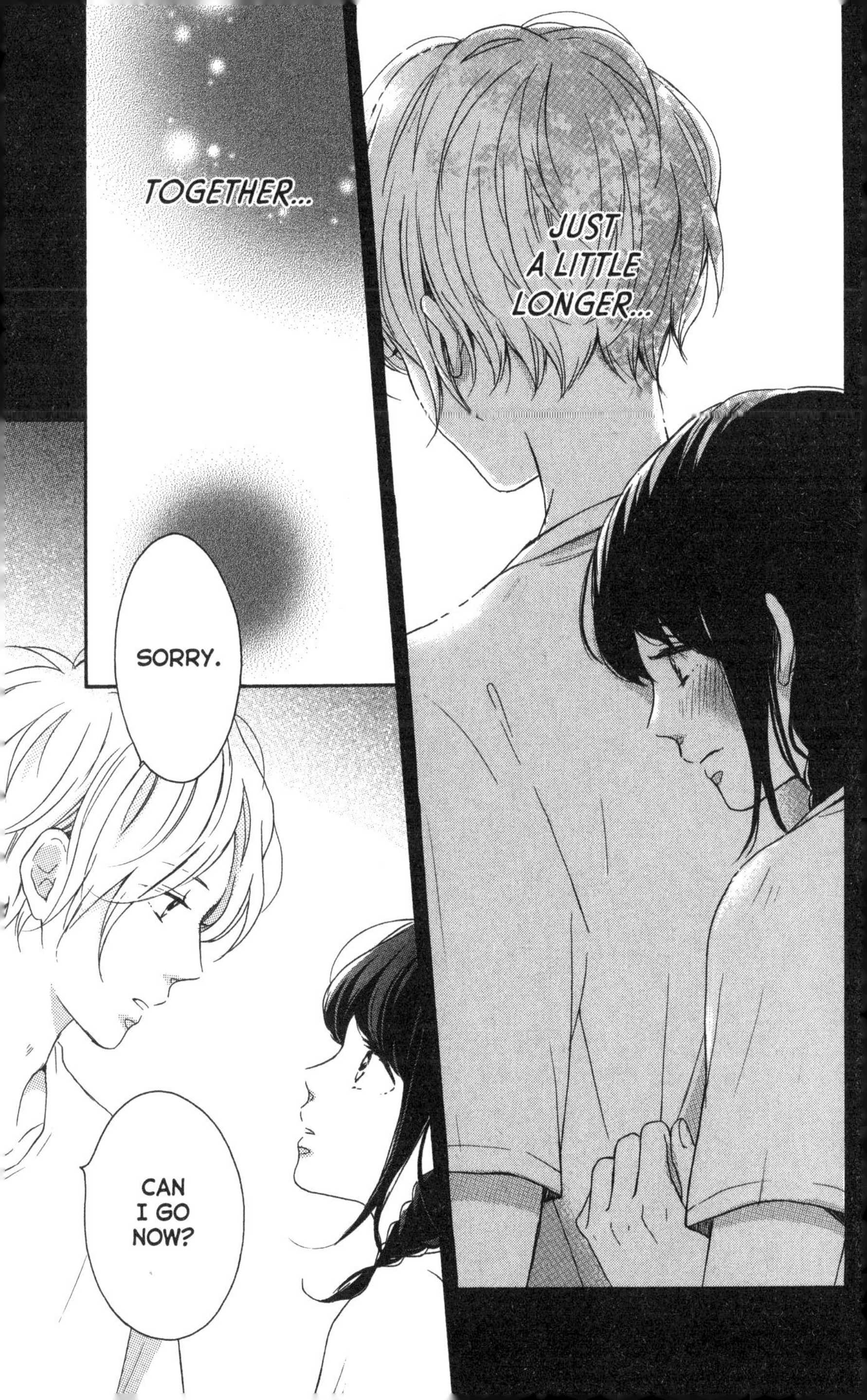
JUST A LITTLE LONGER...
TOGETHER...
SORRY.
CAN I GO NOW?

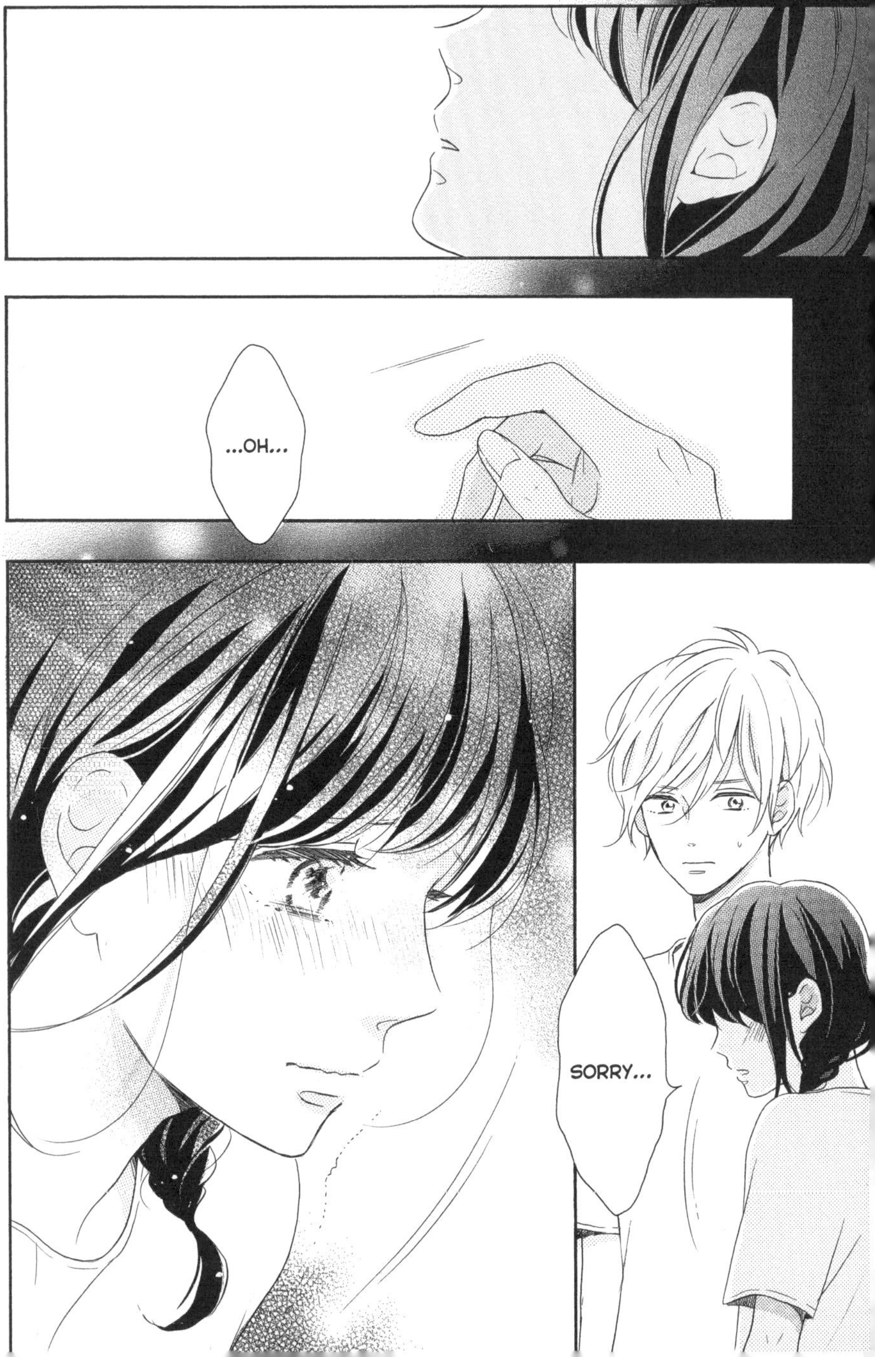
...OH...
SORRY...

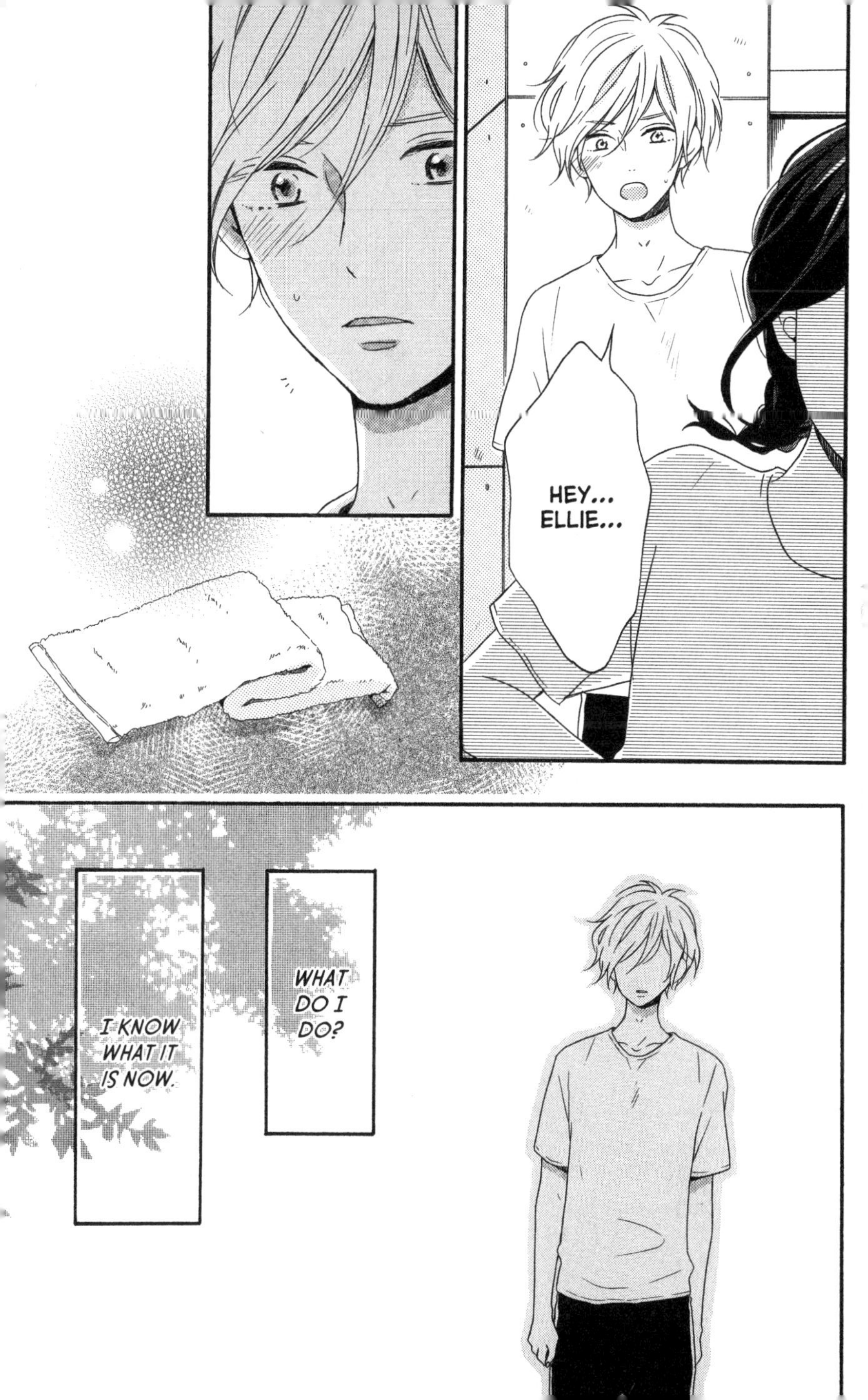
HEY... ELLIE...
WHAT DO I DO?
I KNOW WHAT IT IS NOW.

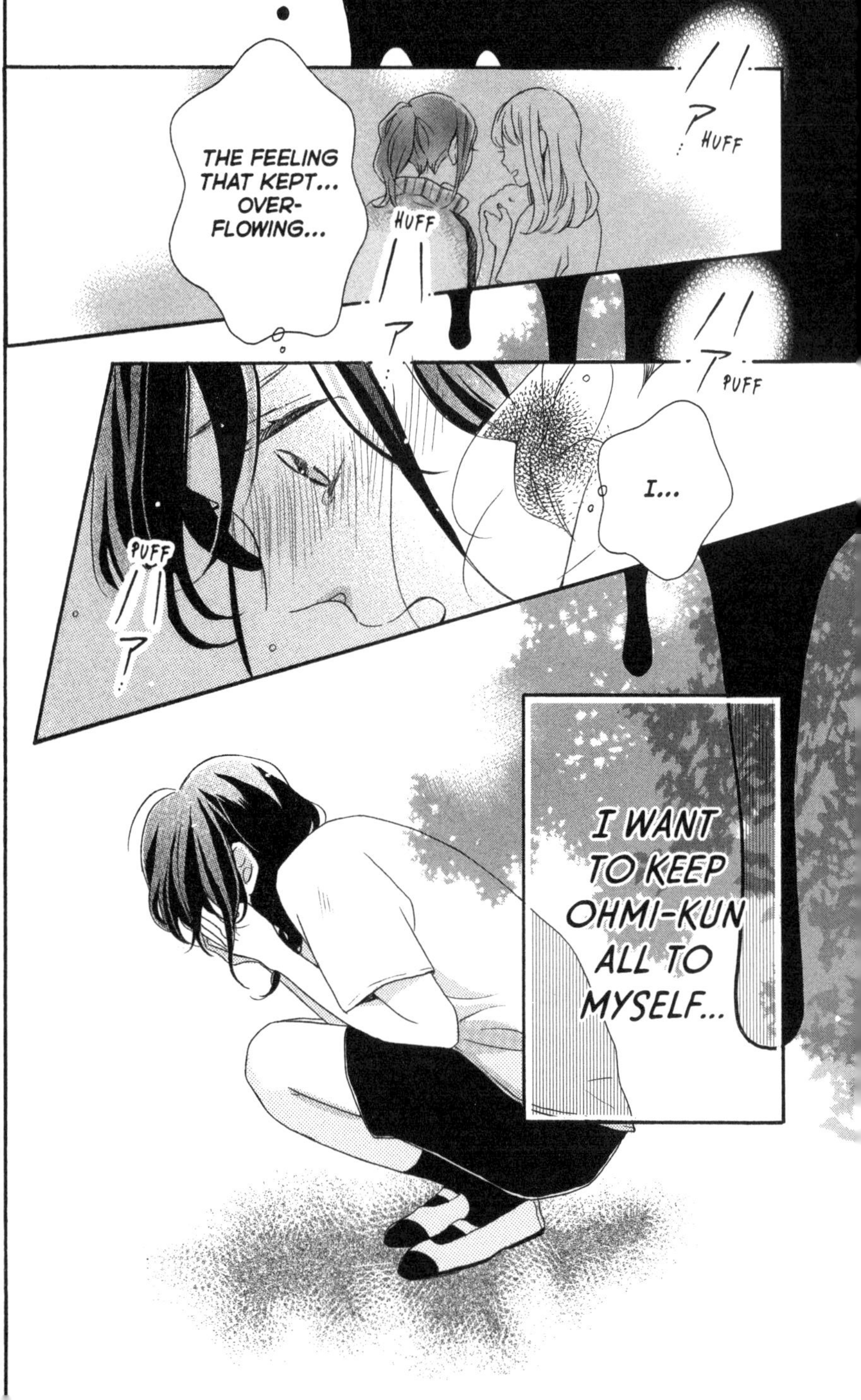
HUFF
THE FEELING THAT KEPT... OVER-FLOWING...
HUFF
PUFF
I...
PUFF
I WANT TO KEEP OHMI-KUN ALL TO MYSELF...

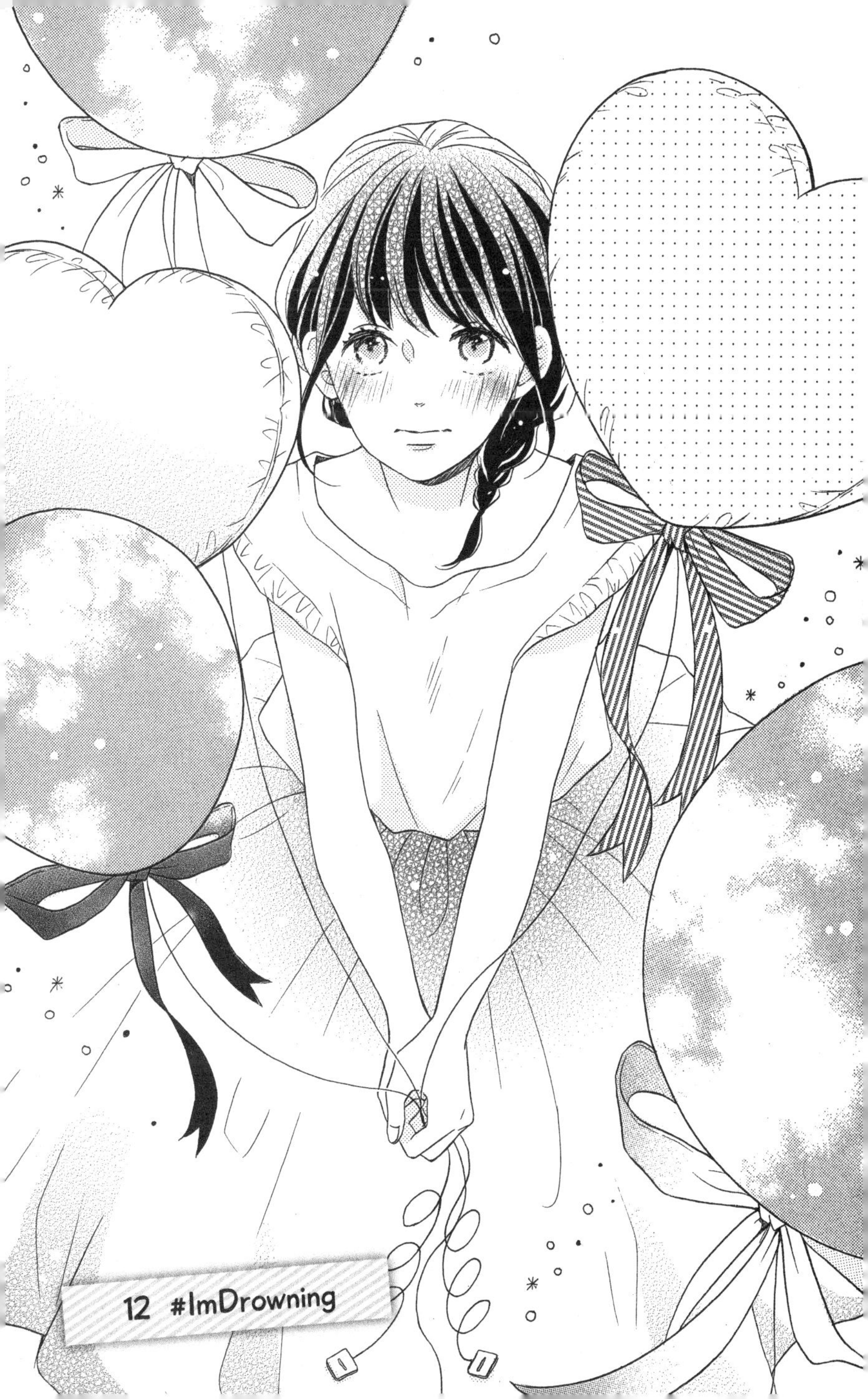
12 #ImDrowning

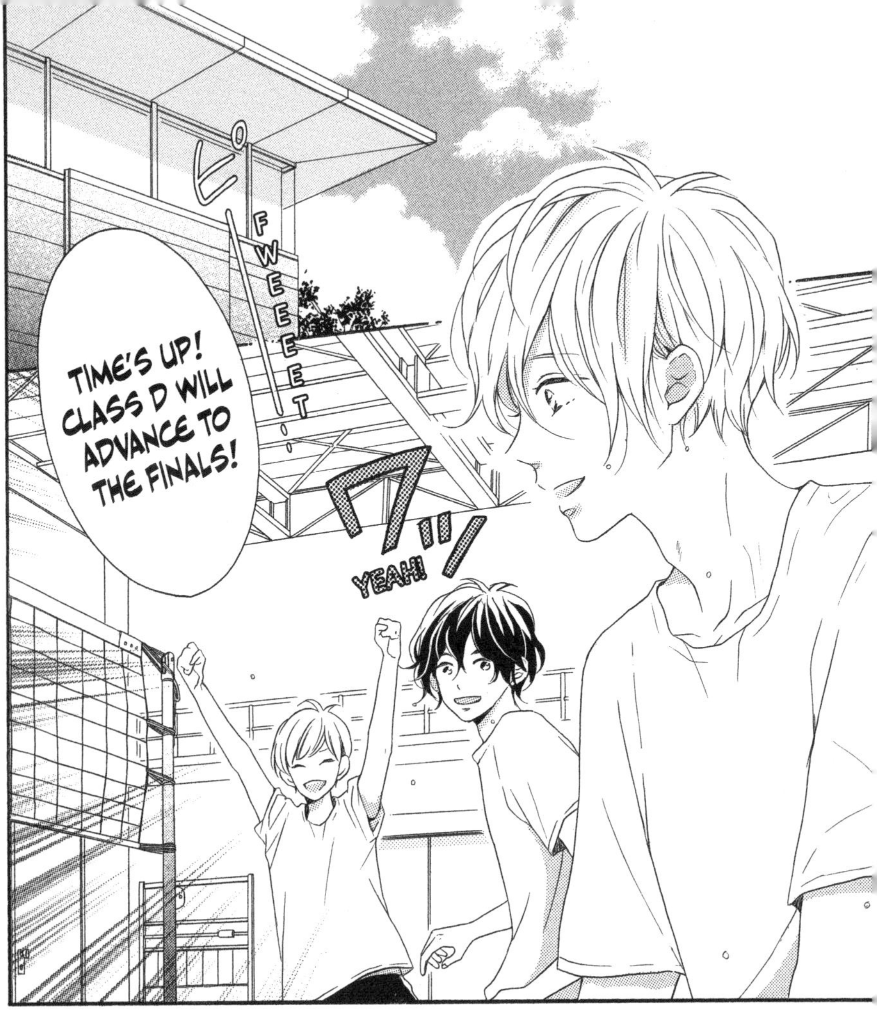
FWEEEET
TIME'S UP! CLASS D WILL ADVANCE TO THE FINALS!
YEAH!

Lovesick Ellie was originally supposed to be a one-volume short serial, but thanks to everyone's support, I was able to keep going to volume 3! And then...on to volume 4. Thank you so much, really!

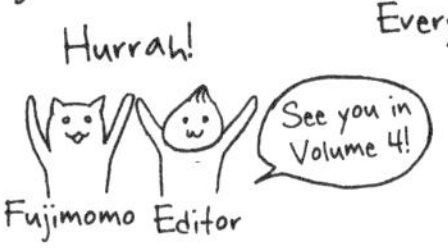
Hurrah!
See you in Volume 4!
Fujimomo
Editor

• Special Thanks •

Kuumii, Nagasaki, Takesu
Editor Minchi   Designer Osawa
Everyone at Dessert Editorial Department
And all my readers

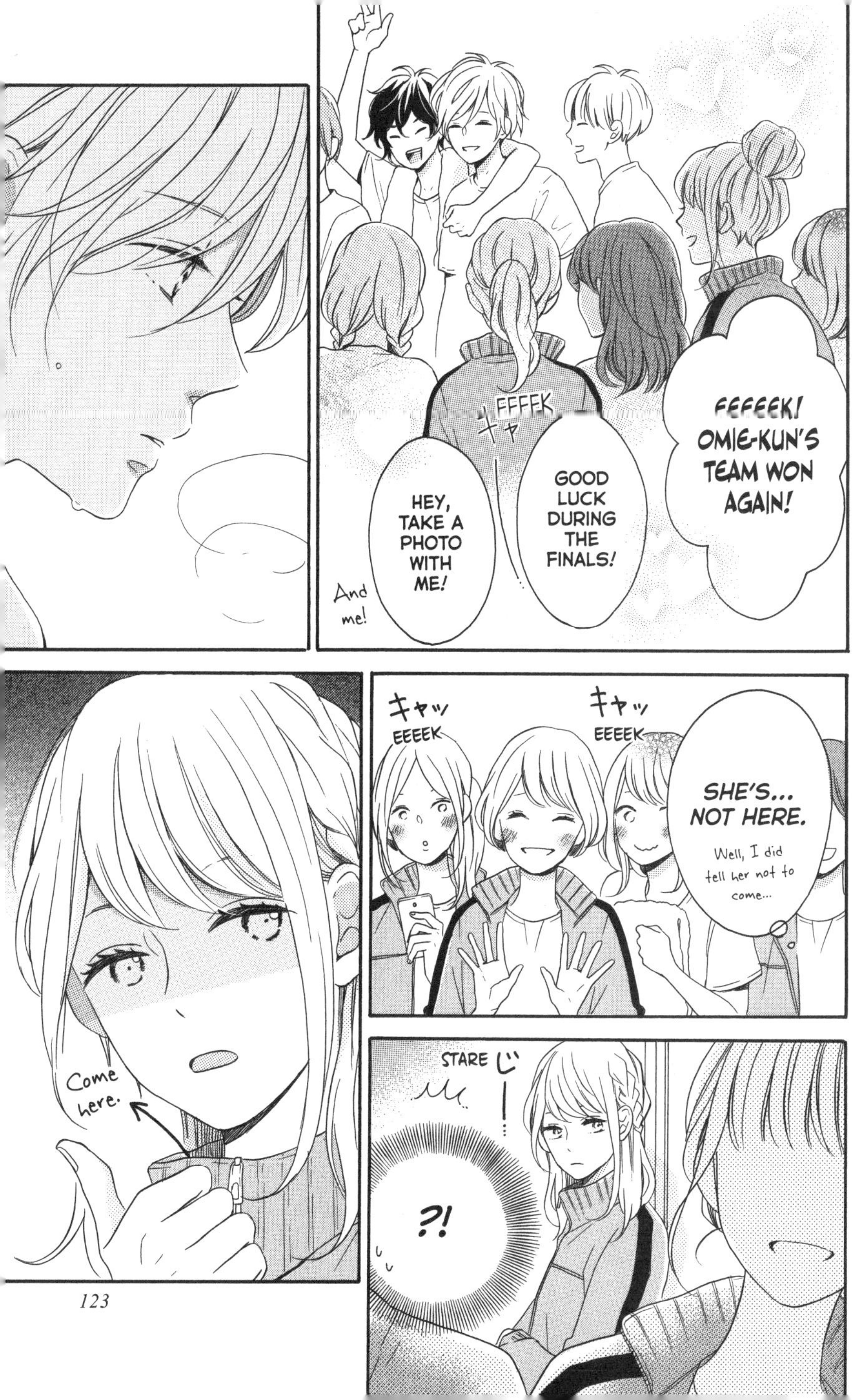
EEEEEK! OMIE-KUN'S TEAM WON AGAIN!
EEEEK
キャ
GOOD LUCK DURING THE FINALS!
HEY, TAKE A PHOTO WITH ME!
And me!
SHE'S... NOT HERE.
Well, I did tell her not to come...
キャッ
EEEEK
キャッ
EEEEK
STARE
じー
?!
Come here.

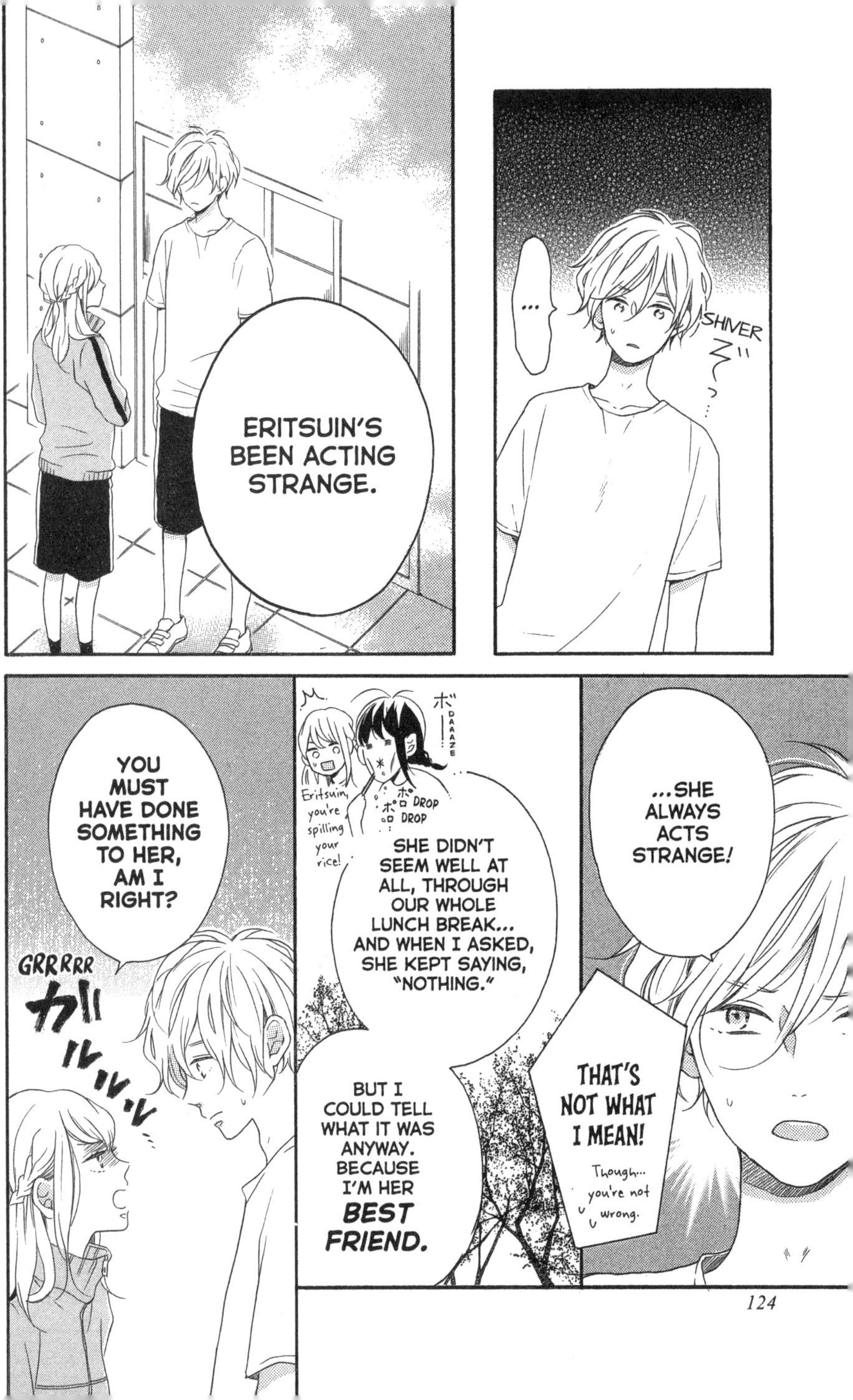
...
SHIVER
ERITSUIN'S BEEN ACTING STRANGE.
...SHE ALWAYS ACTS STRANGE!
THAT'S NOT WHAT I MEAN!
Though... you're not wrong.
DAAAZE
DROP DROP
Eritsuin, you're spilling your rice!
SHE DIDN'T SEEM WELL AT ALL, THROUGH OUR WHOLE LUNCH BREAK... AND WHEN I ASKED, SHE KEPT SAYING, "NOTHING."
BUT I COULD TELL WHAT IT WAS ANYWAY. BECAUSE I'M HER BEST FRIEND.
YOU MUST HAVE DONE SOMETHING TO HER, AM I RIGHT?
GRRRRR

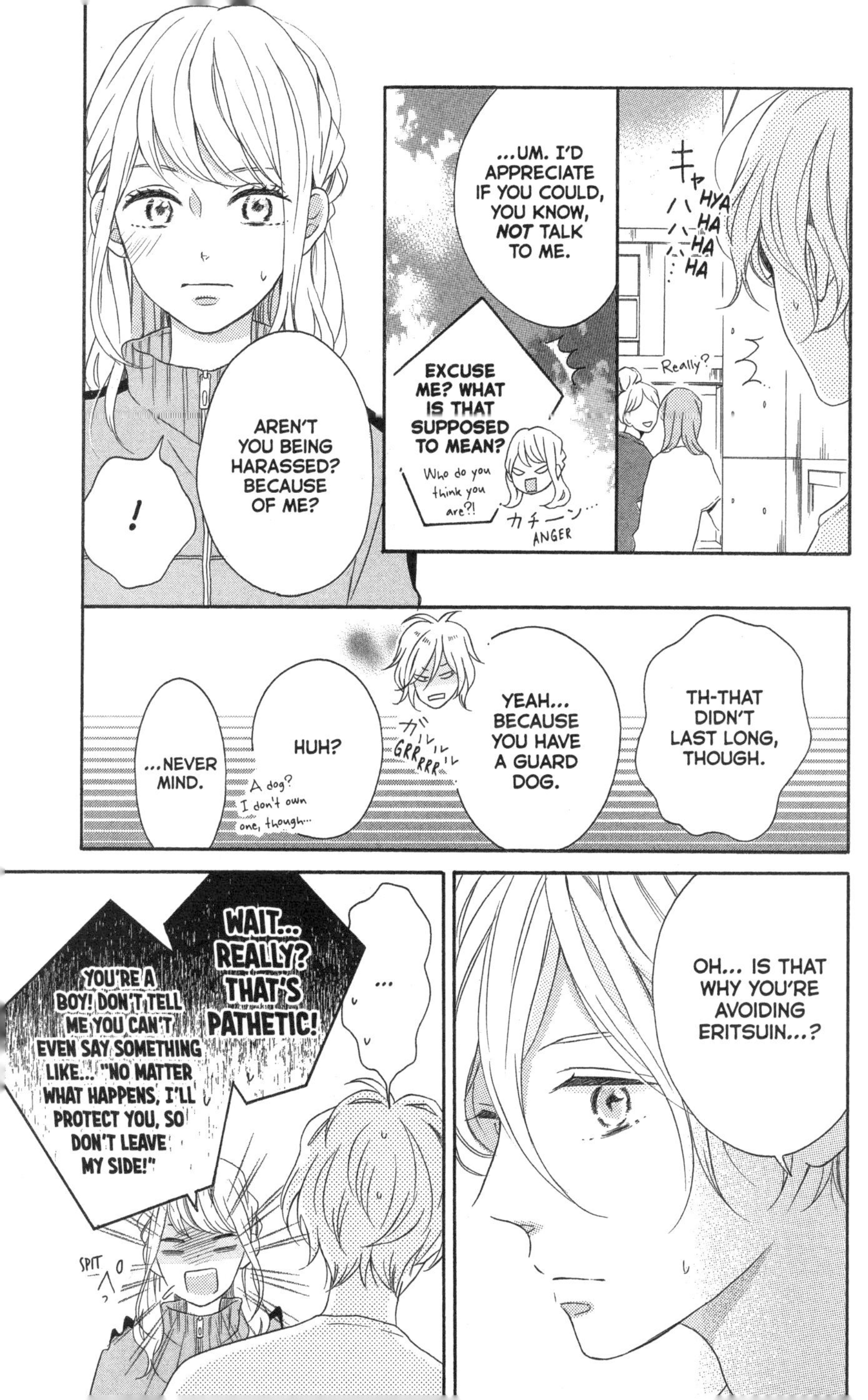
キャハハハ
HYA HA HA HA
Really?
...UM. I'D APPRECIATE IF YOU COULD, YOU KNOW, *NOT* TALK TO ME.
EXCUSE ME? WHAT IS THAT SUPPOSED TO MEAN?
Who do you think you are?!
カチーン…
ANGER
AREN'T YOU BEING HARASSED? BECAUSE OF ME?
!
TH-THAT DIDN'T LAST LONG, THOUGH.
YEAH... BECAUSE YOU HAVE A GUARD DOG.
ガルルル
GRRRRR
HUH?
A dog? I don't own one, though...
...NEVER MIND.
OH... IS THAT WHY YOU'RE AVOIDING ERITSUIN...?
WAIT... REALLY? THAT'S PATHETIC!
...
YOU'RE A BOY! DON'T TELL ME YOU CAN'T EVEN SAY SOMETHING LIKE... "NO MATTER WHAT HAPPENS, I'LL PROTECT YOU, SO DON'T LEAVE MY SIDE!"
SPIT

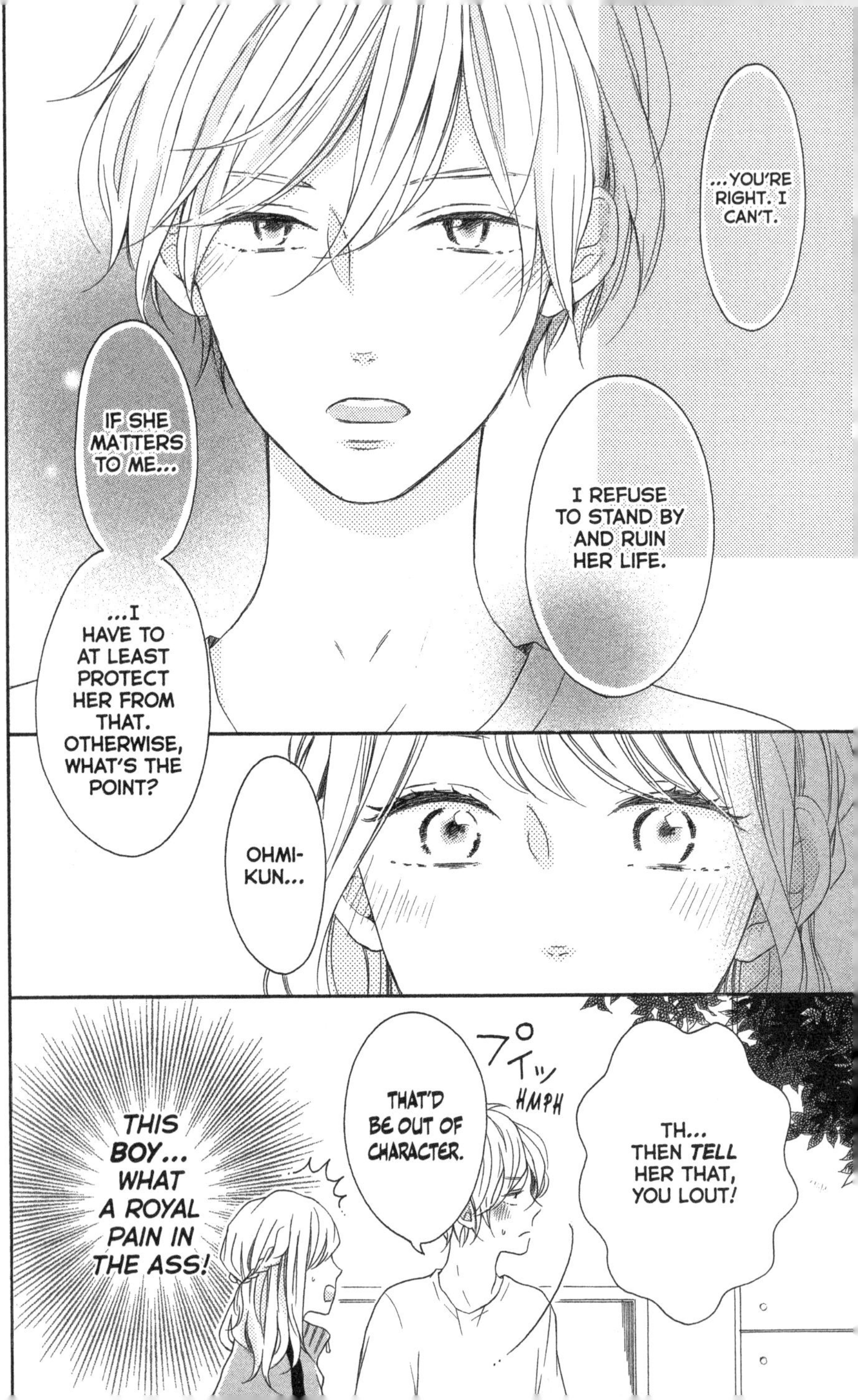
...YOU'RE RIGHT. I CAN'T.
I REFUSE TO STAND BY AND RUIN HER LIFE.
IF SHE MATTERS TO ME...
...I HAVE TO AT LEAST PROTECT HER FROM THAT. OTHERWISE, WHAT'S THE POINT?
OHMI-KUN...
TH... THEN *TELL* HER THAT, YOU LOUT!
プイッ
HMPH
THAT'D BE OUT OF CHARACTER.
THIS BOY... WHAT A ROYAL PAIN IN THE ASS!

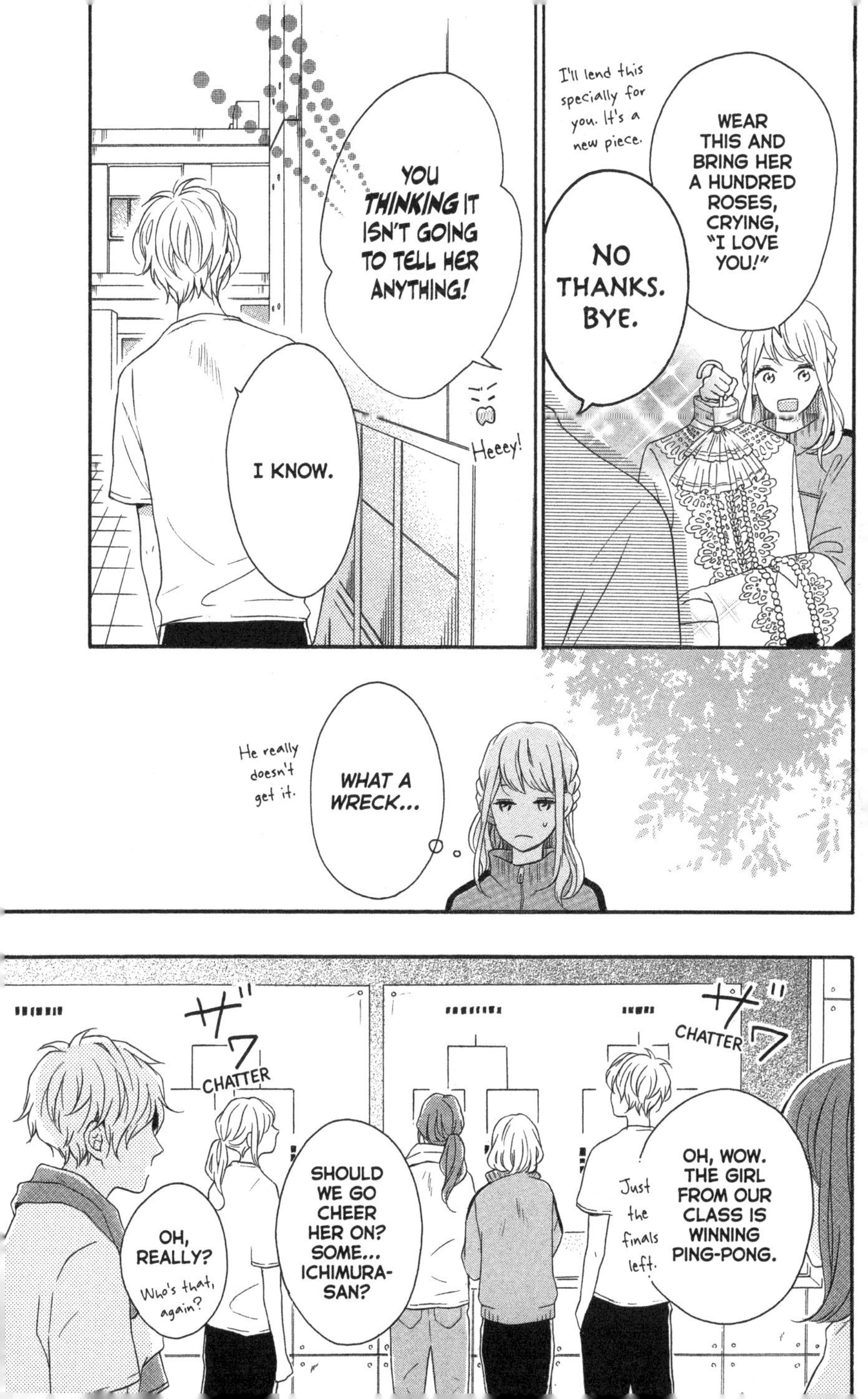

I'll lend this specially for you. It's a new piece.
WEAR THIS AND BRING HER A HUNDRED ROSES, CRYING, "I LOVE YOU!"
NO THANKS. BYE.
YOU *THINKING* IT ISN'T GOING TO TELL HER ANYTHING!
Heeey!
I KNOW.
WHAT A WRECK...
He really doesn't get it.
ザワ
CHATTER
OH, WOW. THE GIRL FROM OUR CLASS IS WINNING PING-PONG.
Just the finals left.
SHOULD WE GO CHEER HER ON? SOME... ICHIMURA-SAN?
ザワ
CHATTER
OH, REALLY?
Who's that, again?

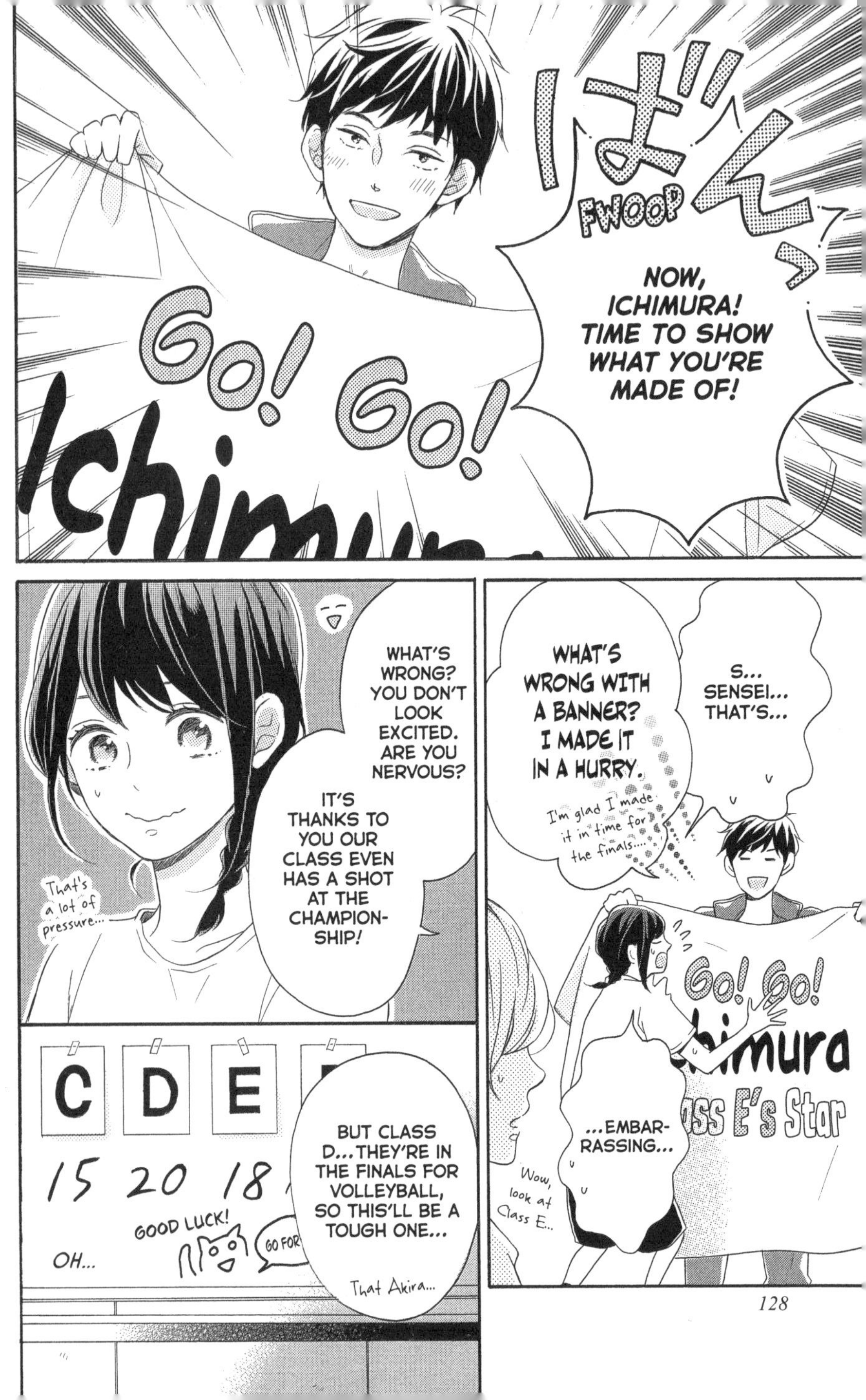
ばん
FWOOP
NOW, ICHIMURA! TIME TO SHOW WHAT YOU'RE MADE OF!
Go! Go!
S... SENSEI... THAT'S...
WHAT'S WRONG WITH A BANNER? I MADE IT IN A HURRY.
I'm glad I made it in time for the finals....
Go! Go!
...EMBARRASSING...
Wow, look at Class E...
WHAT'S WRONG? YOU DON'T LOOK EXCITED. ARE YOU NERVOUS?
IT'S THANKS TO YOU OUR CLASS EVEN HAS A SHOT AT THE CHAMPIONSHIP!
That's a lot of pressure...
C D E
15 20 18
BUT CLASS D... THEY'RE IN THE FINALS FOR VOLLEYBALL, SO THIS'LL BE A TOUGH ONE...
That Akira...
GOOD LUCK!
GO FOR
OH...

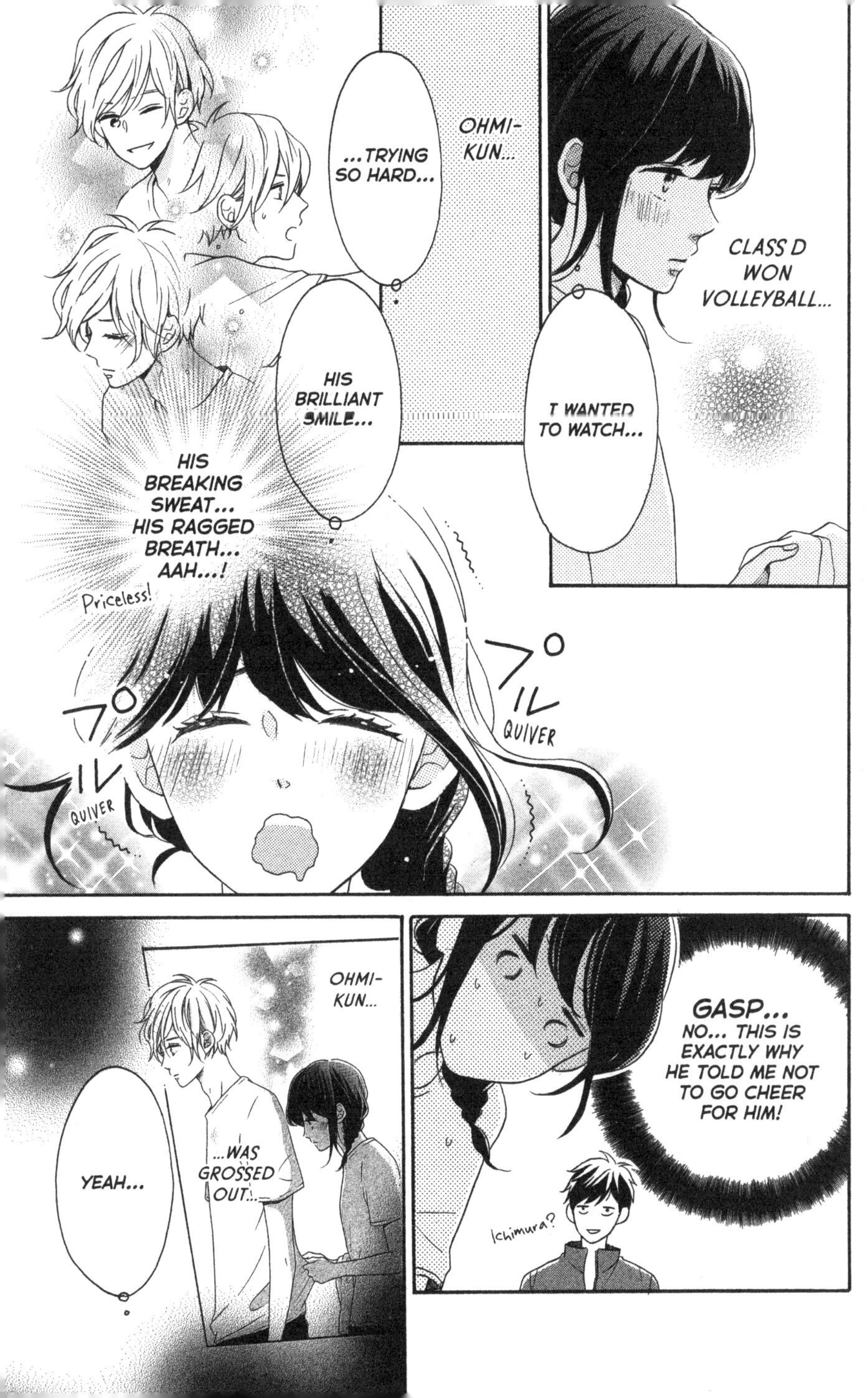
CLASS D WON VOLLEYBALL...
I WANTED TO WATCH...
OHMI-KUN...
...TRYING SO HARD...
HIS BRILLIANT SMILE...
HIS BREAKING SWEAT... HIS RAGGED BREATH... AAH...!
Priceless!
QUIVER
QUIVER
GASP... NO... THIS IS EXACTLY WHY HE TOLD ME NOT TO GO CHEER FOR HIM!
Ichimura?
OHMI-KUN...
...WAS GROSSED OUT...
YEAH...

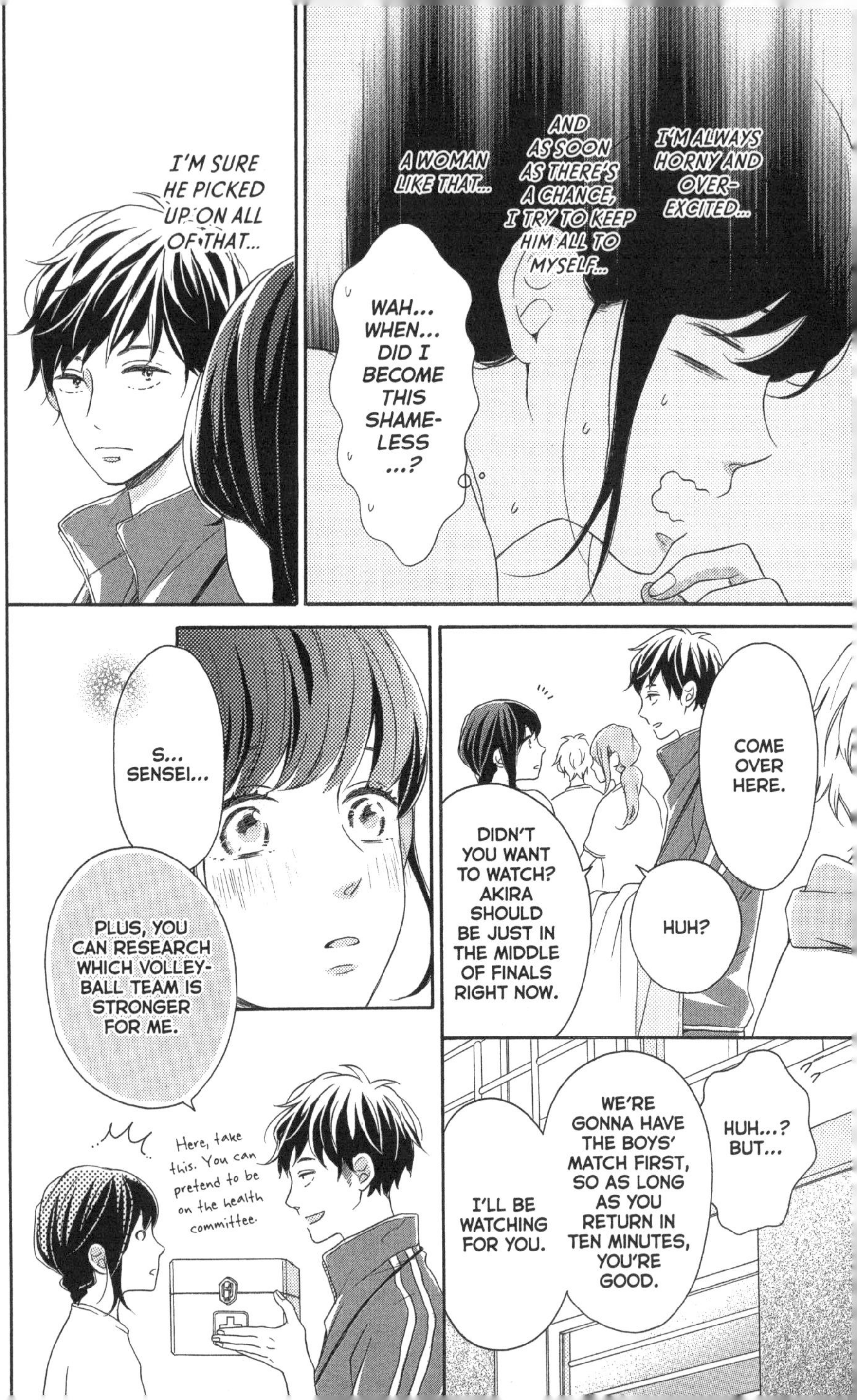
I'M ALWAYS HORNY AND OVER-EXCITED...
AND AS SOON AS THERE'S A CHANCE, I TRY TO KEEP HIM ALL TO MYSELF...
A WOMAN LIKE THAT...
WAH... WHEN... DID I BECOME THIS SHAME-LESS ...?
I'M SURE HE PICKED UP ON ALL OF THAT...
COME OVER HERE.
HUH?
DIDN'T YOU WANT TO WATCH? AKIRA SHOULD BE JUST IN THE MIDDLE OF FINALS RIGHT NOW.
HUH...? BUT...
WE'RE GONNA HAVE THE BOYS' MATCH FIRST, SO AS LONG AS YOU RETURN IN TEN MINUTES, YOU'RE GOOD.
I'LL BE WATCHING FOR YOU.
S... SENSEI...
PLUS, YOU CAN RESEARCH WHICH VOLLEY-BALL TEAM IS STRONGER FOR ME.
Here, take this. You can pretend to be on the health committee.

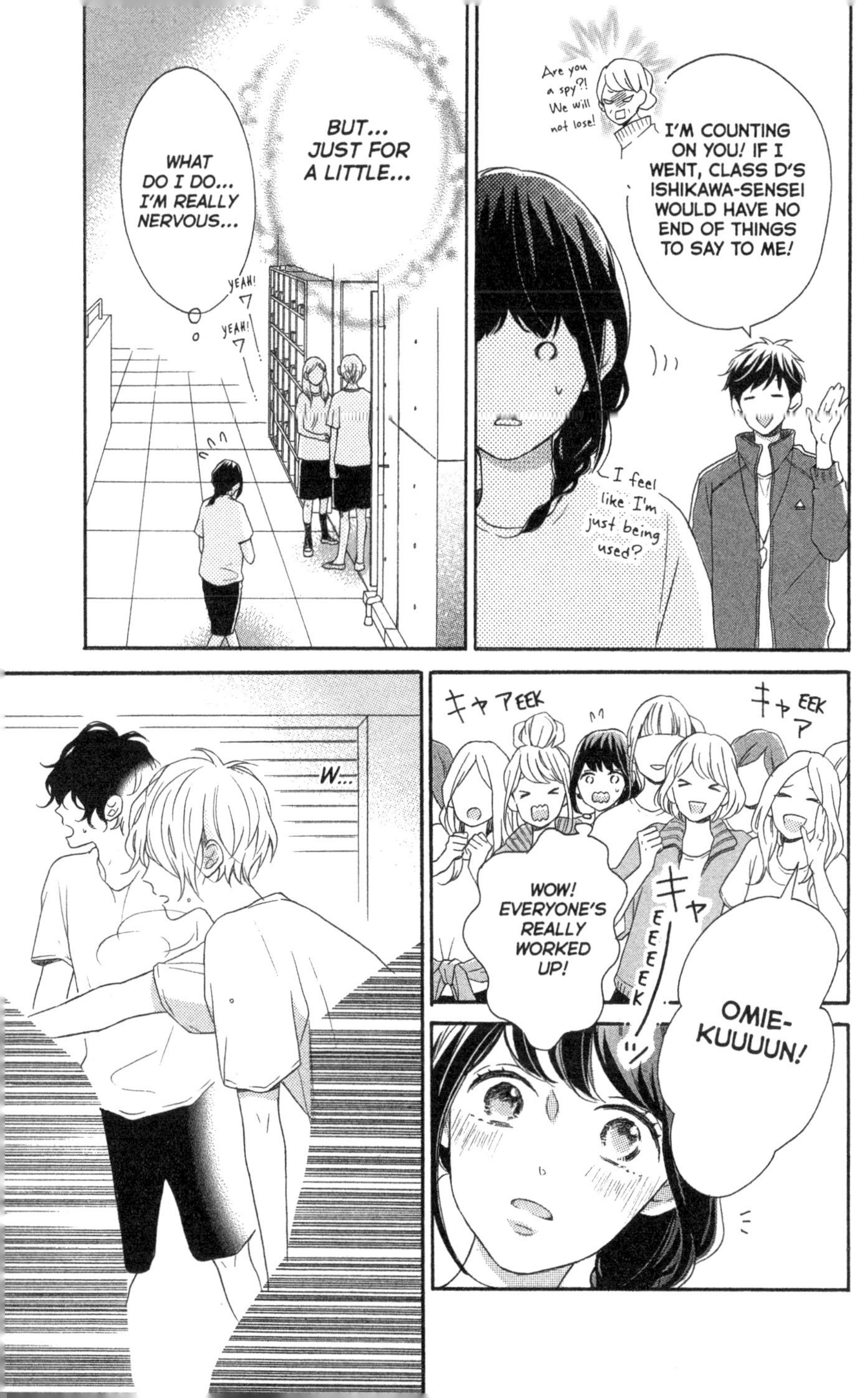
Are you a spy?! We will not lose!
I'M COUNTING ON YOU! IF I WENT, CLASS D'S ISHIKAWA-SENSEI WOULD HAVE NO END OF THINGS TO SAY TO ME!
I feel like I'm just being used?
BUT... JUST FOR A LITTLE...
WHAT DO I DO... I'M REALLY NERVOUS...
YEAH!
YEAH!
キャアEEK
キャアEEK
WOW! EVERYONE'S REALLY WORKED UP!
キャEEEEEK
OMIE-KUUUUN!
W...

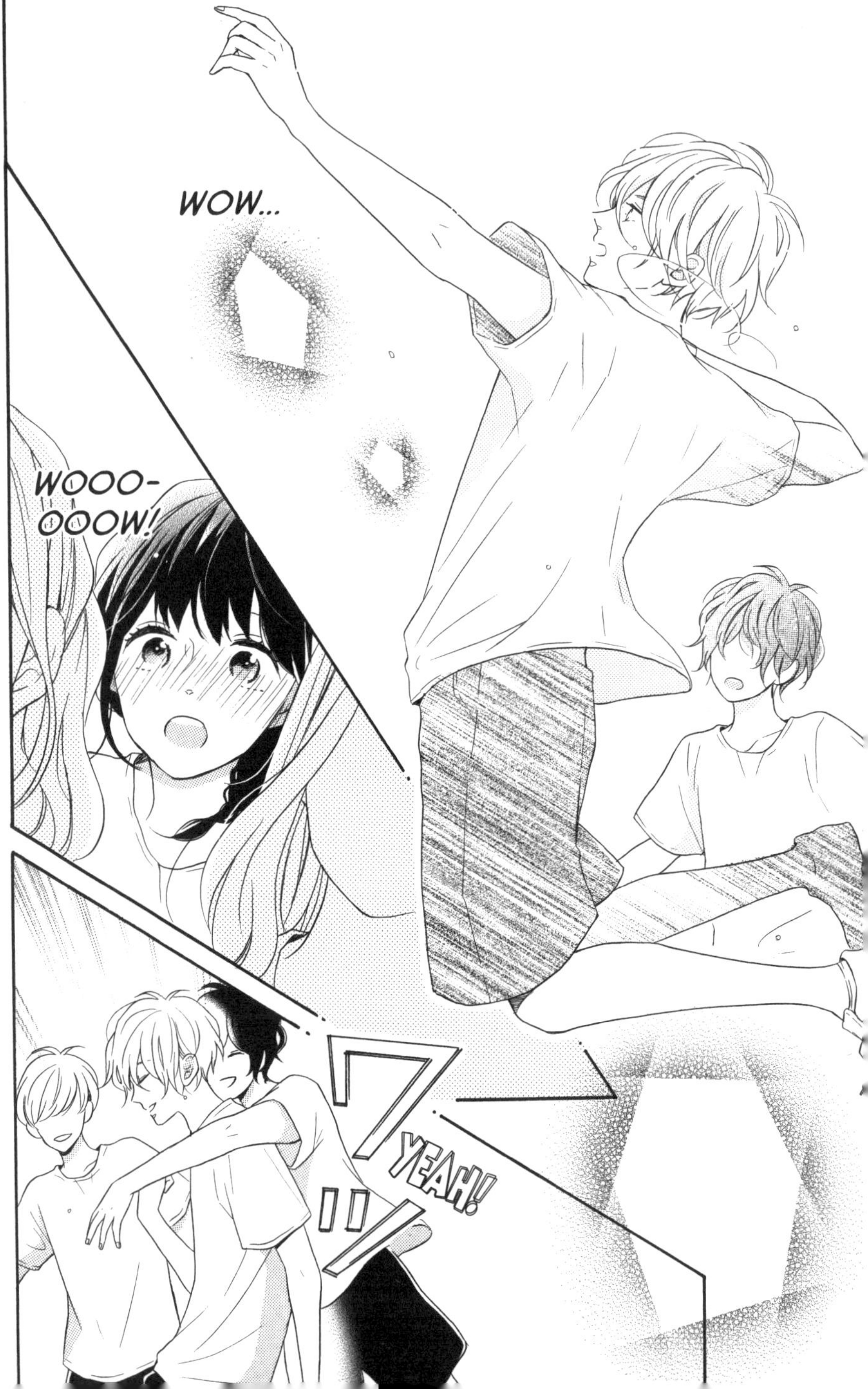
WOW...
WOOO-
OOOW!
YEAH!

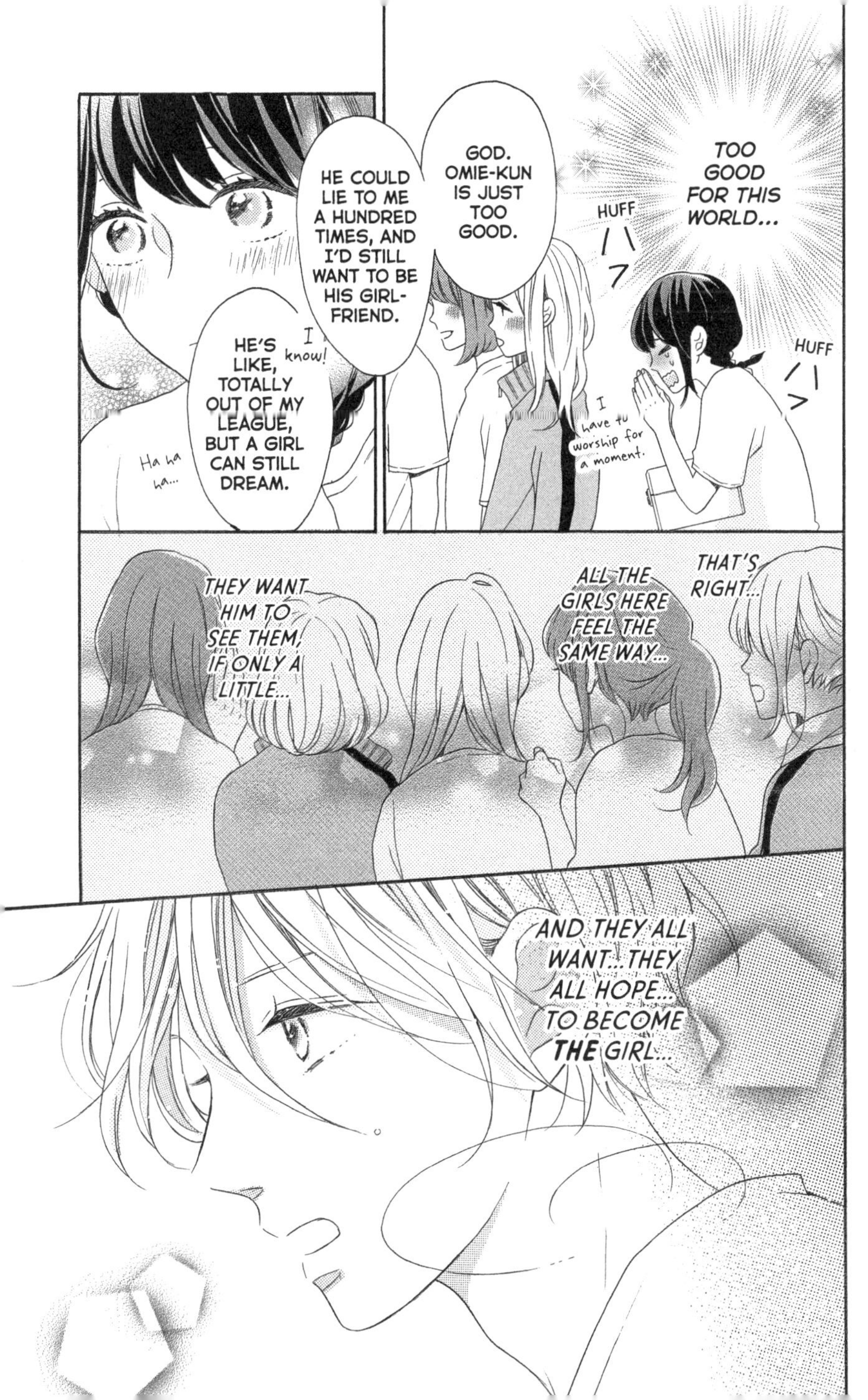
TOO GOOD FOR THIS WORLD...
HUFF
HUFF
I have to worship for a moment.
GOD. OMIE-KUN IS JUST TOO GOOD.
HE COULD LIE TO ME A HUNDRED TIMES, AND I'D STILL WANT TO BE HIS GIRL-FRIEND.
I know!
HE'S LIKE, TOTALLY OUT OF MY LEAGUE, BUT A GIRL CAN STILL DREAM.
Ha ha ha...
THAT'S RIGHT...
ALL THE GIRLS HERE FEEL THE SAME WAY...
THEY WANT HIM TO SEE THEM, IF ONLY A LITTLE...
AND THEY ALL WANT... THEY ALL HOPE... TO BECOME **THE** GIRL...

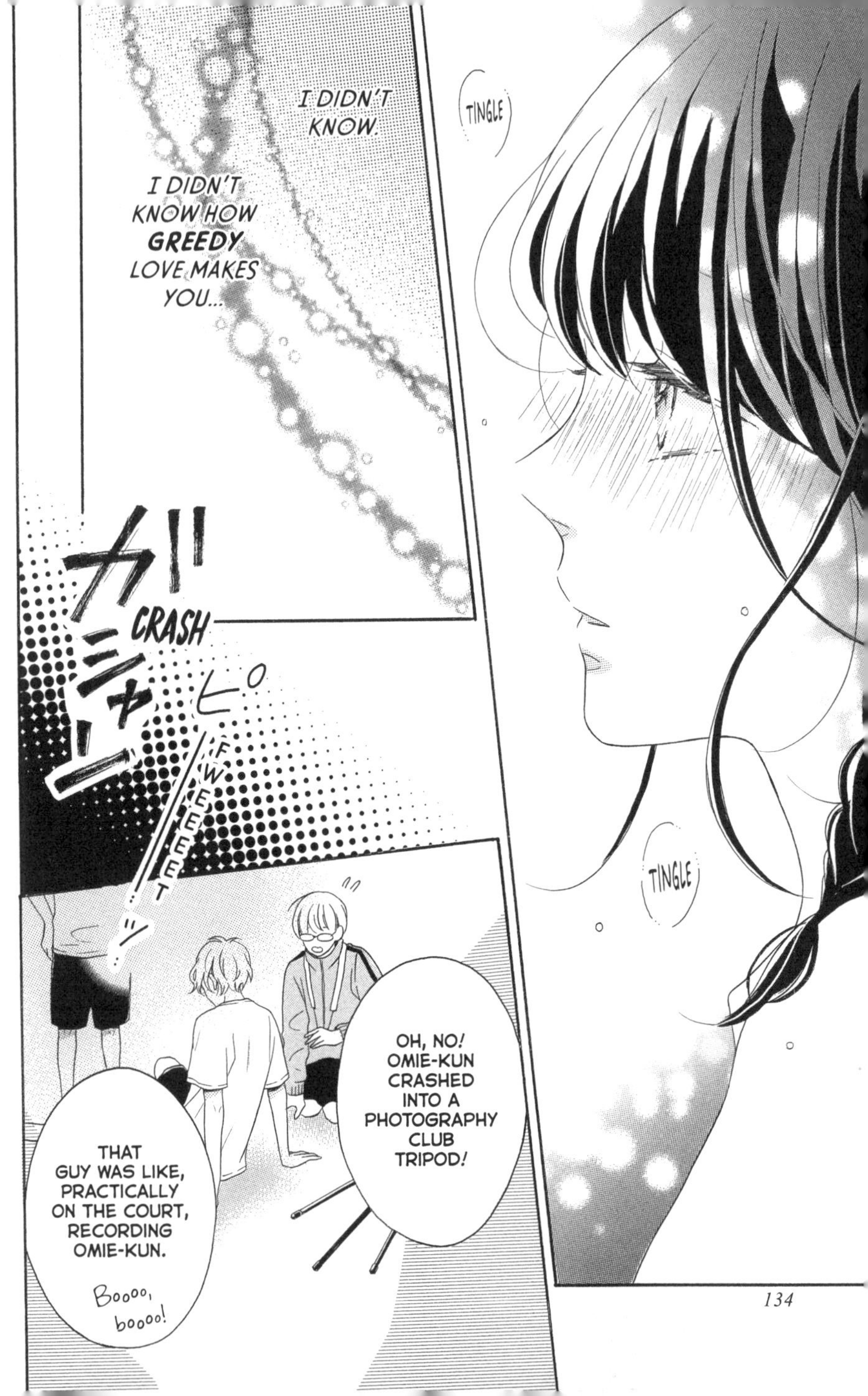
TINGLE
TINGLE
I DIDN'T KNOW.
I DIDN'T KNOW HOW **GREEDY** LOVE MAKES YOU...
CRASH
FWEEEET
OH, NO! OMIE-KUN CRASHED INTO A PHOTOGRAPHY CLUB TRIPOD!
THAT GUY WAS LIKE, PRACTICALLY ON THE COURT, RECORDING OMIE-KUN.
Boooo, boooo!

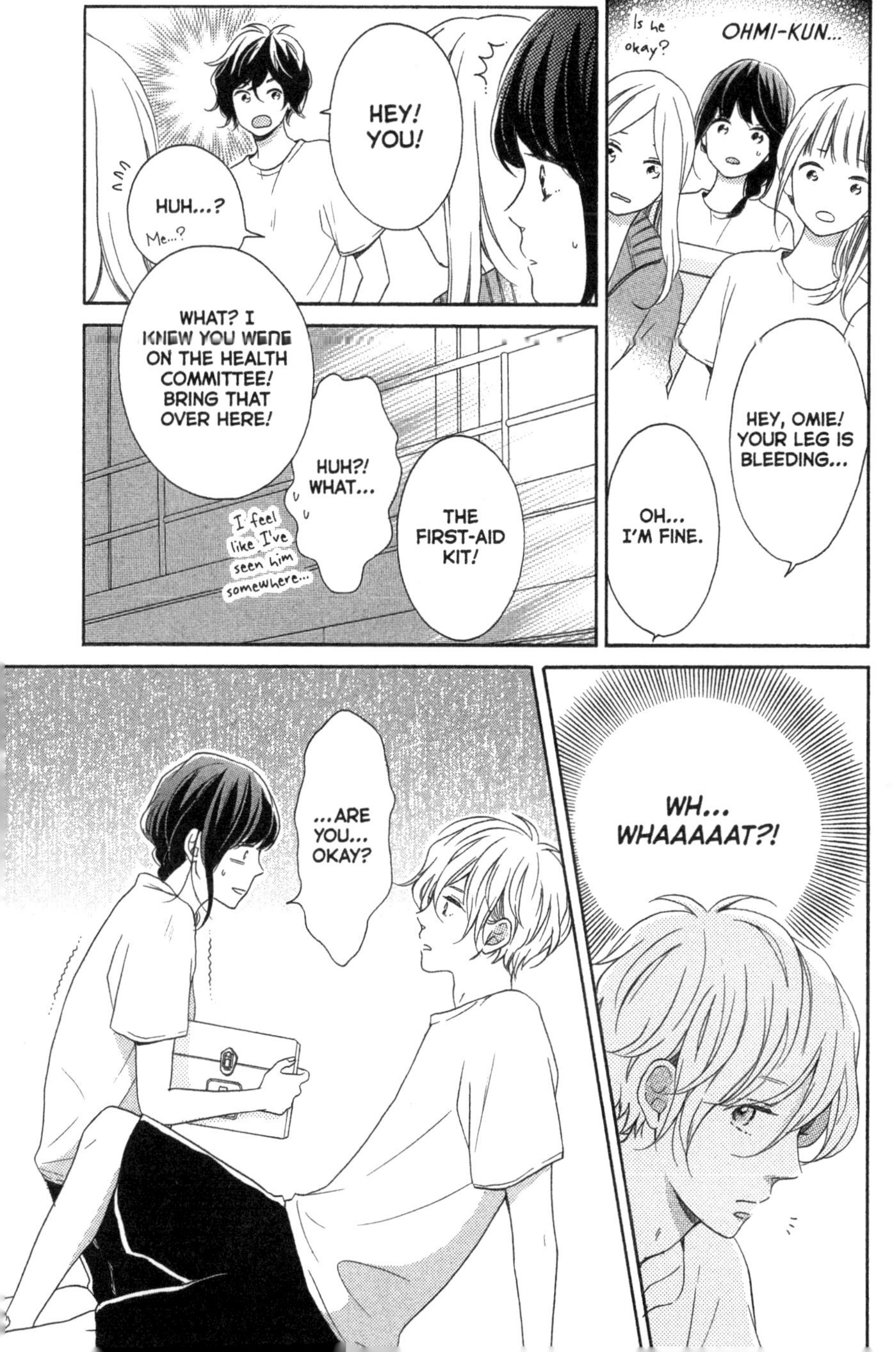
OHMI-KUN...
Is he okay?
HEY, OMIE! YOUR LEG IS BLEEDING...
OH... I'M FINE.
HEY! YOU!
HUH...?
Me...?
WHAT? I KNEW YOU WERE ON THE HEALTH COMMITTEE! BRING THAT OVER HERE!
THE FIRST-AID KIT!
HUH?! WHAT...
I feel like I've seen him somewhere...
WH... WHAAAAAT?!
...ARE YOU... OKAY?

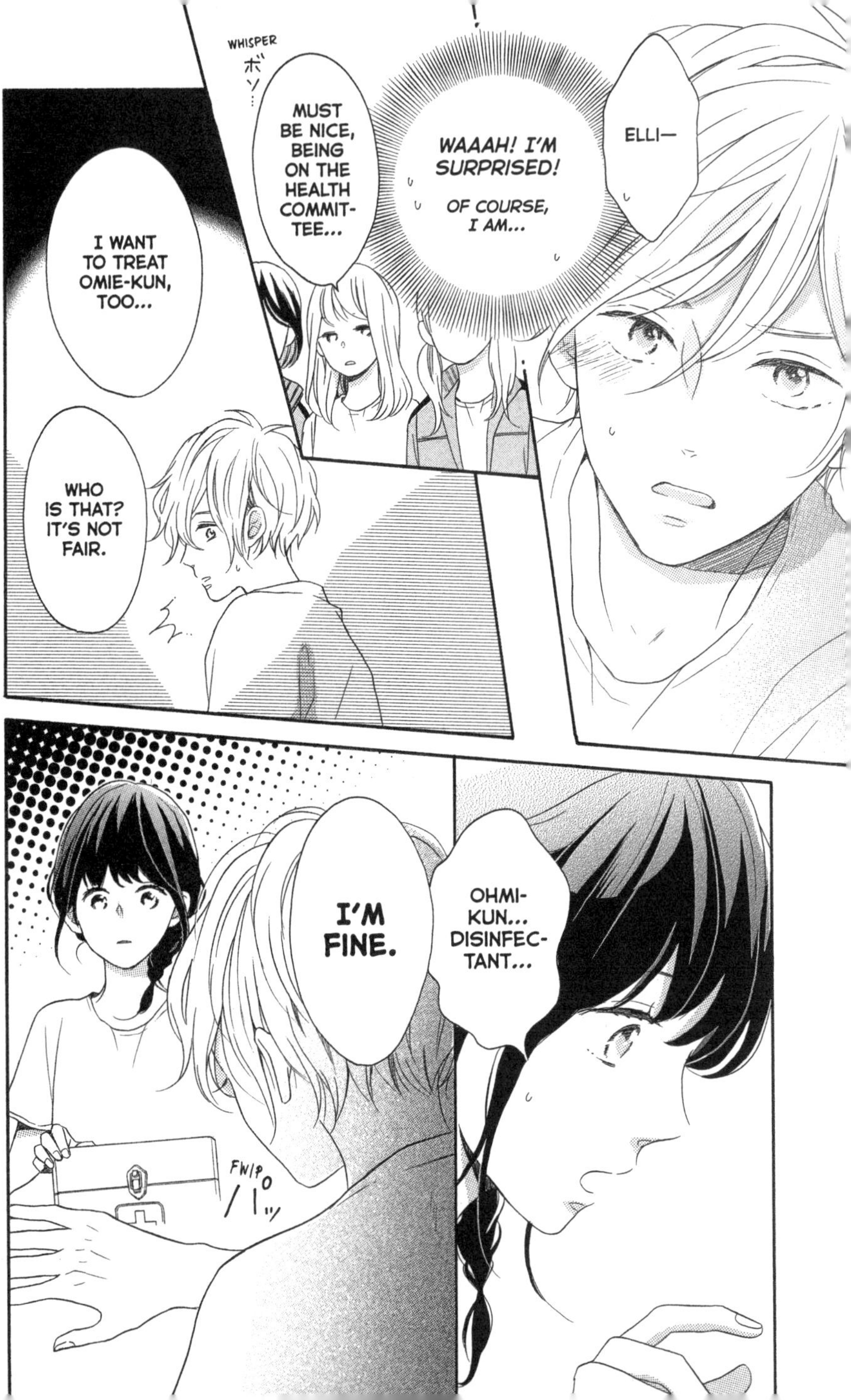
ELLI—
WAAAH! I'M SURPRISED!
OF COURSE, I AM...
WHISPER
ボソ…
MUST BE NICE, BEING ON THE HEALTH COMMIT-TEE...
I WANT TO TREAT OMIE-KUN, TOO...
WHO IS THAT? IT'S NOT FAIR.
OHMI-KUN... DISINFEC-TANT...
I'M FINE.
FWIP
パッ

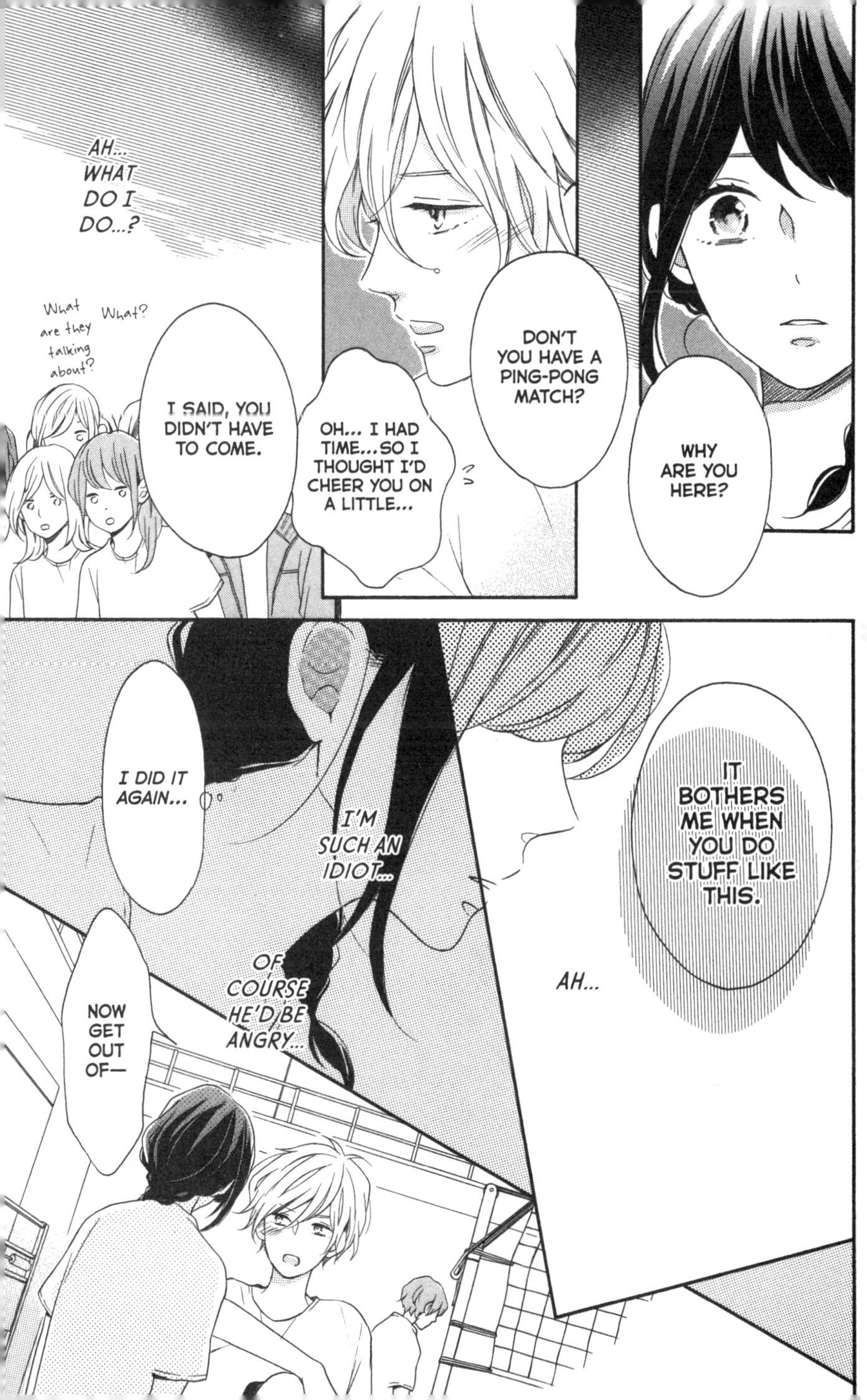
WHY ARE YOU HERE?
DON'T YOU HAVE A PING-PONG MATCH?
OH... I HAD TIME...SO I THOUGHT I'D CHEER YOU ON A LITTLE...
AH... WHAT DO I DO...?
What?
What are they talking about?
I SAID, YOU DIDN'T HAVE TO COME.
IT BOTHERS ME WHEN YOU DO STUFF LIKE THIS.
AH...
I'M SUCH AN IDIOT...
I DID IT AGAIN...
OF COURSE HE'D BE ANGRY...
NOW GET OUT OF—

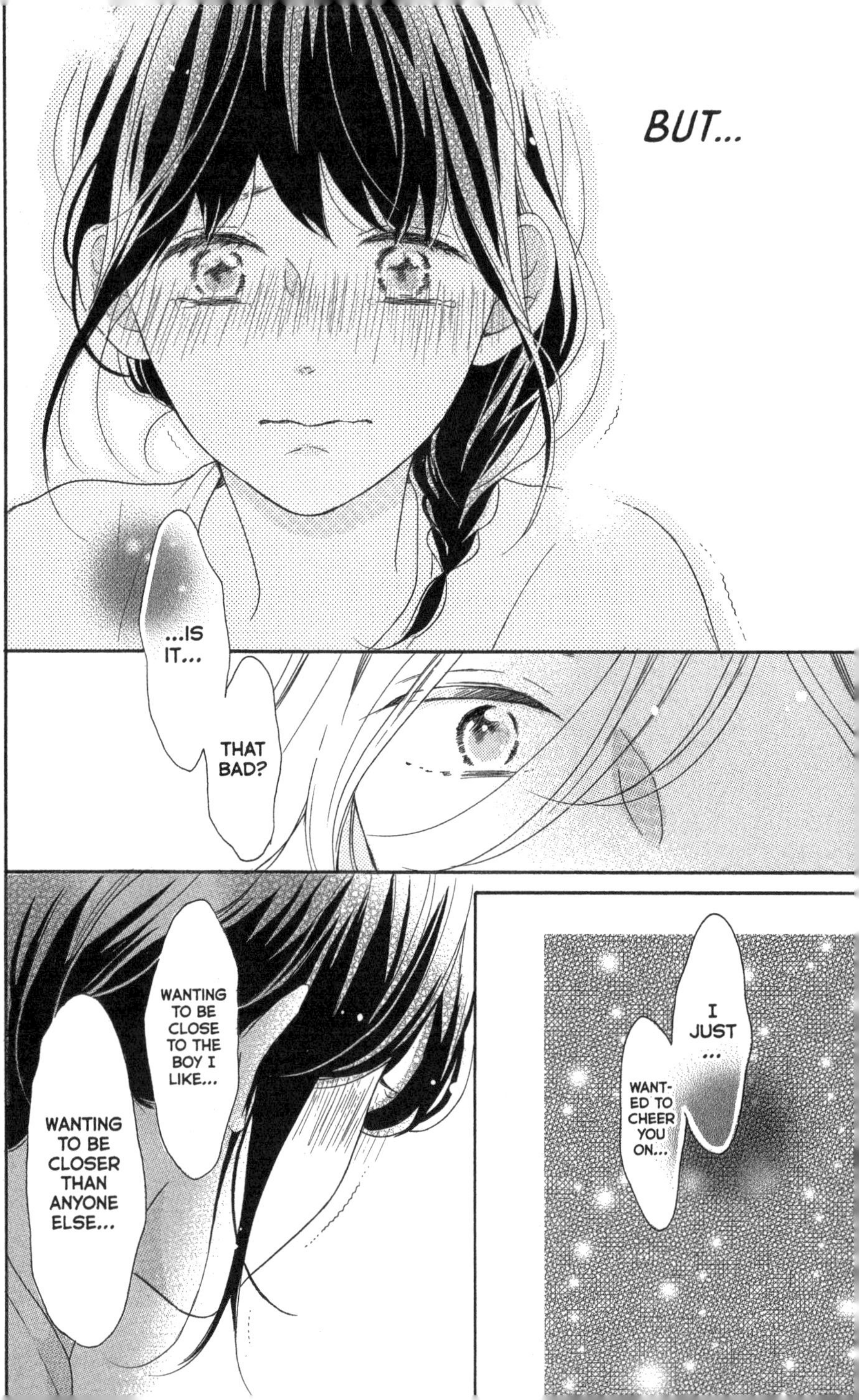
BUT...
...IS IT...
THAT BAD?
I JUST...
WANTED TO CHEER YOU ON...
WANTING TO BE CLOSE TO THE BOY I LIKE...
WANTING TO BE CLOSER THAN ANYONE ELSE...

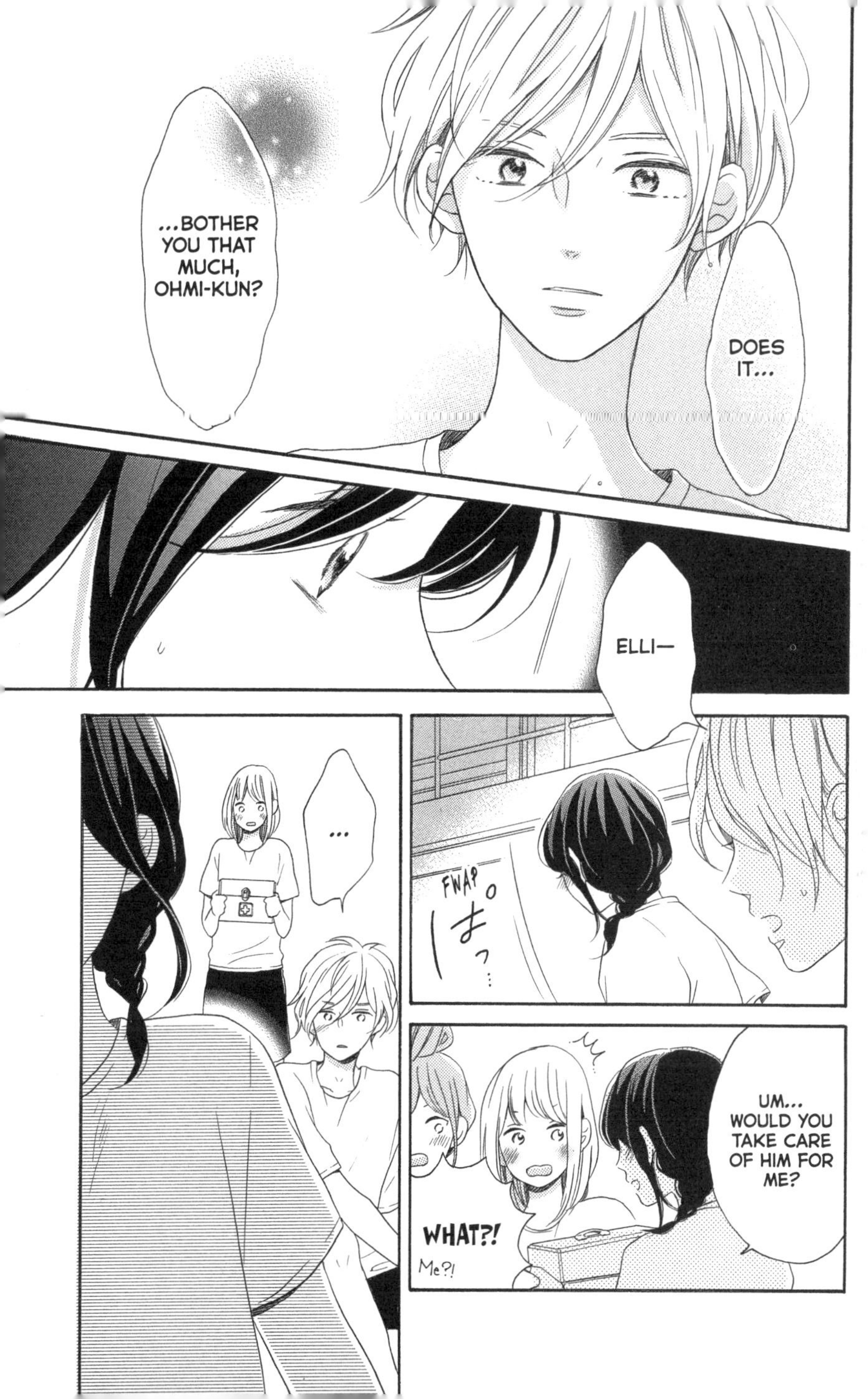
DOES IT...
...BOTHER YOU THAT MUCH, OHMI-KUN?
ELLI—
FWAP
UM... WOULD YOU TAKE CARE OF HIM FOR ME?
WHAT?!
Me?!
...

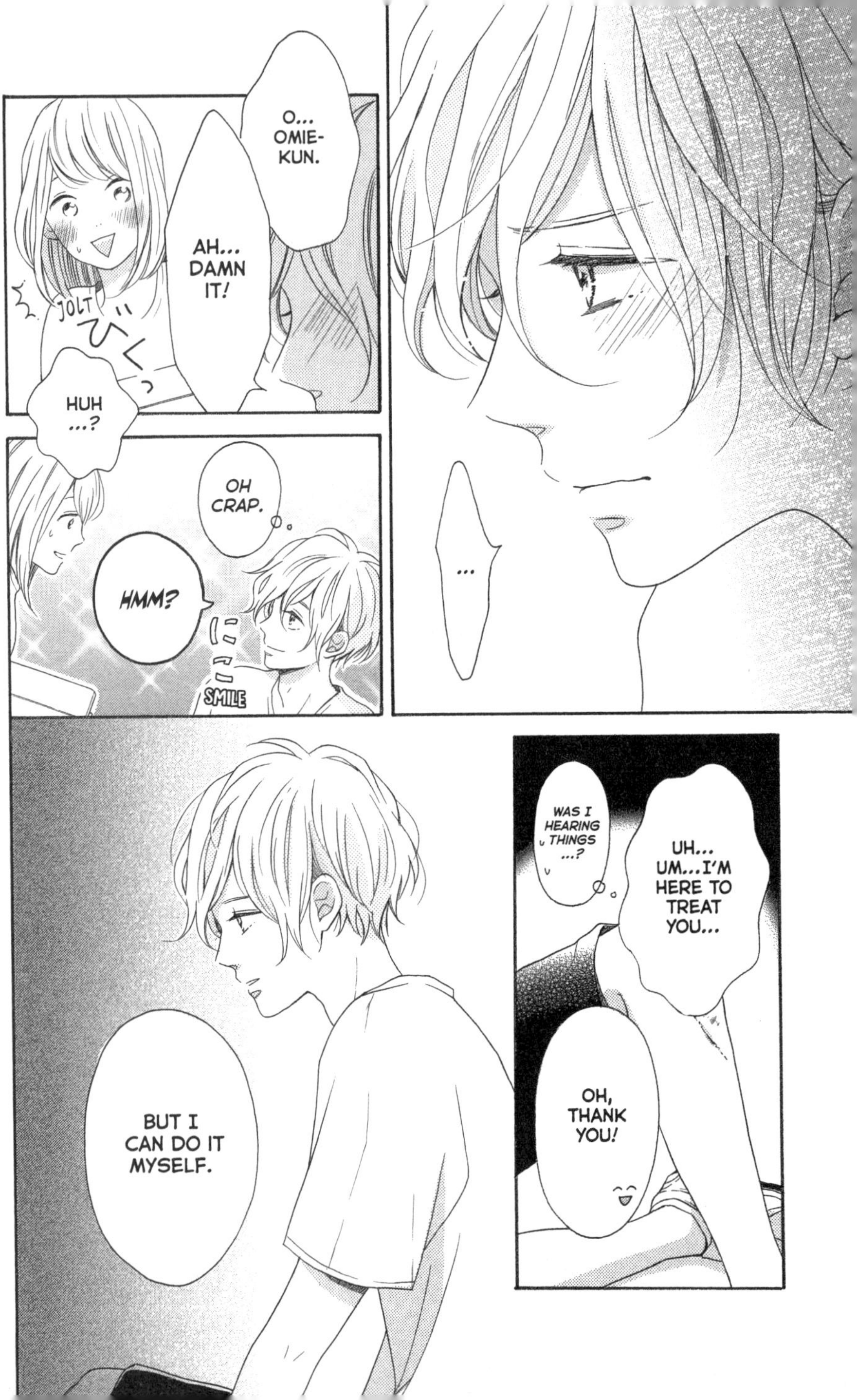
...
O... OMIE-KUN.
AH... DAMN IT!
JOLT
HUH ...?
OH CRAP.
HMM?
SMILE
UH... UM...I'M HERE TO TREAT YOU...
WAS I HEARING THINGS ...?
OH, THANK YOU!
BUT I CAN DO IT MYSELF.

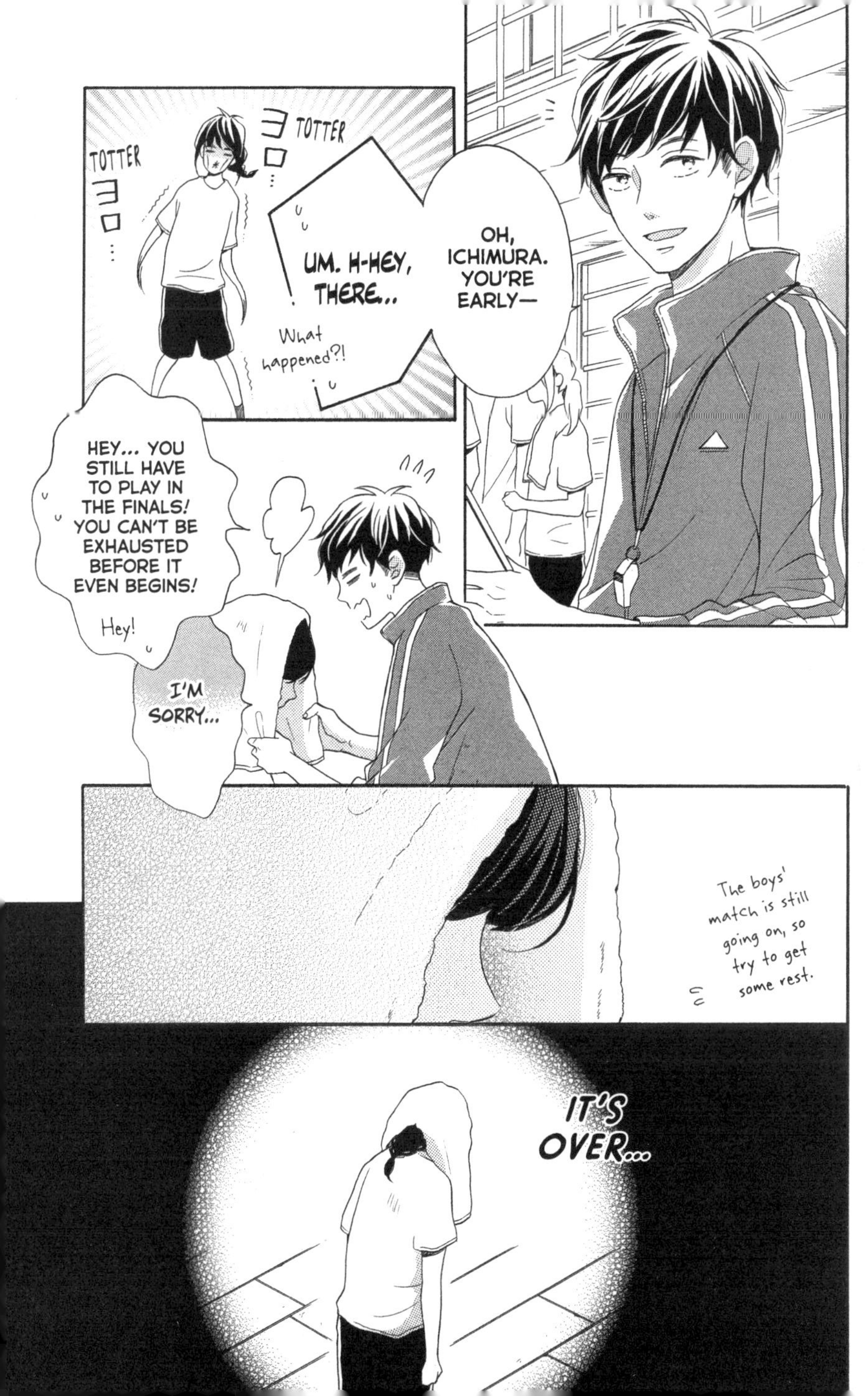
OH, ICHIMURA. YOU'RE EARLY—
TOTTER
ヨロ…
UM. H-HEY, THERE...
What happened?!
TOTTER
ヨロ…
HEY... YOU STILL HAVE TO PLAY IN THE FINALS! YOU CAN'T BE EXHAUSTED BEFORE IT EVEN BEGINS!
Hey!
I'M SORRY...
The boys' match is still going on, so try to get some rest.
IT'S OVER...

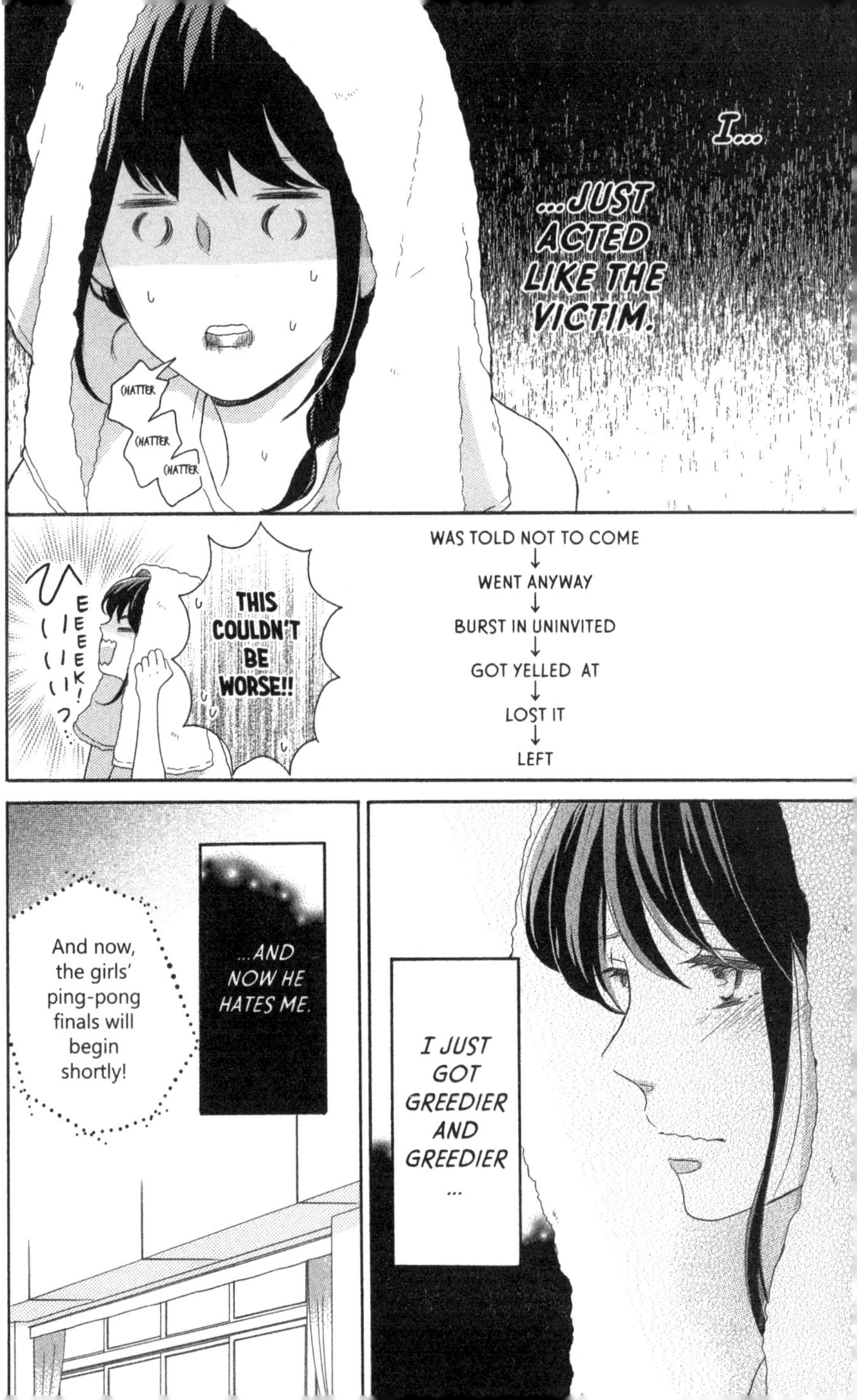
I...
...JUST ACTED LIKE THE VICTIM.
CHATTER
CHATTER
CHATTER
WAS TOLD NOT TO COME ↓ WENT ANYWAY ↓ BURST IN UNINVITED ↓ GOT YELLED AT ↓ LOST IT ↓ LEFT
THIS COULDN'T BE WORSE!!
EEEEK!
I JUST GOT GREEDIER AND GREEDIER ...
...AND NOW HE HATES ME.
And now, the girls' ping-pong finals will begin shortly!

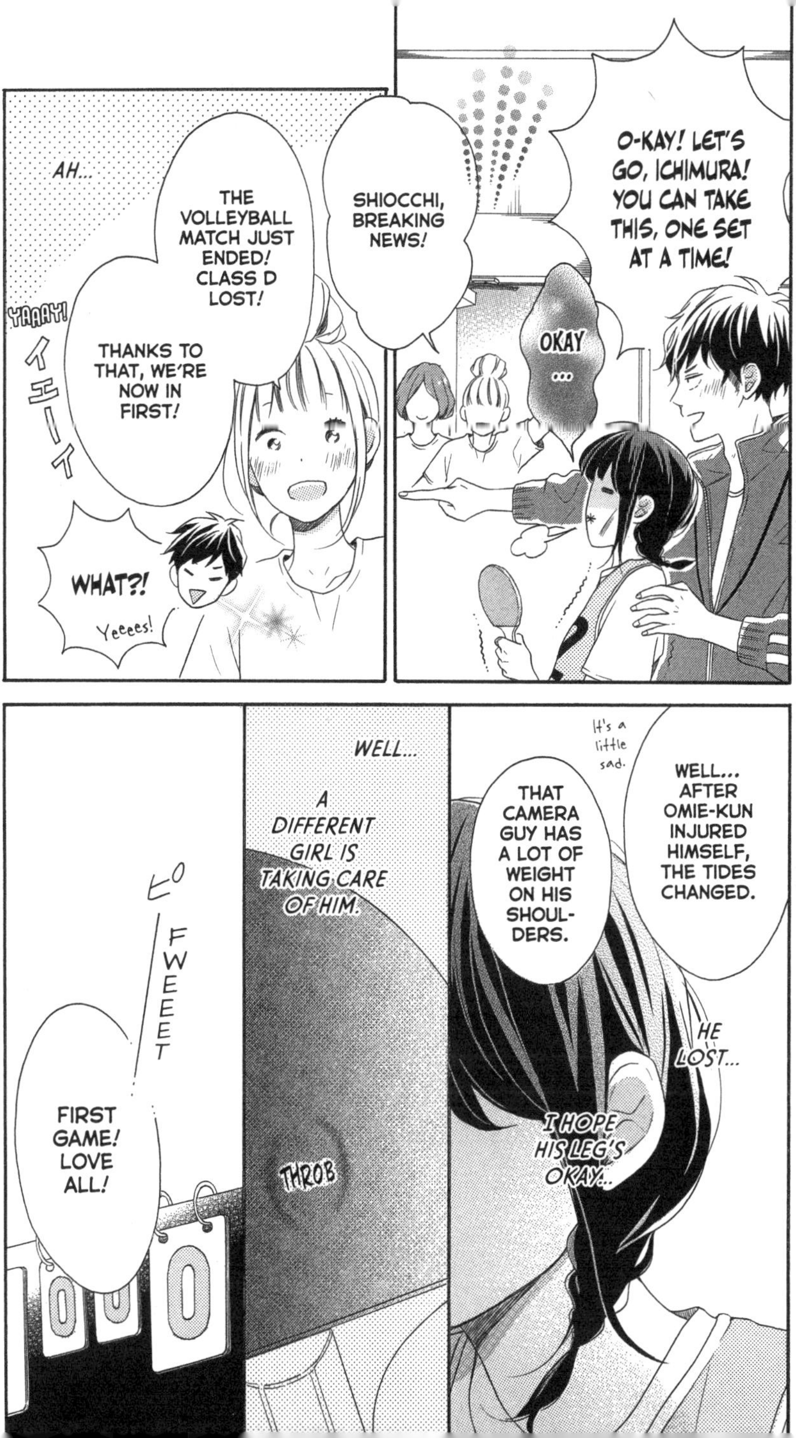
O-KAY! LET'S GO, ICHIMURA! YOU CAN TAKE THIS, ONE SET AT A TIME!
OKAY ...
SHIOCCHI, BREAKING NEWS!
THE VOLLEYBALL MATCH JUST ENDED! CLASS D LOST!
THANKS TO THAT, WE'RE NOW IN FIRST!
AH...
YAAAY!
イエーイ
WHAT?!
Yeeees!
It's a little sad.
WELL... AFTER OMIE-KUN INJURED HIMSELF, THE TIDES CHANGED.
THAT CAMERA GUY HAS A LOT OF WEIGHT ON HIS SHOULDERS.
HE LOST...
I HOPE HIS LEG'S OKAY...
WELL...
A DIFFERENT GIRL IS TAKING CARE OF HIM.
THROB
ピ
FWEEET
FIRST GAME! LOVE ALL!

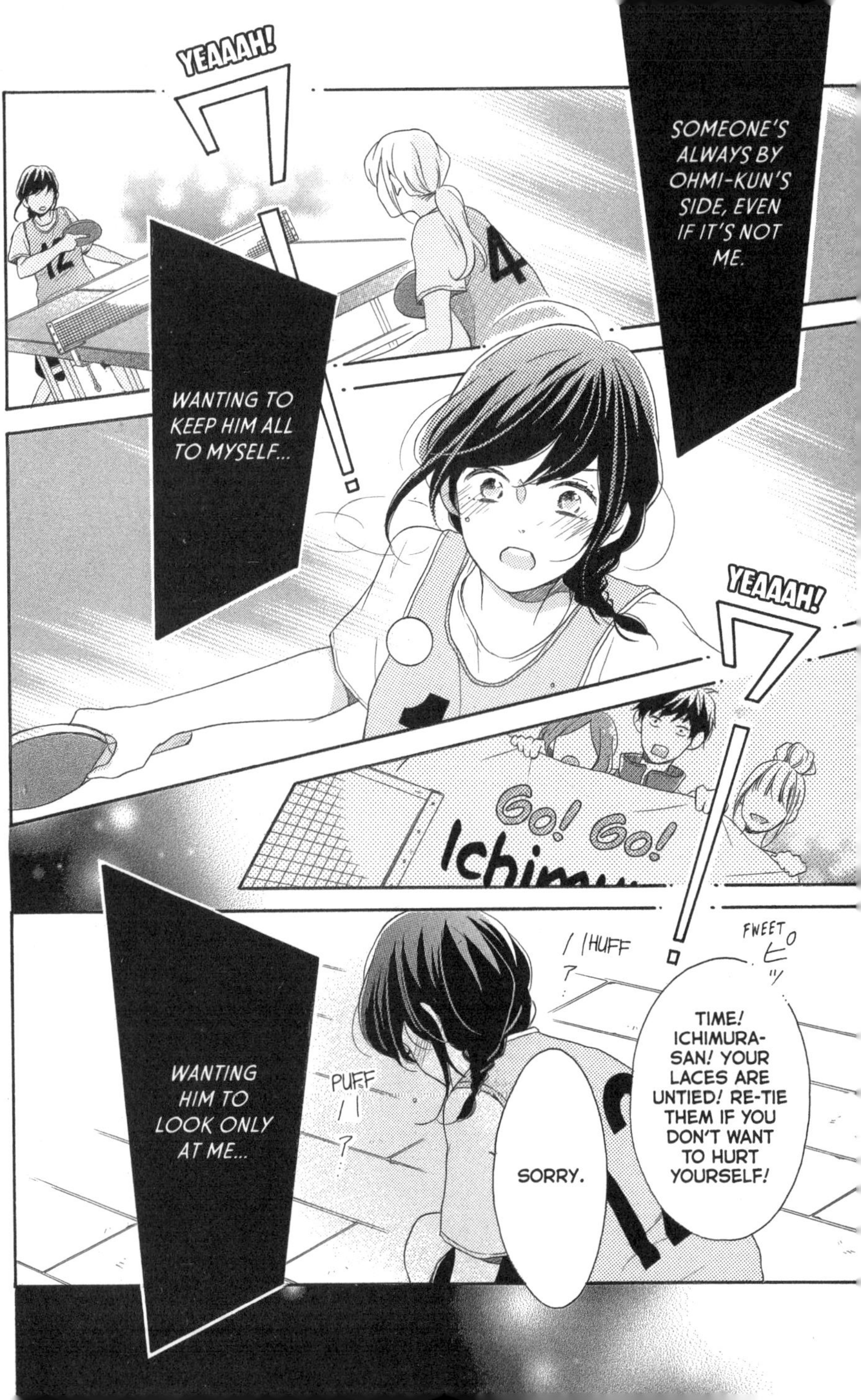

SOMEONE'S ALWAYS BY OHMI-KUN'S SIDE, EVEN IF IT'S NOT ME.
YEAAAH!
WANTING TO KEEP HIM ALL TO MYSELF...
YEAAAH!
Go! Go! Ichimu...
FWEET
TIME! ICHIMURA-SAN! YOUR LACES ARE UNTIED! RE-TIE THEM IF YOU DON'T WANT TO HURT YOURSELF!
HUFF
SORRY.
PUFF
WANTING HIM TO LOOK ONLY AT ME...

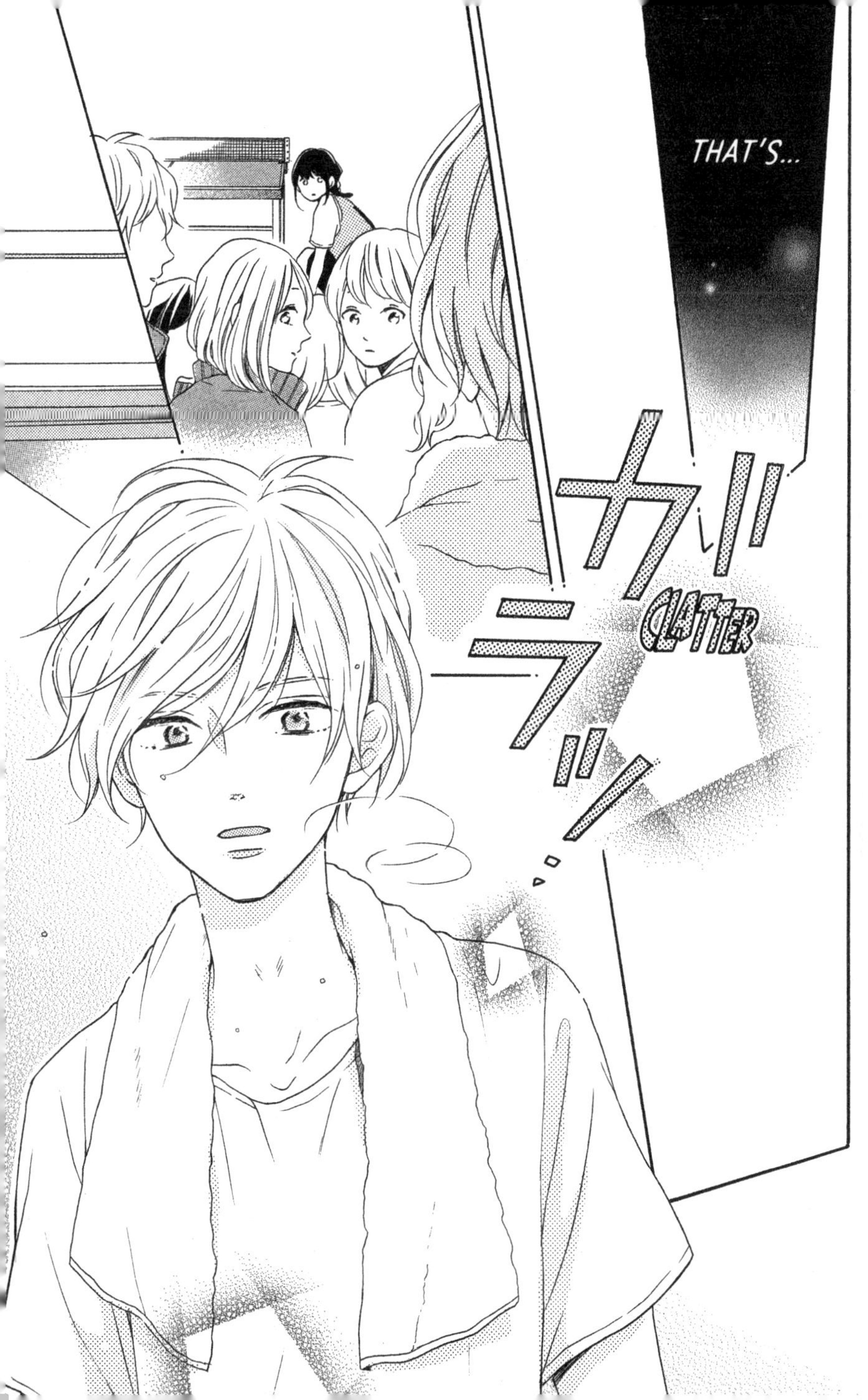
THAT'S...
カラッ
CLATTER

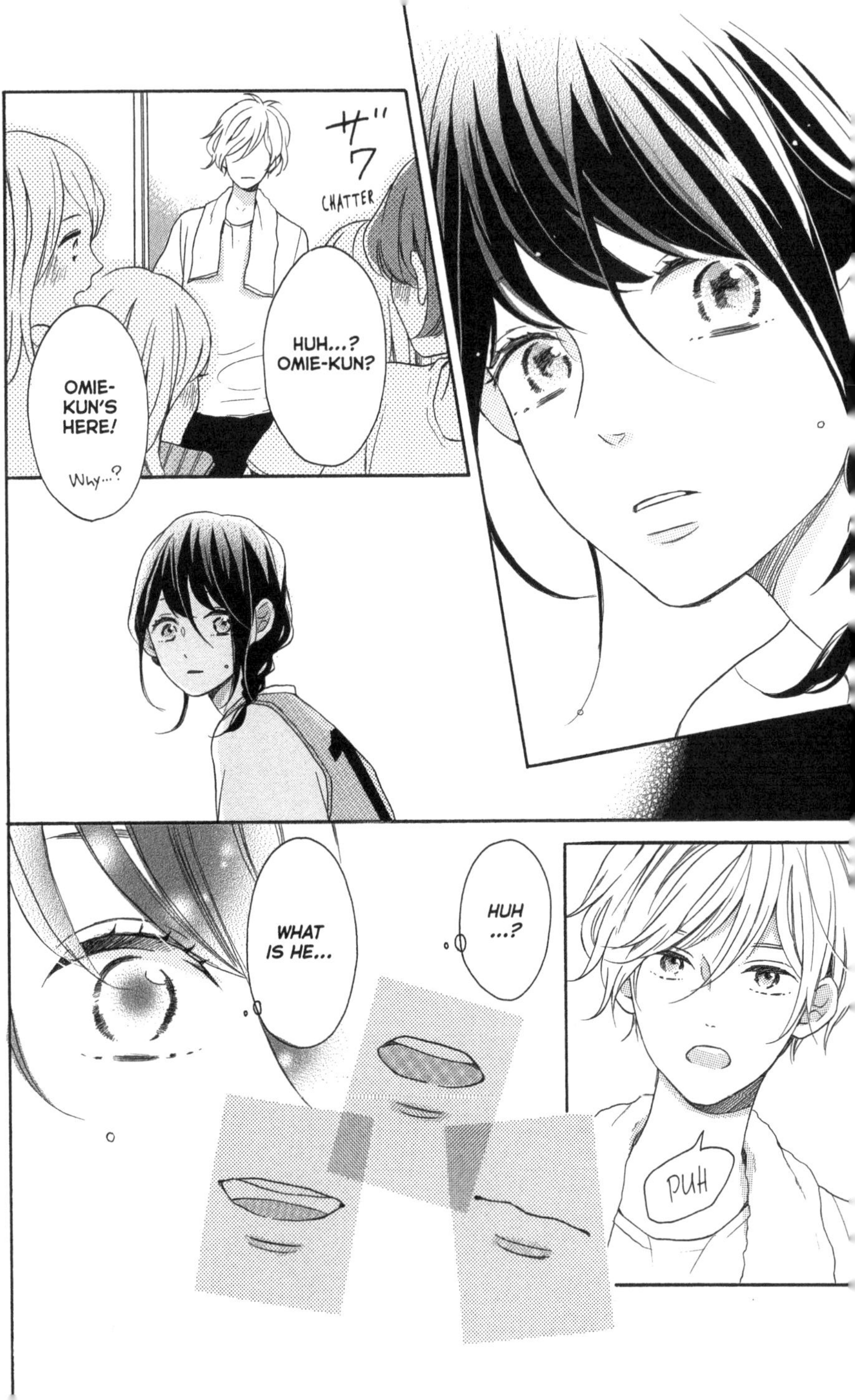
ザワ
CHATTER
HUH...? OMIE-KUN?
OMIE-KUN'S HERE!
Why...?
PUH
HUH ...?
WHAT IS HE...

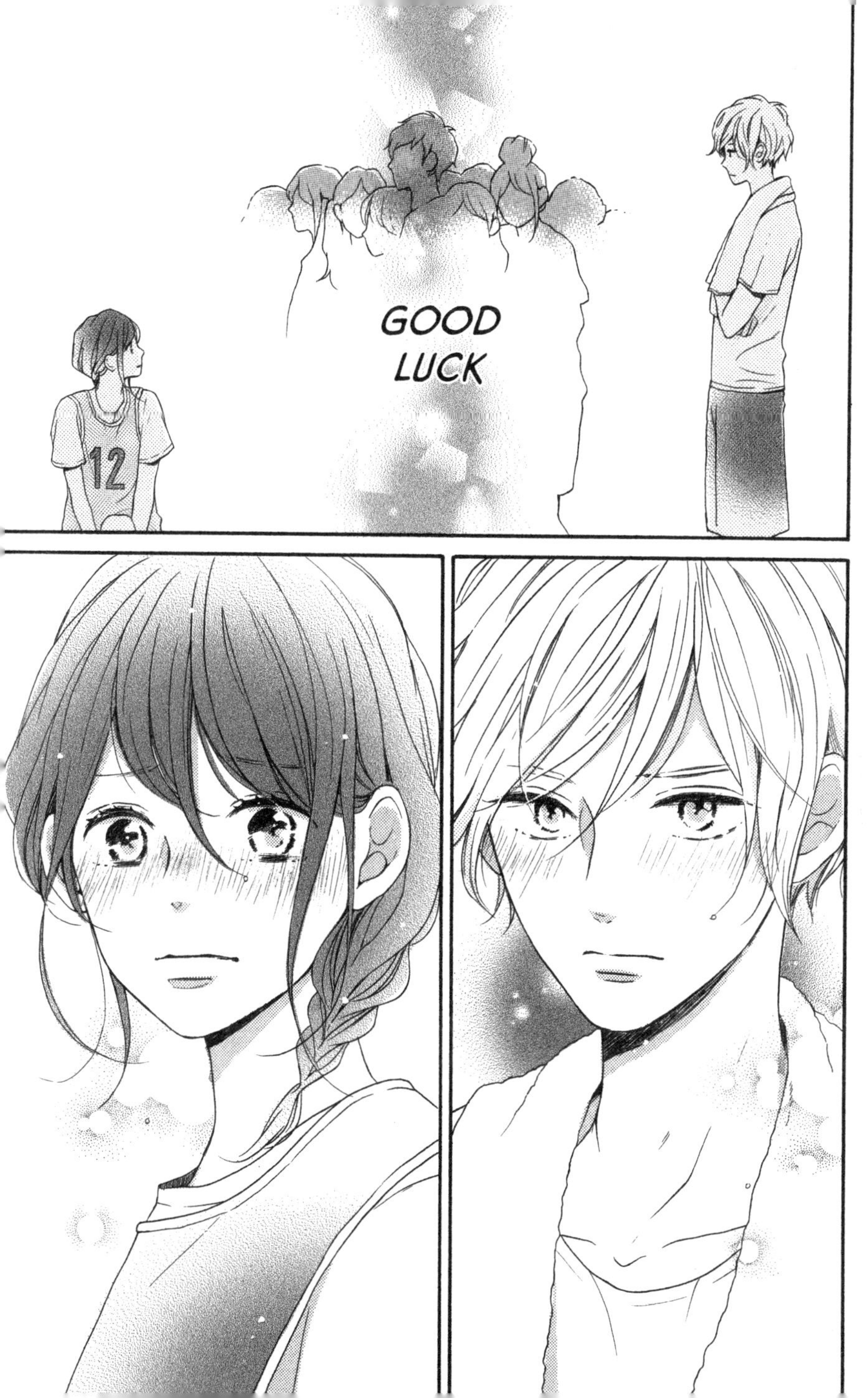
GOOD
LUCK

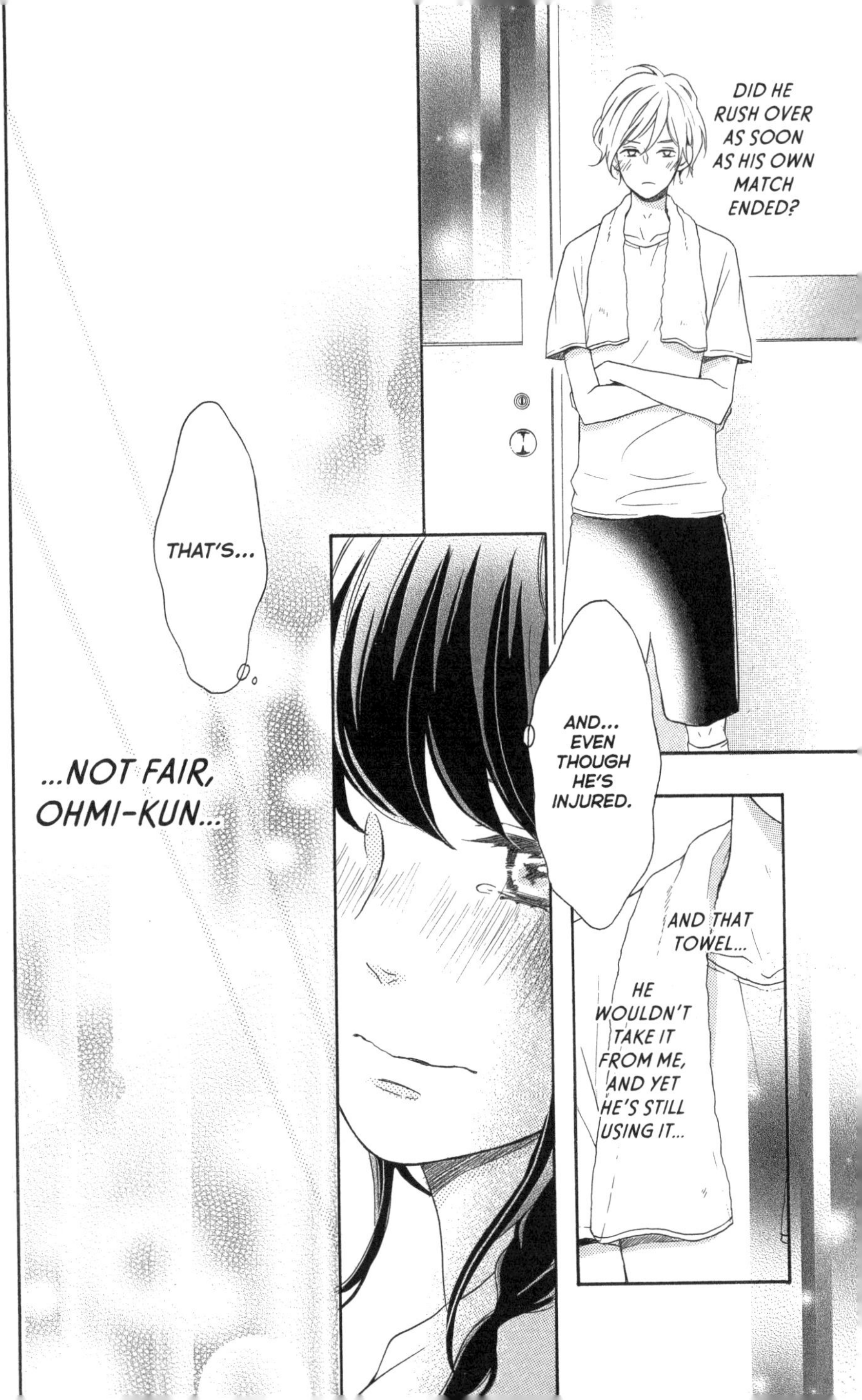
DID HE RUSH OVER AS SOON AS HIS OWN MATCH ENDED?
AND... EVEN THOUGH HE'S INJURED.
AND THAT TOWEL...
HE WOULDN'T TAKE IT FROM ME, AND YET HE'S STILL USING IT...
THAT'S...
...NOT FAIR, OHMI-KUN...

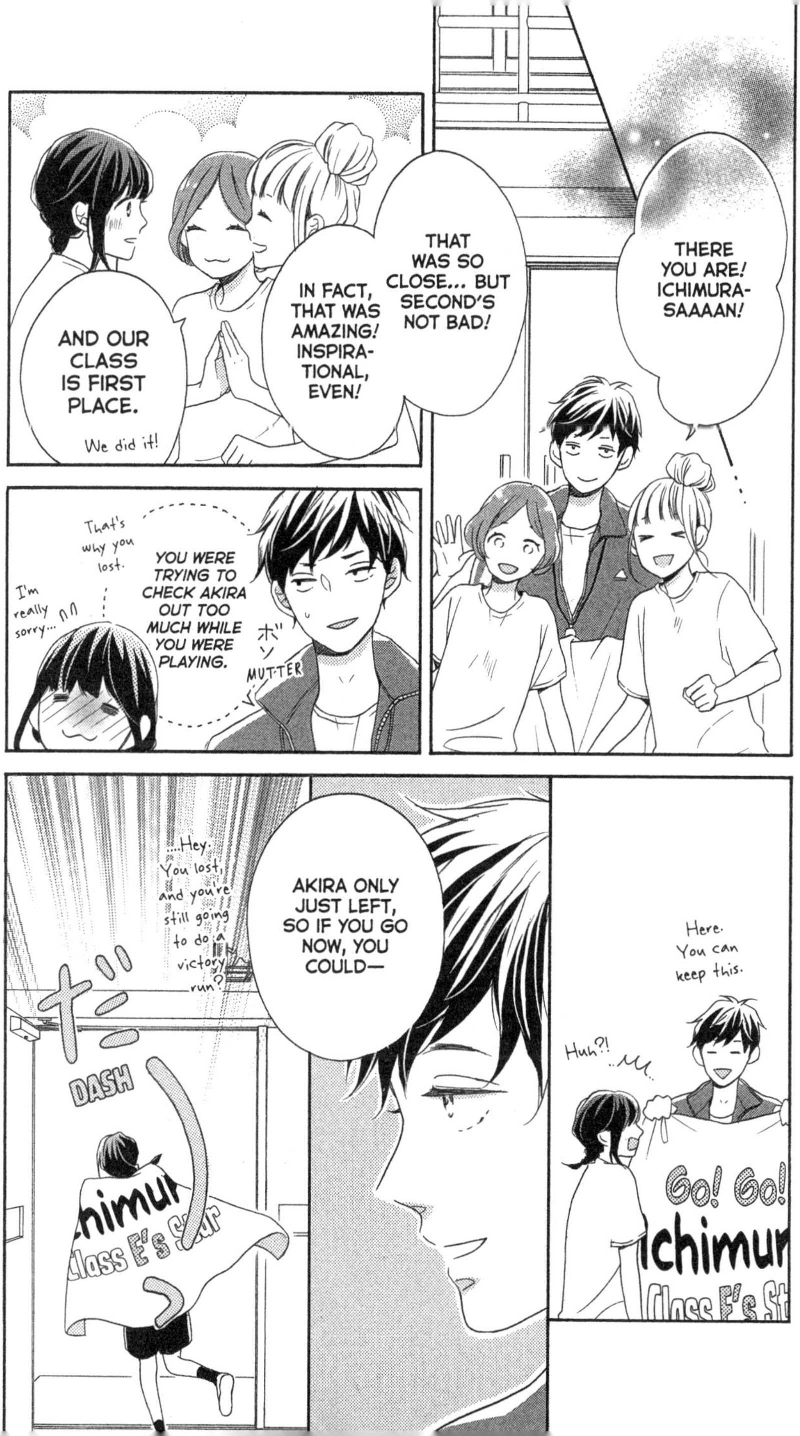
THERE YOU ARE! ICHIMURA-SAAAAN!
THAT WAS SO CLOSE... BUT SECOND'S NOT BAD!
IN FACT, THAT WAS AMAZING! INSPIRATIONAL, EVEN!
AND OUR CLASS IS FIRST PLACE.
We did it!
YOU WERE TRYING TO CHECK AKIRA OUT TOO MUCH WHILE YOU WERE PLAYING.
ボソ
MUTTER
That's why you lost.
I'm really sorry...
Here. You can keep this.
Huh?!
Go! Go!
AKIRA ONLY JUST LEFT, SO IF YOU GO NOW, YOU COULD—
...Hey. You lost, and you're still going to do a victory run?
DASH

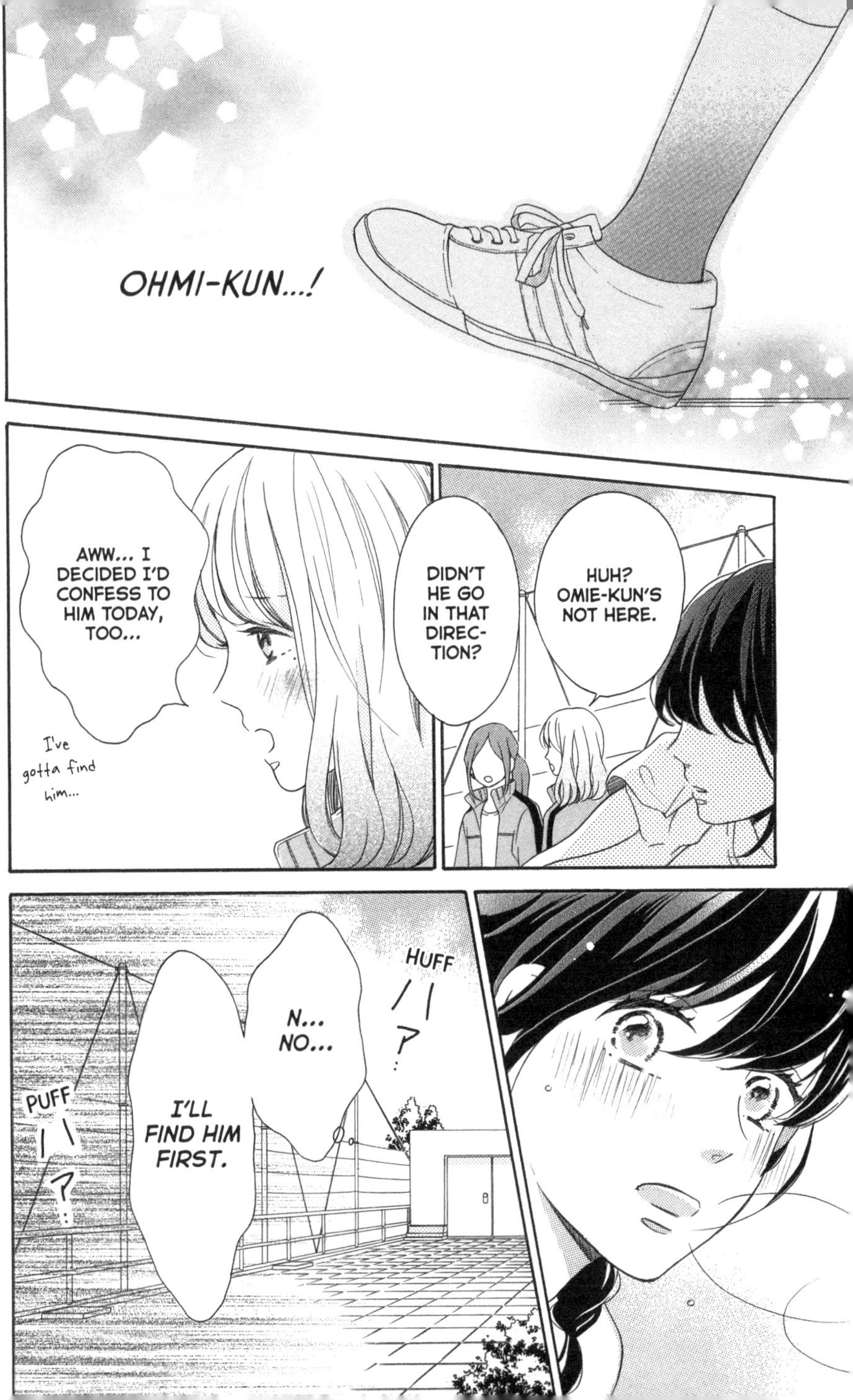
OHMI-KUN...!
HUH? OMIE-KUN'S NOT HERE.
DIDN'T HE GO IN THAT DIREC- TION?
AWW... I DECIDED I'D CONFESS TO HIM TODAY, TOO...
I've gotta find him...
HUFF
N... NO...
I'LL FIND HIM FIRST.
PUFF

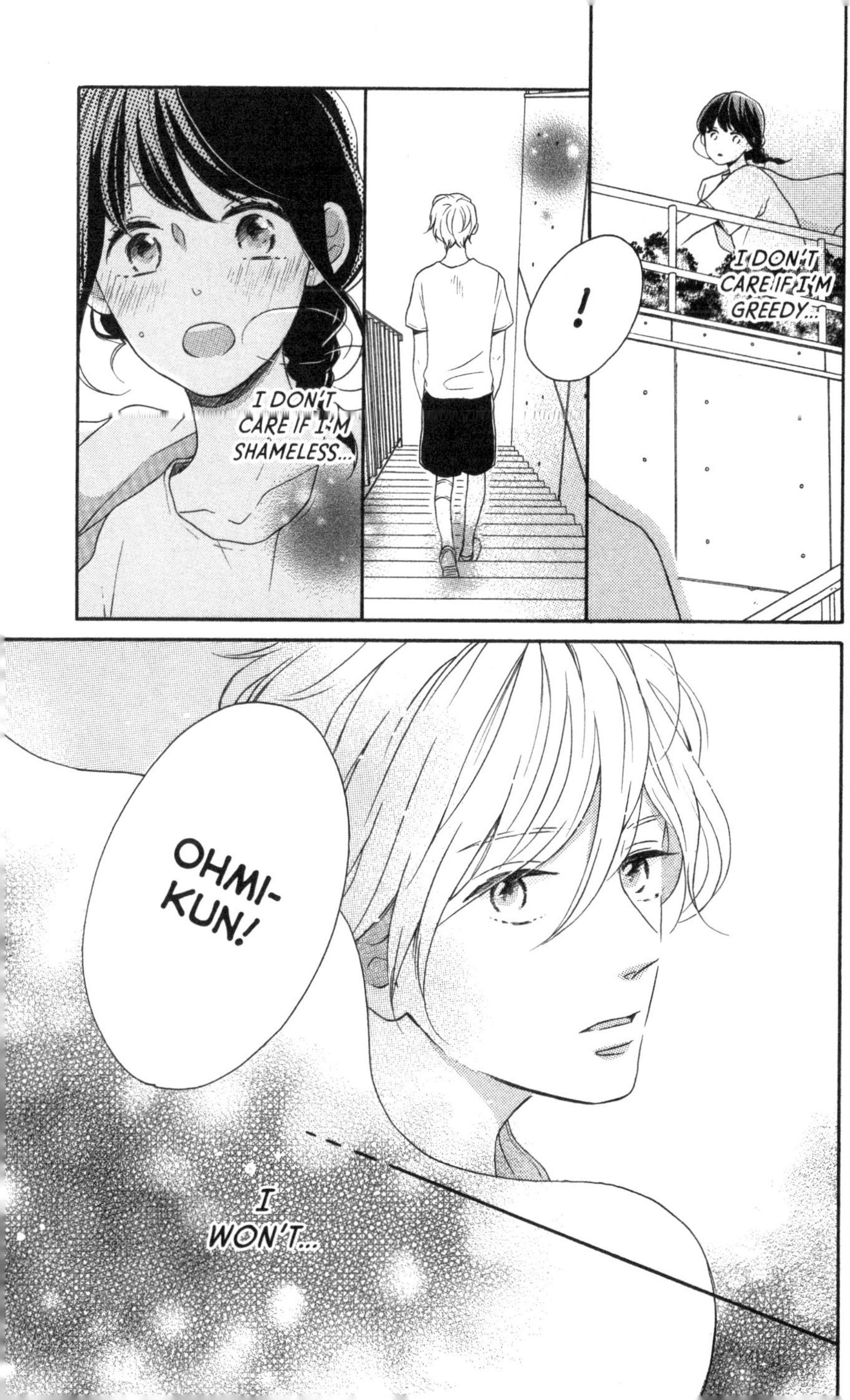
I DON'T CARE IF I'M GREEDY...
!
I DON'T CARE IF I'M SHAMELESS...
OHMI-KUN!
I WON'T...

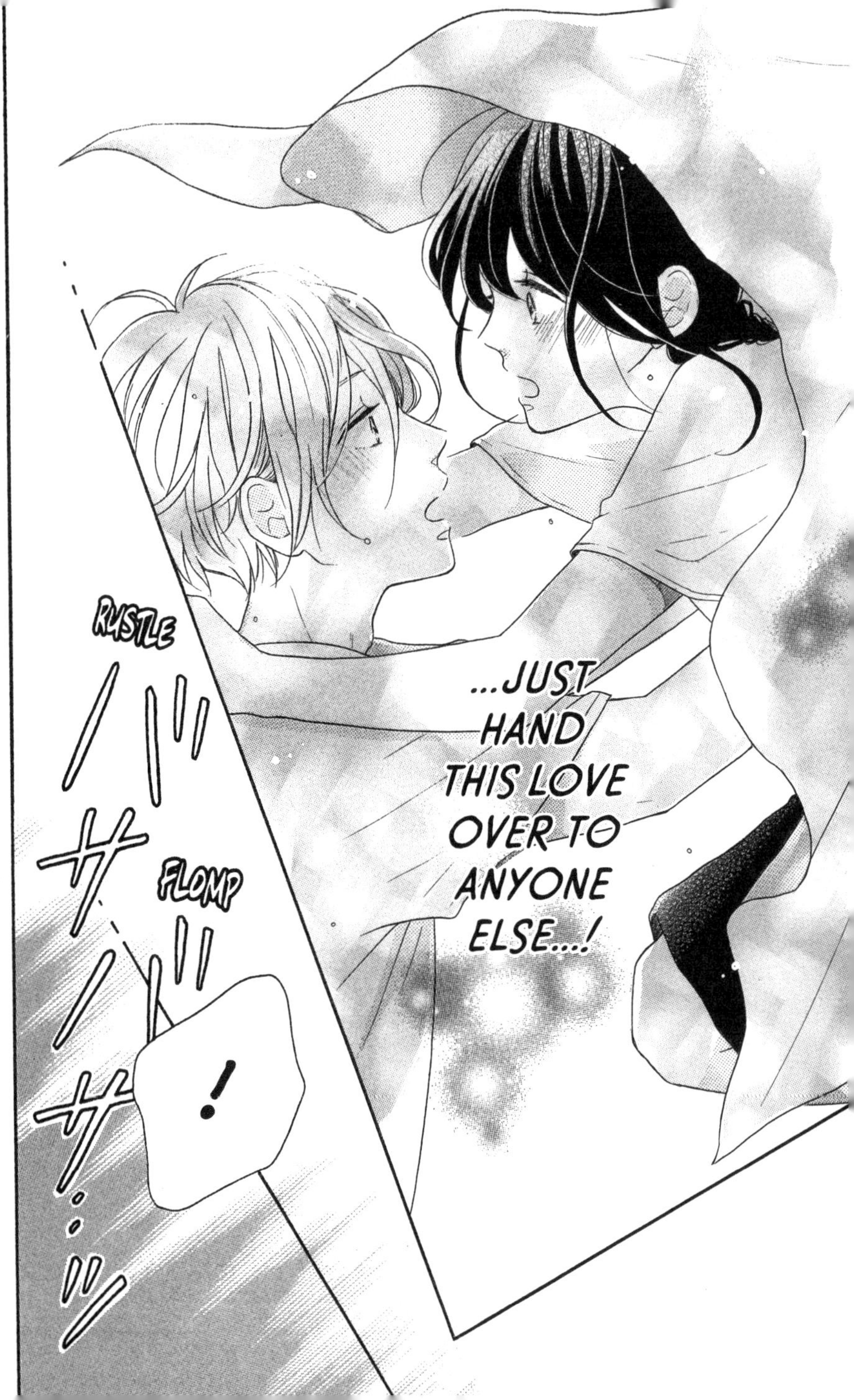
...JUST HAND THIS LOVE OVER TO ANYONE ELSE...!
RUSTLE
FLOMP
!

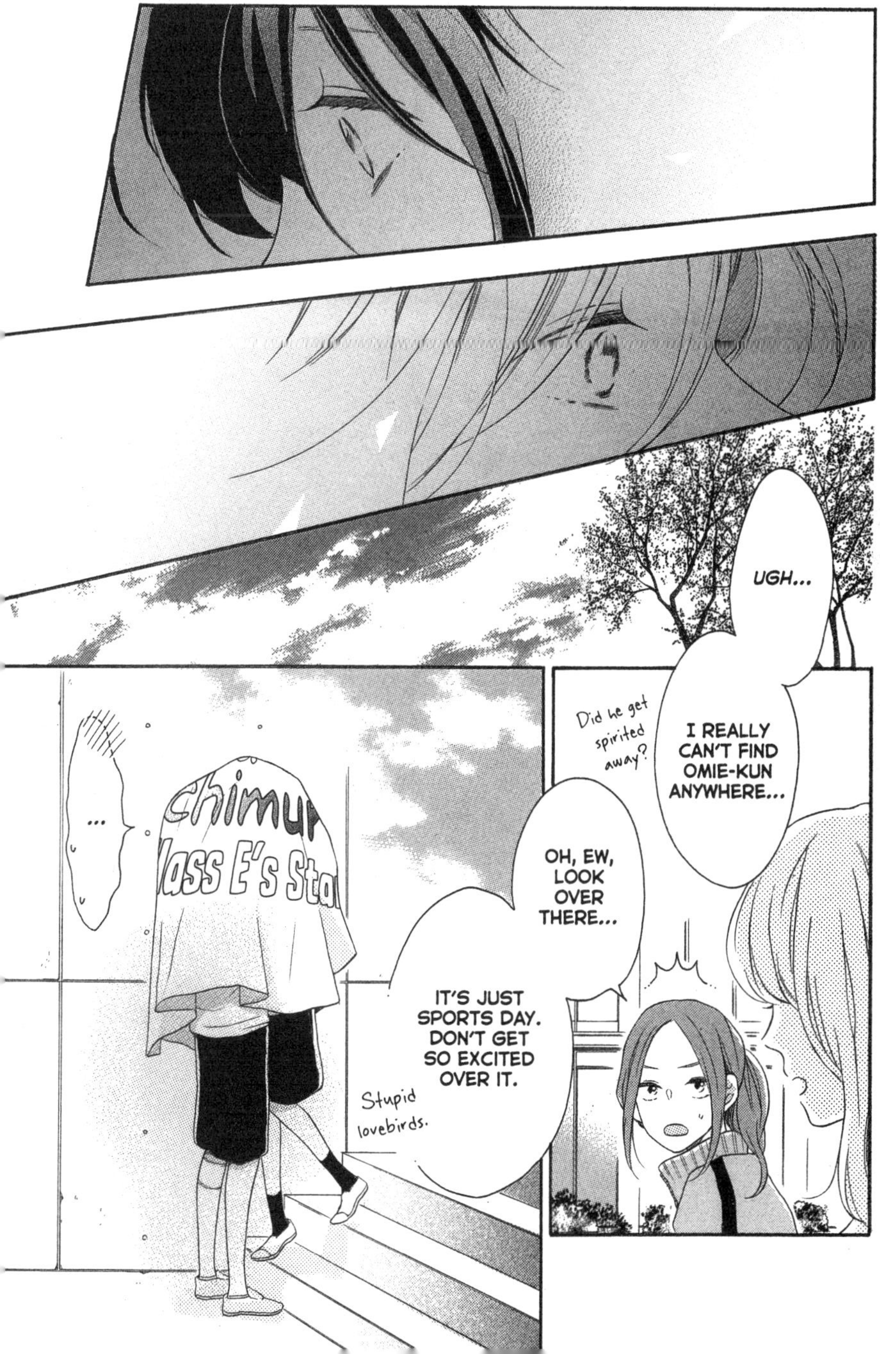
UGH...
I REALLY CAN'T FIND OMIE-KUN ANYWHERE...
Did he get spirited away?
OH, EW, LOOK OVER THERE...
IT'S JUST SPORTS DAY. DON'T GET SO EXCITED OVER IT.
Stupid lovebirds.
...

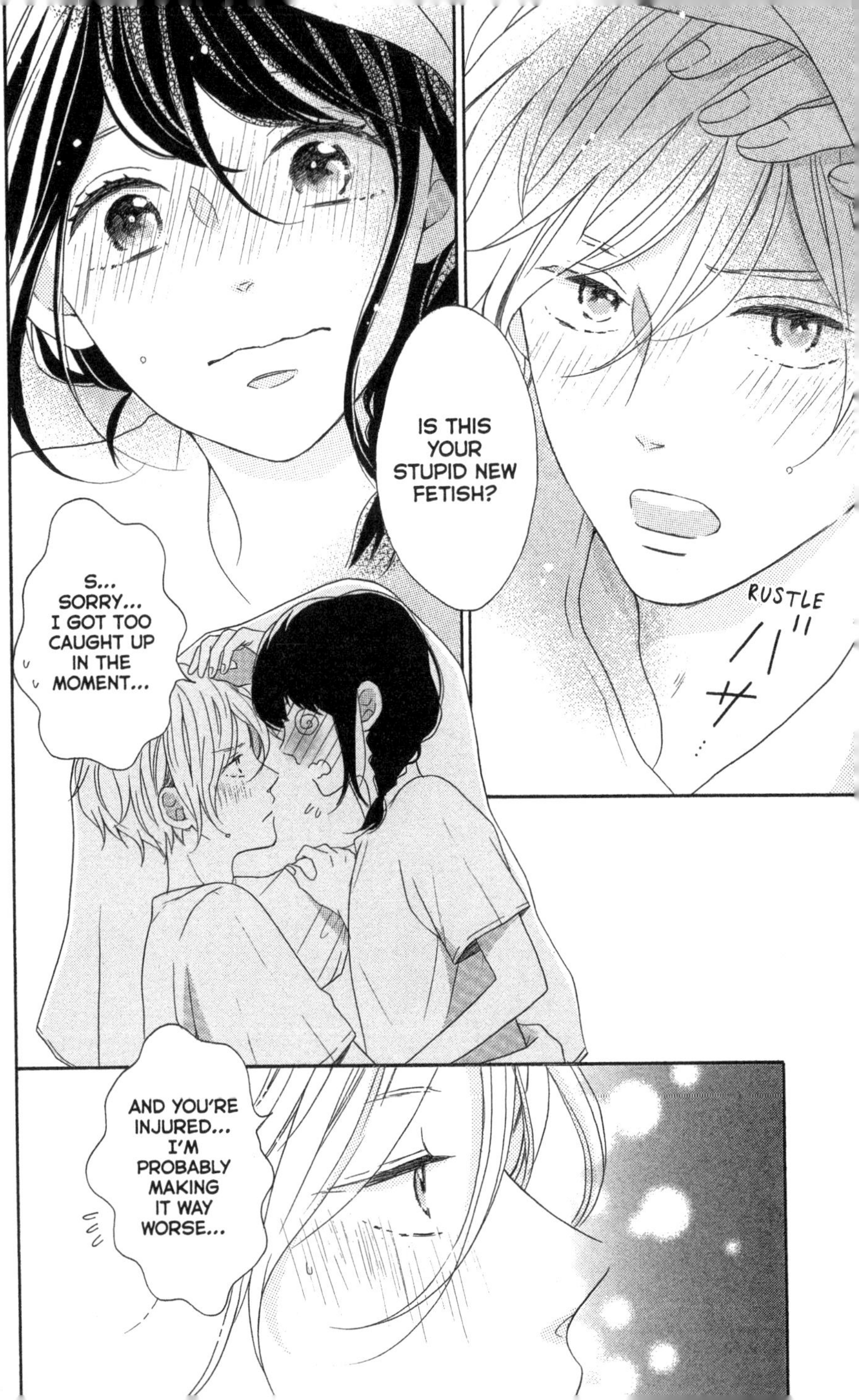
IS THIS YOUR STUPID NEW FETISH?
RUSTLE
S... SORRY... I GOT TOO CAUGHT UP IN THE MOMENT...
AND YOU'RE INJURED... I'M PROBABLY MAKING IT WAY WORSE...

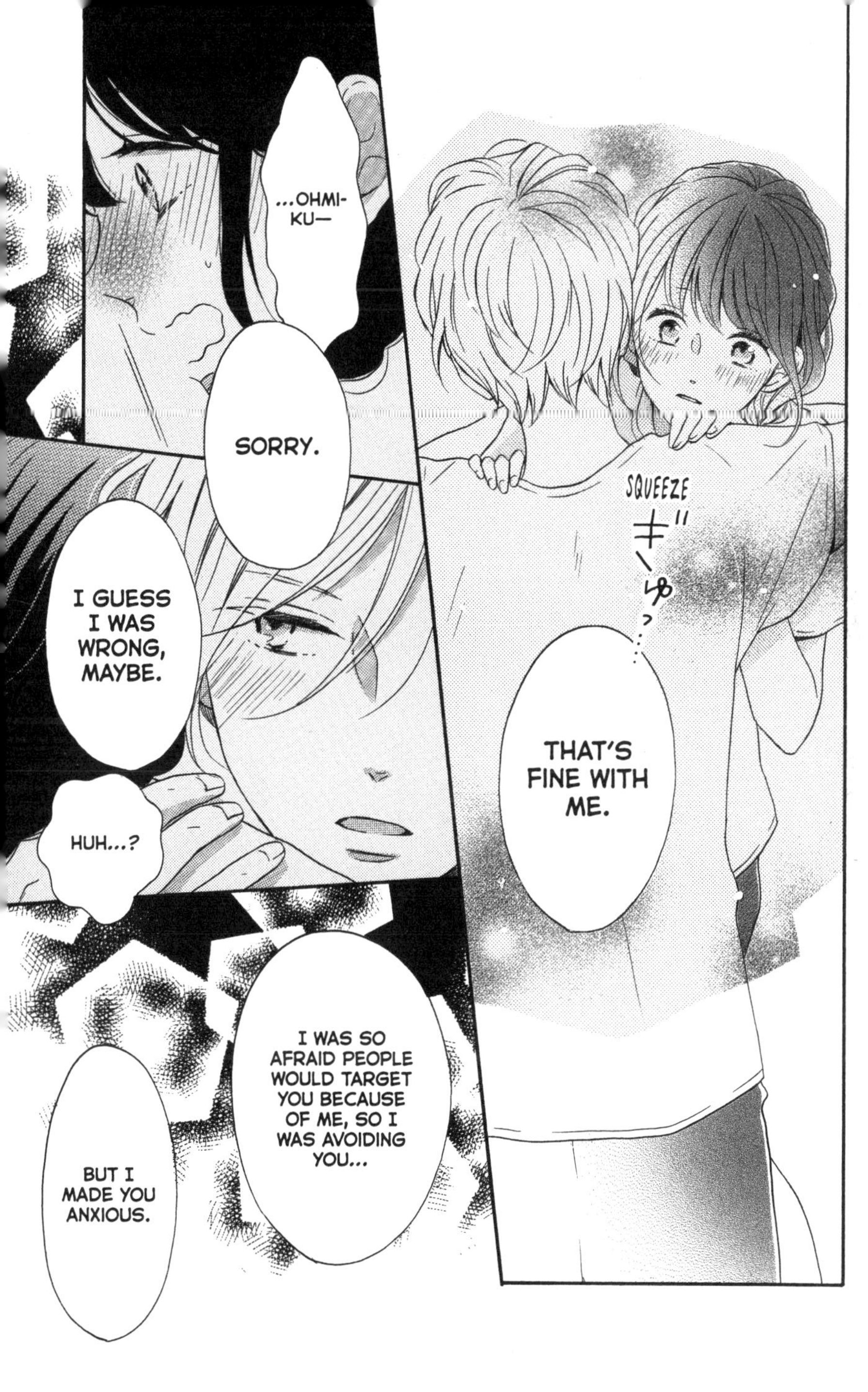
SQUEEZE
THAT'S FINE WITH ME.
...OHMI-KU—
SORRY.
I GUESS I WAS WRONG, MAYBE.
HUH...?
I WAS SO AFRAID PEOPLE WOULD TARGET YOU BECAUSE OF ME, SO I WAS AVOIDING YOU...
BUT I MADE YOU ANXIOUS.

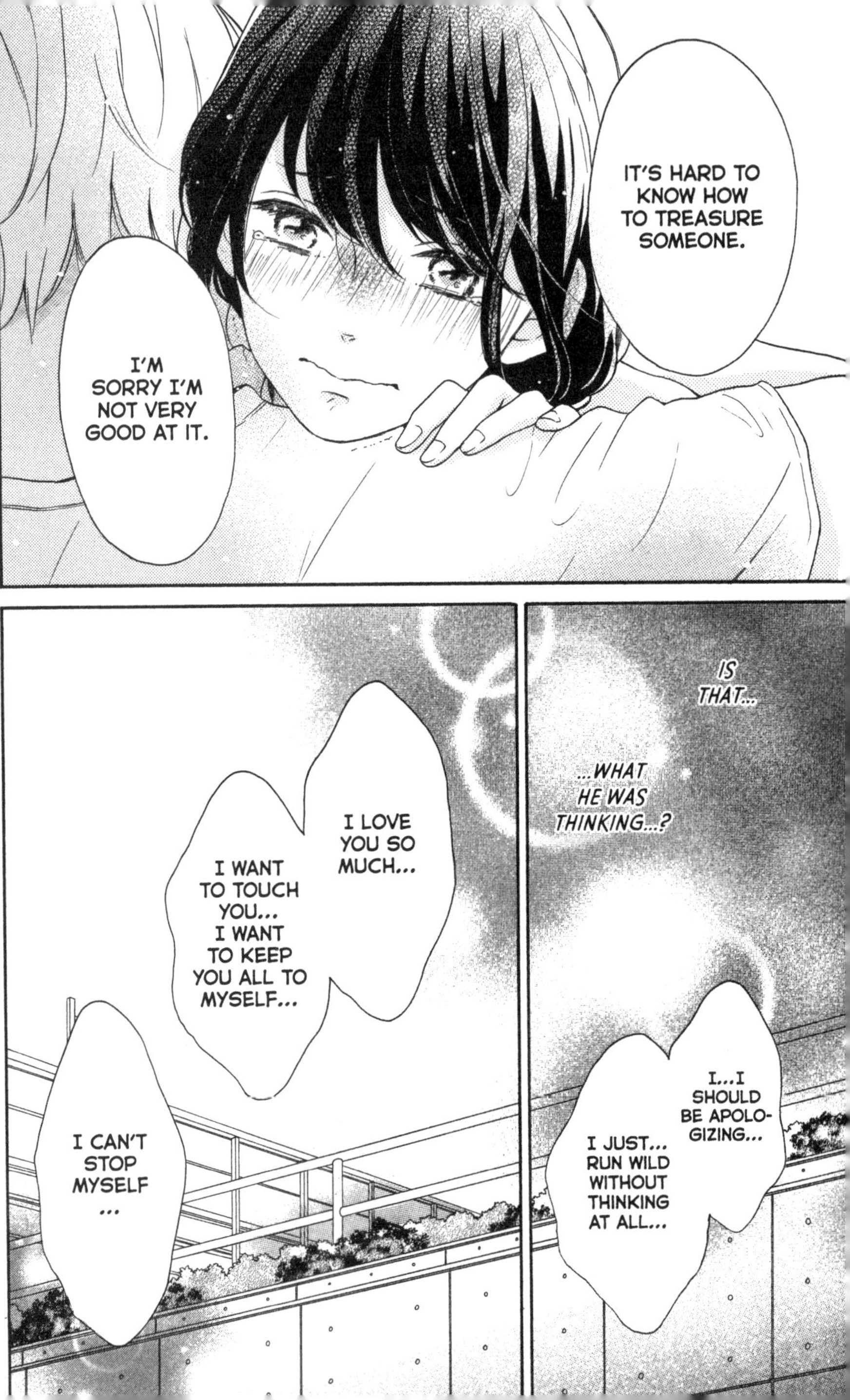
IT'S HARD TO KNOW HOW TO TREASURE SOMEONE.
I'M SORRY I'M NOT VERY GOOD AT IT.
IS THAT...
...WHAT HE WAS THINKING...?
I...I SHOULD BE APOLO-GIZING...
I JUST... RUN WILD WITHOUT THINKING AT ALL...
I LOVE YOU SO MUCH...
I WANT TO TOUCH YOU... I WANT TO KEEP YOU ALL TO MYSELF...
I CAN'T STOP MYSELF ...

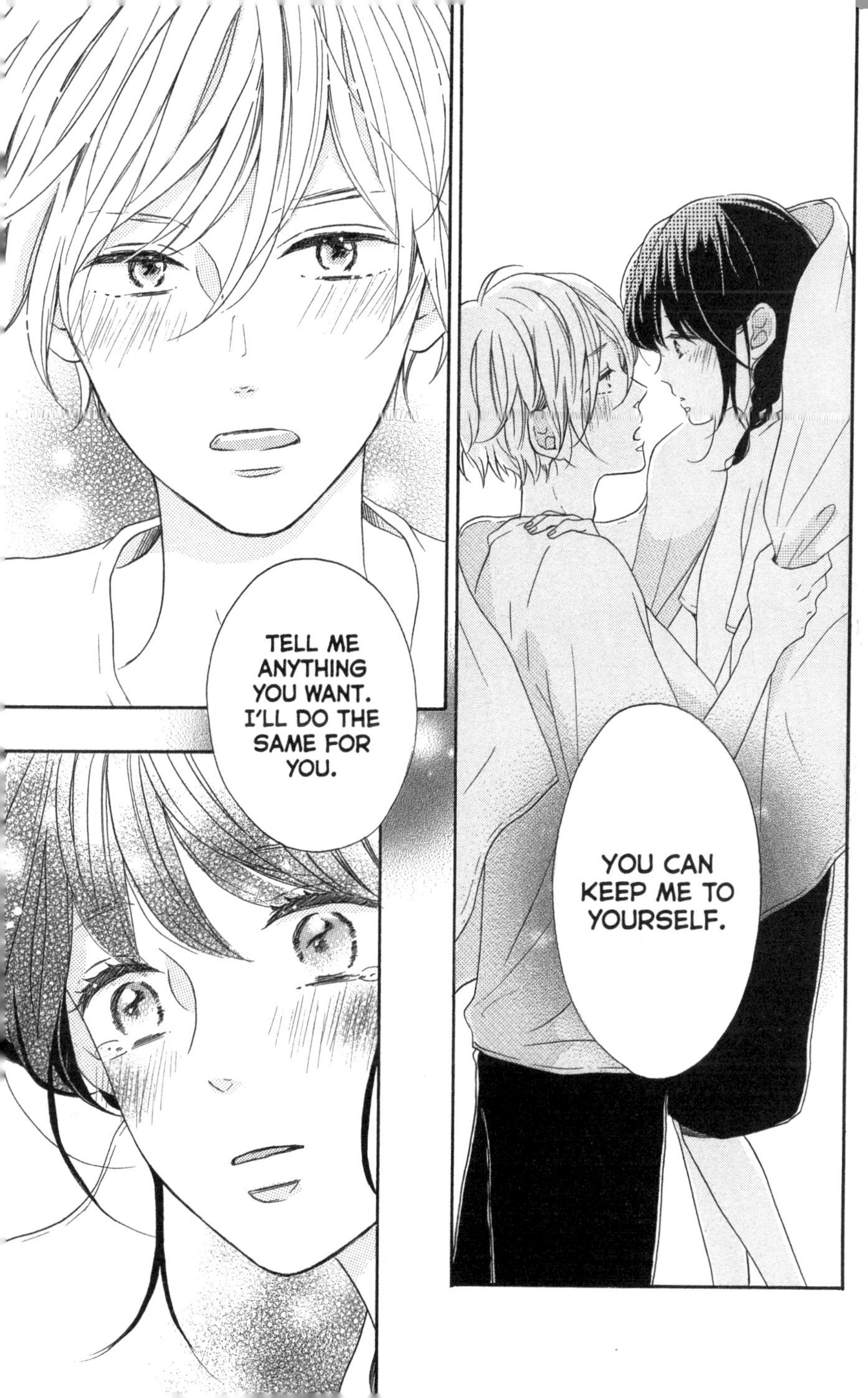
YOU CAN KEEP ME TO YOURSELF.
TELL ME ANYTHING YOU WANT. I'LL DO THE SAME FOR YOU.

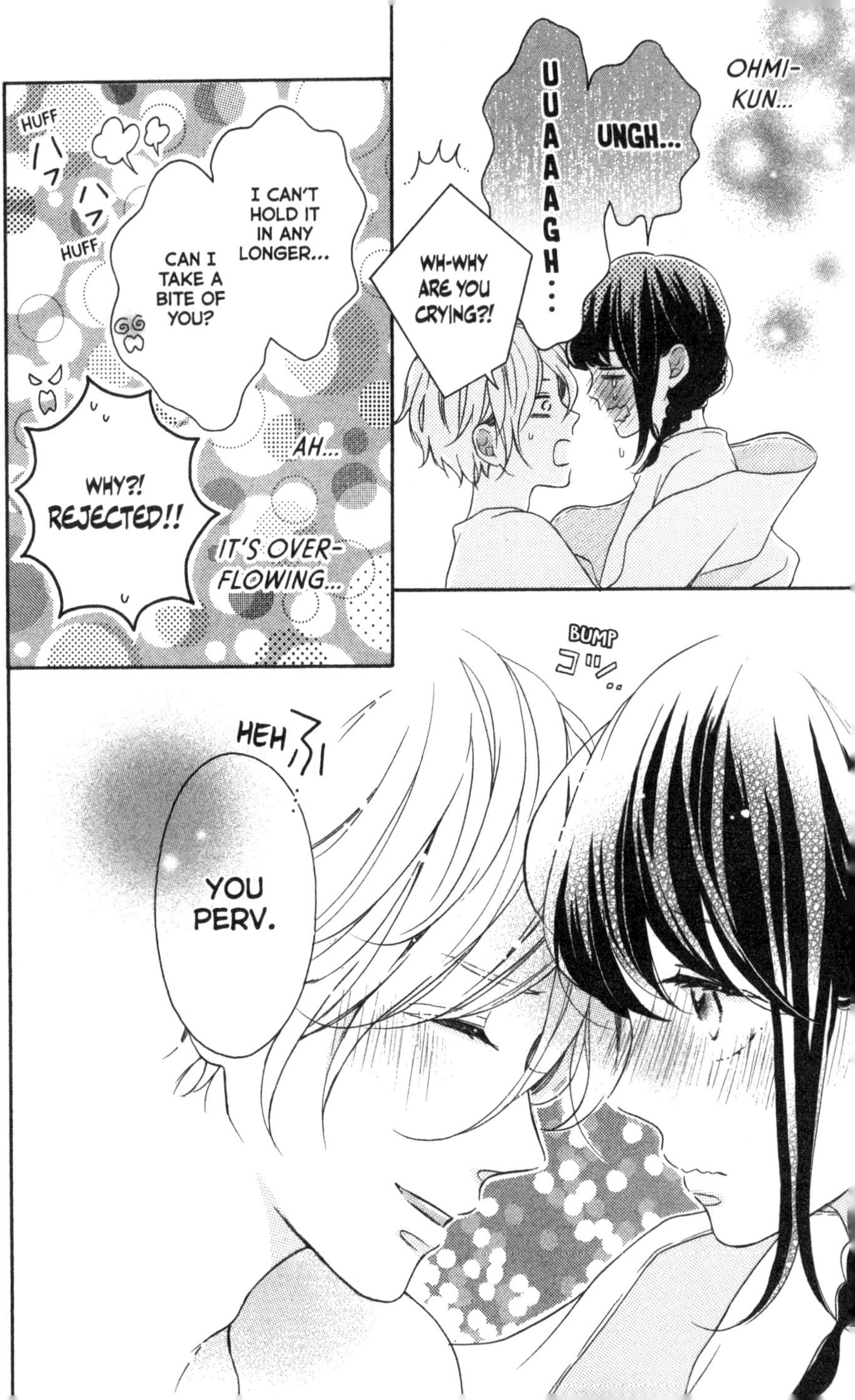
OHMI-KUN...
UNGH...
UUAAAAGH...
WH-WHY ARE YOU CRYING?!
I CAN'T HOLD IT IN ANY LONGER...
CAN I TAKE A BITE OF YOU?
HUFF
HUFF
AH...
IT'S OVER-FLOWING...
WHY?! REJECTED!!
BUMP
HEH
YOU PERV.

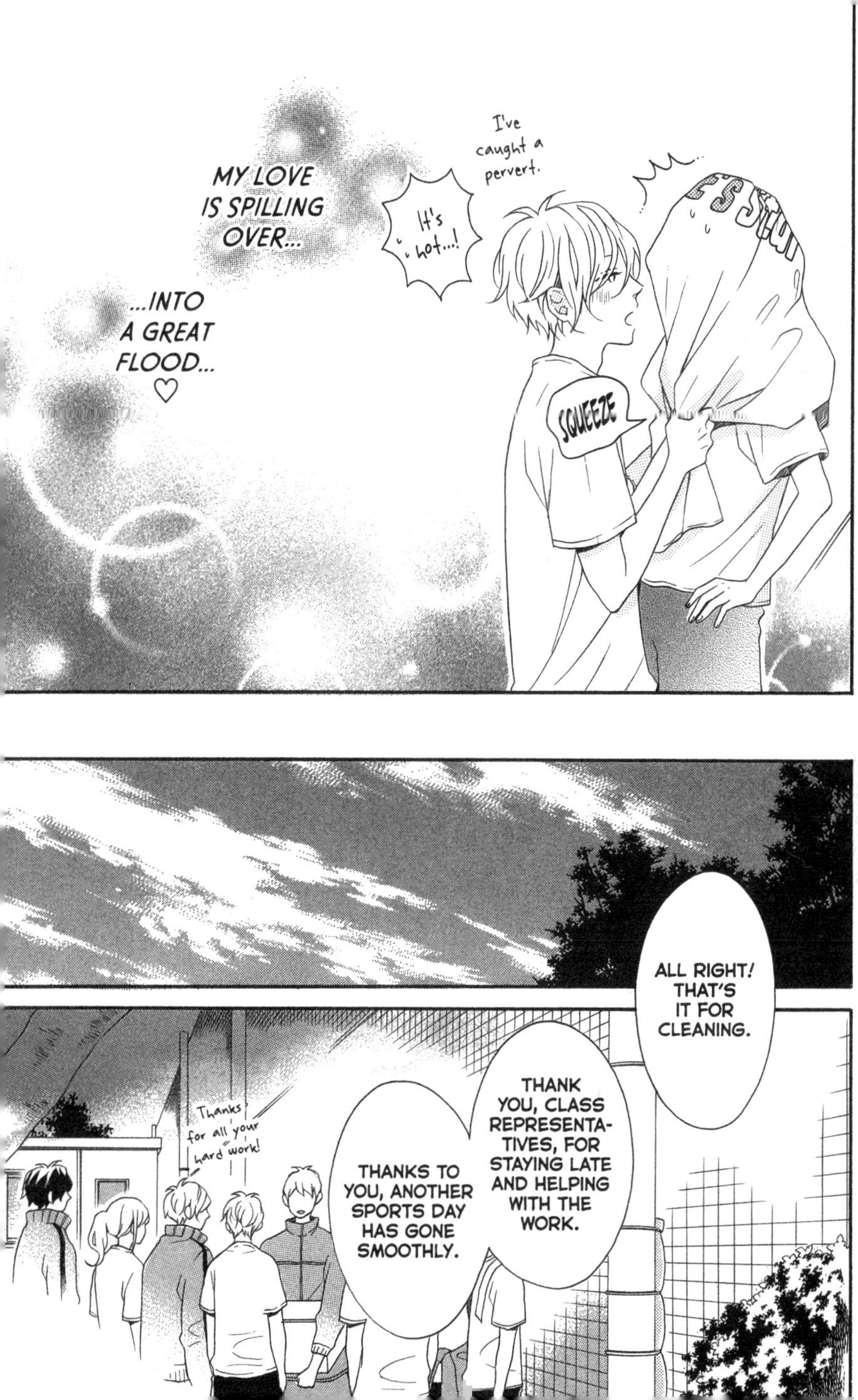
I've caught a pervert.
It's hot...!
MY LOVE IS SPILLING OVER...
...INTO A GREAT FLOOD... ♡
SQUEEZE
ALL RIGHT! THAT'S IT FOR CLEANING.
THANK YOU, CLASS REPRESENTA-TIVES, FOR STAYING LATE AND HELPING WITH THE WORK.
THANKS TO YOU, ANOTHER SPORTS DAY HAS GONE SMOOTHLY.
Thanks for all your hard work!

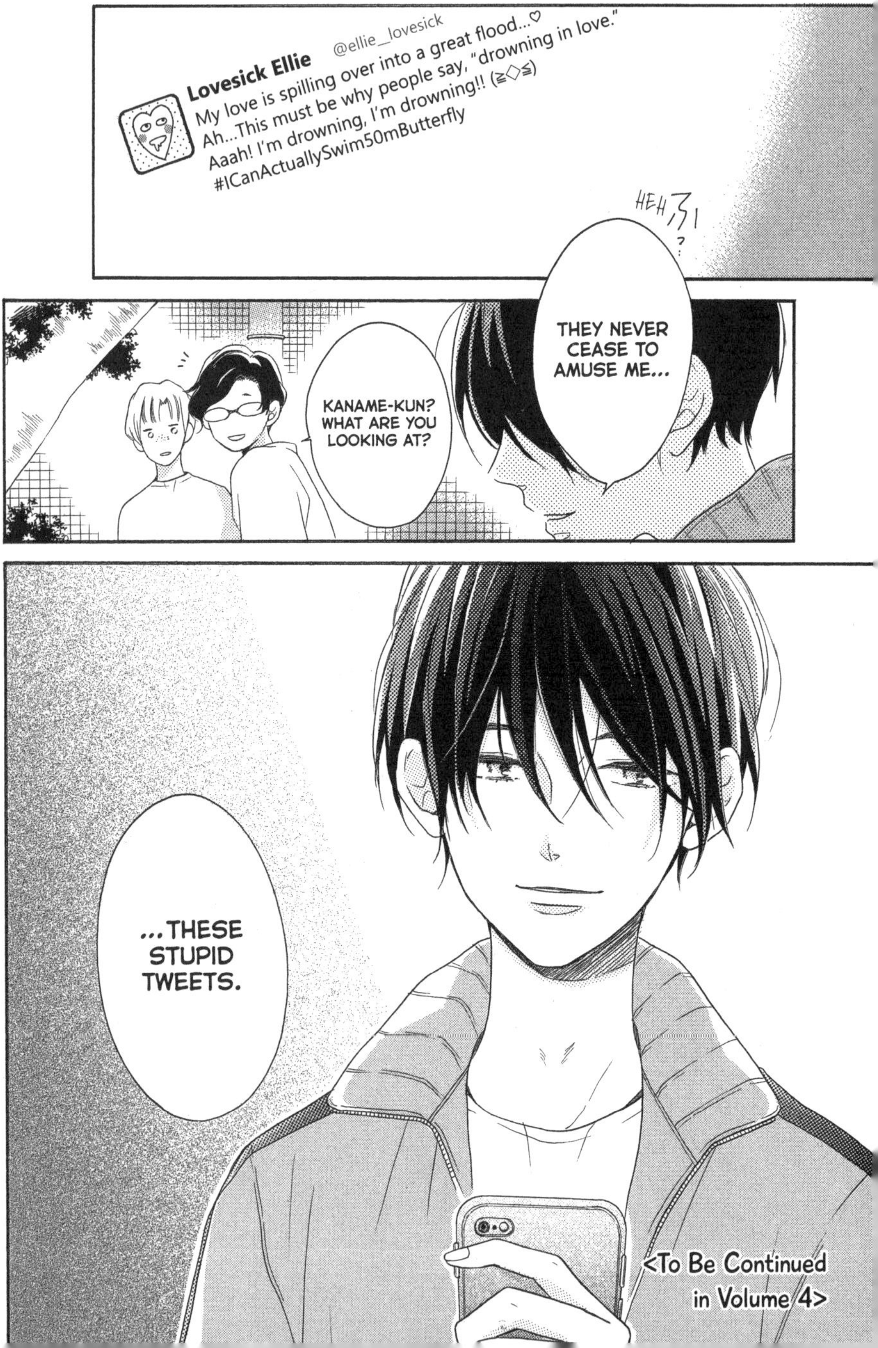
Lovesick Ellie @ellie_lovesick
My love is spilling over into a great flood...♡
Ah...This must be why people say, "drowning in love."
Aaah! I'm drowning, I'm drowning!! (≧◇≦)
#ICanActuallySwim50mButterfly
HEH
THEY NEVER CEASE TO AMUSE ME...
KANAME-KUN? WHAT ARE YOU LOOKING AT?
...THESE STUPID TWEETS.
<To Be Continued in Volume 4>

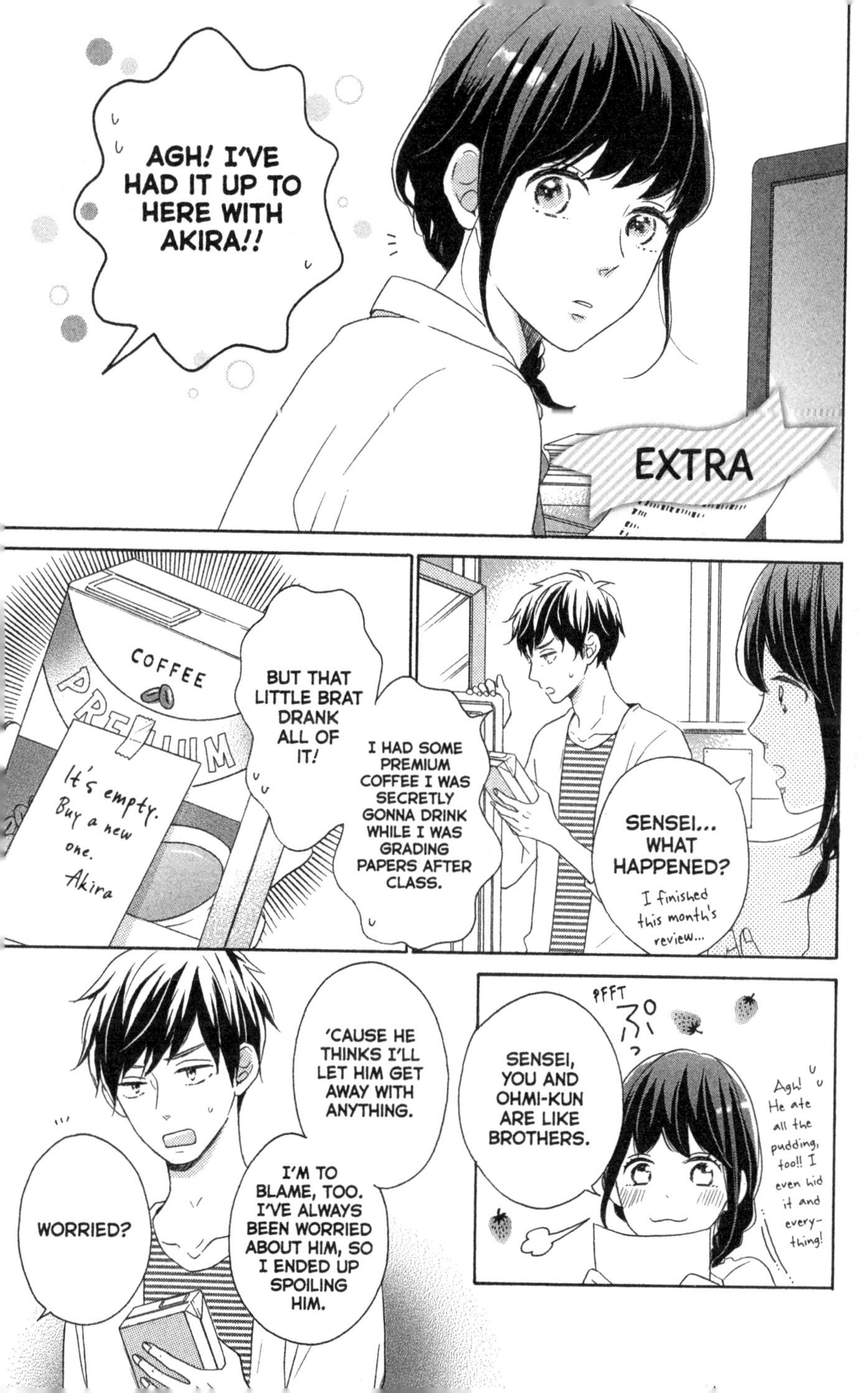
AGH! I'VE HAD IT UP TO HERE WITH AKIRA!!
EXTRA
SENSEI... WHAT HAPPENED?
I finished this month's review...
I HAD SOME PREMIUM COFFEE I WAS SECRETLY GONNA DRINK WHILE I WAS GRADING PAPERS AFTER CLASS.
BUT THAT LITTLE BRAT DRANK ALL OF IT!
COFFEE
It's empty. Buy a new one. Akira
PFFT
SENSEI, YOU AND OHMI-KUN ARE LIKE BROTHERS.
Agh! He ate all the pudding, too!! I even hid it and everything!
'CAUSE HE THINKS I'LL LET HIM GET AWAY WITH ANYTHING.
I'M TO BLAME, TOO. I'VE ALWAYS BEEN WORRIED ABOUT HIM, SO I ENDED UP SPOILING HIM.
WORRIED?

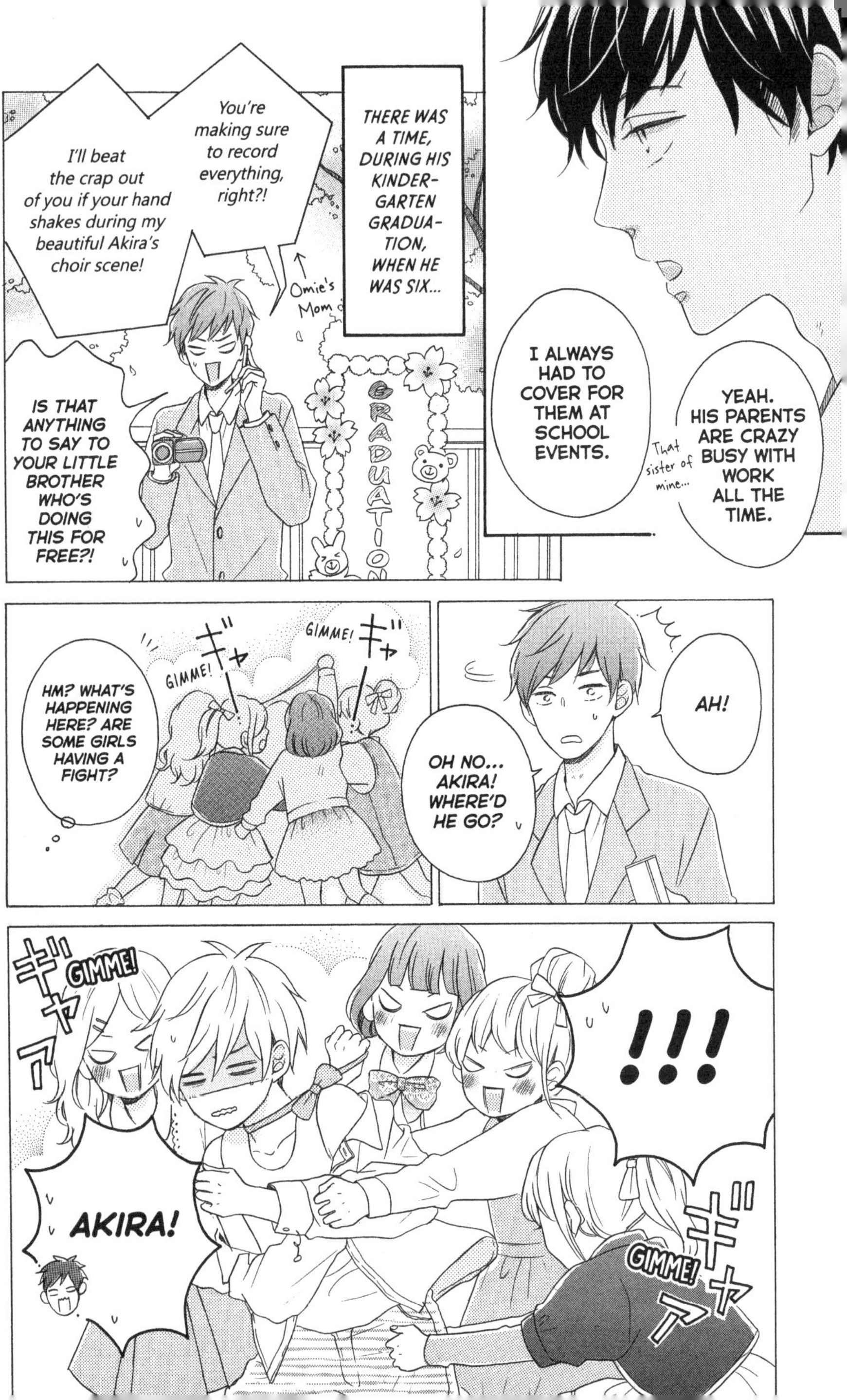
YEAH. HIS PARENTS ARE CRAZY BUSY WITH WORK ALL THE TIME.
That sister of mine...
I ALWAYS HAD TO COVER FOR THEM AT SCHOOL EVENTS.
THERE WAS A TIME, DURING HIS KINDER-GARTEN GRADUA-TION, WHEN HE WAS SIX...
You're making sure to record everything, right?!
I'll beat the crap out of you if your hand shakes during my beautiful Akira's choir scene!
Omie's Mom
GRADUATION
IS THAT ANYTHING TO SAY TO YOUR LITTLE BROTHER WHO'S DOING THIS FOR FREE?!
AH!
OH NO... AKIRA! WHERE'D HE GO?
GIMME!
ギャ
GIMME!
ギャ
HM? WHAT'S HAPPENING HERE? ARE SOME GIRLS HAVING A FIGHT?
!!!
ギャア
GIMME!
ギャア
GIMME!
AKIRA!

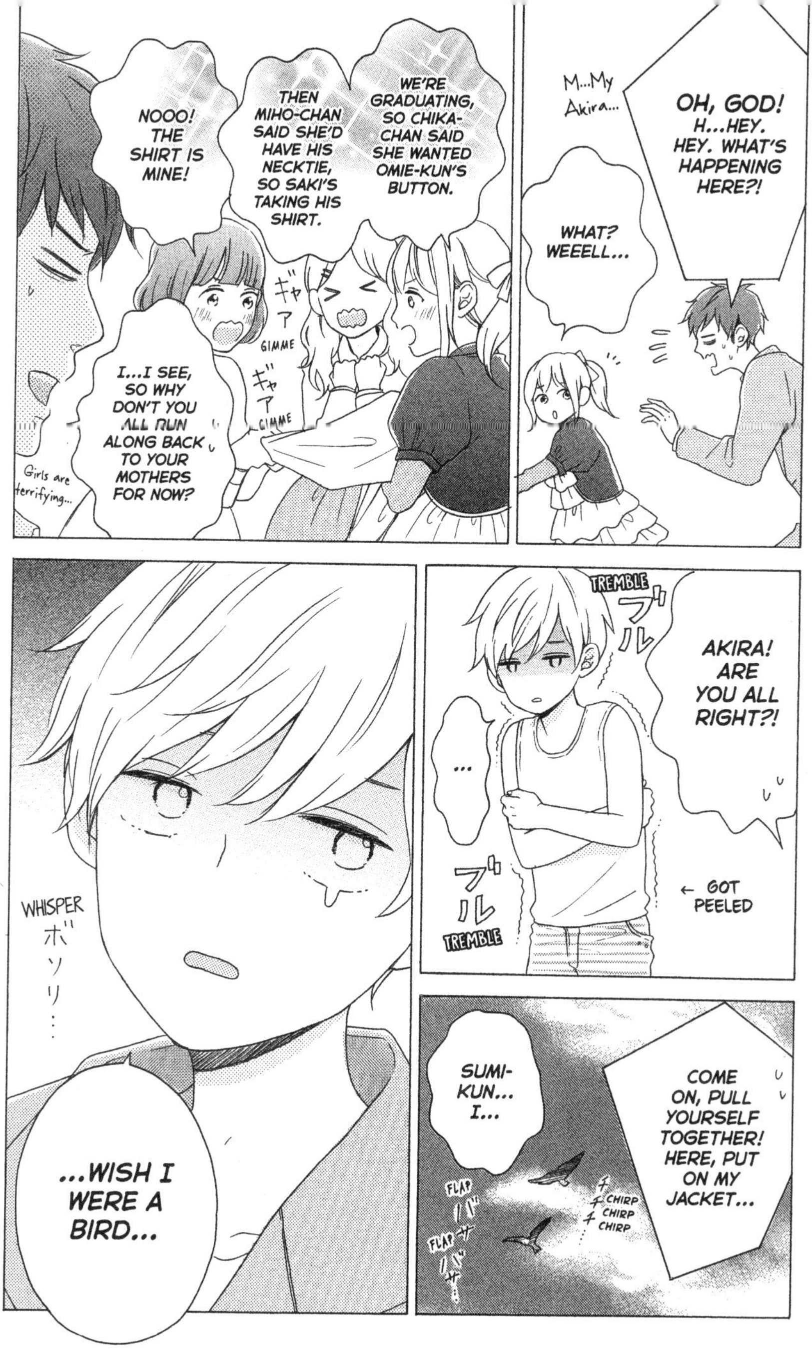
OH, GOD! H...HEY. HEY. WHAT'S HAPPENING HERE?!
M...My Akira...
WHAT? WEEELL...
WE'RE GRADUATING, SO CHIKA-CHAN SAID SHE WANTED OMIE-KUN'S BUTTON.
THEN MIHO-CHAN SAID SHE'D HAVE HIS NECKTIE, SO SAKI'S TAKING HIS SHIRT.
NOOO! THE SHIRT IS MINE!
GIMME
GIMME
I...I SEE, SO WHY DON'T YOU ALL RUN ALONG BACK TO YOUR MOTHERS FOR NOW?
Girls are terrifying...
AKIRA! ARE YOU ALL RIGHT?!
TREMBLE
...
← GOT PEELED
TREMBLE
COME ON, PULL YOURSELF TOGETHER! HERE, PUT ON MY JACKET...
SUMI-KUN... I...
CHIRP CHIRP CHIRP
FLAP
FLAP
WHISPER
...WISH I WERE A BIRD...

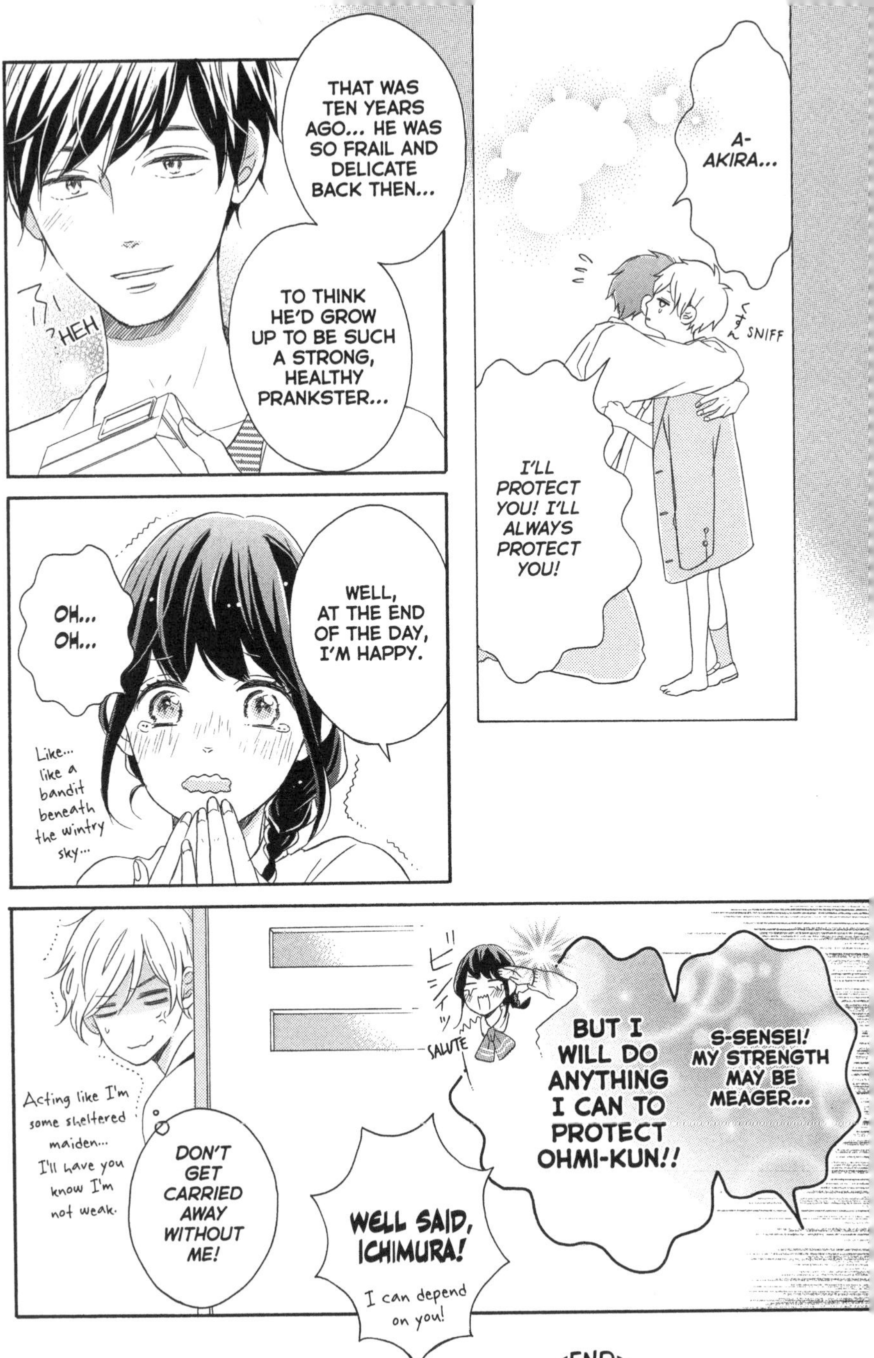
A- AKIRA...
SNIFF
I'LL PROTECT YOU! I'LL ALWAYS PROTECT YOU!
THAT WAS TEN YEARS AGO... HE WAS SO FRAIL AND DELICATE BACK THEN...
TO THINK HE'D GROW UP TO BE SUCH A STRONG, HEALTHY PRANKSTER...
HEH
WELL, AT THE END OF THE DAY, I'M HAPPY.
OH... OH...
Like... like a bandit beneath the wintry sky...
S-SENSEI! MY STRENGTH MAY BE MEAGER...
BUT I WILL DO ANYTHING I CAN TO PROTECT OHMI-KUN!!
SALUTE
WELL SAID, ICHIMURA!
I can depend on you!
DON'T GET CARRIED AWAY WITHOUT ME!
Acting like I'm some sheltered maiden... I'll have you know I'm not weak.

<END>

★ BONUS ★

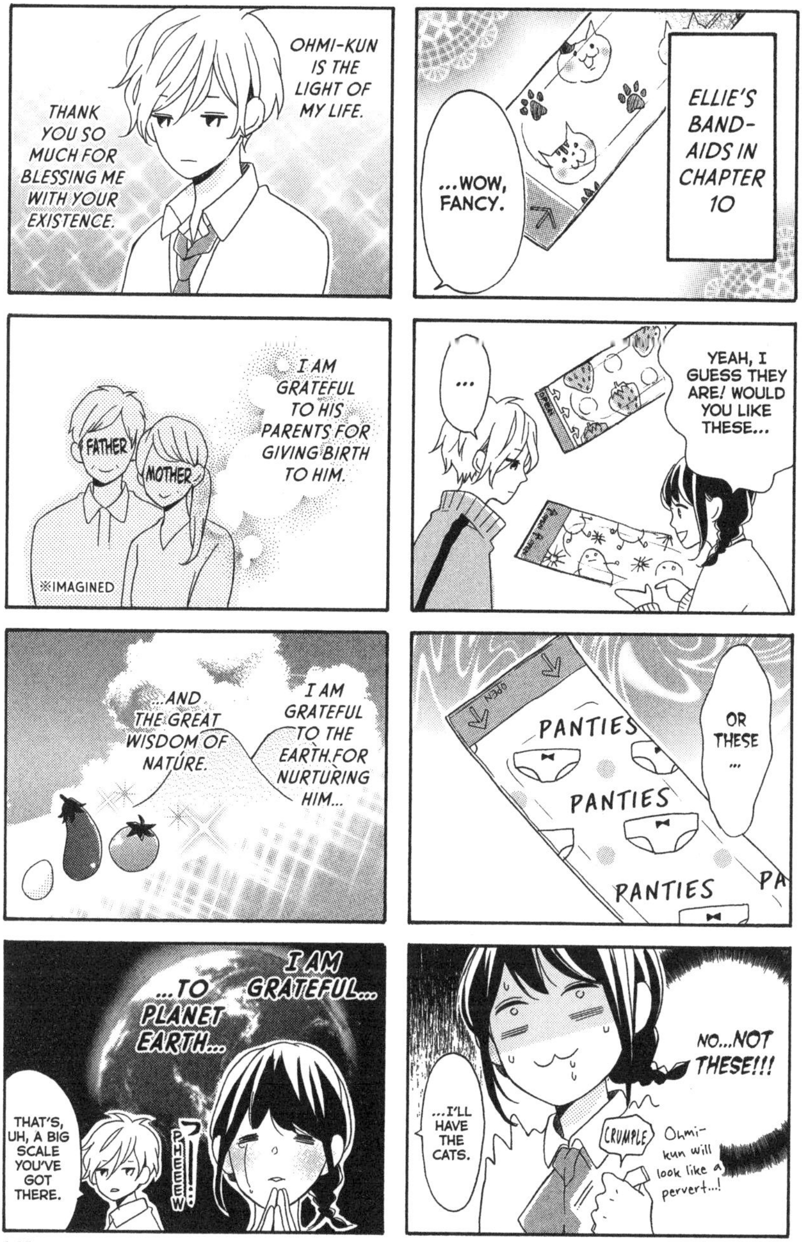
ELLIE'S BAND-AIDS IN CHAPTER 10
...WOW, FANCY.
YEAH, I GUESS THEY ARE! WOULD YOU LIKE THESE...
...
OR THESE...
OPEN
PANTIES
PANTIES
PANTIES
PA
NO...NOT THESE!!!
Ohmi-kun will look like a pervert...!
CRUMPLE
...I'LL HAVE THE CATS.
OHMI-KUN IS THE LIGHT OF MY LIFE.
THANK YOU SO MUCH FOR BLESSING ME WITH YOUR EXISTENCE.
I AM GRATEFUL TO HIS PARENTS FOR GIVING BIRTH TO HIM.
MOTHER
FATHER
※IMAGINED
I AM GRATEFUL TO THE EARTH FOR NURTURING HIM...
...AND THE GREAT WISDOM OF NATURE.
I AM GRATEFUL...
...TO PLANET EARTH...
PHEEEW
THAT'S, UH, A BIG SCALE YOU'VE GOT THERE.

Lovesick Ellie

#Preview

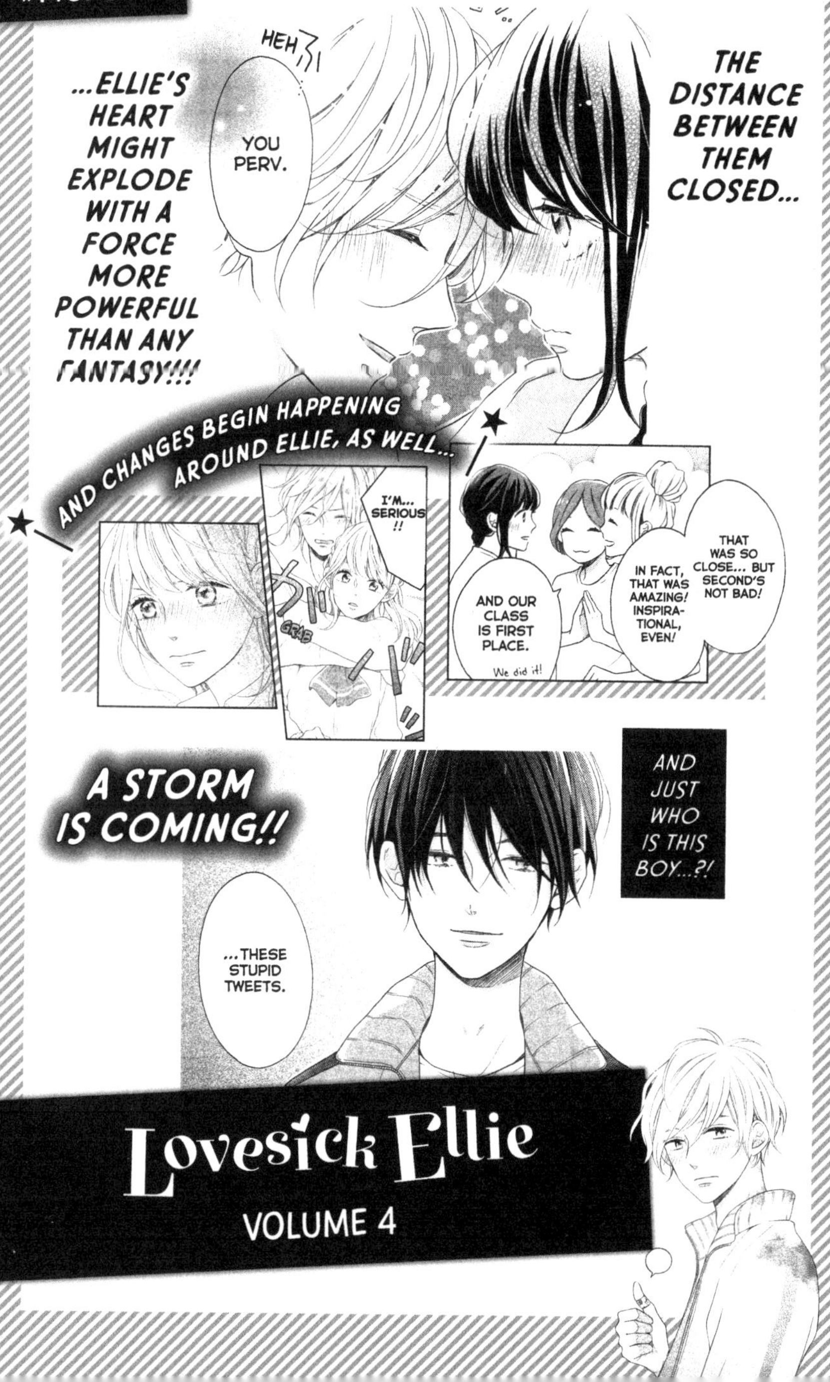
THE DISTANCE BETWEEN THEM CLOSED...
HEH
YOU PERV.
...ELLIE'S HEART MIGHT EXPLODE WITH A FORCE MORE POWERFUL THAN ANY FANTASY!!!
AND CHANGES BEGIN HAPPENING AROUND ELLIE, AS WELL...
THAT WAS SO CLOSE... BUT SECOND'S NOT BAD!
IN FACT, THAT WAS AMAZING! INSPIRATIONAL, EVEN!
AND OUR CLASS IS FIRST PLACE.
We did it!
I'M... SERIOUS!!
GRAB
AND JUST WHO IS THIS BOY...?!
A STORM IS COMING!!
...THESE STUPID TWEETS.

Lovesick Ellie

VOLUME 4

Lovesick Ellie

@Translation_Notes

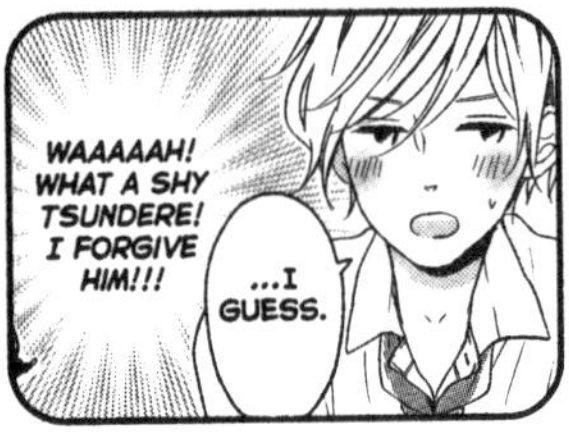
...I GUESS.
WAAAAAH! WHAT A SHY TSUNDERE! I FORGIVE HIM!!!

Tsundere @page 12
A *tsundere* is a personality type where a person can be initially cold or temperamental.

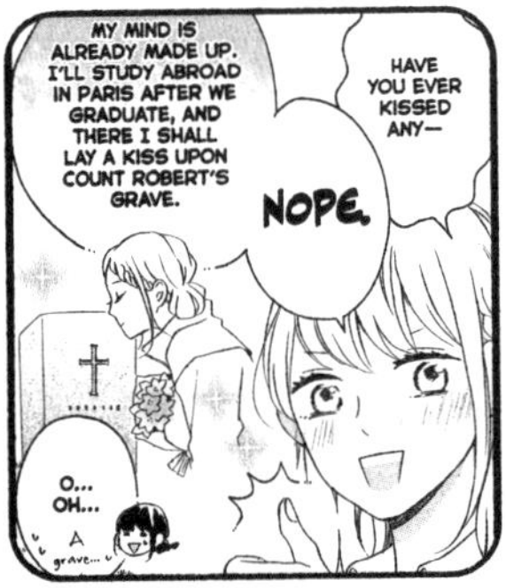
MY MIND IS ALREADY MADE UP. I'LL STUDY ABROAD IN PARIS AFTER WE GRADUATE, AND THERE I SHALL LAY A KISS UPON COUNT ROBERT'S GRAVE.
HAVE YOU EVER KISSED ANY—
NOPE.
O... OH...
A grave...

Count Robert @page 22
Sara references Comte Robert de Montesquiou (1855-1921), who was a French aesthete, poet, art collector, and dandy. He is reputed to be the inspiration for the character Baron de Charlus in Marcel Proust's *In Search of Lost Time.*

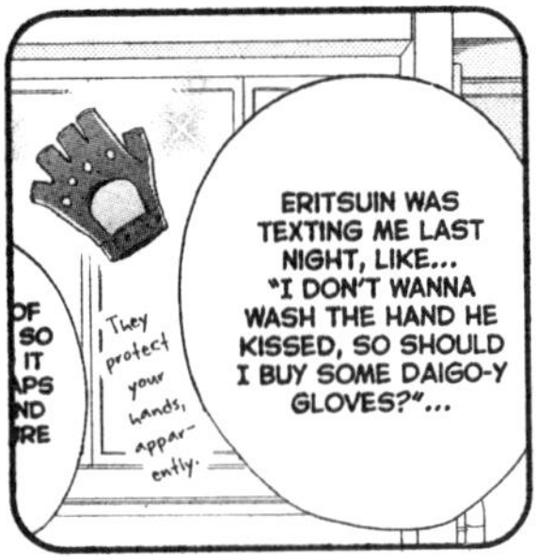
ERITSUIN WAS TEXTING ME LAST NIGHT, LIKE... "I DON'T WANNA WASH THE HAND HE KISSED, SO SHOULD I BUY SOME DAIGO-Y GLOVES?"...
They protect your hands, apparently.

Daigo-y gloves @page 51
Daigo Naito, known by his stage name DAIGO, is a Japanese singer-songwriter and actor well known for wearing fingerless gloves almost all the time.

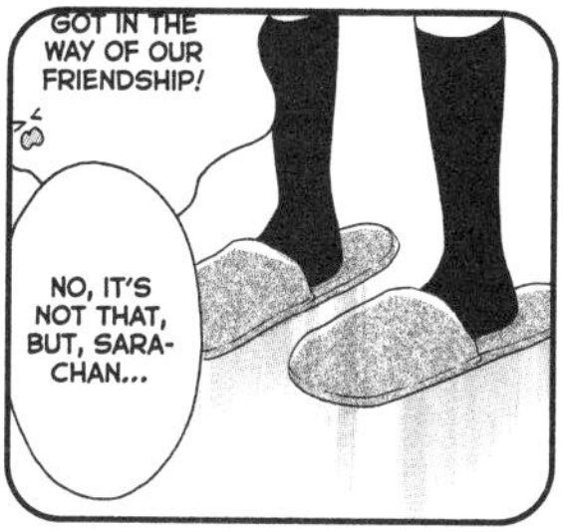
GOT IN THE WAY OF OUR FRIENDSHIP!
NO, IT'S NOT THAT, BUT, SARA-CHAN...

Slippers @page 58
Outdoor shoes are not allowed in Japanese schools, so students have school-issued indoor shoes. For visitors, there are vinyl slippers. Usually these are pretty large in size and can be a bit difficult to walk in. If you ever visit a Japanese school, do not expect to run up stairs in these slippers– you might slip!

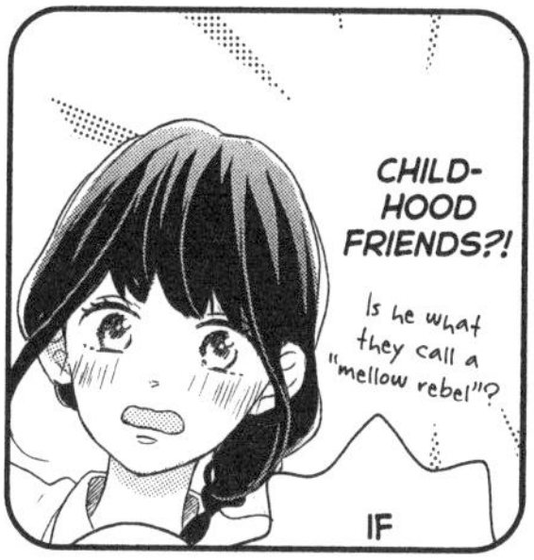
CHILD-HOOD FRIENDS?!
Is he what they call a "mellow rebel"?
IF

Mellow Rebel @page 61
A "mellow rebel," or in Japanese a "mild yankee," is someone who partakes in Japanese yankee fashion (dyed hair, piercings, baggy clothes), loves cars, and shopping malls and values friendship and family; however, they are not associated with delinquency as would be found with a typical yankee.

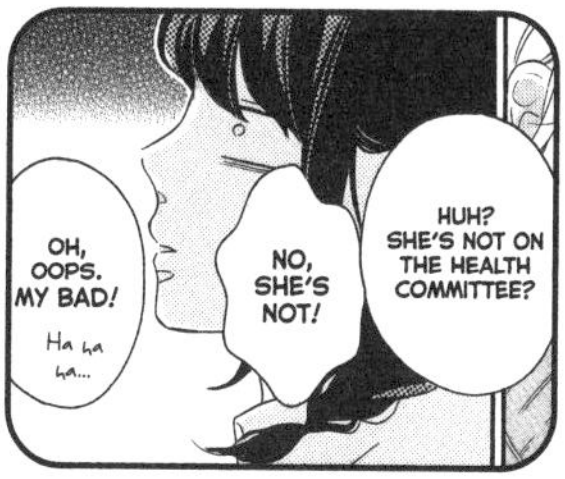
HUH? SHE'S NOT ON THE HEALTH COMMITTEE?
NO, SHE'S NOT!
OH, OOPS. MY BAD!
Ha ha ha...

Health committee @page 78
Students are assigned to specific task committees in their homeroom class, which can include assistance in any health-related tasks. This can include doing a weekly hygiene check where students in the health committee will check to see if everyone has a handkerchief and tissues, and if fingernails are clipped short.

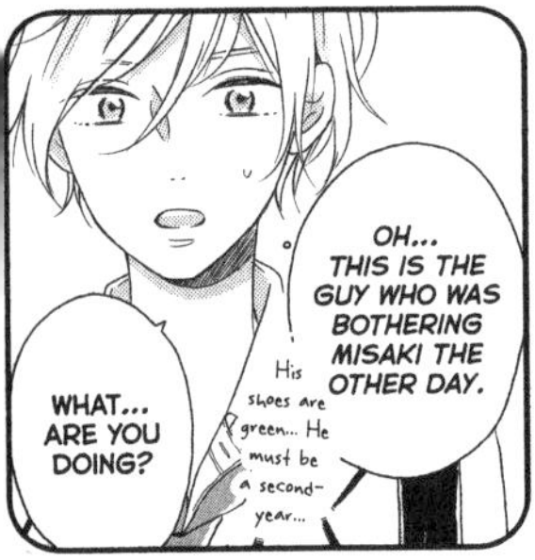
OH... THIS IS THE GUY WHO WAS BOTHERING MISAKI THE OTHER DAY.
His shoes are green... He must be a second-year...
WHAT... ARE YOU DOING?

Indoor shoes (green, must be a second-year) @page 99
Outdoor shoes are not allowed in Japanese schools, so students have school-issued indoor shoes, which are usually white in color. These are called *uwabaki* in Japanese. On the sole, the shoes are colored to indicate the student's grade level.

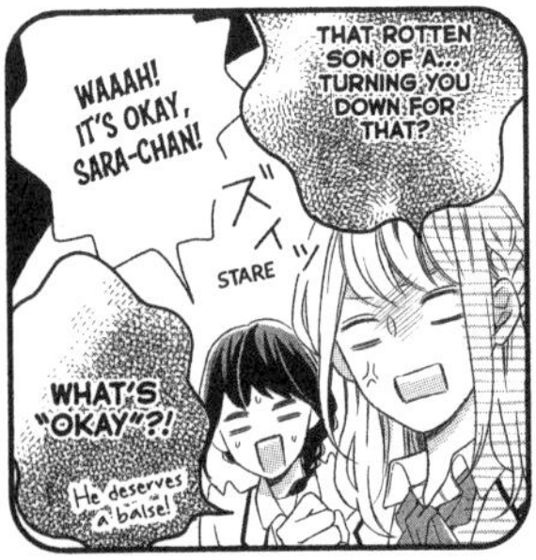
THAT ROTTEN SON OF A... TURNING YOU DOWN FOR THAT?
WAAAH! IT'S OKAY, SARA-CHAN!
ズイ
STARE
WHAT'S "OKAY"?!
He deserves a balse!

Balse @page 107
The incantation used to destroy the castle at the end of the Studio Ghibli film *Castle in the Sky*. It has since become a prominent and beloved meme on 2ch and Twitter.

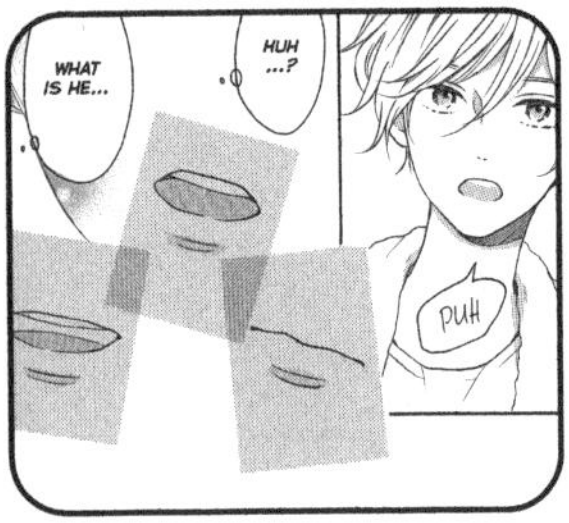
PUH
HUH ...?
WHAT IS HE...

"Good Luck" @page 146
If you read Ohmi's lips in Japanese, he says *ganbare* (がんばれ) which means "Good luck" or "You can do it."

OH...
OH...

WE
AT TH
OF TH
I'M H

Like...
like a
bandit
beneath
the wintry
sky...

A bandit beneath the wintry sky
@page 164

Ellie fantasizes in a (sometimes) poetic way in which she references the *oihagi* (おいはぎ). An English equivalent would be the highwayman, who were robbers who stole from travelers by horseback and were common sights until the mid or late 19th century. *Oihagi*, or bandits, in Japan would do similar, especially along routes like the coastal Tokaido and the inland, mountainous Nakasendo between Kyoto and Edo (modern-day Tokyo). These bandits would typically steal goods carried by travelers, followed by violent attacks. Ohmi further alludes to this imagery by insisting that he is not "some sheltered maiden" as female travelers would usually ride by horseback or inside of a palanquin (called a *kago* for non-samurai citizens and *norimono* for the warrior class and nobility). One romantically tragic version is in the short story *In a Grove* by Ryunosuke Akutagawa.

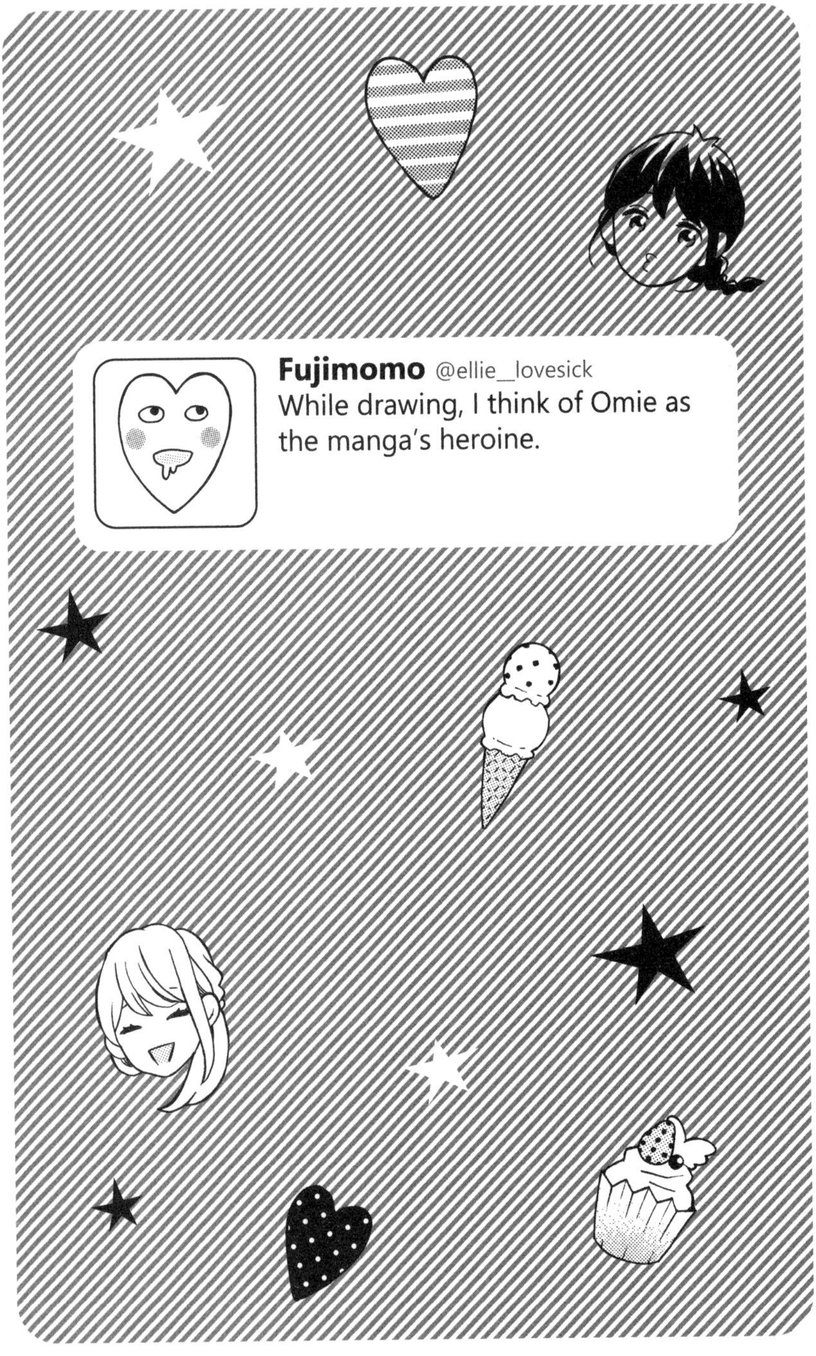
Fujimomo @ellie__lovesick
While drawing, I think of Omie as the manga's heroine.

A SMART, NEW ROMANTIC COMEDY FOR FANS OF *SHORTCAKE CAKE* AND *TERRACE HOUSE*!

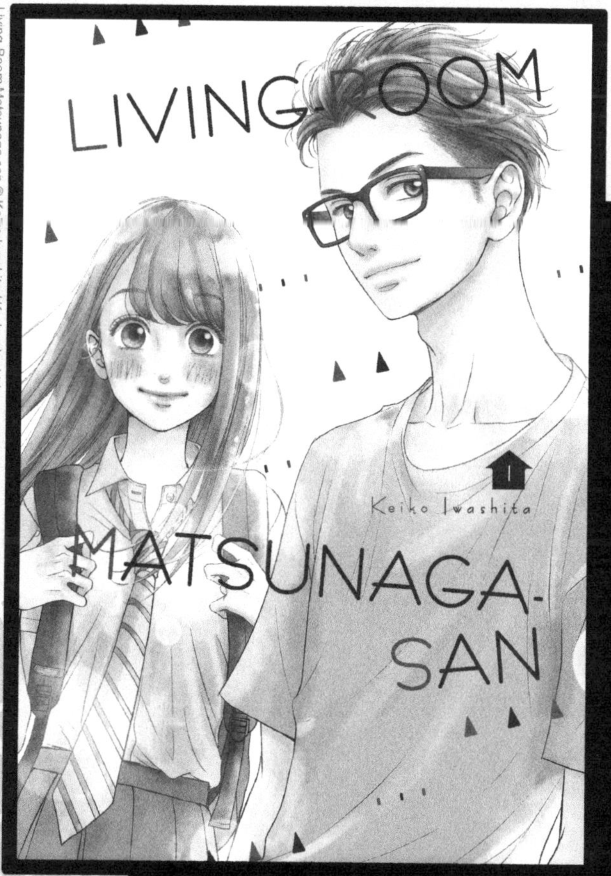
LIVING-ROOM
1
Keiko Iwashita
MATSUNAGA-
SAN

KC KODANSHA COMICS

A romance manga starring high school girl Meeko, who learns to live on her own in a boarding house whose living room is home to the odd (but handsome) Matsunaga-san. She begins to adjust to her new life away from her parents, but Meeko soon learns that no matter how far away from home she is, she's still a young girl at heart — especially when she finds herself falling for Matsunaga-san.

1 PERFECT WORLD

Rie Aruga

A TOUCHING NEW SERIES ABOUT LOVE AND COPING WITH DISABILITY

An office party reunites Tsugumi with her high school crush Itsuki. He's realized his dream of becoming an architect, but along the way, he experienced a spinal injury that put him in a wheelchair. Now Tsugumi's rekindled feelings will butt up against prejudices she never considered — and Itsuki will have to decide if he's ready to let someone into his heart...

"Depicts with great delicacy and courage the difficulties some with disabilities experience getting involved in romantic relationships... Rie Aruga refuses to romanticize, pushing her heroine to face the reality of disability. She invites her readers to the same tasks of empathy, knowledge and recognition."
—Slate.fr

"An important entry [in manga romance]... The emotional core of both plot and characters indicates thoughtfulness... [Aruga's] research is readily apparent in the text and artwork, making this feel like a real story."
—Anime News Network

KC
KODANSHA
COMICS

A Kodansha Trade Paperback Original

Lovesick Ellie 3 copyright © 2016 Fujimomo
English translation copyright © 2022 Fujimomo

Published in the United States by
Kodansha USA Publishing, LLC, New York.

Publication rights for this English edition arranged through
Kodansha Ltd., Tokyo.

First published in Japan in 2016 by Kodansha Ltd., Tokyo
as *Koiwazurai no Ellie,* volume 3.

ISBN 978-1-64651-319-2

Printed in the United States of America.

9 8 7 6 5 4 3 2 1

Translation: Ursula Ku
Lettering: Allen Berry
Additional Lettering and Layout: Lys Blakeslee
Editing: Sarah Tilson, Maggie Le
Kodansha USA Publishing edition cover design by Matthew Akuginow

Publisher: Kiichiro Sugawara

Director of Publishing Services: Ben Applegate
Associate Director of Publishing Operations: Stephen Pakula
Publishing Services Managing Editors: Alanna Ruse, Madison Salters
Production Managers: Emi Lotto, Angela Zurlo

KODANSHA.US